THE DICTIONARY OF INTERIOR DESIGN

THE DICTIONARY OF INTERIOR DESIGN

BY MARTIN M. PEGLER,
ASID & ISP

FAIRCHILD PUBLICATIONS • NEW YORK

F.I.T.
COLLECTION

Fairchild Book Division wishes to thank Verna Small for
her assistance and expertise on this Dictionary. Ms. Small
has been a writer and editor during much of her adult life.
She has done editorial work for both the U.S. and N.Y.
State Department of Labor, has specialized on vocational
and career subjects for such magazines as *Mademoiselle,*
has written extensively on architectural subjects, and
worked as a civic leader in the struggle to preserve important
landmarks in New York City, currently representing the
Mayor on the New York City Historic Preservation Fund.

Designed by Karen Wiedman

Standard Book Number: 87005-447-3

Library of Congress Catalog Card Number: 83-80666

Printed in the United States of America

To Suzan
for her faith and hope

To Karen, Lisa, and Adam
for their charity

INTRODUCTION

The historic and the contemporary go hand in hand in the language of design, since design is the continuous re-use and revitalizing of forms so that they always have meaning for our way of life. There is no design that cannot find its way back into history: at any moment a dormant historical motif may be given a renaissance by the avant-garde. This perpetual rejuvenation means that design terms and ideas survive from many sources and often have more than one interpretation. A word originally used in the French Gothic period might today be applied to a sophisticated element on a Park Avenue skyscraper. A classical architectural ornament might be used by an eighteenth-century cabinetmaker on a piece of furniture. Newly excavated classical remains might form the basis of an entirely new style.

The name of a sixteenth-century architect is given to an eighteenth-century movement in furniture and ornament as well as architecture, and then his name becomes synonymous with a classically elegant mid-twentieth-century style. A frivolous little Gothic castle built by a romantic in the late eighteenth century gives impetus to a revival of the medieval in early-nineteenth-century building and art.

New and exciting concepts are constantly being derived from old or antique motifs of designs. The "chair and a half" is really a contemporary revision of the early-eighteenth-century "drunkard's chair." The long-popular director's chair is an only slightly altered version of the chair that satisfied many a Roman. Our present-day convertible couches are refinements of our forefathers' trundle or truckle beds. The architectural furniture and cabinets of medieval times are having a renaissance as built-ins, storage-wall units, modular furniture, etc. The stone curtain wall of the Gothic period is no different in concept from the light glass and aluminum curtain wall of today.

Architects, artists, building, ornaments, materials, fabrics, construction devices, accessories, woods, styles, periods, etc., all contribute to the language of design, a multilingual common language used by designers in many lands. You will find French, Italian, German, Spanish, Indian, and other exotic words in this dictionary. I have tried to achieve a lucid and comprehensive collection of these terms, illustrated wherever a picture helps define them, and I have endeavored to show their historical origins and the current meanings.

Martin M. Pegler

A

AALTO, ALVAR (1898–1961) Finnish architect and furniture designer. In a strong expressive style he adapted Finnish traditions to modern European techniques, concerning himself with satisfying particular requirements. He became famous as a furniture designer with his creations in laminated wood.

AALTO STOOL A simple stool designed by Alvar Aalto in the early 1930's. Originally made of birch, its seat is a round disc of banded wood with three legs made of solid wood which has been sliced (kerfed), bent, and glued to the seat. The legs form a radius curve extending out beyond the seat. Inexpensive copies are made of plywood sheets glued together and curved.

AALTO STOOL

AARNIO, EERO A 20th-century Finnish architect and designer noted for his molded fiberglass furniture. His Cognac Chair and doughnut-shaped eros table are among his well known designs. The Gyro Chair is another; it resembles a flattened sphere with a shaped depression contoured to hold the human body. It is also made of reinforced molded fiberglass. See *Cognac Chair*.

ABACA The technical name for Manila hemp, a hard fiber used for woven matting, carpeting, wall covering, and also for making rope.

ABACHI A wood. See *Ayous*.

ABACUS The slab or pillow that forms the top of the capital of a column. In Greek Ionic, Roman Doric, and Tuscan classical orders it may be square in plan with a molded lower edge. In other orders it may have concave sides with chamfered edges.

ABATTANT

GYRO CHAIR
BY EERO AARNIO

ACANTHUS

ROMANESQUE ROMAN

GREEK RENAISSANCE

The abacus in the Gothic style is sometimes round or octogonal.

ABATTANT The French term for a drop lid or fall front, as in "secrétaire à abattant" (a drop leaf secretary). A Chippendale design is illustrated.

ABOUDIKROU An African wood that resembles mahogany and sapele. See *Sapele*.

ABRASION RESISTANCE The degree to which a fabric, floor covering, etc., resists wearing out from rubbing or applied friction.

ABSTRACT ART An art expression in which the artistic values reside in the forms and colors rather than in the reproduction or presentation of recognizable objects.

ABSTRACT EXPRESSIONISM Art movement expressing the subconscious through rapid renderings of shapes and the free use of color. The English version is known as "action painting."

ACACIA A figured wood that varies from light brown to shades of red and green, similar to the American locust, used as a veneer in France and England during the 18th century.

ACAJOU The French word for Mahogany.

ACAJOU MOUCHETÉ A fine-quality mahogany with wavelike markings and small dark spots in the grain, popular in the late Louis XVI period for tables and commodes.

ACANTHUS (AKANTHOS) LEAF A carved or painted ornament that resembles the foilage or leaves of the acanthus. A clas-

1

sic design used by the Greeks and Romans, it appears in Gothic art and architecture, and was revived in the Renaissance. The acanthus leaf appears in the Corinthian and Composite capitals. The Greek design has pointed leaf edges, but the Roman version is rounder and broader with more vigorous curves. In Byzantine and Romanesque decoration, the acanthus is stiffer and less delicate. It becomes rounder and more bulbous in the early Gothic period, then becomes bizarre with long thistle-like foliage in the late Gothic. With the Renaissance, the acanthus and tendril motif reaches its highest degree of refinement and elegance.

ACCENT COLOR   Usually a sharp, intense color used as a pickup for a color scheme to add excitement to an effect.

ACCESSORIES   The small items necessary to utility and comfort in a room, often accents to the general color scheme. Ashtrays, vases, plants, lamps, books, etc., are usual accessories, along with throw pillows, pictures, and sculpture.

ACCOTOIR   The French word for arm stump, the wood stile that extends from the frame of the chair seat up to support the arm of the chair. Illustrated is a 17th-century Flemish Renaissance chair. See *Arm Stump*.

ACCOUDOIR   The French word for elbow rest, rail, or balustrade. See *Accotoir*.

ACETATE   A generic name for a cellulose acetate fiber. Textile fibers, yarns, threads, and fabrics made from these fibers are also called acetate. The fabric drapes and dyes well, but has limited abrasion resistance and strength.

ACETYLATION   A chemical reaction that changes cellulose linters (cotton) into cellulose acetate. This reaction improves the heat and rot resistance of the fiber yet does not adversely affect the other good properties of cotton.

ACHECH   A fantasy animal, half lion and half bird, in ancient Egyptian art. See *Hieracosphinx*.

ACORN   A wood turning that resembles the fruit of the oak tree, used as a finial, drop pendant, or furniture foot in the Jacobean furniture of the early 17th century in England.

ACORN CHAIR   A 17th-century Jacobean oak chair with acorn-shaped pendants decorating the cross rail of the back.

ACOUSTICAL PANELS   Panels made of sound absorbing materials, decoratively covered in fabrics or vinyls, used as dividers or sound-deadeners in an open office plan. They may be equipped with "feet" to stand

ACCOTOIR

ACROTERIA

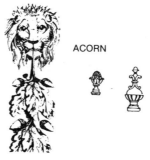

ACROTERIA

ACORN

independently, or can be applied directly to hard wall surfaces of masonry, brick, cement block, etc. or suspended from the ceiling to act as a blanket over a particularly noisy area.

ACOUSTICAL TILE   Rectangular panels, usually 12″ × 12″, made of pulped wood, Fiberglas, compressed Styrofoam pellets, asbestos, or mixtures of the above. Used for quieting down sounds in a room (some tiles are perforated for greater sound absorption), greater insulation, or as a cosmetic over a poor ceiling. In areas where greater sound control is required, the walls may be covered with acoustical tiles. Now available in assorted colors and with various embossed patterns.

ACOUSTICS   The science of Sound and Sound Reception including the implementing of sound, the reinforcement of sound, or the controlling or reduction of sound transmission. See *Acoustical Panels, Acoustical Tiles*.

ACRILAN   A trademark for acrylic fiber composed of 85 percent or more acrylonitrile, a liquid derivative of natural gas and air. Acrilan fibers have stability, strength, and a luxurious wool-like feel. Fabrics made with acrilan hold a pressed crease, and have characteristics similar to those of Orlon. Also used as a carpeting fiber, and is manufactured by the Chemstrand Company.

ACROLITH   A classic Greek statue which had the heads, legs, and arms carved of marble, while the body, which was often sheathed in gold, was made of wood.

ACROTERIA   Greek for summit or extremity (acroterion is the singular form). In classic architecture, the blocks or flat pedestals at the apex and the lowest ends of a pediment. They were often used to hold carved ornaments or statues. The term is sometimes applied to the carved ornament itself, which resembled a stylized palmette leaf. See *Akroter*.

In English and American 18th-century furniture, the acroteria refers to the end blocks of the pediment top of a secretary or bookcase, or the central block in a broken pediment which might hold an urn, vase, finial, or other ornament.

ACRYLICS   Synthetic polymer fibers made of natural materials: coal, air, water, limestone, petroleum and natural gasses. The fibers are strong, durable, and have excellent resistance to strong sunlight and changing weather conditions. Acrylics are also chosen for their insulating qualities. Acrylic fibers make soft, bulky, wool-like fabrics and carpets. Produced under the following registered trademarks: Acrilan (Monsanto), Creslan (American Cyanide),

Orlon (DuPont), Zefran (Dow Chemical).

ACT OF PARLIAMENT CLOCK A mid-18th- to early-19th-century English hanging clock with a short trunk and a large wooden dial, without a glass cover, usually painted black and accented with gold numerals. The trunk design varied: oblong and paneled, bulbous or fiddle-shaped. The overall measurement varied from 3′9″ to 5′ tall.

ADAM BROTHERS, John (1721–1792); Robert (1728–1792); James (1730–1794); William (1739–1822) Four Scottish architect-designers who greatly influenced English interiors and furniture design during the middle and latter half of the 18th century. Robert and James were the most famous; they designed important buildings and interiors in a restrained, classic manner, much influenced by the discoveries at Pompeii and Herculaneum. These classic motifs appear frequently in their work: honeysuckle, swags, husks, oval paterae, flutings, wreaths of flowers festooned between rams' heads. The classic *urn* appears as a decoration and was also used as a cutlery container and wine cooler. Amorini, sphinxes, and arabesques were painted on Adam furniture by such artists as Pergolesi, Zucchi, and Angelica Kauffman. The Adams also used inserts of Wedgwood medallions, which were frequently designed by John Flaxman, as well as composition ornaments for bas relief ceilings and friezes. See *Adelphi* and *Composition Ornament.*

ADAPTATION The changing or adjusting of a design or scale to suit another purpose. For example, oriental furniture is adapted in size and scale to conform with occidental habits and usage.

ADELPHI Greek for brothers. The trademark name of the Adam Brothers of England, in the latter part of the 18th century. See *Adam Brothers.*

ADMIXTURES Water-repellent or coloring agents added to mortar. Also any additives which may speed up or retard the setting time of mortar. See *Panel Wall.*

ADOBE A Spanish word for sun-dried brick. Also the clay used. A building material in Mexico and the Southwest U.S.A.

AEDICULE From the Latin aedicula, a small temple. A niche into which a statue was placed. A pediment resting on two columns usually enframed the opening.

AEGICRAMES The heads of skulls of rams used as decorative elements in classic Greek and Roman sculpture.

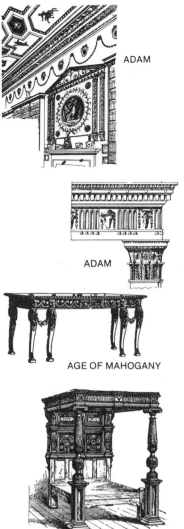

ADAM

ADAM

AGE OF MAHOGANY

AGE OF OAK

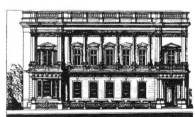

AGE OF REVIVALS

AGE OF SATINWOOD   AGE OF WALNUT

AFARA A wood. See *Korina* and *Limba.*

AFFLECK, THOMAS One of the Philadelphia school of cabinet-makers of the mid-18th century in America, known for his highboys and lowboys, and chairs executed in the Georgian and early Chippendale styles.

AGATE WARE Originally an 18th-century pottery produced by Wedgwood and others in England. The finish was made to resemble agate or quartz.

AGE OF MAHOGANY The period of interior and furniture design in England lasting from approximately 1710 to 1765. Mahogany was favored by designers and clients as well, and much of the Georgian and Chippendale furniture was produced in this wood. Illustrated is a Chippendale mahogany sideboard table of about 1760.

AGE OF OAK The period of the English Renaissance (about 1500–1660) when oak was prominently used for furniture and interior paneling, wainscoting, etc. It encompasses the Tudor, Elizabethan, Jacobean, and Cromwellian periods. Illustrated is a carved oak Elizabethan bedstead of the late 16th Century.

AGE OF REVIVALS The 19th century was in both design and building essentially a time of revivals of styles of the past. The Classic, Renaissance, Rococo and Gothic revivals followed and overlapped one another. See *Victorian* for the various furniture style revivals.

AGE OF SATINWOOD The elegant period in England from about 1765 to 1800, when the cabinetmakers and designers favored the light, delicate-toned satinwood for furniture. The Adam brothers used it extensively in their work, as did Hepplewhite, Shearer, and Sheraton, whose corner washstand of the late 18th century is illustrated. See *Satinwood.*

AGE OF WALNUT The Restoration, Stuart, William and Mary, and Queen Anne periods in England, which ran from about 1660 to 1714. Walnut was the dominant furniture and interior show wood. A William and Mary walnut secretary is illustrated.

AIGRETTE French for egret, a beautifully plumed bird. A decorative feather or plume.

AIR BRICK A brick perforated with holes, allowing air to enter and pass through a wall.

AIRFOAM Goodyear's trademark name of rubber foam latex material used for cushions and padding.

AISLE A passageway usually giving access to seats.

AJARCARA A Spanish word for brickwork with a decorative relief surface.

AJOURÉ A design produced by piercing holes in a definite set pattern in ceramics, wood, metal, etc. Now used to decorate dark parchment lampshades, the pierced design having a brilliant, jewel-like effect when the lamp is lit. See *Pierced Work.*

AKANTHOS See *Acanthus Leaf.*

AKANTHOS

AKARI LAMPS Folding rice-paper Japanese lanterns of varied shape, and size. Many exciting lanterns were designed by Noguchi in the mid-1950's, based on traditional Japanese designs but adapted to modern concepts and use. See *Noguchi, Isamu.*

AKO See *Chen Chen.*

AKROTER An ornamental finish for the apex of a gable. On ancient Greek and Roman structures, the akroter, which decorated the top angle of the pediment, was usually a variation of the palmette ornament, though griffins, figures, and other sculptured devices were used. See *Acroteria.*

ALENÇON LACE

AKROTER

AKUME A wood. See *Bubinga.*

ALABASTER A fine-textured, compact, marble-like mineral, a variety of sulfate of lime or gypsum, (milky white or semitranslucent) used for ornaments and sculpture.

ALAE Latin for wings. Recesses opening out from the central atrium in a classic Roman house. See *Atrium.* (The word "aisle" has its origin in *alae.*)

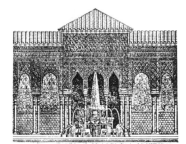

ALHAMBRA

ALBERTI, LEONE BATTISTA (1404–1472) A noted Florentine architect, sculptor, painter, musician, and poet of the Renaissance. Alberti wrote books on architecture, perspective, and painting which greatly influenced later craftsmen. His *De Re Aedificatoria* was the first book on architecture ever published.

ALBERTOLLI, GIOCENDO (1742–1839) An Italian Neoclassic designer of ornaments greatly responsible for the rise and spread of the Neoclassic style in Italy.

ALCAZAR A magnificent castle built in Seville, Spain, in the middle of the 14th century, noteworthy for its blend of Gothic and Moresque, or Moorish motifs.

ALLEGORY

ALCOVE A recess in a room, or a small room attached to a larger one, often designed to accommodate a bed, piano, etc. A niche for a statue or a seat. Originally a Spanish concept: a private area separated from the main room by an estrade or parti-

ALCOVE

tion of columns. Illustrated is an Elizabethan interior of the late 16th century; an alcove is created by the oriel window. The window-seat arrangement makes it a secluded area away from the main activity of the room.

ALCOVE CUPBOARD An 18th-century English corner cupboard, often part of the paneling of the room. See *Coin* and *Quoin.*

ALDER, RED An American hardwood which has a maple-like figure but can be stained to imitate mahogany or walnut. Because of its strength it is often used for plywood cores. In 18th-century England, the alder wood was used for country or provincial furniture.

ALENÇON LACE A decorative fabric with a solid design outlined in cord on a sheer net ground.

ALETTÉ A small addition or wing to a building. Also a door jamb.

ALEXANDRE A 17th-century French painter of historical scenes who worked in the Gobelins Factory during the period of Louis XIV.

ALHAMBRA A citadel and palace, a masterpiece of 13th-century Spanish-Moslem art, near Granada in Spain, begun in 1248 and enlarged in 1279 and 1306. Much of the decoration is in the tile and stamped plaster with exquisite geometric patterns, intricate arabesques, and Arabic characters intertwined. See *Stalactite* for the unusual ceiling treatment in the Wall of the Abencerrages. See also *Mauresque.*

ALHAMBRA VASES Tall, amphora-shaped vases of luster earthenware done in the Hispano-Mauresque style, made in Valencia in about the 11th century, usually decorated with arabesques and Arabic inscriptions.

ALKYD PAINT Paints with a synthetic resin, alkyd, used as the vehicle for the pigment, which can be thinned with either turpentine or mineral spirits. Alkyd paints have replaced oil paints to a large extent.

ALLEGORY A symbolic representation such as the sun for Louis XIV, a dolphin for the Dauphin, or a fearless leader represented as an eagle or a lion. Illustrated is an equestrian statue of Louis XIV dressed as a Roman emperor.

ALLOY A mixture of two or more metals to create a new metal with characteristics of the original metals but also new qualities produced by the blend. See *Bronze.*

ALMERY Originally a cupboard set into the thickness of a wall of a medieval structure, later a cupboard to contain the portion of food set aside for servants and pensioners. See *Ambry*.

ALMIRAH An Anglo-Indian term for a mobile wardrobe or cupboard.

ALMON A Philippine wood used for veneer. Its color varies from tan to a soft reddish tone and it usually has an interrupted stripe figure. Almon is sometimes sold as white luaun.

ALMOND A two-pointed, oval-shaped pendant of cut glass or crystal used to embellish a chandelier.

ALPACA A hard, shiny-surfaced fabric made of wool from an alpaca, a llama-like animal found in the mountains of Chile and Peru. Its wool is long, fine, and usually dark. The cloth may be woven completely of the alpaca wool, or mixed with sheep wool, cotton, or silk.

ALTARPIECE Illustrated is a German Romanesque altarpiece from the Wiesenkirche in Soest.

ALTO-RILIEVO A high-relief sculpture. The carved area projects well out beyond the main surface and appears almost full round. An early French Renaissance carved medallion is shown. See *Robbia* and *High Relief*.

ALUMINUM An extremely light yet strong silvery blue metal which resists oxidation and tarnishing. As hard as zinc, it is malleable, can be made into threadlike wires, and is a good heat conductor. Used for furniture frames and outdoor furniture.

AMARANTH A wine-red or dark violet mahogany of Central and South America, especially Brazil and the Guianas. Its brilliant, exotic coloring is apt to fade when exposed to light. A hard, strong wood also called violet wood, purpleheart and bois violet, it was popular during the latter part of the 18th century in France for veneer and marquetry.

AMBIENCE The overall effect of an interior, the "look," the atmosphere. The effect created by the combination of color, line, form, textures, lighting, decorative items, and accessories.

AMBIENCE LIGHTING or AMBIENT LIGHTING Atmospheric lighting. Soft lights with shadows used to create an effect rather than for better visibility. See *Indirect Lighting, Secondary Lighting*.

AMBOYNA A rich golden brown to orange wood, highly mottled and marked with a "bird's-eye" figure. Adam and Hepplewhite used amboyna as a veneer in the second half of the 18th century in England.

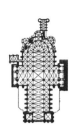

AMBULATORY

ALTARPIECE

ALTO-RILIEVO

AMBRY From the Latin for chest or cupboard. In ecclesiastic work, the ambry or aumbry was a small cupboard used to hold the sacred vessels, books, and altar linens. Also called an almery.

AMBULANTES A French term for small, portable serving tables, such as tea tables. This type of furniture became popular in the Louis XV period in France. See *Rafraîchissoir* and *Serviteur Fidèle*.

AMBULATORY A walking area, like an aisle, or in a cloister. It particularly refers to the aisle around an apse in a church. The ambulatory is indicated on the plan for the Chartres Cathedral in France.

AMERICAN CHIPPENDALE The furniture made by American craftsmen in the Colonies in the mid-to-late-18th century, based on the Queen Anne and Georgian designs as well as those in the Thomas Chippendale books on furniture design. Many of these fine pieces were produced in Philadelphia, Pennsylvania, and are sometimes called Philadelphia Chippendale. See *Chippendale, Thomas*.

AMERICAN EAGLE PERIOD The early part of the Federal period in America, immediately after the Revolutionary War (late 18th, early 19th century), when the eagle was a popular motif on mirrors, and was carved on the bases of couches or other furniture. The eagle also appeared on finials, standards and the exteriors of public buildings.

AMERICAN EMPIRE MIRROR See *Constitution Mirror*.

AMERICAN EMPIRE PERIOD The style of furnishing and design popular in the United States from about 1820 to 1840, basically the French Empire style and the later Sheraton designs interpreted in crotch-grain mahogany veneers, cherrywood, curly maple, and maple. Duncan Phyfe was the leading designer of the period, and ancanthus leaves, pineapples, cornucopias, and *stencil* gliding were important decorative motifs and techniques. See *Butcher Furniture*.

AMERICAN QUEEN ANNE FURNITURE See *American Chippendale*.

AMERICAN SOCIETY OF INTERIOR DESIGNERS (A.S.I.D.) This organization celebrated its 50th anniversary in 1981. Originally (1931) the American Institute of Interior Decorators, in 1936 it became the American Institute of Decorators. In 1958 a split created two groups: the American Institute of Decorators (A.I.D.) and the National Society of Interior Designers (N.S.I.D.). The two groups reunited in 1975 as the American Society of

Interior Designers (A.S.I.D.). The organization is dedicated to protecting interior designers and promoting their recognitions as contributors to environmental design. It also sets a level of excellence and professionalism for aspirants to the field of interior design. The Educational Foundation, Inc., is a separate corporation established by the A.S.I.D. to support grants, scholarships, and awards to interior design students, educators and institutions. See *Foundation of Interior Design Education Research (F.I.D.E.R.) and National Council for Interior Design Qualification.*

AMILAN A Japanese synthetic fiber of the nylon type. See *Nylon.*

AMORINI The plural of amorino. See below.

AMORINO The Italian word for little love. A small cupid or cherub used as a carved or painted decoration in the Italian Renaissance period, and again in Louis XV ornament. The Adam brothers used the amorino in wall-panel designs and ceiling decorations, and these elements were often painted by artists like Pergolesi and Zucchi. See *Adam Brothers.*

AMPHITHEATRE or AMPHITHEATER An oval or circular structure with seats, or steplike ledges, rising above and behind each other and surrounding a central open space, stage, or arena.

AMPHORA A large, two-handled earthenware vase of ancient Greece, with a narrow neck and an ovoid body.

ANAGLYPH A type of relief sculpture or ornament with more depth than a bas-relief, but is not as deep as a high relief. See *Mezzo-Rilievo.*

ANAGLYPHA A metal urn, vase, or vessel with raised or relief ornamentation.

ANAGLYPTA The Greek word for raised ornament. Raised ornaments have been made in gesso and plaster compounds. They are now being produced of rag stock which is liquefied, then poured into a form and molded. The molded pieces are then applied to walls and ceilings to simulate a carved, bas-relief effect. It is, in effect, similar to the Adam brothers' 18th century technique of "composition ornament" or "carton-pierre." Illustrated is an Adam design for a ceiling and cornice to be executed in carton-pierre for the Duke of Richmond's home Goodwood. See *Composition Ornament.*

ANALOGOUS COLORS Colors which are next to each other on the color wheel, i.e., orange, red-orange, red; or yellow, green-yellow, green.

ANCONA

ANCONES

ANDROSPHINX

ANAGLYPHA

ANAGLYPTA

ANCHOR BOLT A long metal device used for reinforcing cornices and pinnacles to ensure greater stability.

ANCON A Greek word for bend. A corner of a wall. See *Ancones.*

ANCONA An Italian word for a group of pictures or one major painting formally arranged, or a recess or niche architecturally framed and used for the setting of a piece of sculpture. Illustrated is an ancona with a madonna and child, attributed to Michelangelo, located in the Notre-Dame of Bruges in Belgium.

ANCONES The brackets used on either side of a door or opening capped with a cornice, serving to support the cornice. See *Console.*

ANDIRONS A pair of upright metal supports with a transverse rod which holds logs for burning on an open hearth. The French word for andirons is chenets. See *Fire Dogs.*

ANDROSPHINX In Egyptian art, a sculptured lion with a human head like the great sphinx at Giza. Illustrated is an androsphinx in the Tuileries Garden in Paris.

ANDROUET, JACQUES See *Du Cerceau.*

ANGEL BED An 18th-century French bed with a canopy that usually extends only partially over the bed. There are no front pillars, the canopy being supported by back pillars or posts. The side draperies continue down to the floor and are pulled back at either side. See *Lit d'Ange.*

ANGLE IRON A metal bar which forms a right angle or L-shape. Usually made of rolled mild steel.

ANGORA A yarn made from the fleece of the angora sheep, used in weaving mohair. See *Alpaca* and *Mohair.*

ANGUIER, GUILLAUME (1628–1708) One of the French painters employed by Le Brun at the *Gobelins Factory.* He created many painted interior decorations, and was also an architect. His brothers, François and Michel, were famous sculptors.

ANILINE DYES Any dyes chemically obtained from aniline or other coal-tar derivatives.

ANIMAL COUCHANT FOOT An antique furniture leg or support sculptured to resemble an animal lying down. Found in ancient Egyptian, Greek, and Roman furniture, and successfully revived in the Empire period in the early 19th century.

ANNEALING A method of slowly cooling off heated glass or metal to decrease the brittleness of the material.

ANNULET A ring. One of the fillets around the lower part of the Greek Doric capital. A band of molding around a Norman column, or the ring of molding joining a group of column shafts in Gothic architecture.

ANODIZED ALUMINUM Aluminum which has been coated to give it a sheen and smooth feel. (See *Anodizing*.)

ANODIZING The process of coating metal with a hard, protective oxide film by means of electrochemical treatment.

ANTA A type of projecting pier (like a pilaster) placed behind a column at the end of a side wall of a Greek temple. The base and capital differ from those of the column. "Anta" may also refer to the short wall which partially or wholly encloses the side of the portico. Illustrated is the northwest view of the Erechtheum at Athens (c. 420–393 B.C.). Note the caryatid figures at the far right of this Greek temple.

ANTEFIX An upright, conventionalized, fanlike ornament, like a spreading leaf. It was originally used in antique Greek and Roman decoration to conceal the end of a roof tile.

ANTEPAGMENTA Molded jambs on either side of an opening or door. The overdoor and lintel moldings are called the "supercilia."

ANTHEMION Greek for flower. A classic Greek and Roman decoration; a conventionalized honeysuckle or a flower or leaf ornament which appears to radiate from a single point. It was used to enhance cyma recta moldings. A popular motif during the French Empire period in the early 19th century.

ANTIMACASSAR A mid-19th century favorite; a crocheted or knitted doily placed over the upholstered backs of chairs and sofas to prevent them from being soiled by the macassar hair dressing used by men of the Victorian era. It became a symbol of gentility and elegance. Matching doilies were often used on the arm rests.

ANTIQUE According to U.S. Customs, a work of art dating from before 1840, or furniture made before 1840. Carpets and rugs must have been made before 1700 to be considered antique.

ANTIQUE FINISH A furniture-finishing technique used on wood to give it an aged look; an artificially created patina. A darker shade of paint or stain may be ap-

APOPHYGE

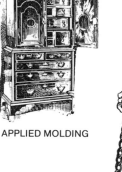
ANTEFIX

APPLIED MOLDING

APPLIQUE

APRON

APSE

plied over a lighter tone, and then rubbed off, or a lighter tone may be used over the darker wood. Wood can also be "antiqued" by artificial weathering, distressing, gouging, or nicking.

ANTRON III AND XL A trademark name for a DuPont nylon fiber which is tough, abrasion resistant and has built-in static control, available in a wide range of colors. Used to loom carpets of various textures and patterns.

APOPHYGE The slight concave curve or sweep at the top and bottom of the shaft of a column. It does not appear in the Greek Doric column. Apophyge is Greek for a flying off.

APOTROPAIC EYE In Greek art, the symbolic representation of an eye on the prow of a boat, on the side of a chalice, etc. It was meant to ward off evil spirits.

APPAREIL EN ÉPI French term for bricks laid in a herringbone pattern.

APPARTEMENT DE PARADE A French term for the best or showiest room in a home. A reception room.

APPLEWOOD An American fruitwood used for provincial styles of furniture.

APPLIED MOLDING A geometric-shaped molding applied to the face of furniture to create a paneled effect. Also called Jacobean ornament, it was popular in the late-17th-century English cabinet and cupboard designs.

APPLIQUE A French word for a wall bracket, sconce, or candelabrum applied to a wall. See *Girandole* and *Sconce*.

APPLIQUÉ A French term for a shape cut out and sewed or pasted onto the surface of another material as a decorative trim.

APRON The structural part of a table directly beneath and at right angles to the top, connecting with the legs, often shaped, carved, or ornamented. On a chair, the surface below and perpendicular to the seat. The apron, on case furniture is the perpendicular face below the lowest drawer, also called the frieze or skirt.

APSE The semicircular or angular extension at the east end of a Christian church. It is typical of all basilica plan (or style) churches. See *Nave* and *Transept*.

AQUARELLE A true watercolor painting produced by using transparent colors and water. The painting surface reflects through the applied paint, and affects the tonal quality of the painting. Water colors dry very rapidly, and the technique calls for speed and dexterity.

AQUATINT A form of intaglio etching which produces tones. It renders a transparent effect similar to that of watercolor. It was first used by Paul Sandby, but Goya (late 18th, early 19th century) is considered the greatest aquatinter. See *Engraving*.

ARABESQUE (Arabian) The complicated ornamental designs based on plant growth fancifully intertwined with lines and geometric patterns used by the Moors, who were prohibited by their religion from representing animal forms. In Greek, Roman, and Renaissance art, the arabesques are used in carvings, paintings, and inlaid work, combining plant and animal forms in complicated intertwining vertical patterns. Mohammedan arabesques are geometrical, and may go in any direction.

ARAZZO Italian for arras or tapestry.

ARBOR A framework, sometimes latticed, used as a support for vines. See *Trellis Work*.

ARBRAUM A red ocher material sometimes used to color mahogany.

ARC EN ACCOLADE An ogree arch.

ARC EN FER À CHEVAL French for horseshoe arch.

ARCA A Spanish term for a storage chest of the early Renaissance period.

ARCADE A series of adjoining arches with their supporting columns or piers.

ARCADED BACK A furniture back with an arcade effect between the top rail and the seat. A Louis XVI motif, it was also used by Sheraton in the late 18th century in England.

ARCADED PANEL A popular motif in early English Renaissance woodwork. The field or face of a panel is ornamented with small piers supporting an arch form. Also used as a decorative device on chests in the French Renaissance. Illustrated is a Jacobean carved chest with a guilloche band trim (17th century). Also see *Bedstead* for Jacobean headboard with arcaded panel.

ARCEAU French for a sculptured trefoil ornament or the curved surface of a vault or arch.

ARCH A curved or arched structural device spanning an opening. May span the space between two walls, columns, or piers. May be flattened, and be ornamental as well as structural. The inner surface of the arch is called the "intrados," the exterior face the "extrados." Also used as decorative features on furniture. See *Intrados, Keystone*.

ARCHAIC

ARCH RIB ROOF

ARCADED BACK

ARCHED STRETCHER

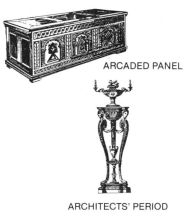
ARCADED PANEL

ARCHITECTS' PERIOD

ARCHITECT'S TABLE

ARCH BRICK The wedge-shaped bricks used in the construction of an arch. See *Voussoir*.

ARCH LAMP A floor or table light fixture with the light source (the bulb) some distance away from the base, i.e., the bulb and its housing is cantilevered, being at the far end of an arc which is firmly connected to a weighted base.

ARCH RIB The projecting band on the edge of an arch in a ceiling or an arch vaulting.

ARCH RIB ROOF A 19th-century cast-iron-girder construction technique. The roof thrust was carried down the arch-like ribs. The interior of the Diana Bath in Vienna by Etzel, built in the late 19th century, is shown.

ARCHAIC Ancient, antiquated. Some pieces of ancient Greek furniture are illustrated.

ARCHEBANE-COUCHETTE A 16th-century Renaissance combination coffer and bench. The slight upward projections of the sides can be similar to armrests, or a headrest.

ARCHED MOLDING A simple, undecorated half-round convex molding, sometimes used in pairs.

ARCHED STRETCHER An arc shaped or hooped stretcher used between the legs of tables, chairs, or case furniture in the English Restoration period. It was introduced into England from Spain, where it was popular in the 17th century. See *Rising Stretchers*.

ARCHITECT From the Greek master builder. The designer, detailer, and often engineer of buildings and other structures.

ARCHITECTIVE FURNITURE A contemporary group of office and residential furniture designed for the John Stuart Company in New York by Lindquist and Van der Lanken. It is basic and slablike, with sophisticated lines and light supports.

ARCHITECTS' PERIOD Term for the furniture and decoration of the 18th century in England, dominated by architects: Christopher Wren, James Gibbs, William Kent, Isaac Ware, and the Adam brothers. Their work was characterized by the use of architectural motifs and concepts in furniture and interior design. Marble was a popular material, and the classic orders appear over and over again. Illustrated is an Adam tripod and candleholder.

ARCHITECT'S TABLE A combination drawing table and desk with an adjustable lid that lifted up to make an inclined surface, an 18th century English innovation.

ARCHITECTURAL LIGHTING Built-in light fixtures considered essential parts of the design of an area; e.g., set into the ceiling in a chosen position.

ARCHITECTURAL TERRA-COTTA Machine-extruded or hand-molded hard burned clay building blocks, usually larger than bricks. May be plain, or decorated, glazed or unglazed.

ARCHITECTURE The art of science of building edifices for human use. John Ruskin defined it as "the art which so disposes and adorns the edifices raised by man —that the sight of them contributes to his mental health, power and pleasure."

ARCHITRAVE In architecture, the lintel, in the classic entablature, the lowest of three main divisions. The architrave supports the frieze, rests directly on the column, and spans the space between columns. A molding around a door may be called an architrave molding. Illustrated is the Italian Renaissance Grimani Palace in Venice.

ARCHIVOLT The ornamentation and/ or moldings on the face of an arch. An architrave molding applied to an arch. See *Architrave.*

ARCUATE Arched or archlike. Illustrated is a late-17th century English chest; note the arched base arrangements. See *Arch.*

ARCUATED ARCHITECTURE Architectural styles which emphasize the use of the arch, the Romanesque, Gothic and Renaissance styles, for example.

ARDABIL RUG Originally, a Caucasian design with geometric figures, the traditional designs having either a single, central medallion surrounded by characteristic figures, or a central design of three diamonds. The background is usually ivory or a combination of strong, vivid colors with red, green, blue and salmon predominant.

ARDISH An East Indian form of decoration. Bits of colored glass were embedded in the ceiling or wall plaster to create a sparkling effect.

AREA RUG A rug, sometimes shaped irregularly, sometimes rectangular, used to highlight one section or area of a room. Usually patterned, more decorative and more highly colored than "wall to wall" broadloom. Usually placed directly over wood, tiled, or ceramic floors.

AREA WALL A brick or stone wall surrounding an area. It also refers to the retain-

ARKWRIGHT

ARCHITRAVE

ARCUATE

ARMOIRE

ARMOIRE
À DEUX CORPS

ing wall around basement windows below grade.

ARFE OR ARPHE 15th- and 16th-century German silversmiths whose work influenced the Plateresco architectural ornament in Spain. See *Plateresco.*

ARGAND LAMP A lamp invented in 1783 by a Swiss named Argand. The lamp had a round wick with provisions for introducing air into and around the outside of the wick. This increased the draft and produced a much brighter flame.

ARKWRIGHT A late Gothic term for a cabinetmaker and his products, which were usually more like carpentry than cabinetry. Illustrated is a late Gothic trestle table.

ARM PADS The partial upholstery on the wooden arms of a chair, which serve as padded armrests. In French they are called manchettes.

ARM STUMP The vertical element which supports the front part of a chair arm. It may be a turning, a carved device, or a shaped piece of wood. In French it is called the *Accotoir.*

ARMADI Italian for a large wardrobe. See *Armoire.*

ARMARIUM A bookcase or cupboard. Originally the armarium was a bookcase near the entrance to a church in the cloister of a monastery.

ARMCHAIR A chair with armrests or arm supports as distinguished from an armless side or pull-up chair. Armchairs as we know them today were introduced into popular use in the late 17th century. See *Cacqueteuse.*

ARMOIRE A French word for a large, movable clothes wardrobe or closet, originally one used to store armor. Usually an important case piece of furniture. An 18th-century French Régence armoire is illustrated. See *Lebrun, Charles,* for an illustration of a Louis XIV armoire. See *Garderobe.*

ARMOIRE À DEUX CORPS A Renaissance cupboard having two parts. The lower, formerly only a supporting base, functioned as a larger cupboard, with a smaller cupboard set on top. Illustrated is a 16th-century Dutch piece. See *Beaufait.*

ARMURE A raised satin (nonreversible) pattern on a fabric with a rep background. The pattern usually consists of small, isolated, conventional motifs arranged to form an all-over design. Originally a fabric woven with a small interlaced design of chain armor, used during the crusades (11th and 12th centuries.)

ARNEL A trademark name for triacetate yarns and fibers produced by Celanese Corporation of America. It drapes well, is soft in hand, colorfast, and holds its shape.

ARQUETA A Spanish term for a small chest, or box, usually to hold jewels, which was kept on a table. The box was often highly ornamented.

ARRAS A rich Gothic tapestry (used as a wall hanging, usually with figures as part of the design, produced in Arras, France, in the 14th and 15th centuries. Had a particular heavy texture, often with precious metals woven into the design. Illustrated is a 15th-century French interior with arras on the wall.

ARRAZZI Italian for arras. See above.

ARRICCIATO An Italian term for the second coat of plaster applied to a wall which will eventually have a fresco decoration.

ARRIS In architecture, the sharp edge produced by two surfaces forming an angle. The sharp edge between two adjoining concave flutings of a column shaft.

ARROW A slender shaft with a triangular pointed tip at one end and a "feathered" end at the back, used as a decorative motif in the classic revival periods starting with Louis XVI and continuing through the Directoire, Empire, and Biedermeier periods.

ARROW SPINDLE A decorative flattened spindle with an arrow tip used in Sheraton chair backs and also in American Federal furniture. It also appeared in some American Windsor chairs.

ART MODERNE The "modern" concept in furniture and decoration, briefly prevalent in America during the 1920's, not a truly contemporary style, so much as an affectation of one.

ART NOUVEAU The "new art" that took hold in Europe and America in the 1890's. A style of decoration which used flat patterns of twisting plant forms based on nature, sometimes tortured. It was strongly influenced by Japanese and Gothic art forms. Aubrey Beardsley, the illustrator, William Morris, the designer, and James Ensor, the Belgian painter, were prime forces. Horta and Van de Velde were outstanding names in the interiors done in this style as were Charles Rennie Mackintosh in Scotland, Hector Guimard in France, and Antonio Gaudí in Spain. See *Gaudí i Cornet, Antonio,* and *Horta, Victor.*

ARTE POVERA (poor man's art) An 18th-century form of decorating furniture similar to the French découpage. Engraved

ARRAS

ARTISAN

ARTESONADO

ARUNDEL MARBLES

ARROW SPINDLE

ART NOUVEAU

prints were hand-colored and applied to wooden furniture in imitation of the fine painted embellishments of the court furniture of the period. See *Découpage.*

ARTESONADO Moorish woodwork or joinery, usually made of Spanish cedar. The wood used for paneling, ceilings, and doors was often left in its natural state, but was painted or gilded in important public buildings. Illustrated is a painted balustrade in the Spanish Gothic tower of Santo Domingo, Moorish in design.

ARTIFACT An article made by man, such as a carving, a pot, or a tool.

ARTISAN A skilled worker in an industrial art, e.g., cabinetmaker, or weaver. Illustrated is a silver gilt jug by a master craftsman, Johann Heinric Mannlich, who worked in Augsburg, Germany, till 1718.

ARTS AND CRAFTS MOVEMENT See *Morris, William; Pre-Raphaelite Brotherhood; and Webb, Philip Speakman.*

ARUNDEL MARBLES A collection of Greek and Roman statues and fragments that belonged to the Earl of Arundel in England during the reign of Charles I (first half of the 17th century). Arundel, a great patron of art, brought the symmetrical planning of Renaissance architecture into England. Illustrated is an artist's conception of the gallery of Arundel Marbles in the Arundel mansion, which was destroyed in 1678.

ARYBALLOS A rounded or globe-shaped ancient Greek wine jar. See *Lagynos* and *Oinochoe.*

ASBESTALL A trademark name for fire-resistant fabrics woven of asbestos and nylon yarns, manufactured by the United States Rubber Company.

ASBESTOS A nonmetallic mineral fiber which is noncombustible. Woven with other yarns, asbestos fiber makes flameproof fabrics.

ASBESTOS CEMENT A fire-resistant material made of Portland cement and fibers of asbestos.

ASH A handsomely figured blond wood with a pleasing texture. It takes dark stains well, but is very hard and not easy to work.

ASH, ENGLISH A native English wood sometimes called olive burl. It has an unusual lateral grain known as fiddleback or ram's horn. It was used for country-made or provincial furniture in 18th-century England. See *Olive Wood.*

ASHBEE, CHARLES ROBERT (1863–1942) An English craftsman-designer and disciple of William Morris and the

Arts and Crafts movement. He was a "medievalist" and in 1888 founded the Guild and School of Handicraft, believing that "the constructive and decorative arts are the real backbone" of any artistic culture.

A.S.I.D. See *American Society of Interior Designers.*

ASPEN An American wood of the poplar family, light-colored and silky-textured with light brown stripes. The crotch cut is extremely decorative. A soft, easy-to-work-with wood, tools well, and has a natural sheen. Similar to the European white poplar.

ASPHALT TILE A synthetic floor covering material, nonporous, easy to maintain, fairly fire-resistant and fade resistant. It can be ruined by oil, paint, grease, and certain organic solvents; a greaseproof asphalt tile is available. Affected by extreme temperature changes, becoming soft under extreme heat and brittle under extreme cold. Can be laid on wood or concrete floors, and comes in a multitude of colors and patterns, in assorted size squares or strips, and varies in thickness from ⅛" to ⅜".

ASPIDISTRA STAND A late-19th century jardinere or plant stand, usually a tripod made of bamboo, three to four feet in height, and reinforced near the bottom with bamboo stretchers. The open top of the stand was made to receive a flowerpot, often for the poplar aspidistra plant.

ASSYRIAN The art form of an ancient civilization contemporary with ancient Egypt (c. 1275–538 B.C.) Many Egyptian motifs appear in Assyrian works. The winged bull, the lion, and the eagle are the motifs most typically Assyrian. And the first true arch was developed here. Glazed tile and bricks were used in building, since stones were scarce. Illustrated is an Assyrian bas relief of King Asshubanipal in repose. Note the furniture. See *Babylonia* and *Mesopotamia.*

ASTER CARVING A decorative carving of three flowers on the central panel of Connecticut chests made in New England during the 17th and 18th centuries. Sunflower carvings also appeared on these chests.

ASTRAGAL In architecture, a small torus molding which is semicircular in section. When decorated with beads or olive or laurel berries, it is called a barquette, chaplet, or bed molding. In furniture, the small convex molding used on the edge of an overlapping door of a cabinet, chest, secretary, etc., to keep dust out. See *Torus.*

ATELIER

ASSYRIAN

ATTIC STYLE

ASTRAGAL

ASTRAKHAN CLOTH A heavy pile fabric with curled loops that simulates the caracul lambskin fur.

ASTRAL LAMP An early-19th-century oil lamp with the burner set on a swinging tubular arm positioned lower than the fuel reservoir. Made of brass, cast iron, silver plate, or china, and sometimes adorned with prisms. They were usually equipped with an Argand burner. See *Argand Lamp.*

ASYMMETRICAL The opposite of symmetrical. Unequal. Not evenly proportioned or balanced. A favorite decorative line device of the Rococo period. See *Symmetrical.*

ATAUJIA A Spanish term for a form of Moorish inlay work somewhat like boulle work. Gold, silver, other metals, or colored enamels were set into a metal surface. See *Boulle Work.*

ATELIER French word for a studio or workshop, usually of a designer, artist, or artisan. Illustrated is a mid-18th-century furniture atelier.

ATHÉNIENNE A small tripod table of the Louis XVI and Empire periods. It was sometimes used as a basin stand.

ATLANTES Full- or half-relief male figures used in place of columns to support an entablature; or in place of furniture legs to support chests, tabletops, etc. The Atlantes are male versions of the caryatids and were popular in Renaissance architecture and interior design. See *Caryatid.*

ATRIUM In classic Roman and contemporary architecture, a central room or courtyard of a home, with a central opening in the roof.

ATTIC A garret or room constructed inside the roof. In certain Louis XIV chambers, the area above the entablature was called the attic.

ATTIC BASE A scotia (concave) molding between two torus (convex) moldings used as a column base in Greek and Roman Doric and Corinthian orders.

ATTIC STYLE A pure, elegant, classic style associated with Athens. Illustrated is a Doric capital and entablature.

AUBERGINE A French term for eggplant and a deep purplish color.

AUBUSSON A rug with no pile, woven like a tapestry, the motifs usually French floral and scroll designs. The name originally referred to a famous French tapestry works in the town of Aubusson, dating back to the 15th century.

AUDITORIUM A hall, enclosure, or theatre, usually equipped with seats. A meeting place or an area for presentations which depend upon sound and acoustics.

AUDRAN, CLAUDE II (1658–1734) A French painter, of historical murals and carver in bronze, gold, and silver. Employed at the Gobelins works during the reign of Louis XIV.

AUDRAN, CLAUDE III (1658–1734) A French painter, decorator, and designer, who created wall murals and tapestries. He made the decorations for the Luxembourg Palace in the period of the Régence and was a teacher of Watteau.

AUDRAN, GÉRARD (1640–1703) A celebrated engraver. The third son of Claude Audran I (1597–1675).

AULA A Roman hall. In Germany, the term is applied to a large hall or a university hall.

AUREOLE From the Latin word for gold. A circular, elliptic, or quadrangular halo around a Christ figure, Madonna, or saint, depicted in art. Also called a mandorla or vesica piscis.

AUSTRIAN DRAPE A shirred fabric treatment for windows which gives the effect of vertical rows of swags from top to bottom. The bottom edge then makes a horizontal band of semicircular scallops. It may be made to work on a pulley cord like a Roman shade, with the drape drawn up in a series of poufs. See *Austrian Shade Cloth*.

AUSTRIAN SHADE CLOTH A crinkled woven striped cotton fabric produced by weaving alternating groups of slack and tight warp ends. May be made of silk, cotton, or some of the synthetic fibers. Used for window shades.

AUTHENTIC Genuine, real, actual.

AWNING WINDOW

AUREOLE

AUSTRIAN DRAPE

AVANTURINE LACQUER A lacquer finish which imitates the color and sparkling quality of the mineral avaturine. Used during the 18th century in France, sometimes for lining drawers in small chests or cabinets.

AVODIRE An African blond wood with strong, dark brown vertical streaking and a medium hard texture, with a pronounced mottled figure and a lustrous quality that makes it a popular veneer and modern cabinet wood.

AWNING WINDOWS Wide horizontal panels of glass, in frames, set one over the other inside the window frame. Each panel is hinged onto the frame and can be opened outward, with the lower end projecting out beyond the building line. Permits air and ventilation along with protection from rain or snow.

AXMINSTER A type of carpet. Originally a rug woven at Axminster in England in the mid-18th century, where Turkish carpets were imitated on special looms that made possible an almost unlimited number of colors, designs and patterns. The Axminster carpet is tightly woven and the pile is usually cut. The back of the weave is heavily ribbed.

AYACAHUITE A satiny pinewood of Mexico and Central America with very little pine graining, used for furniture, and often given a painted or lacquered finish.

AYOUS An African westcoast wood, creamy white to pale yellow, similar to primavera. In veneers, the regular strips are somewhat like mahogany. The wood is soft, lightweight, and has an even texture. Also called abachi.

AZULEJOS Spanish or Portuguese wall tiles decorated with scenes of sports or bullfights, usually done in blue on white. These tiles were used in the late Gothic period to cover the walls in place of tapestries.

B

BABYLONIA The center of the ancient Mesopotamian empire which reached its cultural peak in architecture, art, and learning in about 1800 B.C. It had its renaissance under the Assyrian rule (1275–538 B.C.). The ziggurats were the major architectural accomplishments of the Babylonian rule in Mesopotamia. See *Ziggurat.*

BACCARAT Originally a French card game. The name of a fine crystal made in France and used to decorate chandeliers and sconces, and for table service.

BACHELOR CHEST A simple chest of drawers, usually 24″ to 36″ wide by 30″ to 36″ tall, traditional or contemporary in style. The wood or veneer varies with the design. Sometimes used in pairs, and sometimes in place of sofa tables.

BACK ARCH A concealed arch that carries the inner part of a wall while the exterior facing material is carried by a lintel.

BACK FILLING In masonry, the rough masonry behind the facing material, or the filling in the extrados of an arch. When brickwork is used to fill in between studs in a frame building, it is also called brick nogging.

BACK POST The two rear uprights of a chair which are continuations of the rear legs. Usually connected by a top rail and may have a splat between them.

BACK STOOL An upholstered chair without arms, or literally a stool with a back. This term was used to describe the simple seats of the 15th and 16th centuries.

BACK-CUT VENEER Veneer from a log sliced in a manner similar to half-round slicing. (See *Half-Round Slicing Veneer.*)

BAHUT

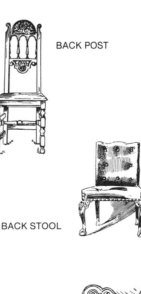

BACK POST

BACK STOOL

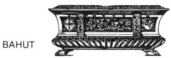

BAIL HANDLE

The result is a striped figure, with the sapwood included on the edges.

BACKUP The masonry wall behind the exterior facing.

BACON CUPBOARD A late-17th-century English cupboard for holding bacon, usually the back of a settle which had an ornamented drawer under the seat.

BAG TABLE A small 18th- and early-19th-century worktable, usually distinguished by the cloth bag or pouch under one or two drawers. Popular in England and America. See also *Pouch Table.*

BAGHEERA A fine uncut pile velvet with a roughish, crush-resistant finish.

BAGNELL An early-18th-century Boston manufacturer of tall case clocks in the Queen Anne style. The works were of brass or wood and the cases of mahogany or maple.

BAGUETTE A very small, convex bead molding. See also *Barquette Molding.*

BAHUT A large-footed chest of the Middle Ages, used to hold tapestries, cushions, etc. It eventually evolved into a high cabinet. A 16th-century Italian Renaissance design is illustrated. See *Cassone.*

BAIGNEUSE A tub-like upholstered daybed introduced during the French Empire period. The back piece sloped down and turned to form the sides; thus the arms or sides angled from the back down to the front of the seat. Similar to a *Méridienne.* See also *Grecian Sofa* and *Récamier.*

BAIL HANDLE A handle or drawer pull which hangs downward in a reversed arch or half moon. Usually the brass drop handles introduced in the William and Mary period in England. Illustrated is a bail handle from a walnut side table of the late 17th century.

BAIZE   A wool fabric originally from Baza, Spain, similar to felt in feel and appearance. Made of wool or cotton, it is a plain, loosely woven fabric with soft twist filling yarns. The longish nap is sometimes frizzed on one side. It found great acceptance as a cover and for inserts on card tables as well as for linings of drawers and case furniture.

BAKED FINISH   A painted or varnished finish which has been baked at a temperature of over 150° F. This heating produces certain desired characteristics: toughness and durability.

BAKELITE   A trademark name for vinyl resins manufactured by Union Carbide Corporation, a group of thermo-plastic resins and plastics used for moldings, extrusions, castings, and adhesives. Popular at one time as a tabletop material.

BAKU   A lightweight, very fine, dull-finished straw fabric.

BALCONY   A platform projecting out from a wall of a building, usually surrounded by a balustrade. Also, the upper section of an auditorium, a shelf-like projection over the ground floor of the hall.

BALDACHINO   A canopy resting on columns, used over altars or thrones in Italian Renaissance churches. Originally described a fine, embroidered cloth of gold and silk used as a portable canopy over shrines and statues in processions. See *Canopy.*

BALDAQUIN BED   The French term for a canopy or tester bed. A late-18th-century French or English canopy or crown bed. The fabric canopy was attached to the wall rather than supported by pillars or bedposts extending up from the four corners of the bed frame.

BALINE   A plain woven, coarse fabric used for stiffening and for underwork in upholstery.

BALKENTRÄGER   German for corbel.

BALL-AND-CLAW FOOT   A furniture foot in the shape of a bird's or dragon's claw grasping a ball or jewel, believed to be an old Chinese motif symbolizing world power. It appeared in Europe in Romanesque furniture and in the Dutch designs of the 17th and 18th centuries, and was popular in Georgian England in the first half of the 18th century. A carved Queen Anne chair of the early 18th century is illustrated.

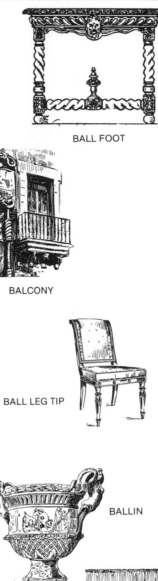

BALL FOOT

BALCONY

BALL LEG TIP

BALLIN

BALLOON CURTAINS

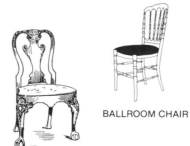

BALLROOM CHAIR

BALL-AND-CLAW FOOT

BALL AND RING   A 17th-century turning used for furniture legs and decorations, consisting of a series of ball-like turnings separated by flattened discs or rings.

BALL-AND-STEEPLE FINIAL   A wood turning popular in 18th-century American furniture. The lowest element of the finial was a sphere surmounted by a series of rings of graduated sizes which created a tapered, steeple-like peak.

BALL FLOWER   A carved Gothic ornament, circular in shape, with a three-lobed or petal effect in the center. Often a carved enrichment in the hollow or convex part of a molding. Popular during the latter part of the 13th and most of the 14th century.

BALL FOOT   A turned furniture foot of a spherical or nearly spherical shape with a narrow disc-like pad at its base. Used extensively in 17th-century Flemish and English furniture. Similar to a *Bun Foot.*

BALL LEG TIP   A small, ball-shaped foot with a cup or ferrule, usually made of brass. It fits over the end of a chair or table leg. A French Directoire chair of the early 19th century, from Malmaison, is illustrated.

BALL TURNING   See *Knob Turning*

BALLIN, CLAUDE (1614–1678)   A celebrated French metal worker of the Louis XII and Louis XIV periods. He created many vases and urns of great beauty, including this bronze vase from the park at Versailles.

BALLOON   A globelike element topping a pillar or gatepost.

BALLOON BACK   The arced, or hoop-shaped chair back of the Hepplewhite period. The curved line starts in a concave form at the seat rail, then sweeps up in a bold convex arc creating a smooth loop. Similar to the Montgolfier chair of the late 18th century in France. Again popularized during the Victorian era. See *Montgolfier Chair.*

BALLOON CURTAINS   Window coverings of pouffy, billowing panels of fabric shirred or gathered at regular intervals. The area between the gathers "poufs" or "balloons" out in an exaggerated fullness.

BALLROOM CHAIR   A small-scaled armless chair popular in the late 19th century and the early 20th. Often had an arcaded back filled with delicate spindles, and turned wooden legs, and was often finished in a gold color, with an applied seat covered in red velvet.

BALUSTER A turned spindle column that supports a railing and is part of a balustrade, or is used as a stretcher between chair legs, or part of a chair back. Commonly an elongated urn or vase shape. Split or half balusters were a favorite applied ornament in the English Restoration furniture. A baluster is also called a banister.

BALUSTRA A dense South African hardwood of a light tobacco brown color.

BALUSTRADE A continuous ornamental railing of stone, wood, or metal. A series of balusters topped with a rail, and serves as a decorated enclosure for balconies, terraces, and stairways. Also used as a decorative motif on 18th-century English architect-designed furniture.

BAMBINO The Christ child portrayed as an infant often in swaddling clothes, in sculpture and painting of the early Renaissance period.

BAMBOO A woody tropical plant used for furniture and ornament. Its distinctive nodular look became very popular in Europe in the 17th and 18th centuries because of the Chinese influence and the Oriental quality of bamboo. Reproduced as a wood turning in Europe and America. See *Bamboo-turned Chair.*

BAMBOO SHADES Rolldown shades made of thin strips or slats of bamboo wood. May be left in a natural yellowish finish, treated to resemble malacca or stained or lacquered a color.

BAMBOO-TURNED Wood *turnings* that simulate the nodular or jointed look of natural bamboo, favored in the late 18th and early 19th centuries for furniture.

BAMBOO-TURNED CHAIR A refinement and development from the *spool furniture* of the mid-19th century in America. It was usually made of maple or other light hardwoods, and was often gilded or painted a light, fanciful color. The *turnings* resemble a stylized bamboo.

BANCONE A 15th- or 16th-century Italian writing table which consisted of a flat writing surface over two paneled drawers. A recessed section, with drawers in its end, supported the two drawers. The entire piece rested on stretcher-connected pairs of legs called "running feet." See *Runner Foot.*

BANDED COLUMN A column which has a lower drum of a larger diameter than the shaft itself. This bottom drum may be more richly decorated than the rest of the shaft. Popular in the French Renaissance period.

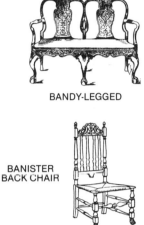

BANDY-LEGGED

BANISTER BACK CHAIR

BAMBOO-TURNED CHAIR

BANJO CLOCK

BANQUETTE

BANDEROLE A ribbon-like motif, carved or painted; often the flat part of the ribbon was filled with an inscription. A Renaissance decoration. See *Ribbon Back.*

BAN-DEW A process devised by the John Bancroft and Sons Co. to make fabrics mildew resistant.

BANDING A narrow strip of veneer used as a border or edging on tabletops, drawer fronts, etc. Usually made of a contrasting inlay, it was popular in 18th-century furniture.

BANDY-LEGGED A colonial American term for bowlegged or cabriole-legged furniture of England and America in the early 18th century. Illustrated is a Queen Anne marquetry settee with bandy legs and ball-and-claw feet. Note the shell carving on the knees of the cabriole legs. See *Cabriole Chair* and *Cabriole Leg.*

BANISTER See *Baluster.* In furniture, usually the split turned splats that make up a banister-back chair of the late 17th century.

BANISTER-BACK CHAIR A late 17th-century English or American chair with split turned spindles or flat bars for the uprights of the chair back. A more elegant and polished variation of this type of chair back was popular in the Hepplewhite period (later 18th century). See *Bar Back.*

BANJO CLOCK A 19th-century wall clock which resembles, in contour, an inverted banjo. See *Barometer Cases.*

BANK A long Gothic bench. See *Banquette.*

BANK OF ENGLAND CHAIR A 19th-century English Regency chair, similar to a tub chair in that the arms start at the front post and sweep around the back in a continuous rising curve. The legs are usually cabriole, and the front edge of the seat is serpentine in form.

BANNER SCREEN An adjustable fire screen. In the mid-18th century, it became a popular accessory, and the banner or shield was often made of tapestry or needlework. It was called, also, a "pole screen," since the screen moved up and down the pole. Some fire screens were made of carved mahogany in cheval form. See *Cheval Screen.*

BANQUETTE The French term for an upholstered bench. Illustrated is an early 18th-century English example.

BANTAM WORK A Dutch and English lacquer technique of the late 17th century. The design was usually etched into a black ground. Originated in Bantam in Dutch Java.

BAR BACK Hepplewhite's term to describe the carved and shaped upright bars that are curved to fit the shield of an open shield-back chair or sofa. A barbacked sofa would be a three- or four-chair-back sofa.

BAR FOOT See *Runner Foot.*

BAR TRACERY Late Gothic tracery in which the stone was cut into bars and arranged in a variety of geometric patterns. It was a refinement from "plate tracery." See *Tracery.*

BARBER'S CHAIR An 18th-century English corner or writing chair. A headrest was sometimes perched over the semicircular top rail. Sometimes the headrest was a continuous broad splat which extended up from the seat frame and was supported by the arms of either side. See *Triangle Seat.*

BARBET,T. A 17th-century late French Renaissance designer of elegant fireplaces and mantels.

BARBIZON SCHOOL A mid-19th-century group of landscape painters who portrayed romanticized scenes of peasant life and the countryside. Included were Jean-François Millet, Théodore Rousseau, and Narcisse Diaz de la Peña.

BARCELONA CHAIR A late-17th-century and early-18th-century ladder-back type of chair of Spain. The top cross-slat was usually greatly enlarged and elaborately carved. The stretchers were ornamented with carved rosettes and chiseled grooves. Also, a 20th-century chair design by Ludwig Mies van der Rohe. The front leg curves up and back to become part of the chair back. The rear leg sweeps up and forward to support the seat. The side view is a graceful X shape. The seat and back are often tufted leather pillows.

BARCLITE A trademark of the Barclite Corporation of America for rigid Fiberglas panels, translucent and patterned with embedded fabrics, foilage, etc. The panels, depending upon the gauge, can be rigid enough to be used as room dividers, sliding doors, cabinet inserts, dropped ceilings, and skylights.

BARDI, LINA BO A modern Italian architect who in 1953 designed a plastic bowl-shaped chair set into a steel base. In her revolutionary steel and glass house in Brazil, cagelike interiors enclosed a garden, and the floors were paved with glass mosaic tiles.

BAREFACED TENON A shaped piece used in the joinery of furniture and cabinets. The tenon usually has two angled

BAR BACK

BARLEY-SUGAR TURNING

BARBER'S CHAIR

BARCELONA CHAIR

BARQUETTE MOLDING

BARRED DOOR

edges or "shoulders." A barefaced tenon has one shoulder only.

BAREFACED TONGUE JOINT In furniture and cabinet joinery, a tongue, flush on only one side of a board, set into a grooved piece of wood. Also called a groove and rabbet joint.

BARÈGE A sheer, gauzelike fabric of wool combined with cotton, silk, and other fibers.

BARJIER OR BARJEER Hepplewhite's term for an armchair or bergère. See *Bergère.*

BARLEY-SUGAR TURNING A spiral turning that resembes a twisted rope, much used in the mid- and late-17th century for furniture legs and stretchers. Illustrated is an upholstered chair of the Cromwellian period (mid 17th century in England).

BAROCCO Italian for baroque.

BAROCKSTIL German for baroque style.

BAROMETER CASES In the 18th century, usually elegant mahogany cases banded with satinwood or boxwood and topped with a broken or swan's neck pediment. The dial was often surmounted by a circular mirror in a reeded frame. The banjo type was formed by a wide circular dial topped by a bulbous upper part. Adam and Chippendale designed many beautiful cases for this popular household accessory.

BAROQUE French for curious, odd, or strange. The Portuguese barroco means a large irregular pearl. The Baroque period in architecture, painting, and sculpture in the 17th and 18th centuries created an overwhelming and direct appeal to the senses of the beholder. It was a blend of illusionism, light and color, and movement with a new approach to classic art. Characterized by large-scale, bold details, sweeping curves, and a wealth of ornament. It was a period of religious emotionalism, and Bernini was one of its great architects. The furniture and decoration of Louis XIV period is also termed baroque. See *Bernini, Gian Lorenzo.*

BARQUETTE MOLDING A small semi-circular molding ornamented with beads or olive berries. See also *Astragal.*

BARRÉ A barred or striped effect running horizontally across knitted or woven fabric.

BARRED DOOR Glass cabinet, secretary, and bookcase door with wood fretwork. Because of the high cost of glass, the small precious pieces were set into the intricate, cutout, lacy wood framework. Illustratcd is a Chippendale mahogany bookcase of about 1760. See also *Fretwork*.

BARREL CHAIR   A semicircular chair, usually upholstered. It resembles a cylinder which has been cut in half vertically. An early-19th century English Regency chair is illustrated.

BARREL-SHAPED SEAT   See *Garden Seat*.

BARTÉLEMY, JEAN SIMON   An 18th-century French painter and decorator of the Louis XVI period. He created a famous series of panels for Marie Antoinette's boudoir entitled "Love Assisting at the Toilet of Grace."

BASALT   A dark green or brown stone with columnar strata used in Egyptian statues. A favored material in the Empire period because of the Egyptian association and its rich, strong coloring.

BASALT WARE   A black porcelain pottery developed by Josiah Wedgwood in 18th-century England.

BASE   The series of moldings at the bottom of the shaft of a column, which helps to distribute the weight. In sculpture, the base can be any block or molding at the bottom of a piece. In furniture, the lowest supporting part of a piece of case furniture.

BASE WOOD   The basic construction wood or carcass (also called the carcase) of a piece of furniture, veneered with a more costly or more beautifully grained wood. Oak and beech are often used in European furniture, native softwoods in the United States.

BASEBOARD   The horizontal board placed at the bottom of the wall and resting directly on the floor, usually trimmed with moldings. Illustrated is a wall area designed by Gilles Marie Oppenords, who introduced the Rococo style in France in the first half of the 18th century.

BASEMENT   In classical and Renaissance architecture, a story below the main level of a building, not necessarily below ground level. Illustrated is a section of the French Renaissance Hôtel de Ville at Anvers. In contemporary usage the basement is a story partially or entirely below ground level.

BASIN STANDS   Small Chippendale and Hepplewhite 18th-century washstands, designed to hold minute handbasins.

BASKET STAND   A late-18th-century two-tiered work table. The tiers were surrounded by galleries composed of small turnings or spindles, and the unit rested on a tripod base. Similar to a Canterbury and

BARREL CHAIR

BAS-RELIEF

BASSES

BASEMENT

BASEBOARD

BASIN STAND

a dumbwaiter. Sheraton designed many such tables.

BASKETWEAVE   A textile woven with large similar-sized warps and wefts. The weft crosses over alternate warp threads, creating an effect like that of a woven rccd basket. Used to make homespun and monk's cloth. Also an inlay technique that simulates the woven quality of a basket.

BASON STAND   See *Basin Stand*.

BAS-RELIEF   French for low relief. A form of sculpture in which the design is raised only slightly from the background. Illustrated are bas-relief panels by Jean Goujon for the Fountain of Innocents, 1549.

BASSES   The lower part of 17th-century English and French beds. Also the elaborate fabric treatments used to cover the basses, similar to what is today called the dust ruffle. Illustrated is a state bed from Hampton Court Palace (late 17th-century England).

BASSET TABLE   A Queen Anne gaming table for the playing of five-handed basset, a popular 18th-century card game.

BASSO RELIEVO   Low-relief carving. See *Bas-Relief*.

BASSWOOD   A lightweight, light-colored wood used extensively for core stock and crossbanding in plywood panels. It does not warp readily, and is moderately strong. Basswood, found in the northern United States and Canada, is related to the linden of Europe.

BAST FIBERS   Fibers obtained from stalk plants like jute, flax, and ramie. The stalks are retted (steeped in water to cause a weakening of the stalks) and decorticated (the hard outer covering removed).

BAT   In masonry, a part of a brick. A half bat is a half of a brick.

BATHTUB   A tub, vat, or container in which a person may bathe or wash, usually connected to water pipes and a drain. See *Labrum*.

BATIK   A Javanese process of resist dyeing on cotton or silk. The design is waxed on the cloth, and the cloth is then dyed. The waxed areas resist the stain, and the pattern appears in the background color of the fabric. The process can be repeated several times for multicolored effects. Streaked effects are obtained when the stain crawls through cracks in the wax. Batik can be imitated by machine printing.

BATISTE   A sheer, fine fabric, usually made of cotton, with a lengthwise striation. May also be made of wool or in silk, where it resembles mull and is called "batiste de soie." Can also be made of rayon and decorated with woven stripes and jacquared florals.

BAT'S WING BRASSES   An early American hardware design which resembles a conventionalized silhouette of a bat's wing outstretched, used on handle plates and escutcheons.

BATTEN   A long piece of sawed wood used for flooring or wainscoting, or as uprights for lathing. It is usually fastened to one or more boards as a cleat.

BATTING   Carded cotton prepared in sheets or rolls and used for stuffing and padding upholstered pieces.

BAUGHMAN, MILO   A 20th-century furniture designer who has combined fine craftsmanship and mass production, often using steel and chrome with wood, and producing interesting textures and colors.

BAUHAUS   An influential school of architecture, art, and design located in Weimar, Austria, and later at Dessau. During its short life (1919 to 1933) the Bauhaus declared that the artist and craftsman were inseparable, and craftsmanship was the main source of creative design. Famous associates were Walter Gropius, who organized it with Lászó Moholy-Nagy, Johannes Itten, Marcel Breuer, Paul Klee, and Wassily Kandinsky.

BAY   The space between columns or supports, or the compartment in a structure which is separated from the rest of the building by an arch, buttress, or vaulting. A bay is also called a severy.

BAY WINDOW   A window which projects outward from the perpendicular wall surface of a building.

BAYADÈRE   A fabric of strongly contrasting multicolored horizontal stripes, originally the garment worn by the dancing girls of India.

BAYEUX TAPESTRY   A famous and extraordinary French Romanesque embroidered tapestry commemorating the victory of the Normans in England, 213 feet long.

BAYWOOD   Also called Honduras mahogany. Lighter in color and softer than Cuban or Spanish mahogany, with fine markings. A desirable veneer wood.

BEACH CLOTH   An imitation linen crash made of a lightweight cotton warp and mohair (or cotton) filling. Often used for draperies in casual or informal rooms.

BEAD   A small cylindrical molding carved to resemble a continuous string of pearls or beads. An *Astragal*.

MILO BAUGHMAN

BEAMED CEILING

BAY WINDOW

BEAU BRUMMEL

BEAD AND BUTT   A panel that is set flush with the stiles and rails that make up the framework of the wall or paneled surface. A bead molding is used along the edges of the panel that butts against the stiles.

BEAD CURTAINS   Individual strings of beads, (glass, wood, plastic, ceramic, bamboo, etc.) hung together to form a curtain over a window, door opening, or arch. May be used as a semitransparent room divider. Originally an Eastern or Near Eastern device.

BEAD FLUSH   A small, almost circular applied molding that runs completely around a panel.

BEAD AND REEL   A decorative half-round or bead molding with alternating circular and elongated oval shapes enriching the surface.

BEAK HEAD   A Norman decorative molding. The carving on this early Gothic enrichment resembles a stylized bird's head and beak.

BEAM   A long piece of timber or metal set horizontally to support a roof or ceiling.

BEAMED CEILING   A ceiling in which the exposed or encased beams are part of the decorative scheme.

BEARDSLEY, AUBREY   An English illustrator and high priest of the Art Nouveau period of decoration in the 1890's, principally known for his work in the *Yellow Book*, 1894, and his illustrations for Oscar Wilde's *Salome*. Beardsley's designs influenced the interior and furniture designs of the time. See *Art Nouveau*.

BEARER STRIP   See *Bearing Rail*.

BEARING PARTITION   An interior wall of one story or less in height which supports a load set upon it from above, in addition to its own weight.

BEARING RAIL   The horizontal carrying member for a drawer in a table or cabinet, also called a "bearer strip."

BEARING WALL   A wall which supports a vertical load in addition to its own weight.

BEAR'S-PAW FOOT   A decorative furniture foot used by French and English designers in the late 17th and early 18th centuries, a carved representation of a furry paw, sometimes combined with a ball. Occasionally used on Chippendale designs.

BEAU BRUMMEL   An early-19th-century Englishman's dressing table with adjustable mirrors, drawers, shelves, and candlestands, named after the famous dandy of the time of George IV. Sheraton designed several units of this type.

BEAUFAIT The original spelling of buffet. Illustrated is a 16th-century French buffet or cupboard. See *Buffet*.

BEAUVAIS An art factory that specialized in textiles and tapestries, begun in France during the reign of Louis XIV. Boucher, during the period of Louis XV, designed many tapestries for the Beauvais looms, including the "Story of Psyche." Toward the end of the 18th century, Beauvais started to produce pile rugs. The most popular motifs used at Beauvais were love scenes and pastorals in soft pastel colors. A Louis XV fauteuil covered in a Beauvais fabric is illustrated. See *Canapé* and *Causeuse* for other examples.

BED CHAIR An early-18th-century Dutch innovation. It was an armed chair with a back that let down and a hidden leg that unfolded to support the lowered back. The legs and the lowered arms came together to make the center firm. The front rail was hinged so that the entire seat and back unit could come over and down. Often made of nut wood or maple inlaid with tulipwood and styled with bandy (cabriole) legs and Dutch feet.

BED FRAME In contemporary use, a steel frame which supports the spring and mattress; generally the frame is set on casters. The frame may be bolted to a headboard. See *Harvard Frame* and *Hollywood Bed*.

BED MOLDING A small molding, or a series of moldings, placed under a projection, as under the corona of a cornice. Illustrated is a late-17th century cornice molding designed by William Penn.

BED RAILS Strips, usually of wood, used to connect the headboard to the footboard and to keep them in a vertical position. Combined with the slats, which are set at right angles to the rails, they support the spring and/or mattress.

BED STEPS An 18th-century English and American device for getting in and out of high beds. The steps were often incorporated into other pieces of bedroom furniture, sometimes with a chamber pot container. Illustrated is a Sheraton bed step unit which converts into a stool with an upholstered top when not in use.

BED STOCK The actual supporting framework of certain 16th-century beds in England and on the Continent. The front posts or pillars that supported the wood tester or canopy stood free of the bed proper, and the bedstock supported the bedding. Similar to the current bed frame.

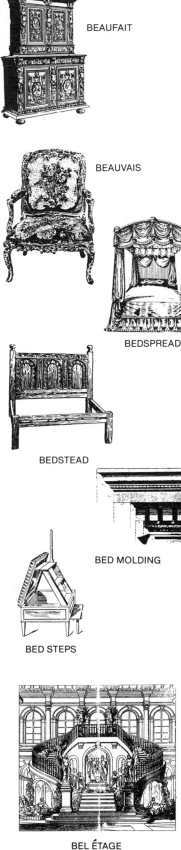

BEAUFAIT

BEAUVAIS

BEDSPREAD

BEDSTEAD

BED MOLDING

BED STEPS

BEL ÉTAGE

BEDFORD CORD A strong, durable rib-weave fabric with raised lengthwise lines produced by warpwise stuffing threads. May be made of wool, silk, cotton, rayon, or a combination. Used for upholstery, and is similar to piqué. Originally woven in New Bedford.

BEDROOM CHAIR A light-frame side chair for use in a bedroom. Sheraton designed this type of chair at the end of the 18th and start of the 19th centuries. Often the frame was made of beech, stained or japanned, and equipped with a rush seat.

BEDSIDE CUPBOARD A small bedside unit which usually contained a chamber pot, also called a pot cupboard. An 18th-century design.

BEDSPREAD A fabric covering for the top and sides of a bed. Can be made of a variety of fabrics and styles: a coverlet with dust ruffles, a fitted top, a loose throw which falls to the floor at the sides. An early-19th-century tester bed by Sheraton is shown.

BEDSTEAD The supporting framework of a bed. Illustrated is an early 17th-century Jacobean oak bedstead with an arcaded head panel.

BEE A stylized bee was the personal emblem of Napoleon I. Along with laurel wreaths, the letter N, stars, and eagles, it was a popular motif of the French Empire period (1804–1814). It has been suggested that the resemblance between the bee and the Bourbon fleur-de-lis made it possible to convert the Bourbon symbol into the Napoleonic symbol without too many drastic renovations when Bonaparte became Emperor.

BEECH A tough, strong, pale, straight-grained wood which resembles birch and maple. Though used for furniture and flooring in the 17th and 18th centuries, it is mainly used today for furniture frames, rocker supports, and bent chair backs. European beech is similar to the American beech but seasons and works better.

BEL ÉTAGE The main story of a building, usually containing salons and reception rooms. Most often the first story above the ground level. Illustrated is the main entrance to a French Renaissance château. See *Piano Nobile*.

BELL (of a capital) The body of the capital between the necking and the abacus.

BELL SEAT A Queen Anne chair seat with a rounded front (early-18th-century England).

BELL AND TRUMPET See *Bell Turning*.

BELL TURNING A conventionalized bell-shaped turning popular during the William and Mary period. Used for furniture legs and pedestal supports (late 17th century).

BELLA ROSA A moderately hard and heavy, pink to yellowish beige wood grown in the Philippines and Malaya. The graining is usually straight.

BELLEEK A fine, ivory colored china produced in Ireland, highly translucent with a marked iridescent quality to the glaze. Most frequently used for small decorative items and tea sets.

BELLFLOWER ORNAMENT A popular 18th-century carved motif used as a furniture and interiors enrichment. Based on conventionalized bell-shaped flowers or catkins, used in a continuous chain or swag or in graduated sizes as a pendant. Similar to the husk ornament. See *Husk Ornament.*

BELLOWS A blowing device used to create a blast of air when contracted, or collapsed, often highly decorated, carved, or embellished and used as a fireplace accessory. Illustrated is a 16th-century Venetian bellows.

BELOW-GRADE FLOORS Floors set below the actual street level or ground level. May be only a foot or two below or one or more stories below.

BELTER, JOHN HENRY (?–1865) A popular New York cabinet and furniture maker of the mid-19th century. He originated and worked with laminated plywood over 100 years ago. Belter's Victorian rococo designs were constructed mainly in rosewood, oak, and walnut. His furniture usually had heavily carved and curved frames, roll moldings, and naturalistic flower details.

BELVEDERE Italian for beautiful view. In Italian Renaissance architecture, the uppermost story of a building open on several sides to allow for viewing the countryside, or to let in the cooling breezes. A lantern atop a building has also been called a belvedere. Shown here is an early English Renaissance structure by Inigo Jones.

BEMBERG A trademark name for *rayon* thread and/or yarns made by a cupramonium process by American Bemberg Company.

BENCH A long stool or rectangular seating device, often backless or with a low back. See *Carreau* illustration.

BENCH TABLES See *Settles.*

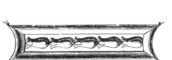

BELLFLOWER ORNAMENT

BELLOWS

BELVEDERE

JEAN BERAIN

BENDED BACK CHAIR See *Fiddleback Chair* and *Spoon Back.* This name is sometimes mistakenly given to a Hogarth chair because of its vase-shaped splat.

BENEMAN, GUILLAUME An 18th- and early-19th-century French master (cabinetmaker for Louis XVI.) He worked for Marie Antoinette at St. Cloud and later executed Percier's designs in the Empire style. Beneman's style was severely, classic, and more in keeping with the Empire look. He used mahogany and elaborate gilt bronze mountings to enrich his designs.

BENGALINE A heavy faille fabric with a fine weave and crosswise ribs. It may be woven of silk, rayon, or wool warp yarns with worsted or cotton fillings (weft).

BENGE An African wood of rich brown with tan or darker brown markings, a hard texture and strong contrasting figure.

BENJAMIN, ASHER (1773–1845) American publisher of handbooks for the guidance of carpenters and builders. He was greatly responsible for the generally high level of building during the Federal period.

BENTWOOD FURNITURE Furniture made of wood softened by steaming and then molded into curving forms. The term is particularly used to describe the furniture made in this manner by the Austrian, Michael Thonet, beginning in 1857. Modern contour furniture such as that created by Eames and Aalto is made in a similar fashion.

BENTWOOD ROCKER A typical rocking chair made by Thonet (at the end of the 19th century). It has swirling bentwood arms, back and support and a scrolly C- and S-shape decorated unit.

BERAIN, JEAN (1636–1711) A great French designer and decorator of the Louis XIV period. He designed furniture, tapestries, wood and metal accessories, and wall panels. Berain's work ranged from the Louis XIII tradition, through the chinoiserie, up to the elegant Régence. He is especially noted for arabesque forms and the designs he created for Boulle's inlay technique. See *Boulle Work* and *Maître-Ébéniste.*

BERBER Originally, the Berber tribes of Morocco in North Africa and their simple, geometrically designed, hand knotted rugs, made of undyed, natural, pure wool yarns. Today the term refers to a coarse, heavy-textured carpet or rug in natural wool or synthetic yarns having the natural, undyed, look of wool and a heavy, pebbley surface texture.

BERGÈRE An all-upholstered low arm-chair, usually with exposed wood frame and enclosed sides. The upholstered arms are shorter than the length of the seat, and a soft loose pillow rests on a fabric-covered seat platform. Introduced in the Louis XV period and also popular in the Louis XVI period. Variations are still produced today.

BERGERIES A popular 18th-century rural scenic design in France and England. Pastoral landscapes were peopled with rustics or elegant gentlepeople dressed as farmers and shepherdesses. Paintings were made in this style, and the popular toile-de-Jouy prints featured it. See *Toile de Jouy*.

BERNINI, GIAN (GIOVANNI) LORENZO (1598–1680) A great Italian architect and sculptor. The roots of his style were in Michelangelo, Caravaggio, and the classic forms. He used many materials together to achieve an exciting and emotional response from the viewer. Bernini did much work in and around St. Peter's and the Vatican in Rome, as well as suggested, but unused, plans for the east colonnade of the Louvre for Louis XIV. See *Baroque*.

BEVEL The edge of a flat surface that has been cut on an angle. See *Chamfer*.

BEWICK, THOMAS (1753–1828) An Englishman, considered to be the "Father of Modern Wood Engravings," who introduced white line engraving. See *Engraving*.

BIBELOTS The French term for trinkets or knickknacks. Small art objects such as paintings, sculptures, snuffboxes, etc., created for personal use or as decorations. See *Objet D'Art*.

BIBLE BOX A 17th-century carved box to contain a family Bible. Later made with a hinged sloping lid, which when closed served as a reading stand. The interior was sometimes fitted with compartments and small shelves. The desk evolved from this item of furniture. An oak piece of the early 17th century (Jacobean period) is illustrated.

BIBLE OR CHANCEL CHAIR English chair dating from 1600 to 1650. The seat lifts up so that a bible can be stored below the seat. Otherwise, the chair is similar to most simple wooden chairs. See *Wainscot Chair*.

BIBLIOTHÈQUE French term for a large bookcase or book press. Illustrated is a 19th-century bookcase by Wright and Mansfield made of juniper wood, and decorated with columns and moldings of ebony. Wedgwood plaques are set into the wood panels.

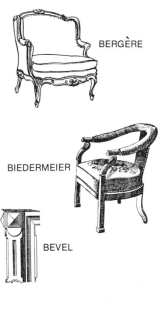

BERGÈRE

BIEDERMEIER

BEVEL

BILLET

BIBLE BOX

BIBLIOTHÈQUE

BIDET French term for a washing unit or a container for a basin, usually associated with feminine hygiene.

BIEDERMEIER An early 19th-century German furniture and decoration style (1815–1848). An unaristocratic, clear and simple style, mainly Empire and classic in line, but rendered "homey" and "bourgeois" with painted details in black and gold to simulate carving. The furniture was made largely of fruitwoods and mahogany, and was characterized by arches, pediments, columns, simple escutcheons, burl woods, lyres, plumes, wreaths and rounded-back chairs. The name was derived from "Papa Biedermeier," a comic symbol of homey comfort, well-being, and middle-class contentment. Biedermeier furniture was also made in Austria and Northern Italy.

BIENNAIS, MARTIN GUILLAUME A noted 19th-century French Empire metalworker.

BILBAO MIRROR A late-18th-century mirror, often with a marble or marble and wood frame, usually with a pair of slender columns on the vertical ends. The name derived from Bilboa, where it originated.

BILDWERK German for sculpture.

BILLET A type of ornament which was peculiarly Norman and consisted of short cylinders and blocks. In 18th-century furniture, inlaid billet banding was used for decoration around cabinet drawers and doors.

BIOTECHNICAL DESIGN See *Ergonomic Design*.

BIRCH A light brown, fine grained American wood. It is strong and hard, and can take a natural finish or be stained to simulate mahogany, walnut, satinwood, and other more expensive woods. Birch is used for doors, trims, and floors as well as furniture. In quartered or flat sliced veneer, it is possible to get a curly figure. European birch is similar but less available.

BIRDCAGE CLOCK A late-17th-century English clock made of brass with exposed pendulum and weights. An openwork clock.

BIRDCAGE SUPPORT In early American furniture, the double-block construction which makes it possible for a tilt-top table to rotate and tilt. It resembles the outline of a cage. In other styles (e.g., 18th-century English) the birdcage was made of turned colonnettes.

BIRD'S BEAK In Greek classic architecture, a supporting molding which resembled the downward curve of a bird's beak. In furniture, a round V-cut on molding corners.

BIRD'S-EYE A figure on wood that resembles small birds' eyes, caused by cutting on a tangent through the indentations which sometimes appear on the annual rings of the log. Often noted on maple wood.

BISECTED VAULT An arch or ceiling vault with one impost only; the crown abuts against the opposite wall. It resembles one quarter of a cylinder or half of a barrel vault.

BISCUIT See *Bisque*.

BISCUIT TUFTING A method of tying back upholstery and padding to create plump, square tufts on chair backs and seats. Buttons are usually sewn back taut in a regular square or diamond pattern. The excess padding is forced into the center of each square or diamond making a small "pillow." A late-19th-century German Victorian sofa is illustrated.

BISQUE Pottery that has been fired once and has no glaze or a very thin one. Dull in color, tan or red terra-cotta, depending upon the clay used. Bisque also refers to white, unglazed porcelain figurines and groups, made at Sèvres in France during the latter part of the 18th century.

BISTRO TABLE A small table, usually not more than 28″ to 30″ in diameter, with a slender upright pedestal that can end in a cast iron, weighted based. The table top may be marble, metal or more recently, laminated with a plastic. The sort of table used by French outdoor cafes.

BLACK GUM See *Tupelo*.

BLACKAMOOR A decorative statue of a Negro, usually in gaudy oriental-type costume. A popular motif during the Italian Renaissance, revived in the Victorian period. The blackamoor was used as a pedestal for tables and for torch holders.

BLACKWOOD A wood similar to acacia and native to Australia and Tasmania. Hardwood painted or stained to look like ebony, frequently used by John Belter in the mid-19th century in his American Victorian furniture. See *Acacia*.

BLACKWORK A technique of embroidery of the English Tudor period (16th century). Patterns were picked out in black and silver thread; these designs inspired many printed linings and wallpapers of the period. Blackwork embroidery became popular again at the end of the Elizabethan reign (after 1603).

BLANC DE PLOMB French for white lead. Some Louis XV furniture which was ordered for the Petit Trianon was originally painted white, but dust and time grayed the

BISECTED VAULT

BISCUIT TUFTING

BLIND ARCADE

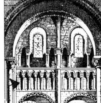

BLACKWORK

BLOCK FOOT

furniture down to gris Trianon, a soft gray color.

BLANKET CHESTS 17th- and 18th-century American chests which had a lidded section on top, and sometimes one or two drawers below. These units were eventually replaced by the lowboy, the highboy, and the chest of drawers. See *Connecticut Chest* and *Hadley Chest*.

BLEACHING The process to remove the natural and artificial impurities in fabrics, to get a pure white for even dyeing or printing. Varies with the fiber content of the fabric which might be bleached by exposure to air and light or by chlorine, etc.

Open-textured woods can also be chemically bleached to lighter tones. Blond walnut and blond mahogany are typical of bleached woods.

BLEEDING The running off or blending together of excess dye from a dyed fabric during washing. In the printing of wallpaper and fabrics, the color or pigment which spreads out beyond the actual printed designs, usually into the selvage.

BLEND A mixture of different fibers in the same yarn or fabric.

BLIND A shade or screen device used over a window area to control light and air. May be made of various fabrics, and work on a roller or on a pull cord like a Roman shade or Austrian shade. May also be made of slats of wood, metal, or plastic. (Venetian or Boston blinds). See *Austrian Shade* and *Roman Shade*.

BLIND ARCADE A decorative, nonstructural arcade applied to a wall surface with no actual opening. Shown is the Romanesque church of the Trinity in Caen, France.

BLIND HEADER In masonry, a hidden brick header inside a wall.

BLIND STITCHING In upholstery, a method of sewing in a particular area of a couch or chair which is eventually covered and therefore impossible to reach. The hidden or blind area is sewn first from the back, then the flap is put into place and finished off by sewing or tacking from the front.

BLISTER A wood-grain effect produced by the uneven contour of the annual ring growth. It presents a bumpy, blistered figure, also called a "quilted figure." This figuration often appears in maple, cedar, poplar, and mahogany.

BLOCK FOOT A cube-shaped foot, usually used with a square, untapered leg. When tapered it is called a spade, taper, or therm foot. The block foot is also known as the Marlborough foot, and was used by Chippendale in mid-18th century England.

BLOCK PRINT Fabric printed by hand, using carved wooden blocks or plates. The dye is rolled over the raised pattern on the block which is then pressed down, usually under pressure, on the fabric. If a two-color design is desired, two separate blocks are used. This technique was also used on early wallpapers and gilded leather tapestries.

BLOCKFRONT A furniture front which is divided vertically into alternating convex and concave panels. The center panel is recessed between the two advancing side panels. Especially associated with John Goddard and the Newport School of 18th-century American chests, secretaries, and highboys. Also called a tub front.

BLOND WOODS Light beige-toned woods like primavera, avodire, aspen, holly, birch, and bleached mahogany and walnut. Also wood clouded with a white pigment or open grains filled in with white pigment to achieve a light look.

BLONDEL, JACQUES FRANÇOIS (1705–1774) A French architect of the period of Louis XV. He designed in a refined Rococo manner, and his interior "boiserie" is recognized by its straight, elegant, lined panels with Rococo corners and cornices.

BLUEPRINT A positive print in white lines on a blue paper (ferroprussiate). The negative is a translucent drawing, usually of building or engineering details or plans.

BLUNT ARROW LEG The leg of an 18th-century American Windsor chair which ends in a ball-like tip. It resembles a spent practice arrow.

BOASTING The rough shaping of a stone by a carver or sculptor before the finished sculptural or architectural details are accomplished.

BOAT BED A bed placed in an alcove with only one long side showing. A low, massive piece popular in the French Empire and Restoration periods, and in American furniture contemporary with these periods. It is similar to the gondola or sleigh bed, boat-shaped and often made in light-colored woods with contrasting wood marquetry. It was often raised on a massive, steplike base.

BOAT-SHAPED TABLE A modern conference and dining table-top shape. The long sides are shaped like parentheses (they bow out gently in the center and taper in toward the short ends). The two short ends are straight. The shape is somewhat

BOBBIN TURNING

BOFET

BLOCKFRONT

BOISERIE

like a long oval with a flattened top and bottom.

BOBBIN TURNING Turned legs and stretchers with bobbin-like swellings, popular in the early 17th century. In the late-18th-century Windsor chair, this type of turning was sometimes used for stretchers. A Jacobean child's chair with bobbin-turned legs is shown.

BOBBINET A sheer, meshlike curtain fabric.

BOBÈCHE A socket with a wide rim for a candle or an electric bulb. Originally used to catch wax drippings, today it is used as a decorative top to a candlestick, or as a device to hook on prisms and crystals.

BOBOTE A tropical hardwood.

BODY In pottery, the clay or other material from which a piece of pottery or porcelain is manufactured. The glaze is applied later.

BODYING IN In wood finishing, the filling in of the coarse grains of wood to permit a more even finish.

BOFET An early form of buffet from the original beaufait. A 15th-century French buffet is illustrated. See *Crédence.*

BOFFET OR BOFFET CHAIR A three-legged, triangular, Scandinavian chair which was produced till the end of the 16th century. They were usually made of turnings and had carved ornaments.

BOFFRAND, GERMAIN An 18th-century French decorator of the Louis XV style. He decorated the Palais Soubise for the Prince de Soubise.

BOG OAK Oak which has been preserved in peat bogs to affect its color, used for banding, paneling, and ornaments.

BOGEN German for arch.

BOGENGANG German for arcade

BOIS DE BOUT Wood cut across the grain, thus appearing darker.

BOIS DE FIL See *Fil de Bois.*

BOIS (or BOISE) DE ROSE A yellowish wood with reddish striped markings. The wood turns blond as it ages. See *Tulipwood.*

BOIS DE VIOLETTE Also called bois de violet and amaranth. See *Kingwood.*

BOISERIE The carved woodwork and paneling of 17th- and 18th-century French interiors, often picked out in gilt. Could become quite elaborate as shown in this Louis XV salon. A gilt console table and mirror are to the left of the door.

Note the trumeau (overdoor paneling with painting).

BOKHARA RUG   See *Turkoman Rug.*

BOLECTION MOLDINGS   A series of rounded moldings which project far beyond the panel or wall to which they are applied. A bolection panel (illustrated) projects from the wall surface, as opposed to a sunk panel. See *Panel.*

BOLSTER   A long, usually cylindrical, stuffed pillow or cushion popular in the late 18th and early 19th century. Also an oversized pillow or back rest and may be wedge-shaped or rectangular.

BOLSTER ARM   A fat, rounded or cylindrical upholstered arm on a chair or couch which resembles a bolster. A 19th-century term.

BOMBAY FURNITURE   Furniture manufactured in India after 1740 (the breakdown of the Mogul Empire). The furniture is a conglomeration of French and Portugese styles and forms which are overlaid with typically elaborate and minute Indian carving. English and Dutch influences also appear.

BOMBÉ   French for convex, arched, or humpbacked. A swelling or flowing curve, a surface which swells outward and then recedes. This line appears in commodes and chests at the end of the Louis XIV and the Régence periods in France, and reaches its height during the Louis XV or Rococo period. The term bombé often is given to the swollen, overblown commodes of this period. The bombé type of cabinet or drawer furniture also appears in the Venetian Rococo and Chippendale's French style. It is typical of a French base.

BONADER   Wall hanging, painted on paper or canvas, of peasant subjects, created by Swedes and Swedish Americans in the 18th century.

BOND   The arrangement of bricks, masonry, concrete blocks, etc., in a pattern that is so arranged that the vertical joints do not come out one directly beneath the other. The pattern can be made more definite by using different colored finishing bricks. See the following: *Checkerboard Bond, Common Bond, English Bond, English Cross Bond, Flemish Bond, Running Bond, Stretcher Bond.*

BOND COURSE   The course of bricks which overlaps the bricks below.

BONDED FABRIC   A non-woven fabric made up of a mass of fibers glued, cemented, fused or otherwise bonded together. Similar to felt. See *Felt.*

BONHEUR DU JOUR

BONNET TOP

BOLECTION PANEL

BOOKCASE

BORNE

BOND

BONHEUR DU JOUR   A small upright lady's desk with a cabinet top and drawers, the desk area usually covered with a let-down front. A small cupboard or bookshelf was often at the rear. A popular design of the Louis XVI period. Illustrated is a design by Reisener (late 18th-century France), which has been enriched with Sèvres plaques.

BONNET TOP   A rounded hat-shaped top portion of a highboy, secretary, etc., prevalent in 17th-century and early-18th-century English and American furniture. Also called a hooded top.

BONNETIÈRE   An 18th-century French cabinet, usually designed tall, narrow and deep enough to hold hats and bonnets.

BOOK BOX   See *Bible Box.*

BOOK TABLE   A rectangular, circular, or hexagonal pedestal with either exposed shelves on all sides, or doors to cover the bookshelves. An 18th-century innovation similar to the pote or pole table.

BOOKCASE   In the late 17th and early 18th centuries, the bookcase resembled the china cabinet of the times. In the mid- and late 18th century, the bookcase took on a new importance, and usually was made in two parts: a glazed door section on top of a closed cupboard. The area below had either additional shelves or drawers. The bookcase top was sometimes used with a writing desk below. Illustrated is a Sheraton design.

BOOK-MATCH VENEERING   Every other sheet of veneer is turned over, as a page in a book, so that the back edge of one meets the front edge of the adjacent panel. This produces a matched joint effect.

BORAX   A slang expression for cheap, commercial furniture, usually poorly constructed, badly styled, and poorly finished.

BORDER   A continuous running motif or ornament used for edging a design, fabric, or panel frame.

BORNE   A round or oval type of French sofa with a separating pillar or rail in the center which serves as a back, popular in public areas during the Victorian period. These upholstered poufs were usually located in the center of a room.

BOSS   The projecting ornament placed at the intersections of moldings or beams. Angel heads, flowers, or foliage and animal heads are common motifs. In Gothic architecture often a hanging, ornamental pendant at the meeting of ribs in vaults. See *Cul-de-Lampe.* On furniture, the boss is a small oval or semicircular applied ornament found in 17th- and 18th-century English and American designs.

BOSSE An African wood used successfully for large veneer. A uniform pink-brown color with a mottled, satiny texture. It is also called African cedar and cedar mahogany. Bosse has a cedar-like aroma when freshly cut. See *Piqua.*

BOSSE, ABRAHAM (1611–1678) A French designer, painter, and architect under Louis XIII and Louis XIV.

BOSSONA A hard Brazilian wood with black and brown streaks on a red-brown ground. See *Gonçalo Alves.*

BOSTON ROCKER A rocking chair, i.e., a chair on curved supports. The wooden seat usually curves upward in the rear and dips down in front. The chair is often spindle-backed and ornamented with a painted design on the wide top *rail.* An early-19th-century American design.

BOTTEGA Italian for shop. The studio or atelier of an artist or artisan.

BOTTLE END GLAZING Glazing of cabinet doors in the 18th century that resembled bottle bottoms leaded together. A bull's-eye-effect in a circular glass disk. See *Crown Glass.*

BOTTLE TURNING A Dutch wood turning which resembles a bottle and appears in William and Mary furniture in late-17th-century England.

BOUCHER, FRANÇOIS (1703–1770) The French boudoir artist and decorator of the 18th century. Boucher specialized in voluptuous and sensuous art, and he was a favorite designer of Mme de Pompadour. In 1765, he was made Court Painter to Louis XV. Among his assignments was that of inspector at the Gobelins Factory, where his style influenced the products, including the use of an oval medallion or frame which appears on tapestries and on Sèvres china.

BOUCHER, JULES FRANÇOIS (1736–1781) The son of François Boucher, the famous painter of the Louis XV period. He painted and designed panels and interiors in keeping with the Louis XVI style. One of his chair designs is illustrated here.

BOUCHON A cork pad covered with baize on one side and leather on the other. It was used, in the 18th century, as a removable cover over the marble top of a bouillotte table. The bouchon filled the space between the actual tabletop and the surrounding brass gallery, thus creating a level surface.

BOUCLÉ French for buckled or crinkled. A plain or twill weave with small,

BOSTON ROCKER

BOUILLOTE TABLE

JEAN-BAPTISTE BOULARD

ANDRÉ CHARLES BOULLE

JULES FRANÇOIS BOUCHER

regularly spaced loops and flat irregular surfaces produced by using specially twisted yarns. It can be made of wool, rayon, silk, cotton, or linen, and the texture is particularly well suited to contemporary furniture upholstery.

BOUDOIR From the French "bouder," "to pout." A woman's private apartment or room where she could go to "be alone." It was the nucleus of the court social life in the period of Louis XV. Guests were received and entertained in these feminine retreats, which were usually lavishly decorated and furnished.

BOUDOIR CHAIR A small-scaled chair, usually fully upholstered, for a woman's bedroom or dressing room. Can be of any style or period, but is often French Rococo.

BOUILLOTTE A foot warmer used in the 18th century.

BOUILLOTTE LAMP A late-18th-century candlestick-like lamp, often a three- or four-armed candlestick set into a brass galleried base. A shallow shade, usually metal, covered and protected the flames of the candles. A decorative brass handle finial above the shade made it portable. Originally associated with the small galleried tables they were set upon. See *Bouillotte Table.*

BOUILLOTTE SHADE A shallow, drum-shaped shade used for a lamp or candlestick. It is sometimes made of decorated metal (tôle). See *Bouillotte Lamp.*

BOUILLOTTE TABLE An 18th-century French small circular gaming table, with a brass or bronze gallery edge. The table usually had two small drawers as well as a pair of candle slides set into the apron, below the marble top. Originally used for playing bouillotte, a card game. See *Bouchon.*

BOULARD, JEAN-BAPTISTE (1725–1789) A cabinetmaker (ébéniste) and sculptor of the Louis XVI period, noted for the magnificent bed he created for Fontainebleau.

BOULLE, ANDRÉ CHARLES (1642–1732) Boulle and his four sons were French master cabinetmakers. Boulle designed rich, ornate, massive pieces, often in his own veneer technique of tortoiseshell and brass inlay. In 1672, Boulle was appointed head cabinetmaker to Louis XIV. Besides his noted Boulle-work technique, he also designed the parquet floors, mirrored walls, and inlaid panels in the Versailles Palace. His designs were opulent and full of scrolls, flowers, and arabesques. See *Boulle Work.* An armoire of Boulle work is used to illustrate Le Brun, Charles. Here illustrated is a Boulle commode in the Régence style.

BOULLE, P. Born in France in 1619. The head cabinetmaker to Louis XIII. See *Ébéniste*.

BOULLE WORK The special inlay technique of Charles André Boulle, using tortoiseshell and German silver, brass, or pewter. A sheet of metal (usually brass) and a sheet of tortoiseshell were glued together, and the design was cut out of both pieces at the same time. The piece of brass which dropped out during the cutting could then be set into the tortoiseshell, making a decorative inlay (première partie); or the tortoiseshell could be used to fill in the brass sheet (contrepartie). Boulle work is most often associated with the Louis XIV and Régence periods. See also *Première Partie, Contrepartie,* and *Marquetry.*

BOURBON PERIOD The classic part of the French Renaissance period, dating from about 1589 to 1730. It encompasses the reigns of Henry IV, Louis XIII, and Louis XIV, and the Régence. Illustrated is a chair of the Louis XIII period done in the Italian style.

BOURBON PERIOD

BOW BACK An 18th-century Windsor chair with the hooped or curved back continuing in its sweep to the arms or chair seat.

BOW FRONT A convex or "swell front" shape, typical of mid- and late-18th-century chests, commodes, sideboards, etc. This curved line was especially popular in England with Adam (illustrated) and Hepplewhite.

BOW TOP The top rail of a chair with an unbroken curve between the uprights.

BOW WINDOW A large projecting curved or semicircular window. See *Bay Window.*

BOWFAT An 18th-century American term for a buffet. See *Buffet.*

BOWTELL or BOUTELL A round or roll molding, used as an enrichment on Gothic architecture.

BOX BED A bed enclosed on three sides, or sometimes a bed that folds up against the wall. In the French Gothic period, the open side was usually draped or shuttered to provide privacy and keep out the drafts. Illustrated is a 10th-century Anglo-Saxon box bed showing drapery used as a screen. See *Lit Clos.*

BOX MATCH A veneering pattern similar to the diamond match but angled to

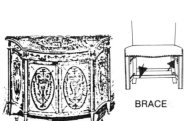

BOX STRETCHER

BOW FRONT   BRACE

BOX BED

BRACED BACK

create a series of consecutive squares radiating out from the center.

BOX PLEATING A technique in which fabric is folded back on itself and then folded back again in the opposite direction, creating a partially hidden panel of fabric. Similar to a *Linenfold* motif.

BOX SETTLE A chest or box that functions as a seat and has a hinged lid that serves as the seat. This piece was popular in the early English Renaissance (Tudor and Elizabethan), and also in 17th- and 18th-century Provincial American furniture.

BOX SPRING A sleeping unit made of spiral steel springs encased in a box-like frame. A layer of cotton felt, hair, rubberized hair, or foam is placed over the springs and tightly covered with ticking. Usually used in conjunction with a mattress to provide the mattress with greater resiliency.

BOX STOOL A Renaissance simple seating unit consisting of a box with a flat hinged top that functioned as a seat.

BOX STRETCHER A square or rectangular reinforcement at the furniture base, created by the turned or squared stretchers between the legs of a table, chair, or cabinet.

BOXWOOD A very dense, light-colored, and grained West Indian wood used almost entirely for inlays and small decorative articles. During the 16th century it was used as an inlay wood on walnut and oak, and in the late 18th century for border edge work on satinwood pieces.

BOZZETTO Italian for sketch. Though it is usually applied to models for sculpture, it may also refer to painted sketches.

BRACCIO Italian for wing of a building.

BRACE The part of a piece of furniture used to give added strength or rigidity. Stretchers on the legs of a piece of furniture would be considered braces. In construction, an angled device used to transmit the weight from one part of a structure to another. It is often a piece of wood angled between two major timbers to keep them set in place and to preserve the angle they create. A reinforcement.

BRACED BACK A Windsor chair whose back is reinforced by two spindles projecting up from an extension behind the seat up to the chair rail. Also called a fiddle-braced back.

BRACKET In furniture, a shaped support between the leg and the seat of a chair, or the leg and the top of a table. A bracket is also a decorative wall-hung shelf and a sconce or wall fixture. In architecture, a supporting element which projects from a wall or pier at a right angle, and helps to carry the weight of a beam or architectural member.

BRACKET CANDLESTICK A sconce or applique. A decorative wall-hung unit with a candlestick projecting forward. Illustrated is a late French Renaissance design from the Versailles Palace. See *Bronze-Doré* illustration.

BRACKET CLOCK A small clock designed to be set on a projecting wall-hung bracket. A shelf clock rather than a wall-hung clock.

BRACKET CORNICE An ornamental cornice supported by a series of brackets. An interior wooden version of a corbel table. See *Corbel Table.*

BRACKET FOOT In cabinetry, a popular furniture leg in 18th-century English and American designs, with a straight corner edge and a curved inner edge. In English furniture the leg is usually longer than it is high. Also called a console leg.

BRAD A small, thin nail with little or no head and usually less than one inch in length, often used for finishing work.

BRADSHAW, GEORGE AND WILLIAM Cabinetmakers and upholsterers of the mid-Georgian period in England.

BRAGANZA TOE See *Spanish Scroll Foot.*

BRAID A narrow strip made by intertwining several strands of silk, cotton or other fabric, used as a trimming, a binding, or a finishing edge. A late-17th-century footstool is illustrated. The pillow is edged with braid.

BRAIDED RUGS Provincial rugs, oval or round in shape, made of strips of fabric twisted and/or braided into a thick coil. The coil is laid flat and stitched together, usually in the traditional oval shape. Braided rugs are associated with Early American interiors. See *Rag Rug.*

BRASS An alloy of one part zinc and three to seven parts copper.

BRASS, ANTIQUED Brass given an aged look through oxidation. Can be artificially produced on new brass.

BRASS, POLISHED Brass given a bright mirror-like finish.

BRASSES Hardware or decorative handles, escutcheons, hinges, etc., made of brass.

BRATTISHING A cresting like an ornamented or pieced parapet. A decorative leaf design used as a cresting device on the top

BREAKFAST TABLE

BRACKET CANDLESTICK

BREAKFRONT

BREWSTER CHAIR

BRACKET FOOT

MARCEL LAJOS BREUER

BRAID

of English Tudor screens or paneling. The motif is also called Tudor Flower.

BRAZIER A pan, on legs, which held hot embers and was used for heating through the 19th century. The brazier is also called a brasero or brasera. A man who works in brass is called a brazier.

BRAZILWOOD A reddish-colored wood similar to mahogany.

BREAKFAST TABLE Chippendale's name for an elegant, small four-legged table, often with a pierced gallery and fretwork trim. The table sometimes had a long narrow drawer.

BREAKFRONT A case piece of furniture whose front is formed on two or more planes; the central portion is either advanced or recessed from the two ends. Particularly descriptive of bookcases, cabinets, and secretaries of the 18th century in England and America. Also see *Blockfront.*

BREEZE BRICKS Standard-sized bricks made of coke breeze concrete instead of baked clay. It is possible to nail or screw breeze bricks.

BREUER, MARCEL LAJOS A 20th-century architect and designer of the Bauhaus School, born in Hungary in 1902. At Harvard, he took on a teaching assignment under Walter Gropius, also of Bauhaus fame. Breuer created the "Butterfly" house in 1949 for the Museum of Modern Art in New York, which presented a vital form of split-level construction, and designed many beautiful residences based on traditional American "frame" construction. Illustrated are the tubular metal cantilevered chairs designed by Breuer in 1925.

BREWSTER CHAIR An early New England chair with turned spindles and a rush seat. Named after Elder Brewster. The chair usually has a double row of spindles on the back. Resembles Provincial Jacobean furniture and is similar to the *Carver Chair,* which, however, has horizontal rails on the back.

BRICK A hardened rectangular block of clay, dried and baked in a kiln. The brick is used as a building material, and can be stacked in a great variety of designs to create wall and floor patterns. Brick patterns are also reproduced in paper, embossed paper, plastic, vinyl, etc. The standard brick size is 8¾″ × 4¼″ × either 2″, 2⅝″ or 2⅞″. Some common types of bricks are: blue or engineering, fletton, glazed, London stock, and sand lime. There are also special facing bricks which are more interesting and colorful.

BRICK, ADOBE Large clay bricks of varying sizes which are roughly molded and sundried.

BRICK, ARCH See *Voussoir*.

BRICK, BUILDING Also called a common brick. Not especially textured or surfaced.

BRICK, CLINKER A very hard burned brick.

BRICK, COMMON See *Brick, Building*.

BRICK, ECONOMY 4″ × 4″ × 8″, with one course laying up every 4″.

BRICK, ENGINEERED 3.2″ × 4″ × 8″, laying up five courses in every 16″.

BRICK, FACING Specially treated, colored or textured bricks used for exterior or decorative facing.

BRICK, FIRE A ceramic brick which resists high temperatures.

BRICK, GAUGED A specially dimensioned brick like an *Arch Brick or Voussoir*.

BRICK, NORMAN 2⅔″ × 4″ × 12″, laying up three courses to every 8″.

BRICK, ROMAN 2″ × 4″ × 12″, laying up two courses in every 4″. The Roman brick is sometimes made up to 16″ long.

BRICK, SALMON A soft, underburned, pinkish brick. It is also called a chuff or place brick.

BRIDAL CHEST A "hope chest." A chest to hold linens, dower, etc. See *Cassone, Connecticut Chest*. A 17th-century Flemish Renaissance bridal chest is illustrated.

BRISEAUX, CHARLES ÉTIENNE (1680–1754) A French Rococo architect and interior designer. In his boiserie panels he preferred straight sides with a moderate amount of curvature on top.

BRITISH COLONIAL The Georgian-like furniture, interiors, and architecture of the 18th century which was developed by the English Colonials in the West Indies, India, and parts of Africa. It resembled the styles current and popular in England at that time, but was interpreted by native craftsmen in native woods with native details.

BROADCLOTH A lustrous cotton cloth with a tight, plain weave and a crosswise rib. Can also be woven of wool, rayon, or silk.

BROADLOOM A seamless carpet woven in widths of 6′ or more, usually 9′,

BRIDAL CHEST

BROKEN ARCH

BROKEN FRONT

12′, 15′ and 18′ widths and in a variety of textures, weaves, colors, and fibers.

BROCADE From Low Latin for to embroider or to stitch. Originally a fabric of silk, satin, or velvet, variegated with gold and silver or raised and enriched with flowers, foliage, and other ornaments. The fabric resembles embroidery and is woven on a jacquard loom. The threads do not appear on the surface, but are carried across the width on the reverse side. Much favored for drapery and upholstery in period and traditional rooms.

BROCADE, CARPET A fabric in which the pattern is formed by heavy twisted yarn tufts on a ground of straight fiber yarns. An engraved appearance results, though the yarns are often of the same color.

BROCATELLE Originally an imitation of Italian tooled leather. A heavy fabric which resembles damask, with a pattern which appears to be embossed. The pattern is usually a silk weave against a twill background. Also, a calcareous stone or marble having a yellow ground, flecked with white, gray, and red.

BROCATELLE VIOLETTE The most French of all marbles. A stone or marble with a purplish undertone, usually richly grained and patterned.

BROCHÉ A silk or satin ground fabric similar to brocade, with small raised floral designs made to resemble embroidery. Threads that are not used on the surface design are carried only across the width of the design on the reverse side, rather than across the entire reverse side in brocade.

BROKEN ARCH A curved or elliptical arch which is not completed or joined at its apex. The open center section is sometimes filled with a decorative device like an urn, finial, etc. Illustrated is a late-17th-century English china cabinet. See also *Gooseneck* and *Swan Neck Pediment*.

BROKEN FRONT Like a blockfront or breakfront, the front of the piece of furniture is made up of different planes. The center section may project beyond the side sections. Illustrated is an English bookcase of the first half of the 18th century, with a typical classical pediment on top. See *Blockfront* and *Breakfront*.

BROKEN PEDIMENT An architectural element frequently used on 18th-century English furniture on top cabinets, bookcases, curio cabinets, corner cabinets, highboys, etc. The triangular pediment is interrupted at its apex and the open central area often filled with a decorative urn, finial, shell, etc.

BRONZE A compound metal originally used for sculpture in ancient Greece and Rome as well as China and Africa, made up mainly of copper and tin. As bronze ages and reacts with chemicals, it takes on a greenish tint and matte surface called a patina. A patina can be chemically induced. Bronze has been a popular material for cast sculpture since the 15th century. Illustrated is an ancient Pompeiian bronze figure.

BRONZE D'AMEUBLEMENT
Bronze furniture mounts: handles, escutcheons, drawer pulls, etc.

BRONZE FURNITURE Metal furniture used by the ancient Greeks and Romans. The designs could be light and open since the material was so strong. In the late Renaissance and Empire period, bronze was again popular for tables, bases, etc., as well as for mounts, hardware, and trim. Illustrated is a Roman bronze lampstand found in Pompeii. See *Bronze-Doré* and *Ormolu or Ormoulu.*

BRONZE-DORÉ Gilded bronze. Illustrated is an 18th-century Italian bracket candlestick with a bronze-doré finish. See *Ormolu or Ormoulu.*

BRUSSELS CARPET An uncut wool loop-pile fabric woven on the Wilton loom, with a cotton back. It is also called a "round wire" carpet. Distinguished by its long pile and unusual wearing qualities.

BUBINGA An African wood with a beautiful, purple, closely striped grain, on a pale to red-brown ground. The figure is either narrow broken stripes or mottled. Also called *akume.*

BUCKET ARMCHAIR A Regency armchair, similar to the spoon-back chair. The arms rise in a scroll from the middle of the side rails of the seat, then form a continuous curve to create the top rail of the chair. The rounded back is often filled in with caning.

BUCKLAND, WILLIAM An indentured servant brought to America from England in 1755 to serve as "architect" for Gunston Hall near Mount Vernon in Virginia, the home of George Mason, author of the Virginia Declaration of Rights. Buckland was responsible for the exterior and interior woodwork, some of the most beautiful of the period. He also designed the exquisite woodwork in Edward Lloyd's house in Annapolis, Maryland. The Hammond-Harwood House in Annapolis is considered his masterpiece.

BUCKRAM A stiffly finished, heavily sized plain weave fabric, used as a stiffening for valances, etc.

BRONZE

BRONZE FURNITURE

BUFFET

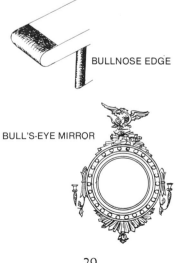

BRONZE-DORÉ

BUILDING BLOCK

BUILT-IN FURNITURE

BULLNOSE EDGE

BULL'S-EYE MIRROR

BUCRANIUM A decorative sculptured ox skull which sometimes appeared on the friezes of Roman structures.

BUEN RETIRO See *Capo di Monte.*

BUFFET A cupboard or sideboard. A side table sometimes with cupboards or shelves. Early Renaissance buffets resembled medieval cupboards and were supported on bases. The entire piece was usually decorated with columns, medallions, and arabesques. Illustrated is a late-18th century Sheraton buffet. See *Crédence, Desserte.*

BUHL WORK The English term for *Boulle Work,* André Charles Boulle's inlay technique using brass and tortoiseshell.

BUILDING BLOCK A hollow block made of concrete, terra cotta, or extruded burnt clay. Illustrated are late-19th-century hollow bricks.

BUILDING BOARD Also called plasterboard. Made from repulped paper, shredded wood, gypsum, and other plaster composition and then sandwiched between sheets of kraft paper. Usually placed on lathing strips to create partitions, walls, or ceilings. The panels are usually made 4' × 8'.

BUILT-IN FURNITURE Elements of furnishing (cabinets, seats, beds, chests) built into the room as an integral part of the interior architecture, a practice that dates from the earliest interiors. In contemporary usage, elements of furniture constructed into the actual walls or a false wall, designed with the aim of economy in the use of floor space. Illustrated is an early-18th-century Norse interior with built-in beds and Dutch-type chairs of the period.

BULBOUS FORM A heavy, melon-like wood turning that was popular for furniture supports and bases during the early Renaissance in Holland, England, France, and Italy.

BULLION See *Bull's Eye.* Also a type of fringe made of thick cord wrapped in gold or silver thread.

BULLNOSE EDGE A deep, almost half-round edge on a piece of wood furniture. A thick slap or marble used as a table or desk top having an exposed, rounded edge that approximates 180°.

BULL'S-EYE A circular or oval window. A circular distortion in the center of a disk of crown glass. In French it is known as "oeil-de-bouef." See *Crown Glass.*

BULL'S-EYE MIRROR A round mirror, often with a convex or concave glass set in an ornamental frame. The period of decoration of the frame may vary. A *Girandole*.

BUN FOOT or Flemish Foot A furniture support resembling a slightly flattened ball, used on Flemish, late French Renaissance, and English late 17th-century furniture.

BUNDLE A unit of wallpaper, usually delivered in single, double, or triple rolls.

BUNK BED Two sleeping units set one directly over the other, separated by vertical frames or uprights in the four corners. Each unit has its own spring and mattress; a built-in ladder or steps makes access to the upper bed easier.

BUNTES FENSTER   German for stained-glass window.

BUREAU Originally the fabric used to cover a table which was to be used as a writing surface. A desk. A writing table with "pigeonhole" compartments. According to Sheraton, in late-18th-century England, "a common desk with drawers." In the 19th and 20th centuries in America, a chest of drawers used in a bedroom, or part of a bedroom suite.

BUREAU À CYLINDRE French for a rolltop desk. Illustrated is the famous bureau du roi (king's desk) begun by Oeben and completed by Riesener for Louis XV. The roll-top desk is also called a bureau à rideau.

BUREAU À PENTE French for a folding, slant-lid desk.

BUREAU À RIDEAU   French for a rolltop desk. See *Bureau À Cylindre*.

BUREAU BOOKCASE A desk with a cabinet over the writing surface, according to Chippendale in 18th-century England.

BUREAU COMMODE A Louis XIV large writing table with drawers.

BUREAU EN DOS D'ÂNE A Louis XV drop leaf desk which took its name from its contour. The top of the desk resembled the back of an ass. The desk stood on tall cabriole legs with a slant-fronted unit on top. The slanted front dropped down to become a flat horizontal writing surface.

BUREAU PLAT A flat writing table or desk. Illustrated is a Louis XVI design by Riesener with decorative hardware and mounts by Gouthière.

BUREAU TABLE A kneehole table designed by Goddard of Newport, Rhode Island, in the late 18th century.

BUREAU À CYLINDRE

BUREAU BOOKCASE

BUREAU PLAT

BUST

BURGOMASTER CHAIR See *Roundabout Chair.*

BURGUNDIAN STYLE A provincial French Renaissance furniture style of the Rhone Valley area. Typically Renaissance in its use of architectural elements, it was noteworthy for its massive construction and high-relief carved decoration. The two-tiered cupboard *(cabinet à deux corps)* with carved human or allegorical figures is typical of the Burgundian style. Hughes Sambin of Dijon, the architect, is believed to be largely responsible for the Burgundian style. In 1570 he published a book of engraved ornaments, architectural details, etc. See *Cabinet à Deux Corps* and *Sambin, Hughes.*

BURJAIR   A Chippendale term for a *Bergère.*

BURL A growth in the bole or root of a tree. The wartlike protuberance, which is sliced to obtain veneer wood, contains dark pith centers and many underdeveloped buds which produce a pitted "little eye" or "knotted effect" on the surface. The burl often appears in walnut. See *Carpathian Elm Burl.*

BURLAP A plain weave of cotton, jute, or hemp which is coarse and loosely woven, used to cover springs in upholstered furniture and also as webbing. In informal, contemporary settings, it can be used for draperies, bedspreads, etc.

BURLING A final checking and finishing in broadloom production. Long tufts may be clipped or hidden, sunken tufts may be straightened out, etc.

BURNT WORK Line designs drawn on wood by means of a heated metal instrument, or shaded with hot sand.

BURNT-OUT or ETCHED-OUT FABRIC A fabric in which patterns are produced by chemically burning out one of the two types of yarns used in making the fabric. This technique is used in the production of brocaded velvet.

BURO TABLE An early American (early-18th-century) term for a bureau on legs, and usually with drawers.

BURR A veneer made from transverse slices of the gnarled roots of the walnut tree, popular in England from the mid-17th century to the beginning of the 18th. See *Burl.*

BUST   A painting or sculpture of a human head and shoulders, sometimes including the chest or breast. It may be used as a freestanding piece of art, or incorporated into an architectural niche, set on a pedestal, or used as a finial in a broken pediment. Illustrated is a section of a room designed by James Paine in the mid-18th century.

BUTCHER FURNITURE   The heavy, architectural furniture produced by Duncan Phyfe after 1825. The massive scrolled quality that was characteristic of the Second or Late Empire in France. See *Second Empire* or *Late Empire.*

BUTLER'S TRAY TABLE   A small side table with hinged sides that lift up to form the edges of a tray. Cut-out sections in the hinged flaps make it possible to lift up the whole table and move it about as one might carry a tray.

BUTT HINGE   A simple hinge with two leaves. When the hinge is attached to a door and a vertical frame, the pin joint is visible.

BUTT JOINT   The simplest and cheapest type of joint, but one that will not take much strain. One piece of wood is set perpendicular and at right angles to another (the pieces butting up against each other), and then glued, nailed, or screwed together.

BUTTERFLY   A popular oriental motif that became associated with the Second Empire period in France (1848–1870). Many of the symbols of the first Empire period were revived under Louis Napoleon Bonaparte, but the bee was replaced by the butterfly. It seemed better suited to the romantic and naturalistic tendencies of the

BUTTERFLY TABLE

BUTT HINGE

BUTTERFLY

period. Illustrated is a 17th-century Japanese textile.

BUTTERFLY TABLE   A Colonial American drop-leaf table with a broad butterfly-winglike bracket to support the raised leaf.

BUTTERFLY WEDGE   A double V-shaped fastener used to hold adjoining boards together. The V's connect at their points to form a butterfly shape.

BUTTERNUT   An American wood also known as white walnut. The wood resembles black walnut in fine graining, carvability, polishability, etc., but is lighter in color, hard and durable. The annual rings form a beautiful figured pattern.

BUTTWOOD VENEER   In wood grains, the section of the tree toward the root where the trunk fibers swing out and produce, in cross-section, a crinkly texture in addition to the long grain. Also called a stump grain.

BYZANTINE   Related to the Byzantine Empire, centered at Constantinople from 476 until 1453. The name is derived from the original town of Byzantium, which was renamed Constantinople by the Emperor Constantine. Byzantine designs were composed of Roman forms overlaid with Near Eastern motifs. The dome on pendentives, the rounded arch, and mosaics play an important part. Some Byzantine motifs still appear in Russian and south European decoration.

C

CABBAGE ROSE A flamboyant, overblown rose extremely popular in the Victorian era on carpets, wallpapers, silks, and chintzes. Often combined with lovers' bowknots, doves, and cherubs.

CABINET A general term from the French for closet or receptacle. In current usage, a unit of case furniture with shelves and/or cabinets, or a wooden or metal housing to contain an object (i.e., television set, radio, etc.) Illustrated is a 16th-century French Renaissance cabinet with carved door panels and architectural motifs.

CABINET À DEUX CORPS A late-16th-century Renaissance case piece consisting of one cupboard or cabinet set upon a second and usually larger one. Often carved and ornamented with classic motifs, and had caryatid supports at the corners of the lower unit.

CABINET BED See *Murphy Bed.*

CABINET SECRÉTAIRE A desk with a cabinet set above the writing surface. The cabinet may have glass, metal, grill, or wood-paneled doors. It was a popular innovation of the 18th century in France and England. A late-18th-century Sheraton design is illustrated.

CABINET VITRINE A cabinet with glass doors, essentially a display case, first popularized in the late 17th and early 18th centuries when procelain from China was rare and precious, and collections of "China" articles were worthy of display. Illustrated is an 18th-century Hepplewhite design which served as a bookcase.

CABINETWORK Furniture and finished interior woodwork, as opposed to construction work or rough carpentry.

CABINET

CABLE FLUTING

CABINET SECRÉTAIRE

CABINET VITRINE

CABRIOLE LEG

CABLE A twisted-rope motif often used as a molding enrichment in Norman and Romanesque architecture, still used for wood moldings, frames, and carved furniture embellishments.

CABLE FLUTING A semirounded molding worked into the hollowed-out channels of a column. The cables usually rise about one-third of the way up the shaft. This enrichment was originally used by the Romans in the classic times, but was greatly emphasized in the Renaissance period in France and Italy. Illustrated is a column from the interior of Chesterfield House in London designed by Isaac Ware in the mid-18th century. Cable fluting is also called cannelation.

CABOCHON From the French for a hobnail. A round or oval convex polished stone. A concave or convex shape used as a carved enrichment on furniture, sometimes surrounded by ornamental leaf carvings. It is found in *Rococo* furniture and decoration.

CABRIOLE CHAIR A small chair with a stuffed back made in the mid-18th century in England during Chippendale's French period. The term is an anglicized version of cabriolet. It does not refer to the cabriole leg. See *Cabriolet* and *French Chair.*

CABRIOLE LEG From the French for to leap or caper. A conventionalized animal's leg with knee, ankle, and foot adapted in wood as a furniture leg or support. Greatly favored by designers in the late 17th and 18th centuries for French, English, Flemish, and Italian furniture. The leg curves outward toward the knee and then in and downward to the ankle, making an S shape. In the Queen Anne period the knee was often adorned with a shell, in early Georgian furniture with lion masks, satyr masks, or cabochon and leaf ornaments. The cabriole leg reached the height of refinement and ornateness during the Louis XV Rococo period, and is considered a typical Rococo feature. An 18th-century Chippendale secretary is illustrated.

CABRIOLET A small Louis XV chair with a concave back and cabriole legs. In the Louis XVI period the name was applied to a chair with an oval, hollowed-out back. The top of the frame was often decorated with a ribbon and bow as though the chair back were a frame ready to be hung. Illustrated is a Hepplewhite adaptation. A cabriolet is also a two-wheeled, one-horse carriage. See *Cabriole Chair*.

CABRIOLET

CACHE-POT A pot made of china, wood, or porcelain, used as a container or flowerpot holder.

CACQUETEUSE (chaise de femme) An early French Renaissance conversational chair with a high, narrow back and curved arms. A prototype for the smaller-scaled fauteuils of the 18th century. A 16th-century French Renaissance chair is shown. See *Caqueteuse* and *Caquetoire*.

CADUCEUS A wand or staff, entwined by two serpents, and surmounted by a pair of wings, in classic times the symbol for Mercury's rod. The motif appears in carved and painted form in the Louis XVI period. Currently the symbol of the medical profession.

CACQUETEUSE

CAFÉ CURTAINS Short curtains, usually made with a scalloped top. The top points of the scallops are hooked, clipped, or slipped over a rod, usually decorative, sometimes by means of fabric loops sewn on the curtains. Café curtains are often used in pairs, one set below the other, most often for an informal, country-style window treatment.

CAFÉ CURTAINS

CAFFIERI, JACQUES (1678–1755) A French cabinetmaker and sculptor in bronze, who worked for Louis XV in the Rococo style.

CAFFIERI, JEAN-JACQUES (1725–1792) A great French artisan of ormolu metal mounts for Rococo furniture. He worked under Jean-François Oeben, the king's cabinetmaker to Louis XV.

PHILIPPE CAFFIERI

CAFFIERI, PHILIPPE (c. 1634–1716) A French sculptor in metal, wood, and marble, considered the greatest metal carver of his time. He specialized in decorative furniture mounts. Caffieri worked under Le Brun at the Gobelins Factory during the reign of Louis XIV. The illustrated pedes-

CAMELBACK

tal was designed by Boulle, the metalwork was executed by Caffieri.

CAFFOY A rich 18th-century fabric of silk and cotton used for hangings and draperies in state rooms.

CAISSONS Sunken panels in a ceiling or dome, also called coffers or lacunaria. They are found in classic Greek and Roman architecture. Simulated in wood in English Renaissance interiors, and interpreted in plaster composition or gesso in Adam brothers interiors in mid-18th-century England. This ceiling, arch, or dome enrichment is also found in French and Italian Renaissance structures, especially in domed buildings.

CALAMANDER A wood from Ceylon used for banding and veneering in 18th-century furniture. See *Coromandel*.

CALATHOS The basket- or bell-shaped element which supports the acanthi of the Corinthian capital; also the name of the basket-like element on the head of a caryatid figure. See *Caryatid*.

CALCIMINE A painting mixture often used on ceilings and as a whitewash. It is a cold-water mixture of whiting, glue, and coloring matter.

CALENDERING A finishing process for fabrics which produces a flat, smooth, glazelike finish when the fabric is passed between hollow, heated cylinders.

CALICO A plain weave, printed cotton fabric originally produced in Calcutta, India, similar to percale.

CALLIGRAPHY The art of free rhythmic handwriting. The brushstrokes used for Chinese, Japanese, or Arabic written characters. In painting, free and loose brushwork suggesting letters.

CAMAÏEU French for monochromatic. Shades and tints of a single color.

CAMBER The slight convexing or bellying on the lower surface of a beam to accommodate for the optical illusion that the beam appears to sag in the center. This technique is also used on horizontal furniture supports. See *Entasis*.

CAMBRIC A soft, white, loosely woven cotton or linen fabric originally from Cambrai, France. True linen cambric is very sheer; coarser versions are used for linings.

CAME The soft metal strip used as the divider between adjacent pieces of glass in a stained or leaded glass window.

CAMELBACK A chair back with a serpentine curved top rail. A late Chippendale (illustrated) or Hepplewhite chair. The term may originally have been applied to the 18th-century shield-back chair.

CAMELBACK SOFA An upholstered sofa in the mid-18th-century Chippendale tradition. The back has a serpentine line which rises from the roll-over arms to a high point in the middle of the couch back.

CAMEL'S HAIR The wool-like under-hair of a camel. Natural color varies from light tan to brownish black. Soft and lustrous, and may be combined with sheep's wool. The yarn produced is sometimes used for Oriental rugs.

CAMEO A low-relief carving. A striated stone or shell which is carved in relief. Used for decoration on English furniture of the late 18th century. Illustrated is a pair of ancient Roman cameos.

CAMEO BACK An oval-framed chair back with an upholstered oval insert, popular in the Louis XVI, Adam, and Sheraton style. The cameo-back chair is similar to the Louis XV "cabriolet," and Hepplewhite's "oval-back-chair." See *Le Medaillon* and *Oval Back.*

CAMERA An arcaded or vaulted roof, or a room with a vaulted roof.

CAMLET A rich fabric made of camel's hair which originated in the Orient. Made in France in the 14th century from hair, wool, and silk, and used and manufactured in England in the 17th and 18th centuries.

CAMP BEDSTEAD See *Field Bed.*

CAMPAGNOLA The Italian term for provincial furniture, furniture made in outlying districts in a simple, unsophisticated manner.

CAMPAIGN CHEST Originally a portable chest of drawers used by officers on military campaigns. The units were reinforced with metal edges and corners to withstand rough traveling conditions. In current usage, somewhat like a "bachelor chest," often lacquered and embellished with metal corner strips, corner pieces, and pronounced hardware. Usually sits flush on the floor.

CAMPEACHY CHAIR A rocking chair made of logwood, also called blood-wood, grown in Campeachy, Mexico. The sloped back is upholstered in leather and finished with nailhead trim. The campeachy chair in Thomas Jefferson's study at Monticello dates back to 1819.

CANAPÉ Originally, a 17th-century small, two-seater couch covered with a canopy. The canopy was later removed but the name still applied to a small sofa. A Louis XVI canapé or sofa covered with Beauvais

CAMELBACK SOFA

CAMEOS

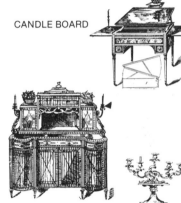

CANDLE BOARD

CANDLE BRACKETS

CANDLESTAND

CANAPÉ

CANED-BACK CHAIR

tapestry is illustrated. See *Tapet* for a 15th-century canapé.

CANAPÉ À CORBEILLE A kidney-shaped sofa. The ends curve in so that the sofa takes on the appearance of a wide topped basket. Corbeille is the French word for a wide basket or breadbasket.

CANDELABRA The plural of candelabrum. See below.

CANDELABRUM A branched, highly ornamental candlestick, lampstand, or hanging lighting unit or chandelier. See *Chandelier.*

CANDLE BOARD A small shelf, under the writing surface of a desk, which slides out and is used to hold a candlestick. An 18th-century English furniture device. Illustrated is a Sheraton drawing table.

CANDLE BRACKETS Brackets set into the base of the upper part of a secretary to be used as candlesticks. Illustrated is a Sheraton design.

CANDLE SLIDES See *Candle Board.*

CANDLESTAND A light table used for candles, vases, and other small ornaments, usually associated with tripod furniture. Made in the early Georgian period, and continued in use through the 18th century. A Chippendale design is illustrated.

CANDLESTICK A socketed holder made of metal, wood, china, or pottery. It can be a simple tube with an opening at one end to receive the candle and a flattened base at the other to set securely on a flat surface, or it can be elaborately decorated.

CANDLEWICK FABRIC Fabric with chenille effect created by making heavy-pile yarn (candlewick) loops on unbleached muslin bed sheeting. The loops are cut to simulate the fuzzy effect of a true chenille yarn. Candlewick fabrics can be used for draperies and bedspreads, and may be obtained in a variety of colors and patterns.

CANE From the Latin for reed. The stems of certain palms, grasses, or plants like bamboo and rattan, plaited or woven into a mesh which is yielding, and therefore comfortable to sit on or lean back against. Cane was used as a decorative and elegant seating and chair-back material in the Louis XIV, XV and XVI periods in France, and in the 17th and 18th centuries in England and Holland. Still a popular material, currently used for decorative inserts in screens and case furniture.

CANED-BACK CHAIR A popular chair back of the latter part of the 18th century. An intricately woven pattern of cane was set into a round or oval frame, which usually had an inlaid wood center. The cane appears to radiate out from the center medallion. A Sheraton design is illustrated.

CANEPHORA   A sculptured female figure with a basket on her head. Originally, used as a classic structural decoration somewhat like a caryatid. (See *Caryatids* and *Atlantes*.) Used as an ornamental support for furniture and shelves in the French and Italian Renaissance.

CANNE   French for cane or reed.

CANNÉ   French for caned, used, for example, in reference to a caned seat.

CANNELLATED   See *Fluting*.

CANOPY   From the Greek for a net to keep out gnats. A covering usually of drapery, over a piece of furniture, like the Sheraton bed illustrated. See *Canapé* and *Tester*.

CANOPY BED   A bed with a fabric roof over it. The canopy is often supported by four posts, one at each corner of the bed, or suspended from above. An early-19th century American version of a Sheraton design is illustrated. See *Angel Bed*, *Four-poster Bedstead*, and *Tent Bed*.

CANOPY CHAIR   A late-15th-, early-16th-century stately chair with a broad back that angles upward over the seat to form a projecting canopy. The design was usually heavily enriched with a carved ornament. It was the probable forerunner of the smaller, wider, and more intimate 17th-century Canapé. See *Chayers à Dorseret*.

CANTED   Slanted or sloped; angled, beveled, or chamfered. This term is usually applied to large elements like the angles of a half-octagonal bow window, illustrated.

CANTERBURY   An ornamental stand having compartments for papers, books, envelopes, etc. A sort of portable magazine rack of the 18th century. It was probably originally designed to carry trays, plates, cutlery, etc., and serve as an auxiliary piece for tea service or dining.

CANTILEVER   A rigid member extending well beyond its vertical support. One end extends out free and unsupported. Originally, the term referred to brackets of stone, wood, or metal which projected out from a building (corbels), and supported shelves, cornices, balconics, or eaves, as seen in Gothic and early Renaissance structures.

CANTON CHINA   A blue-and-white ceramic ware exported from the port of Canton, China, from the 17th century up to modern times. Extremely popular in both America and Britain.

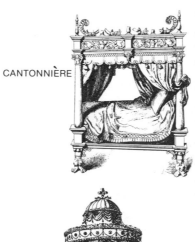

CANTONNIÈRE

CANOPY

CANOPY BED

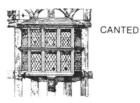

CANTED

CANTONE   Italian for quoin corner.

CANTONED PIERS   Piers decorated with pilasters or columns at the corners or other exposed faces. A classic form of decoration which appeared in Renaissance architecture.

CANTONNIÈRE   The French word for valance. It especially refers to the elaborate valance arrangements used on French state beds in the 16th and 17th centuries. See *Lambrequin* and *Valance*.

CANVAS   A heavy cotton or linen fabric with an even weave. May be bleached or unbleached. A stiff open-weave material used for needlework. A firm, closely woven fabric used as the paint surface in oil painting.

CAPITAL   The head of a column or pillar. The capital is placed directly over the shaft and immediately under the entablature. Each of the classical architectural borders has its own particular capital. The column and capital have been used as decoration and for functional supports on many styles of furniture. See *Composite Order*, *Corinthian Order*, *Doric Order*, *Etruscan Order*, and *Ionic Order*.

CAPITELLO   Italian for capital.

CAPO DI MONTE   A Spanish porcelain factory founded by King Charles III in 1743. In 1760, the plant was set up in Buen Retiro, and this porcelain is also known by that name. Figures and groupings of soft paste were made here, in typically Rococo patterns and vivid colors. Large plaques and wall brackets of Capo di Monte were used to decorate the palaces in Madrid and Aranjuez. The Capo di Monte style is still used today for ornamental lamps and vases.

CAPOMO   See *Satine Rubanne*.

CAPRICCIO   Italian for caprice. A fanciful landscape composition of the 18th century.

CAPROLAN   A trademark of the Allied Chemical Corporation for nylon fibers used in upholstery fabrics which have a high abrasion resistance. Also used as a carpet fiber.

CAPTAIN'S BED   A single bunk-type platform bed with a series of drawers below the wooden surface that supports the mattress. An adaptation of the built-in captain's bed aboard ship.

CAPTAIN'S CHAIR   A sturdy all wood provincial-style chair with a rounded back and curved arms, both supported by tiny spindles. The seat is shaped, the legs are wood turnings joined to each other by means of turned stretchers. Favored by

19th century sailors, especially sea captains, aboard ship.

CAPTAIN'S CHEST A sturdy, straight-lined chest made of wood, usually oak, with recessed pulls and hardware, used on 19th-century sailing vessels.

CAQUETEUSE A conversation chair with a high wood back, with the seat sometimes arranged to turn on a pivot. An early French Renaissance design introduced into England in the 16th century. The front of the chair seat was usually wider than the back. Illustrated is a 16th-century French example. See *Cacqueteuse*.

CAQUETOIRE A small, light, four-legged conversation chair of the mid French Renaissance. The back of the seat is narrower than the front, and the arms are curved inward from the front to the chair back. See *Cacqueteuse*.

CARAVAGGIO, MICHELANGELO DA (1573–1610) A great realist painter of the Italian Renaissance.

CARCASE or CARCASS The base wood framework of a piece of furniture without veneering, carving, ornament, or finish. The term usually refers to case furniture. The skeleton of an upholstered piece of furniture is called a frame. See *Basewood*.

CARD CUT A Chinese-style fretwork or latticework design. The pattern is carved in low relief rather than pierced or cut out. Chippendale used this type of decoration on some of his cabinets and secretaries.

CARD TABLE A small folding table used for gaming. Originated in the 17th century and was especially popular in the William and Mary and Queen Anne periods. Early card tables had depressions at the four corners of the tabletop to hold candles, and often, four additional wells or "guinea holes" for holding the money in use during the gaming. The tabletops were often covered with green baize. The styles of card tables varied with the succeeding periods. Illustrated is a Queen Anne card table with cabriole legs with shell motif on the knee. See also *Dished* and *Mechanical Card Table*.

CARLIN, MARTIN An 18th-century French master cabinetmaker to *Louis XVI.* He produced charming, delicate furniture in rosewood, with Sèvres porcelain inlays. Carlin was also a caster and chaser of metal furniture mounts, and one of the earliest exponents of the Classic Revival. He often used independent, or detached, balustrade columns to support the friezes of cabinets. These columns were made of wood, bronze gilt, or the two combined. Another decora-

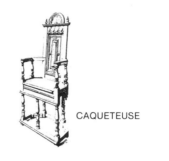
CARLTON TABLE

CAQUETEUSE

CAROLEAN PERIOD

CARPET

CARD TABLE

MARTIN CARLIN

tive device frequently used by Carlin was the fringe of drapery pinched in with small tassels.

CARLTON TABLE A writing table on legs with a raised back and sides, fitted with pigeonholes, small drawers, and fittings for pens and inkwells. The desk made its appearance at the end of the 18th century in England, and was usually made of mahogany or satinwood with inlay trim. Sheraton referred to this as a "ladies' drawing and writing table."

CAROLEAN PERIOD The period in English furniture and interior design which spanned the years 1660–1688, also referred to as the Restoration, Late Stuart, or part of the Jacobean period. Illustrated is an oak chest of the period with geometric panels and lunette carving.

CAROLINGIAN The period in architecture and art in western Europe from about the 7th to the 10th centuries, roughly the dynasties before, of, and after Charlemagne.

CARPATHIAN ELM BURL A decorative, light-brown to brick-red veneer wood with darker brown veins and figurations, often combined with walnut as a decorative accent. Found in the Carpathian Mountains in Europe and in France and England.

CARPET In the 16th and 17th centuries, a woven table covering. Since the late 17th century, a floor covering. See *Tapet.* Illustrated is a carpet pattern of the early-16th century German Renaissance.

CARPET PADDING An undersurface for carpets and rugs. Provides additional softness underfoot, protects the carpet, and insulates against the loss of heat. Also adds sound absorption. The heavier the padding (the greater the "ounces per square yard"), the more expensive it usually is. An 80-oz. padding usually does well under heavy traffic, while 64-oz. will do well in most residential installations.

Padding is made of polyurethane which is non-allergenic, mold resistant, durable, resiliant, and good for heat insulation and sound absorption. Produced in thicknesses of ¼″ to ½″. Also made of sponge rubber, the softest and most porous material, odor resistant and very resilient. At the other end of the scale is a combination of hair and jute, felted in a waffle pattern. This material does insulate but can mildew if water seeps through it.

CARPET TILES Carpet squares precut into definite modules (18″ ×18″, 24″ × 24″, etc.) and laid, like tiles, directly onto a hard floor. May be produced with a spongc-likc backing for extra comfort and resiliency. Their major advantage, especially in areas with heavy traffic and in contract design, is that soiled or worn areas can be replaced without having to pull up and remove the rest of usable carpet. Especially effective in open-office planning, where the movable partitions may be rearranged and areas may require refinishing.

CARREAU From the French for square. A square tile or brick. A loose, stuffed cushion used on chairs and settles before upholstery, as known today, came into use. A squab cushion. Illustrated is a French 15th-century bench with movable backrest. See also *Squab*.

CARREL A bay or study nook separated from the rest of a library by an architectural screen or flanking bookcases.

CARRELAGE ENCAUSTIQUE French for a pavement of inlaid tiles.

CARRIAGES or CARRIAGE PIECES The supporting members for steps in stairway construction.

CARROUSEL A triple-arched construction designed by Percier and Fontaine in the early 19th century and inspired by the Arch of Septimus Severus in Rome.

CARTAPESTA Italian for papier-mâché.

CARTEL (Clock) A hanging wall clock. In the Louis XV and Louis XVI periods it was often highly ornate and fanciful in design, and made of ormolu. See also *Régulateur* and *Regulator*.

CARTER, EDWARD A 17th-century English designer-architect who, with John Webb, executed many of Inigo Jones's designs. His own work was much in the style of Jones, as illustrated.

CARTER, J. A late-18th-century English designer who worked mainly in the Adam brothers tradition. He designed classic-inspired ceilings, panels, chimneypieces, gates, grates, architectural pedestals, shop fronts, and doorways.

CARTER'S GROVE A typical Georgian house of the mid-18th century in America. It was built for Carter Burwell in James City, West Virginia, in 1751. The great central hall opened into four rooms, two of which were coupled with antechambers. The main part of the house was flanked by a kitchen and a service building (flankers). David Minitree was the builder of this brick structure done in Flemish bond.

CARTOCCIO Italian for cartouche or scroll.

CARREAU

CARTOUCHE BACK

EDWARD CARTER

CARVING

CARTONNIER A decorative 18th-century pasteboard box used to hold papers, usually ornamented and lavishly decorated.

CARTON-PIERRE A Robert Adam, mid-18th-century English technique of "carved ornament" using a gesso-like composition applied to the surface of wood, panels, and ceilings. See also *Anaglypta*.

CARTOON From the Italian cartone, a big sheet of paper. A full-sized drawing for a painting, worked out in detail, and ready to be transferred to a wall, canvas, or panel. One of the steps in the preparation for a fresco or wall mural.

CARTOUCHE Usually a sculptured ornament in the form of a scroll unrolled, which often appears on cornices. The cartouche is frequently used as a field for inscriptions, and as an ornamental block in the cornices of house interiors. A conventionalized shield or oval. An ornate frame.

CARTOUCHE BACK An upholstered chair back of a side chair or fauteuil which is cartouche-shaped. Illustrated is a Louis XV fauteuil upholstered in Beauvais tapestry. The tapestry has a multicurved shield effect, and is set into the cartouche frame of the chair.

CARVED RUG A rug on which the pattern is created by having the pile cut at different levels, making lights and shadows. A sculptured look may also be effected by eliminating some tufts, or pulling some pile yarns tightly back to create a pattern or design.

CARVER CHAIR An early American wood-turned chair with a rush seat. A straight, square-looking chair named after a chair belonging to Governor John Carver of Plymouth. The rear legs continued up to form the uprights of the back. A single row of vertical and horizontal spindles was set between the uprights. Mushroom-shaped turnings usually acted as finials on the uprights. Closely related to the Brewster chair. See *Banister Back Chair* and *Brewster Chair*.

CARVING A sculptured, incised, gouged, or appliquéd three-dimensional decoration or ornament. Illustrated is an early Georgian (early-18th-century) sideboard which is heavily carved and gilded.

CARYATIDS Sculptured female figures used in place of columns or pilasters to support entablatures, decorative figures used as supporting members of a design. It appears in classic architecture and decoration, and again in the Renaissance and Empire periods. The male version of the caryatid is the Atlante. See *Canephora*. The famous "Porch of the Maidens" in the Erectheum consists of caryatid supports. See also *Atlantes*.

CASCADE   See *Jabot*.

CASE CLOCK   A clock contained in a wooden housing.

CASE GOODS OR CASE PIECE Furniture designed to contain or store objects: chests, cabinets, desks, bookcases, drawer units, etc. Also called architectural furniture. A contemporary secretary/cabinet is shown here.

CASEIN PAINT   A paint for interior use, in a casein solution instead of the usual drying oils. It is mixed with water. The hiding property of the paint is lime, powdered chalk, and kaolin.

CASEMENT   A frame for glass that forms a window or part of one.

CASEMENT, WILLIAM   A late-18th-century English furniture designer, who contributed to the *Cabinet Makers' London Book* of prices for designs of cabinetwork.

CASEMENT CLOTH   A light-weight, usually sheer drapery cloth of silk, cotton, rayon, mohair, nylon, or mixture of these fibers. It is used as a curtain fabric.

CASEMENT WINDOW   A side-hinged window that swings in and out, rather than one which is pushed up and down.

CASHMERE   A soft wool textile or yarn made from Indian goat hair.

CASHMERE WORK   From the province of Kashmir in India, a "mirror-mosaic" form of decoration in Indian furniture of the 18th and early 19th centuries. Small pieces of mirror were inlaid into the carved geometric patterns of a panel or surface.

CASING   The wood or metal framework around a window, set into the construction of the wall.

CASINO   An Italian word for little house. A summerhouse or an 18th-century dancing salon.

CASKET   A box or miniature chest, usually lavishly ornamented and made of wood, ivory, and precious metals. A container for trinkets, jewels, etc. A Byzantine ivory casket is illustrated.

CASO-RILIEVO   An Italian word for a relief carving in which the highest parts of the sculpture are on a level with the surface that surrounds the relief. It is also called intaglio rilievato.

CASSAPANCA   Derived from the Italian cassone (chest) and banca (bench). A

CASE GOODS

CASSETTE

CASSONE

CASEMENT WINDOW

CASKET

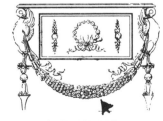

CATENARY ARCH

mid-Renaissance Italian, long, wooden, hinged-top chest with wooden arms and a back. It functioned as a bench as well as a chest. A prototype of the box settle. See *Box Settle*.

CASSAWS   A late-17th-century English wallpaper which resembles a silk damask.

CASSETTE   The French word meaning casket. Sometimes assumed monumental proportions. Illustrated is a 14th-century French wood cassette.

CASSOLET or CASSOLETTE   A small box, made in a variety of shapes, for holding or burning perfumes. The term also applies to a covered urn-shaped vase, sometimes with a top that reverses to become a candle holder.

CASSONE   An Italian decorated hinge-topped chest. It was usually used as a marriage chest to contain the bride's household linens. This 14th- to 16th-century chest was richly decorated and carved with gilt moldings, and often had painted front and back panels, 4' to 6' long and about 18″ in height. See *Cassapanca*, *Chest* and *Marriage Chest*.

CASSOON   A sunken panel in a vault or ceiling. See *Coffered Panel*.

CAST   A reproduction, often made of plaster of Paris, of a piece of sculpture.

CAST ALUMINUM   Aluminum that has been cast in molds. Furniture produced from cast aluminum components looks like cast iron, but it is much lighter and is rust-resistant.

CAST IRON   Iron which contains 3.5 percent of carbon, first made commercially by the Darby family in England in the early 18th century. They smelted iron ore with coke instead of charcoal. In about 1750, using coal, they turned out pig iron of a quality they could forge into bar iron, and mass production became possible. Cast iron columns appear in 1780 as structural elements. During the 19th century, it was an important building material.

CASTERS or CASTORS   Small wheels on swivels which are applied to legs or bases of furniture to make it movable.

CATENARY   Chainlike. A swag or festoon. See *Festoon* and *Swag*.

CATENARY ARCH   The arc or curve formed by a cord or chain of uniform density hanging freely between two points of suspension. The console with the catenary arch trim illustrated was designed by Charles Normand in the French Empire period.

CATHEDRAL CEILING   A high-pitched ceiling in a modern home. The living room in a ranch or split-level house is sometimes enhanced by the extra-high ceiling.

CATHEDRAL GLASS A rolled glass with one surface textured partially to obscure transparency. May be tinted. Many textured patterns available.

CATKINS A decorative 18th-century motif like the bellflower or husk ornament, usually used as a pendant, or as a chain of stylized and graduated bell-shaped flowers. A late-18th-century Hepplewhite girondole is illustrated. See *Bellflower Ornament* and *Husk Ornament.*

CAUCASIAN RUGS Originated with the nomadic tribes of Northern Iran. Hand knotted, made of undyed wool yarns, with a dense, thick pile. Some of the characteristic geometric patterns popularly used are: the swastika, the cross, and the eight-pointed star. Linear figures and animals also appear in these elaborate designs. The favored colors are vivid reds, blues, greens, and bright yellow, and sometimes black. Some of the most popular Caucasian rug designs are: Kabistan, Kazak, Karabagh, and Shirvan.

CAULICOLI The stalks that support the volutes on a classic Corinthian capital.

CAUSEUSE A wide armchair, or a small sofa with open sides. The back and seat were often covered with Beauvais tapestry in the 17th and 18th centuries. Similar to a marquise, love seat, or settee. Illustrated is a typical Louis XVI design.

CAUVET, GILLES-PAUL (1731–1788) A leading French designer of interiors, furniture, and metal ornament in the Louis XVI period. His work is reminiscent of the Louis XV style.

CAVETTO A quarter-round, concave molding. In late-17th-century English furniture, the cavetto molding was often veneered crosswise. See *Cove.*

CAVITY WALL Also called a hollow wall. Two brick walls which are spaced two or three inches apart and connected to each other with metal ties or bonding bricks.

CAVO-RELIEVO Italian for *intaglio.*

CEDAR A fragrant fine-grained wood used for chests and lining closets. Persian cedar is an eastern hardwood used for building. A favorite wood of the Egyptians and ancient Romans.

CEDAR CHEST A long, low chest, either made completely of, or lined only with, cedarwood, used for the storage of linens, blankets, and woolens. It can be styled to suit any period and is often referred to as a

CATKINS

CELLARETTE

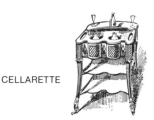

BENVENUTO CELLINI

CAUSEUSE

CEDAR CHEST

"hope chest." Illustrated is a 15th-century carved cedar chest. See *Cassone.*

CEDAR, RED Not a decorative wood. It is mainly used for shingles and as a lining material.

CELADON A light-grayish sea-green color. The word is also used to describe pottery or Chinese porcelain of this color.

CELANESE A trademark for textiles produced by the Celanese Corporation of America.

CELAPERM A trademark name for solution-dyed acetate yarns produced by the Celanese Corporation of America.

CELATURE A method of decorating metal surfaces by embossing or cutting into the metal.

CELLAR In medieval architecture, a storage room above ground level. In contemporary usage, an underground or below-grade storage area.

CELLARETTE A portable or movable cabinet or liquor chest with a place for bottles, glasses, etc. A Sheraton design is illustrated. Also, the drawer of a sideboard fitted with divisions to hold bottles, often lined with lead. See *Sarcophagus.*

CELLINI, BENVENUTO (1500–1571) An outstanding Italian Renaissance goldsmith, sculptor, and adventurer. A beaten silver goblet of his design is shown. See *Tazza* for another illustration of Cellini's work.

CELLULOSE An insoluble starchlike matter taken from plants, used as a basis for many synthetic materials.

CEMENT A natural or artificial lime compound which is burnt and ground, used to make a mortar to bond bricks, stones, etc.

CEMENT BLOCK A building unit of cast cement, usually 8″ × 8″ × 16″.

CEMENT MORTAR A mixture of cement, sand, and water used for binding bricks, stones, etc.

CENTAUR A decorative figure with the torso of a human male, but the body and legs of a horse. It appeared in ancient Greek mythology, and reappeared in Renaissance and later designs.

CENTER OR CENTERING In masonry, a temporary timber framework upon which the masonry of an arch, or a reinforced masonry lintel, is supported till it sets and becomes rigid and self-supporting.

CENTER MATCH Two flitches or log slices butted in the center of a single veneered panel.

CENTER OTTOMAN See *Borne* and *Confidante.*

CENTER TABLE A large table which stands in the center of a hallway or large room, similar in use to a rectangular library table. Illustrated is an Elizabethan room with a center table. See illustration of *Venetian Gilt.*

CENTER TABLE

CERAMIC A product of baked clay, procelain, pottery, tile, earthenware, etc. A 17th-century English stoneware jug is illustrated.

CERAMIC COLOR GLAZE An opaque colored glaze obtained by spraying a clay tile, brick, or object with a compound of metallic oxides, chemicals, and clays, and then heating it in an oven at a high temperature. This fuses the glaze into the clay object.

CERAMIC TILE Thin flat pieces of baked clay (glazed or unglazed). May be used to cover floors and counters, or line walls, etc. A wide range of colors is available, and a multitude of designs and patterns can be created with ceramic tiles.

CERAMIC VENEER An architectural terra-cotta plate with large face dimensions but only 1⅛″ to 2½″ in thickness. Actually an oversized tile applied to a brick, stone, or rough concrete surface as a facing material.

CERCEAU, JACQUES DU A 16th-century French architect and furniture designer under Henry IV. See *Du Cerceau, Jacques Androuet.*

CERTOSINA An Italian term for an inlay of marble, ivory, or blond woods on a darker background. It has an oriental character since it is generally set into small geometric patterns. See *Intarsia* or *Tarsia* and *Intarsio.* The name was derived from the Carthusian monks who excelled in this type of inlay work.

CESCA CHAIR Classic Bauhaus chair designed in the 1920's, which has a continuous metal-tube frame that forms a support for a lightweight and light-looking seat and chair back. Originally the seat and chair back were rectangular wooden frames with softly rounded corners that contained a natural colored caning material. The seat is cantilevered out on the frame which has no back legs or rear base support. The chair back is secured to the metal tube that rises up from behind the seat. The frame angles out and forward to become the supports for the wooden arm rests. Many variations are now on the market.

CHAFFEUSE A low, fireside chair. Originally the seat was so low that the

CHAIERE

CERAMIC

CHAIR RAIL

CHAIR TABLE

CHAISE À BRAS

knees of a seated person were higher than the lap. It was used by nursing mothers to cradle children between their knees and body. Also spelled *chauffeuse.*

CHAIERE OR CHAIRE A French Gothic term for a thronelike wood-carved chair. See *Chaire.* Illustrated is a 14th-century interior.

CHAIR Derived from the Old French *chaiere.* A seat with a back for one person. A chair usually has feet, legs, stretchers, brackets, apron, seat frame, rails, arms, splat, and top rail.

CHAIR AND A HALF An 18th-century English chair with overly generous proportions. The chair usually had wings or cheeks, and the seat was smaller than a two-seater love seat but larger than a regular upholstered chair. It is similar to the French marquise in proportions and was also called a *Drunkard's Chair.*

CHAIR BED A chair or settee with a draw-out arrangement that converts into a bed. An 18th-century English innovation. See *Bed Chair.*

CHAIR RAIL The top molding of a dado, also called a dado cap. Usually placed about 30″ off the ground, and the wall area below the molding is called the dado. The wood strip originally was used to protect the plaster wall from being damaged by the top rail of chairs. An 18th-century English room designed by Halfpenny is illustrated.

CHAIR TABLE A chair that converts into a table when the hinged back is dropped to a horizontal position. Illustrated is a 17th-century Stuart period chair. See *Table Chair.*

CHAIRE A French term for an early Renaissance choir stall. It resembles a chest (or boxlike seat) with a tall, heavily carved back. The arms were also carved. In the Gothic period it was also called a *chayère* and its thronelike proportions made it the special seat for the lord or head of a family.

CHAIRE À HAUT DOSSIER A 16th-century French Renaissance high-back chair, usually ornately carved and covered in leather or tapestry.

CHAISE French for side chair.

CHAISE À ACCOUDOIR See *Cockfight Chair* and *Fumeuse.*

CHAISE À BRAS A Renaissance armchair. Illustrated is an English version from the 16th century.

CHAISE À CAPUCINE A low slipper chair. The name is probably derived from the Capucin nuns who might have used this type of chair.

CHAISE À PORTEURS   A sedan chair. It originally was an enclosed covered chair which seated one person and was suspended between two poles to be carried by porters. Present-day variations are hooded and winged chairs that simulate the enclosed look of the chaise à porteurs. See *Sedan Chair.*

CHAISE BRISÉE   A *Chaise Longue* in two parts, one of which is the footrest. Also, a folding chair.

CHAISE LONGUE   A long chair for reclining or stretching out. A *Duchesse.* It is an upholstered chair with a very elongated seat supported by extra legs.

CHAISE PERCÉE   A chair with an opening cut in the seat over a chamber pot. Originally, a movable toilet styled like a throne or an imposing arm chair in keeping with the current vogue of the period (Louis XIV, XV or XVI). Today, a chair to cover an existing toilet fixture. A *commode.*

CHALICE   A cup or goblet used in church ceremony, and often made of precious metals beautifully ornamented and jeweled.

CHALLIS   A soft fabric woven of wool, silk, rayon, or cotton. Usually has a small allover design, but may be solid color.

CHAMBER HORSE   An 18th-century English exercising mechanism designed by Sheraton, a bellows-like affair made up of several wooden boards separated by coils, and covered over with leather equipped with air vents. This bellows was set on a wood base with arms, and a front step. The individual sat on the bellows-pillow, held onto the arms, and bounced up and down, much as one would ride a vibrator.

CHAMBERS, SIR WILLIAM (1726–1796)   An English architect who designed in the Palladian tradition during the Greek Revival period. Like Chippendale, he adapted Chinese forms to furniture. In 1759, he published *Designs of Chinese Buildings, Furniture, Dresses, Machines and Utensils.* Chambers was chief architect to George III and was a leading authority on the Italian Renaissance. His *Somerset House* in London is a classic in "secular Renaissance" design.

CHAMBLIN, M. DE   Early 18th-century Régence designer and decorator.

CHAMFER   The edge of a corner that is beveled or angled off. A splayed effect. A Chippendale press or wardrobe with chamfered edges is illustrated. See *Bevel* and *Canted.*

CHAMPLEVÉ   A type of enamelware in which the pattern is grooved out in a metal

CHAISE BRISÉE

CHAISE LONGUE

CHANDELIER

CHAPITEAU

CHAPLET

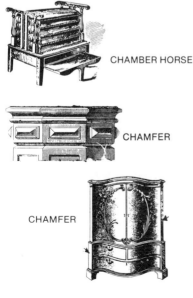

CHAMBER HORSE

CHAMFER

CHAMFER

base and the grooves filled with colored enamels. The thin raised lines that separate the enamel color are similar to the cloisons in *Cloisonné.*

CHANDELIER   A hanging lighting fixture. A pendant unit with branches to hold candles or lights, often decorated with prisms and crystals. Introduced into England by the French émigrés of 1685. See *Candelabra.*

CHANNELS   The long, shallow, concave grooves that run vertically up and down the shaft of a column, and are separated from one another by a narrow edge called a fillet. See *Fillet* and *Fluting.* A channel is also a form of rolled steel.

CHANTILLY LACE   A bobbin lace with a delicate ground. The design is outlined by a cordonnet of thick silky threads. See *Valenciennes Lace.*

CHAPITEAU   French for capital. Illustrated is the capital and base of a cannellated pilaster of the French Renaissance Château d'Aney le Franc.

CHAPLET   A small torus molding with a bead or berry decoration. A Byzantine capital is illustrated. See *Astragal.*

CHARCOAL   Twigs of willow charred away from the air, mainly used for preliminary drawings on a canvas or wall. Can be readily erased.

"CHARLES OF LONDON" SOFA
A heavily upholstered, 20th-century piece, with flat, massive, low armrests, barely rising above the T pillows that are set next to them. The platform is usually upholstered. The Charles of London chair, also a 20th-century innovation, has the same generally massive look.

CHARLES X PERIOD   From 1824 to 1830, part of the Restoration period in France. A mixture of Louis XVI and late Empire styles and Rococo and Renaissance detail.

CHARMEUSE   A soft, silken luster produced on fine cotton-warp sateens by mercerizing and schreinering, or a satin weave fabric (of cotton, silk, or rayon) which has a matte back and a semilustrous face.

CHASE   A long recessed area in masonry, brickwork, or concrete left to accommodate service pipes.

CHASING   A method of ornamenting on any metal surface. The pattern is produced by embossing or cutting away parts of the metal. A burin or graver is also used in this technique. Chasing with a burin is also done on marquetry, on metal mounts for furniture, or on Boulle metal inlays.

Chasing, as a form of metal enrichment, reached its peak during the 18th century in France. See also *Lalonde* and *Repoussé*.

CHAUFFEUSE A small fireside chair with a low seat of the early French Renaissance. See *Chaffeuse*.

CHAYERS À DORSERET Late-14th- and early-15th-century Gothic canopied chairs, usually carved of oak or chestnut, elaborately gilded, and highlighted with color. The chayer (or chaire) was massive and thronelike. Illustrated is a 15th-century French example. The back of the chair was lined with tapestry. See *Canopy Chair*.

CHECKER See *Chequer*. Originally the office of one of the heads of a monastery. The office usually had a checkered tabletop upon which accounts were reckoned with counters. An abbreviated form of the word exchequer.

CHECKERBOARD BOND In masonry, headers, only, laid one directly over the other in vertical lines. A purely ornamental arrangement, as it does not actually bond at all. See *Bond*.

CHECKERBOARD MATCH Veneer or wood panels set so that the stripe figure is vertical in one panel and horizontal in the next. Below the vertical striped panel, a horizontal is set, and a vertical panel is set under the horizontal panel. The pattern is then repeated.

CHECKS In cabinetry, small cracks which may appear in lumber which has not been dried evenly or properly. They appear perpendicular to the annual rings and radiating out from the heart of the trunk.

CHEEK The side pieces of a dormer window. A cheek is also the side post of a gate or door.

CHEEK PIECES The wings or fins of the tall easy chairs designed in 18th-century England, designed to keep draughts from the head of the person seated. See *Draught Chair*, *Grandfather Chair*, and *Wing Chair*.

CHEF D'OEUVRE French for "masterpiece." Also the name of a miniature piece of furniture made by a journeyman as a test of his level of accomplishment and readiness to be considered a master craftsman.

CHEN CHEN A pale, light, soft North-African wood from whitish to pale gray. Works well and has a characteristic stripe pattern. Also called Ako and Quen Quen.

CHÊNE French for oak.

CHENETS French for andirons or fire dogs. See *Andirons*.

CHAYERS À DORSERET

CHERUB

CHEST

CHEST OF DRAWERS

CHENILLE From the French for caterpillar. A woven yarn which has a pile protruding all around at right angles to the body thread. Used for embroidery, fringes, and tassels. Also fabrics woven from chenille yarns, having a plushlike surface. Can be made of cotton, silk, rayon, etc.

CHENILLE CARPET A thick, soft, cut-pile fabric woven on two looms, the weft loom and the chenille loom. Woven in any design, coloring, type, or surface yarn. May be made in any shape or size up to 30′ wide seamless. A variety of textural effects and thickness of pile are available.

CHEQUER One of the squares in a chequered or checkered pattern. An inlay design.

CHERRYWOOD A light to dark reddish grained wood resembling mahogany. It darkens with age. Used for small carved articles and French and American 18th-century Provincial furniture. Also popular for inlays and marquetry. The figure varies from plain to a rich mottle. Black cherrywood is found in the Appalachians, mainly in Pennsylvania and West Virginia. French cherry is found in France and England. Wild cherry is found in England, Europe, and Asia Minor.

CHERUB See *Amorino*. Illustrated here is a section of a Robert Adam 18th-century English design for a pilaster.

CHERUB HEAD A popular decorative motif which appears in Renaissance church or secular architecture, and as furniture decoration. See *Têtes d'Anges*.

CHESS TABLE A tabletop with a checkered pattern either painted or inlaid. In medieval Europe, the tops of chests were sometimes decorated with checkerboards.

CHEST Originally, a container or box with a hinged lid. Drawers were added to the chest in the mid-17th century, and the chest of drawers evolved. Chests in the medieval period were architectural in concept and decoration. Illustrated is a 15th-century Italian chest or cassone.

CHEST OF DRAWERS A box or chest with drawers added. Illustrated is a late-18th-century Hepplewhite design.

CHEST ON CHEST A chest of drawers in two parts, with one set of larger drawers. Also called a double chest.

CHESTERFIELD An overstuffed, heavily upholstered couch or sofa. Usually a large piece of furniture with a continuous back and scrolled, roll-over arms of the same height.

CHESTNUT A soft wood with coarse grain. It resembles oak, and can be used in its place when a quartered effect is not desired. Unsuitable for fine details because the grain is coarse and it has marked annual rings. Certain cuts were used in late-18th century England to imitate satinwood. One form, *Wormy Chestnut*, is popular today.

CHEVAL GLASS OR MIRROR Literally a "horse mirror," a mirror suspended between horses (see *Horse.*) A full-length mirror decoratively mounted so as to swing in a frame and large enough to reflect the whole figure. A French innovation introduced into England in the late 17th century. In the 18th century in England a small table model was introduced. The cheval mirror is also called a "swing glass" and "psyche."

CHEVAL SCREEN A fire screen which stands on two bracketed feet. A Sheraton design is illustrated.

CHEVET French for head of a bed. The head of a bed, or a bolster or pillow. A bedside table or night table.

CHEVIOT A loosely woven, rough-napped woolen cloth originally made from the wool of the sheep of the Cheviot Hills of Scotland.

CHEVRON French for "rafter." In ornament, a zigzag design or molding. A continuous band of V's, frequently used in Norman and Gothic ornament, and also in the 17th century as an inlay motif. See *Churn Molding.*

CHIAROSCURO Italian for light-dark. The balance of light and shadow in a picture. See *Clare-Obscure* and *Grisaille.*

CHIFFON A sheer, gauzelike silk fabric. A term used to describe the light, soft finish of a fabric like chiffon velvet.

CHIFFONNIER A French term for a rag-and-bone man. Originally a unit for collecting and containing assorted odds and ends. In the period of Louis XV, it refers to a tall chest with five drawers; however, in 19th-century England, the term is applied to a sideboard with two doors below enclosing shelves. Sometimes there were shelves at the back and top of the sideboard to hold ornaments, decorative serving pieces, etc. A Thomas Hope, early-19th-century English chiffonier is illustrated.

CHIFFONNIÈRE A sort of sewing table, with a three-sided gallery on top, drawers, and a shelf at the bottom, which was enclosed and used to hold balls of wool. A Louis XV innovation.

CHIFFOROBE A forerunner of what is now called an "armoire." A piece of bedroom furniture which combines hanging space with drawers in a single unit. Part

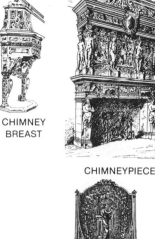
CHIMNEY BREAST

CHIMNEYPIECE

CHEVAL SCREEN

CHINA

CHINA CLOSET

CHIFFONNIER

CHINESE CHIPPENDALE

chiffonier (drawer unit) and part wardrobe (closet unit) thus chifforobe.

CHIMERA A mythical, dragon-like animal, or composite, part human, part animal, used in decoration. Used for legs or furniture supports in the Renaissance, Empire and later-19th-century designs.

CHIMNEY BREAST The projecting stone or brickwork of a fireplace above the fireplace proper to house the flue. The illustrated 17th-century design is from Bolsover Castle in Derbyshire, England.

CHIMNEYPIECE The ornamental structure surrounding the fireplace and the breast above it. A projecting hood, sometimes called the mantel. Many beautiful chimneypieces were designed and decorated by artists and architects of 18th-century England. A 16th-century French chimneypiece is illustrated. See *Mantel.*

CHINA The European name given to porcelains imported from the Orient. A hard, translucent porcelain with a large percentage of bone ash. Illustrated is a late-17th-century Chinese vase of the K'ang Hsi period. See also *Hard Paste* and *Kaolin.*

CHINA CLOSET or CABINET A display cabinet, usually with glass sides and front, used for exhibiting china collections. A popular piece of furniture in the late 17th and early 18th centuries when Oriental china was rare, and avidly collected. The illustrated lacquered design is of the William and Mary period.

CHINA SILK A sheer, plain-weave silk fabric which is nearly transparent. It may be made of rayon combined with silk.

CHINESE BRACKET FOOT or CHINESE FOOT A bracket-type foot with a reverse S-shape curve (cyma recta) on the face of the bracket. Also called an ogee bracket foot. A support favored by Chippendale in the mid-18th century.

CHINESE CHIPPENDALE A period in Chippendale's work, in the mid-18th century, when he was greatly influenced by chinoiserie, Chinese motifs, and the work of Sir William Chambers. See *Chambers, Sir William; Chinoiserie; Fretwork; Lacquerwork.*

CHINESE KEY DESIGN A continuous geometric border design, similar to the Greek key design or meander. Used by Chippendale in fretwork and openwork grille doors for bookcases, secretaries, etc.

CHINESE ROOM An 18th-century English craze. A room decorated "à la Chinoise," with imported Chinese furniture or adaptations such as Chippendale produced. China (or India or Japan) wallpaper or handpainted paper murals would usually cover the walls. Many of these wallpapers were produced in England after Chinese originals. See *Chinese Chippendale* and *Chinoiserie*.

CHINESE RUGS The Chinese rug differs from other rugs made in the Orient in its plainer background, narrower border, and central medallion. The smaller motifs scattered on the open ground are almost always symbolic. Popular background colors are blue and cream; soft yellow, cream, apricot, and gold are preferred top colors. These soft pastels are used to render clouds, dragons, waves, peonies, and other floral motifs. See *Oriental Rugs*.

CHINESE WALLPAPER A wallpaper introduced into Europe in the mid-17th century under the name of "India" or "Japan" paper. It was sold in sets of 25 rolls, each 12′ long and 4′ wide with a studied dissimilarity of detail from panel to panel. In the mid-18th century, chinoiserie had reached the peak of its popularity, and Chinese papers were very much in vogue. Among the favorite motifs were flowering shrubs, trees, flowers, birds, and butterflies. These were later replaced with exotic landscapes and curious "oriental" figures. The authentic Chinese wallpapers were imitated by French and English paper printers. Often contemporary 18th-century occidental figures are portrayed wandering through lush pseudo-oriental scenes. James Minikin of England produced wallpapers of this type.

CHINOISERIE Chinese-style or Chinese-like decorative motifs: gay, picturesque, imaginative occidental versions of oriental designs. Particularly popular in the Louis XV period in France and the 18th-century English styles. See *Chinese Chippendale; Formal; Huet, Christophe; Signerie;* and *Venetian Chinoiserie*.

CHINTZ From the Hindu word for spotted. A fine cotton cloth with a printed design, usually glazed or calendered. The design can be printed by blocks, copper plates, screens, or rollers. Unglazed chintz is called *cretonne*.

CHIP CARVING A simple, low relief form of ornamentation of the 18th and early 19th centuries, on American furniture. The work was accomplished with flat chisels and semicircular gouges. In the early 17th century, chip carving was used to enrich English furniture.

CHIPPENDALE, THOMAS I An early-18th-century English cabinetmaker, and creator of many early Georgian pieces. He was father of Thomas II, most famous of the three Chippendales.

THOMAS CHIPPENDALE

CHINOISERIE

CHURCH-GOING CHAIR

CHIPPENDALE, THOMAS II (1718–1779) The noted Chippendale. An English furniture designer and cabinetmaker. His earliest work was in the refined Georgian style, and in 1754 he published the *Gentleman* and *Cabinet-Maker's Director*. Chippendale's designs had great beauty, and he created in a variety of styles, including the decorated Queen Anne, Chinese, and Rococo French, as well as the Gothic. He was noted for his chairs, girandoles, mirrors, frames, and assorted beds (canopy, Chinese, dome, Gothic, field, and tent). He also designed many stands, side and serving tables, and teapoys. Henry Copeland, William Ince, Thomas Johnson, Mathias Lock, Robert Manwaring, J. Mayhew, and others followed in the styles originated by Chippendale. A Chippendale Chinese sofa is illustrated. See *Teapoy*.

CHIPPENDALE, THOMAS III (1749–1822) The son of the noted Chippendale. He designed and executed furniture in the Regency style. He worked in partnership with Thomas Haig.

CHOIR The area of the church fitted for the singers, or more broadly, the enclosed space for all those engaged in an ecclesiastic ceremony.

CHROMA or CHROME The degree of intensity, brilliance, or saturation of a spectrum color. Yellow is in the center of the spectrum, and is the most brilliant, but the palest chroma because it has the least saturation. Blue is the darkest, and has the greatest saturation. Red has a medium chroma.

CHROME PLATED Covered with a thin deposit of chromium deposited by electrolysis to give the underlying metal a shiny appearance and make it corrosion-resistant.

CHROMESPUN A trademark name for solution-dyed acetate fibers produced by the Tennessee Eastman Company. Used in carpet and upholstery fabrics.

CHRYSELEPHANTINE Made of ivory and gold. Certain ancient Greek statues were so made, the exposed body, face, and hands made of ivory, and the clothing or drapery of gold.

CHURCH-GOING CHAIR A light, portable, folding chair of the 16th and 17th centuries. Similar to today's folding bridge chairs. Made of wood, with a leather or fabric seat. The chair back often had a colonnade motif made up of spiral colonnettes.

CHURN MOLDING The zigzag or chevron molding used to enrich Norman architecture.

CHURRIGUERA, JOSÉ (1665–1725)
A Spanish architect who introduced the Baroque style into Spanish architecture. Heroically scaled motifs were applied onto structures rather than planned as functioning parts of the construction. Columns and pilasters became spiral or baluster-form shafts; voluptuous volutes replaced pediments; and nudes, cherubim, plaster clouds, waterfalls, draperies and such became lost in the mélange of swirls, curves, and fantasy.

CHURRIGUERESQUE The bold and massive Spanish Baroque style of the 17th century. The period was mainly influenced by the architect Churriguera. The Baroque period in Spain ran concurrently with the Rococo and up through the mid-18th century. There are an exuberance of color and an extravagance of ornament in this Baroque period which also had an effect on the Spanish possessions in the Americas.

CHUTE The French for fall or tumble. The chutes were ornate decorative bronze plates that fitted over the exposed angles and on the legs of wood furniture pieces, to protect as well as reinforce these areas. These functional enrichments appear in the 18th- and 19th-century French furniture. Many famous craftsmen like Caffieri made these chased and engraved pieces. Sometimes the chutes were finished as ormolu or as bronze-doré. Illustrated is a typical Louis XV commode. See *Sabots*.

CIBORIUM See *Baldachino*.

CIEL DE LIT French for a bed tester or canopy. Illustrated is an early French Renaissance bed.

CINCTURE The broad fillet below the concave molding (congé) located at the bottom of the shaft of a classic-order column.

CINDER BLOCK A building unit made of cinder concrete.

CINQUECENTO The 16th century.

CINQUEFOIL A five-leaf clover shape; also a motif in Gothic tracery.

CIPRIANI, GIOVANNI BATTISTA (1727–1785) An Italian painter of the Adam period in 18th-century England. He painted many ceiling and wall panels, as well as medallion inserts for Adam furniture. Cipriani did elegant, decorative, classic pieces and many graceful arabesque panels.

CIRAGE A monochromatic painting in yellow.

CIRCA Approximately the year or era given. "Circa 1850" would date an object

CHUTE

HINGE ORNAMENTED BY CISELEUR

CISTERN

CIEL DE LIT

CLAP TABLE

or event as appearing, occurring, or being made sometime near 1850. Often abbreviated, e.g., c. 1850.

CIRCASSIAN WALNUT A highly figured veneer wood that is produced from twisted, gnarled, and warped walnut trees grown in the dry Black Sea area of Europe.

CIRE PERDUE French for lost wax. A method of casting in which a figure is modeled in wax and then coated with hard clay. The figure is heated, the melted wax runs out through holes left in the clay, and molten metal is poured into the clay shell. The final details are often worked directly on the casting.

CISELÉ VELVET A raised, cut velvet, typical of *Renaissance* fabrics of Genoa. The pattern was raised against a flattened background.

CISELEUR A chiseler; a craftsman who ornaments bronze and other metals by chiseling; one who does chasing. Applied to finishers of metal mounts and chutes for 18th-century furniture. A Renaissance metal hinge is illustrated.

CISTERN In furniture, a wine cooler, sarcophagus, or cellarette of the latter part of the 18th century. Most often used to keep bottles on ice, but sometimes used for washing up. A Chippendale cistern is illustrated. See *Cellarette, Sarcophagus,* and *Wine Cooler*.

CITRONNIER French for lemon tree. A pale, honey-colored wood popular for furniture at the end of the 18th century.

CLAP TABLE An early 18th-century English pier or console table which usually had a pier looking glass set over it. Illustrated is a clap table designed by Thomas Johnson.

CLAPBOARD HOUSE The typical 17th-century New England house. Clapboarding (see *Clapboard Wall* below) was originally used as a protection for half-timbered houses in late Gothic—early Renaissance England, and was brought over to the New World. The house of Parson Capen at Topsfield, Massachusetts, (1683) is a typical clapboard house.

CLAPBOARD WALL An exterior wall facing made up of horizontal, slightly overlapping planks. A weatherboarded wall.

CLARE-OBSCURE The 18th-century Anglicised form of the French clair-obscur, a method of painting in lights and shades or chiaroscuro. Similar to *Grisaille* painting.

CLASSIC Referring to the architecture, sculpture, arts, and literary arts of the ancient Greeks and Romans. Something with an antique source or an established degree of excellence. The 18th- and 19th-century architecture and arts based on Greek and Roman elements, usually called Neoclassic or new classic. Illustrated is the Greek Doric order.

CLASSIC REVIVAL The early-19th-century architectural trend in England and the Continent which stressed the revival of classic forms and motifs. Classic prototypes were reexamined and supplied inspiration for new structures. Examples of the Classic Revival are the Royal Exchange in London, the Palais de Justice in Paris, the Court Theatre in Berlin. Greek columns and porticoes were frequently used.

CLAVATED Club-shaped. A type of turning used for furniture legs and stretchers on early Renaissance Spanish furniture. A Louis XIII Renaissance chair done in the Spanish style is illustrated.

CLAVECIN See *Clavichord* and *Pianoforte.*

CLAVICEMBALO A predecessor of the pianoforte which resembled a dulcimer with a keyboard attached to it.

CLAVICHORD A 17th-century forerunner of the piano. A stringed instrument used in England during the Carolean, William and Mary, and Queen Anne periods.

CLAW-AND-BALL FOOT See *Ball-and-Claw Foot.* Illustrated is a roundabout or corner chair of the late 17th century.

CLAY MORTAR MIX A finely ground clay added to mortar as a plasticizer.

CLEAR CERAMIC GLAZE A translucent tinted glaze. See *Ceramic Color Glaze.*

CLEARCOLE A priming or sizing solution made of white lead ground in water with glue, used in Great Britain.

CLEAT A wood strip fastened on a wood surface as a means of joining two adjacent surfaces, or a method of reinforcing the join. Can also prevent warping. See *Butterfly Wedge.*

CLEF PENDANTE French for boss. A hanging or projecting ornamental pendant. See *Boss.*

CLERESTORY A window placed near the top of a wall, originally, above an adjacent roof.

CLOCHE A glass dome fitted over a wood base, usually to protect artificial flowers, a clock, or an objet d'art from dust or harm.

CLASSIC

CLOISONNÉ

CLAVATED

CLAW-AND-BALL FOOT

CLOTHESPRESS

CLOVEN FOOT

CLUB FOOT

CLUSTERED COLUMN LEG

CLODION, CLAUDE MICHEL (1738–1814) A French sculptor who specialized in terra-cotta figures and figurines of satyrs, nymphs, and other decorative and sensual subjects. After the French Revolution, he was able to adapt to the Roman taste.

CLOISONNÉ A type of enamelware in which delicate metal partition filaments hold and separate colored enamels in a pattern. The individual metal partitions are called cloisons. Illustrated is a section of a Japanese copper dish with cloisonné inlay.

CLOSE CHAIR or CLOSE STOOL An enclosed box or stool equipped with a removable chamber pot, in use before the toilet or water closet came into being. Sheraton describes his design in his *Cabinet Dictionary* (1803) as: "made to have the appearance of a small commode, standing upon legs; when it is used the seat part presses down to a proper height by the hand, and afterward it rises by means of lead weights, hung to the seat, by lines passing over the pulleys at each end, all which are enclosed in a case."

CLOSED PLAN An interior with constructed walls and dividers that separate particular areas into sections for special activities. See *Open Planning.*

CLOSER The last tile or brick in a course.

CLOSURE A cut or trimmed brick, usually ¼ or ¾ of a brick. It is used at corners to obtain proper bonding.

CLOTHESPRESS A chest of drawers, sometimes with a cupboard set above it. The cupboard or cabinet has shelves to hold clothes. Illustrated is a Chippendale design.

CLOVEN FOOT Decorative foot for a Louis XIV furniture leg. It resembles a deer's cleft hind foot. See *Pied de Biche.*

CLUB CHAIR A large, roomy, upholstered easy chair. It may or may not be skirted, and the type of arms may vary with period or style, from high to low, from thick to thin, from all-upholstered to partially upholstered and partially framed. An oversized *bergère.*

CLUB FOOT A flat, round pad ending for a cabriole leg, used frequently on early-18th-century English furniture. See *Dutch Foot, Pad Foot,* and *Spoon Foot.*

CLUNY LACE See *Valenciennes Lace.*

CLUSTERED COLUMN LEG A furniture leg made up of several grouped or engaged turnings or columns. Used by Chippendale and William Ince in mid-18th-century England.

CLUSTERED COLUMNS Several columns placed together or having overlapping shafts which form a single support. A Gothic architectural motif.

COAL SCUTTLE A box or bucket used as a coal receptacle. Sometimes made of brass and ornamented. See *Pipkin*.

COAT OF ARMS Originally a lightweight garment, usually embroidered or decorated with heraldic emblems and worn over armor. In more recent terminology, the heraldic emblems of a family or institution. Illustrated is a design by the Adam brothers (mid-18th century) for the English royal family.

COATED GLASS A one-way mirror; a glass pane on one side and a mirror on the other, so that vision through the glass is possible from one direction only.

COBB, JOHN An 18th-century English furniture maker and partner of William Vile.

COBBLER'S BENCH A shoemaker's bench with seat, last holder, and compartments for pegs, etc. Usually made of pine in Colonial America. Reproductions and adaptations are made today and are used as cocktail tables in American Provincial rooms.

COCHIN, CHARLES NICHOLAS (1714–1790) A French designer and engraver who opposed the rococo style and worked in the classic tradition.

COCHOIS, JEAN-BAPTISTE A French master cabinetmaker *(ébéniste)* to Louis XVI. He was an inventor of dual purpose and change-about furniture: e.g., a chiffonière that converted into a night table.

COCK BEADING or MOLDING A small convex or half-round projecting molding used around the edges of drawers. See *Single Arch Molding*.

COCKADE A ribbon rosette or badge popular in the French Revolution. It was much in use in the French Directoire period as a decorative element.

COCKFIGHT CHAIR A saddle-like chair with a small shelf as the top rail of the chair back. The individual straddles the chair facing the back. The top rail, usually padded, functioned as an armrest. Used for reading, writing, and viewing sports events (like cockfighting). An 18th-century English favorite. See also *Fumeuse, Ponteuse, Straddle Chair, Voyelle,* and *Voyeuse*.

COCKLESHELL Also called the escallop or shell ornament. It was used as a carved decorative feature on furniture

COAT OF ARMS

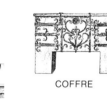

COFFERED PANEL

COFFRE

COCK BEADING

COGNAC CHAIR

knees, crestings, and pendants of chairs and other furniture pieces in early-18th-century English, Louis XIV, and Louis XV period designs. See also *Rococo* and *Scallop Shell*.

COCKTAIL TABLE See *Coffee Table*.

COCO BOLO A fine, uniform-grain, dark brown wood with a purplish cast which takes a fine polished finish. Found in Central America and used for modern furniture and fancy cabinetwork.

COCO WOOD A hard and brittle wood with purplish brown stripes on a medium dark ground, native to India.

COFFEE TABLE A low table, usually placed in front of a sofa or couch, and used to hold ashtrays, magazines, and refreshments. It can be styled to suit any period. In the 18th century, similar tables were designed as tea tables to hold tea service, cups, saucers, etc.

COFFER See *Coffered Panel* and *Coffre*.

COFFERED PANEL A sunken panel in the ceiling of a vault or dome, or in the underside of a cornice, usually ornamented and decorated. Illustrated is the Pantheon in Rome.

COFFIN STOOL A small oak four-legged stool, with stretchers, usually left undecorated. It may have been used originally to hold coffins awaiting interment.

COFFRE (COFFER) A chest or strongbox used for holding valuables. It also served as a seating unit in Gothic interiors. A French Renaissance example is illustrated.

COFFRET A small chest or coffer, often on its own stand or table.

COGGING A form of joinery with the pieces of wood crossing each other at right angles. The lower member is grooved out so that a projection fits into a slot on the underside of the upper member.

COGNAC CHAIR A 20th century molded fiberglass version of the tub or barrel chair, on a pedestal base. It was designed by Eero Aarnio of Finland and resembles in profile, the classic cognac glass. The outer form is fiberglass, while the inner lining and the pillow seat are lightly upholstered.

COGSWELL A 20th-century easy-chair with a fully upholstered back and seat, and a low upholstered platform. The sides are not enclosed. The arm stump rises from the platform and carries an overstuffed arm pad.

COIFFEUSE A hairdressing table or makeup table of the Louis XV and Louis

XVI periods. See also *Poudreuse* and *Table à Coiffer*.

COIGN See *Quoin*.

COIN A triangular cupboard that fits into a corner. See *Encoignure* and *Quoin*. Illustrated is an American corner cupboard, circa 1800.

COLLAGE From the French for gluing. A picture or ornament built up with pieces of paper, cloth, and other materials which are fastened to a canvas or other surface. See *Montage*.

COLLAR An astragal, or molding, which forms a band or ring around a furniture element like a table or chair leg.

COLLECTION A group of related units kept together, such as a *Wedgwood* collection, or a group of furniture by a particular designer, or one based on the same decorative styles or ornaments.

COLONIAL AMERICAN The period in American art and architecture from 1620 up to the Revolution. The period of early settlement in America, it blends English, French, and Dutch influences with native provincial interpretations.

COLONNA Italian for column or pillar.

COLONNADE A row of columns supporting a single entablature. An architectural treatment for a passageway or corridor.

COLONNATO Italian for colonnade.

COLONNETTE A miniature column used in architecture and also as a furniture decoration. In the Sheraton chair back here illustrated, the uprights resemble Corinthian columns. A group or cluster of colonnettes is sometimes used as a support for a pedestal table. A classic motif and a favorite of the Renaissance period.

COLORBOND A trademark name for an oil-in-water resin pigment dyeing technique developed by Dan River Company. It makes cotton, viscose rayon, acetate, nylon and other synthetics or blends colorfast to sunlight, washing, dry cleaning, gases, etc.

COLORFAST A term used to describe the ability of a fabric to retain its color when subjected to normal light, air, gas, and laundering. Little or no noticeable change of shade should take place, though it is almost impossible to produce an absolutely colorfast fabric.

COLORWAYS The various color schemes in which a commercial pattern or design is available for purchase. The number of colorways is the number of color

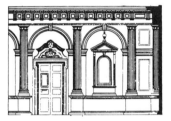

COIN

COLUMNS

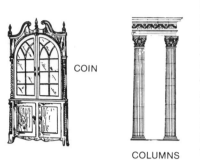

COLONIAL AMERICA

COMB BACK

COLONNETTE

COMMODE

arrangements printed or screened on a paper, fabric, etc., of a particular design.

COLUMBANI, PLACIDO An 18th-century Italian architectural designer of the Adam period. He worked with the Adam brothers in designing decorative mirror frames, and is especially noted for his chimneypieces. Columbani published *A New Book of Ornaments* in 1775, and *A Variety of Capitals, Friezes, Cornices and Chimney Pieces* in 1776. See *Crunden, John*.

COLUMN An upright member which is taller than it is thick, and serves as a support for something resting on its top. In architecture, a shaft set on a base and topped with a capital. Illustrated is a Corinthian column from the Temple of Vesta at Tivoli. Columns are distinguished by the name of the style or period of architecture to which they belong. See *Classic*.

COMB BACK A Windsor chair back in which the central group of spindles extends above the back proper, and is topped with an additional rail (the cresting rail). The top unit is called the comb piece since it resembles the high, Spanish-type combs fashionable in the 18th century. Also called "three-back" Windsor chair.

COMBED YARNS Yarns spun after the longer cotton fibers are combed to make them as parallel as possible. Combed yarn produces a smoother and more lustrous fabric since fewer fiber ends project from the fabric surface.

COMMEDIA DELL'ARTE Traditional form of Italian comedy popular with the artists and designers in the 18th century. Jacques Callot, Claude Gillot, and Antoine Watteau used scenes, costumes, and characters from the commedia dell'arte in their works.

COMMERCE TABLE An 18th-century collapsible or folding X-shaped frame which supported an oval card-table top. It was used to play Commerce, a card game.

COMMESSO A geometric type of mosaic work used in Italy during the Middle Ages.

COMMODE A chest of drawers or a cabinet, usually low and squat. In about 1700, in the Louis XIV period the term "bureau commode" was used to describe a large table with drawers. In the Regency and the Louis XV periods, the commode was often bombé in shape and it is considered the most typical piece of furniture of that time. The finer pieces showed no dividing rail or strip between the upper and lower drawer. The later units often had only two drawers. See illustration for *Chute* for a Louis XV commode. Also see *Cres-*

sent, Charles. A commode is also a night stand, a bedside cabinet or chest. Also a term for a latrine, a toilet.

COMMODE CHAIR   A thronelike chair construction used to camouflage a toilet bowl. A 20th-century conceit.

COMMODE DESSERTE   A French 18th-century sideboard with a center cabinet area and open shelves on either side.

COMMODE STEP   The curved bottom step of a stairway.

COMMODES EN TOMBEAUX   Early Louis XV chest, usually designed with two small drawers on top, and two full-width drawers below. The units were heavy in appearance and the lowest drawer was only inches off the floor; the legs were that short. *Tombeau* is French for tombstone and these designs were massive, squat, and tombstone-like.

COMMON BOND   In masonry, several courses of stretcher bond with the sixth or eighth course made up of headers only. This provides transverse strength to the bond since the headers tie back into the next set of bricks.

COMMON RAFTERS   The rafters that support the roofing of a building. They slope from the top of a wall to the ridge or apex of a pitched roof.

COMMONWEALTH   The Cromwellian period in England, 1649–1660. A puritanical period of chaste, severe forms. Illustrated is the bed of Oliver Cromwell.

COMMUNICATIONS RACEWAY A channel at the bottom of some open-planning panels or acoustical panels for offices, through which telephone and computer wires may be pulled to bring outlets to the machines out on the floor and away from walls and/or columns. See *Acoustical Panels* and *Open Planning.*

COMPANION CHAIR   Three curved upholstered chairs joined together at one point so that they appear to radiate from that central junction. Each chair is large enough to accommodate two persons. It is like a three-part *Tête-à-Tête* or *Siamoise.* Popular in the mid and late-19th century.

COMPARTMENT   In interiors, any area enclosed or bordered by architectural elements: walls, columns, arches, etc. In furniture, a cubicle, pigeonhole, etc.

COMPASS SEAT   An early-18th-century term for a round chair seat. Also referred to as a pincushion seat or chair.

COMPLEMENTARY COLORS   Each of the primary colors (red, yellow, and blue) has its complement, which is produced by

COMPO

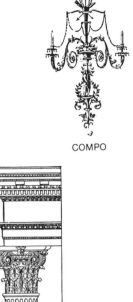
COMPOSITE ORDER

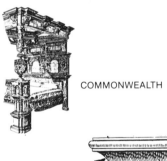
COMMONWEALTH

CONCAVE

CONFIDANTE

mixing the other two. Yellow and blue make green, and green is the complement of red. Violet complements yellow, and orange complements blue.

COMPO   See *Carton-Pierre, Composition Ornament,* and *Gesso.* A plaster or papier-mâché-like material molded or applied to a ceiling, panel, frame, or piece of furniture to create bas-relief enrichment. Illustrated is a late-18th-century girandole, probably designed by Hepplewhite circa 1788, and executed on molded plaster

COMPOSITE ORDER   A variation of the Corinthian order. The capital resembles an Ionic volute placed above rows of Corinthian acanthus leaves. A classic Roman order.

COMPOSITION   A grouping of elements to create a unified whole in a design or work of art.

COMPOSITION ORNAMENT An ornament or enrichment made of plaster or plaster-like material. The material is cast in a mold, and then applied to a surface to make a bas-relief decoration that resembles carving. The material and resulting ornament are also called *gesso* and *yeseria.* Composition ornament was introduced into England by the Adam brothers for the decoration of panels, ceilings, walls, doors, etc. See *Anaglypta, Carton-Pierre, Gesso, Papier-Mâché,* and *Pargework.*

CONCAVE   A sunken or caved-in line. The reverse of a convex line.

CONCRETE   A construction material made of cement, sand, and crushed stone, tile, or brick, mixed with water.

CONDUIT   A pipe or enclosed channel for carrying water, electrical wires, etc.

CONFESSIONAL   An 18th-century large, upholstered French wing chair. Also a small enclosure in which a priest sits to hear a confession.

CONFIDANTE   Three seats attached in a single unit. The two end seats are usually smaller, angled, and separated from the prominent center section by arms. A Hepplewhite design is illustrated.

CONFORTABLE   An early French Renaissance all-upholstered chair. A forerunner of the *bergère.*

CONGÉ   A concave molding similar to a cavetto, but tangent to a plane surface. The astragal under the bell of a capital consists of bead, fillet, and congé moldings. See *Cincture.*

CONNECTICUT CHEST   An early American chest, with two rows of double drawers, which stands on four short legs. It was frequently decorated with split spindles, painted black, and sometimes ornamented with three carved panels (see *Aster Carving*). The Connecticut chests were often made of oak, with pine tops, backs, and bottoms.

CONOIDAL VAULT　See *Fan Vault*.

CONSERVATORY　A greenhouse. Usually a glassed-in room in which plants and trees are grown. The room often has a glass ceiling. Also called a *jardin d'hiver*. A late-19th-century favorite.

CONSOLE　The French term for bracket. A console is a bracket, usually in an S scroll or curve, used to support a cornice or shelf. In furniture, it is more a decorative device than a functional one. The term often applies to a console table, which is actually a shelf supported against a wall by a bracket, a leg, or a pair of legs.

CONSOLE DESSERTE　A small serving table similar to a sideboard.

CONSOLE LEGS　Scroll legs that are bracket-shaped. They are found in late-18th-century furniture and are also called bracket feet. Illustrated is a Chippendale wardrobe.

CONSOLE MIRROR　A mirror that is set over a console or pier table. Illustrated is a German Empire console mirror and table.

CONSOLE SERVANTE　A serving table with a marble top and a shelf below, of the Louis XVI period. It is similar to the console desserte and commode desserte. A Sheraton design is illustrated.

CONSOLE TABLE　A shelflike table attached to a wall, and supported by a receding front leg or legs, or set on an S-shaped curved or caryatid-type bracket. Originally popular in 18th-century France and England, and still in use today in foyers, entries, etc. Also called a *pier table*.

CONSTITUTION MIRROR　A very late-18th, early-19th-century rectangular *Sheraton* mirror frame, usually gilded and had a row of balls under the cornice and a painted upper panel over the mirror area. In the 19th century the painting was often of the frigate Constitution of the War of 1812. Also called a "Tabernacle Mirror." See *Tabernacle Mirror*.

CONSTRUCTION　The assembling of the component parts into an integral unit. Illustrated is the internal construction of a couch, showing the wood framework, springs, filling, and muslin.

CONTEMPORARY　Term for the current, present-day, modern style of decora-

CONSOLE

CONSOLE LEGS

CONSOLE MIRROR

CONSOLE SERVANTE

CONVENTIONALIZATION

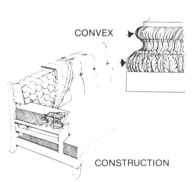

CONVEX

CONSTRUCTION

tion or furniture, as opposed to "traditional," which refers to a conventional past period or an antique style.

CONTOUR　The basic outline of a shape or object, disregarding painted or internal ornaments or decorations.

CONTOUR CHAIR　Any molded, shaped, or upholstered chair that conforms to the contours of the human body. Many modern pieces are so designed in laminated plywood, plexiglass, aluminum, etc. See *Eames, Charles; Saarinen, Eero;* and *Womb Chair*.

CONTRACT DESIGN　The interior design and furnishing of non-residential areas; offices, reception spaces, hospitals, health-care facilities, schools, libraries, restaurants, theaters, hotels, etc. Interior design based on commercial requirements. Contract design often requires quantity purchasing.

CONTRACT FURNITURE Furniture designed for heavy use in non-residential interiors, as for use in public areas by many people. Must be strong enough to withstand exposure to wear and tear over extended periods.

CONTREPARTIE or CONTRE BOULLE　A form of boulle work in which the brass forms the groundwork. The tortoiseshell is set into it, and is the less prominent material. The reverse form of the usual boulle work, or *Première Partie*.

CONVENTIONALIZATION　The simplifying or exaggerating of natural forms to make them reproducible in other materials. *A* is a realistic drawing of an acanthus leaf. *B* is a conventionalized form of it.

CONVERSATION CHAIR　This term has been applied to a variety of chairs; the caqueteuse in the 16th century, the round-about or cockfight chair in the 18th century, and the S-shaped "vis-à-vis" or "dos-à-dos" of the 19th century. Essentially, it is a comfortable chair which is not as low or as deep as an easy or lounge chair.

CONVERSATION PIECE　In current usage, an oddity or unique piece of decoration in a room which may cause comment.

CONVERSATION PIT　In contemporary interiors, a sunken area in a living or family room, surrounded by an architectural ledge, usually covered with upholstery or pillows. The riser to the floor level, above the ledge, serves as the backrest for those seated in the pit. The unit may be rectangular, oval, or circular, but the conversationalists are placed facing one another.

CONVEX　A swelling or outgoing curved line or surface, as opposed to a concave line or surface. Two convex moldings are illustrated.

CONVOLUTE A scroll or paper-roll shape.

COOL COLORS The green-yellows, greens, blue-greens, blues, blue-violets, and violets.

COORDINATED Designed or arranged to be harmonious together. A collection of furniture designed in the same given modules, or with the same trim and decoration, would be coordinated. Several different solid-color fabrics and a plaid consisting of all of these same colors would be a coordinated group.

COPE A method of joining two molded strips at an angle. Instead of the pieces being mitered, one piece fits over the top of the other.

COPELAND, HENRY An 18th-century cabinetmaker of the Chippendale, and then the Adam, school. With Matthias Lock, he published *A New Book of Ornaments.*

COPTIC Referring to the Copts, a Christian group in Egypt. From the 4th to the 7th century, their work included realistic portraits, and ended with flat decorative patterned designs.

COPTIC CLOTH A small-patterned, plain-woven, cotton upholstery fabric which usually has a provincial or rustic appearance.

COPTIC TEXTILE A linen fabric woven and designed in Egypt by the Coptic sect (4th to 7th centuries).

COQUILLAGE A French Rococo shell-like pattern used with birds, flowers, masks, and other carved ornaments to decorate mirrors, frames, clocks, etc. It also appears in Chippendale's French-style furniture as a furniture enrichment.

CORBEIL or CORBEILLE A sculptured representation of a basket of fruit or flowers.

CORBEL In architecture, a bracket or shoulder set in a wall to carry a beam. The corbel was also adapted for use on interiors and on furniture, and was popular in Renaissance designs. See *Bracket* and *Console.*

CORBEL TABLE A slab of stone or masonry supported by a row of corbels.

CORBELED ARCH A span of stonework constructed by regularly advancing the successive courses from either side till the top ones nearly meet. A capstone is set in the center to close the gap. Illustrated is the early Greek Treasury of Atreus at

CONVOLUTE

CORINTHIANESQUE

COQUILLAGE

CORBEL TABLE

CORBELED ARCH

CORNER BLOCK

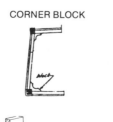

   CORNER BLOCK

Mycenae. Here a dome-shaped ceiling is achieved by the advancing in of the successive courses.

CORDOVAN LEATHER The decorated leatherwork made in the technique and style begun in Cordova, Spain, during the Middle Ages. The leather was often stamped, carved, or embossed with gilt arabesques and Moorish patterns.

CORDOVAN TAPESTRY See *Guadamicil.*

CORDUROY From the French, for the king's cord. A cotton or rayon cut pile fabric with ridges or cords in the pile which run lengthwise, giving a ridged, velvety quality.

CORE In cabinetry, the structural wooden body of a piece of furniture. It usually gets a veneer finish (see *Carcase* or *Carcass.*) The central body of plywood which has crossed layers of veneer or other wood applied to either of its surfaces. This internal layer, or core, is usually made of a porous wood.

CORINTHIAN ORDER The most slender and elaborate of the classic architectural orders. The Romans made the height of the column equal to ten times the diameter of the shaft. The capital is enriched with rows of acanthus leaves and four volutes.

CORINTHIANESQUE A design similar to the Corinthian order, but not an exact reproduction. Illustrated is an Italian Renaissance version.

CORK TILES Pressed cork baked into a solid, homogeneous block, and then cut into rectangular sheets or tiles. The squares may be used for flooring or wall surfacing. It is an extremely resilient material. Resin reinforced, waxed cork tile is less pourous than natural cork tile, and requires less maintenance. The natural cork will stain, and because of its softness is will indent or pit. Cork can be laminated with a thin layer of vinyl or impregnated with vinyl resins.

CORLON A trademark name for sheet vinyl flooring with a hydrocord back, made by Armstrong. Usually comes in 6' widths and can be used over suspended, on grade, and below grade subfloors. Available in a variety of colors, patterns, and textural effects.

CORNER BLOCK In carpentry, a square block of wood used to form a junction, as between the sides and head strip of a door. In cabinetry, a triangular block used as a brace in joining legs to seat rails. A plan of a chair seat is illustrated; the chair legs are shaded.

CORNER CHAIR   See *Roundabout Chair.*

CORNER CUPBOARD   A triangular cabinet or chest originally designed by architects as an integral part of a room. In the 18th century it became a mobile piece of furniture. See *Coin* and *Encoignure.*

CORNER STILES   The corner or end vertical members in a paneled piece of furniture. A late-17th-century cabinet is illustrated.

CORNER CHAIR

CORNER TABLE   A square or triangular table used in a corner between a pair of couches or chairs set at a right angle to each other. The corner table fills in the space that is left when two units join but do not overlap at a 90° angle. Can be of any period or design or material. Usual sizes are 24″ or 36″ square or triangular.

CORNICE   The projecting top portion of a classic entablature consisting of bed fascia and crown moldings. In Renaissance interiors it was used on interior walls directly below the ceiling, without the frieze or architrave moldings. See *Architrave, Fascia,* and *Frieze.* Also, a decorative applied cap to a curtain or drapery arrangement on windows, canopy beds, etc. It is usually made of wood with molding trim, but it may be carved or covered with fabric. Similar to a valance, lambrequin, or pelmet. In the mid-18th century it was called a window mantel.

CORNICIONE   Italian for entablature.

CORNISH   See *Cornice.*

CORNER STILES

CORNUCOPIA   The twisting, spiraling "horn or plenty" of mythology, often represented with fruits and/or flowers pouring forth. As a decorative motif, it was popular in the Renaissance, Empire, and Victorian periods. Arms and legs of sofas were sometimes cornucopia-shaped in 19th-century furniture.

CORNUCOPIA SOFA   An English Regency sofa (circa 1820), with scrolled arms carved in the form of a cornucopia. The sofa back and legs repeat this motif. The foot was often a lion's paw. The cornucopia sofa also appeared in American Empire furniture.

COROLITIC   A term used to describe something decorated with sculptured branches of foliage.

COROMANDEL   Also called coromandel ebony, calamander, and Macassar ebony. A hard, dark, brown wood with black stripes. It resembles black rosewood, and was used for banding and veneering in late-18th-century furniture.

CORNICE

CORNUCOPIA SOFA

COROMANDEL LACQUER   A lacquering technique originally from the Honan province in central China, greatly admired and used in the Louis XV period for finishing commodes and cabinets. The background was a reddish-black which turned brown with age. The lacquer was very thick, applied in successive layers. It was possible to incise designs in it. Panels were decorated with figures, houses, landscapes, etc. See *Coromandel Screen.*

COROMANDEL SCREEN   A Chinese lacquered screen often decorated with an all-over pattern in low relief, or executed with a landscape design. Originally introduced into Europe by the East India Company in the middle of the 17th century. The finest were first made in Peking and Soochow.

CORONIZED   A trademark for a heat-treating finish applied to Fiberglas cloths. The process was developed by the Owens Corning Fiberglas Corporation. It sets the weave of the fabric, and releases strains in the glass yarns. The finish gives the Fiberglas a better hand, and makes it drape better.

CORTILE   An Italian term for an inner court surrounded by an arcade.

COSMATI   The marble and mosaic workers of Rome from the 12th to the 14th century. They created pavements, tombs, pulpits, etc., in marble with inlays of mosaic, gilding, colored stones, and glass. By the 14th century, these workers, many of whom were from the same family, were producing sculpture. *Cosmati Work* is a generic term for work in colored stone.

COSMATI WORK   Generic term for work in colored stone. See *Cosmati*

COSY CORNER   An upholstered couch that fitted into the corner of a room. Forming a complete right angle, it usually had an upholstered and tufted back, and was a popular piece in the late 19th century. It was similar to the corner ottoman, and was sometimes the main furnishing of a Turkish Corner. The mid-20th-century sectional furniture, in a way, fulfills the same purpose: a seating unit for two or more people to sit and talk to one another.

COTTAGE FURNITURE   Mid-19th-century mass-produced Victorian furniture. Inexpensive pieces made of pine and painted and decorated in a Colonial or provincial style. The *Dry Sink* is an example.

COTTAGE ORNÉ   A French term for a pseudo-rustic middle-class dwelling fashionable in the 18th century.

COTTAGE PIANO An upright piano of the 18th and early 19th centuries. It usually had a fretwork panel in front of and above the keyboard. Behind the fretwork was a pleated silk curtain.

COTTAGE-SET CURTAIN A two-tier set of curtains usually made of a sheer or semisheer fabric. The lower tier may be pleated or shirred, and extends across the width of the window. The upper tier is usually ruffled along the edges, and is pulled back to either side of the window, allowing an open center area.

COTTE, ROBERT DE (1656–1735) Cabinetmaker and designer who assumed control of the Gobelins Factory after Mignard. He was first the pupil and later the brother-in-law of Jules Hardouin-Mansart.

COTTON A plant that produces a versatile fiber which makes a popular fabric and blends well and lends its good characteristics to other fibers in a mixture. It combines with rayon, dacron, and Fortisan as well as with wool.

COUCH A lounge chair used for resting, with supports and cushions at one or both ends. It was a French innovation of the early 17th century, and developed into a daybed. In 18th-century America, couch was synonymous with daybed. In common usage, a couch is often confused with a sofa or settee.

COUNT OF CLOTH The number of threads per inch. The lengthwise yarns are called ends, the crosswise yarns are called picks. The density of a fabric may be given in number of ends X number of picks.

COUNTER BOULLE See *Contrepartie.*

COUNTERFLOOR A subflooring under a main floor, made of battens laid on the floor joists.

COUNTERLATHING A layer of laths laid at right angles and on top of a first layer of lath strips. A latticed effect.

COUNTERPANE A quilt, usually the exposed quilt placed on top of a bed. The pattern is raised or "quilted."

COUNTERSINK A depression made in a piece of wood so that the head of a screw, inserted into it can be flush with or below the top surface of the wood. See *Cup.*

COUNTRY CHIPPENDALE A mid-18th-century American provincial version of Chippendale chairs, often made of pine and painted. These were simplified, but were usually very skillfully made.

COUNTRY FRENCH A heavier, sturdier, more countrified version of the

COUPLED COLUMNS

COURT CUPBOARD

COUCH

COURTING CHAIR

COVE

Rococo style than the version usually called French Provincial. The early-American look with a French accent.

COUNTRY-MADE Furniture or cabinets made by country or rustic cabinetmakers. The term usually implies less refined and less finished workmanship, and simplification of design.

COUPLED COLUMNS Columns or shafts grouped in pairs. In classical orders, they are usually spaced half of a diameter (of the column shaft) apart. Illustrated is a Renaissance example, the gateway to Toulouse in France.

COURSE A horizontal row of stones, bricks, tiles, etc., that can be arranged into decorative patterns. A module of masonry.

COURT CUPBOARD Court is French for short. A low cupboard mounted on legs, or a double cupboard, usually heavily carved and massive in appearance. It was originally designed to hold plate, utensils, goblets, etc. In the Tudor period it was a buffet, and probably related to the Italian and French crédence. An oak court cupboard of the Jacobean period (17th century) is illustrated. The panels are decorated with lozenge carvings.

COURTING CHAIR An upholstered double chair or settee, popular in the Louis XIV period. In the Queen Anne style, the design had an open back and looked as though two chairs had been joined together with a common seat. Also called a two-chair back settee. A forerunner of the *love seat.*

COURTING MIRROR A small 18th–19th-century mirror with a simple wood frame with insets of small pieces of glass. The pieces of glass were often painted or decorated. It may originally have been a gift presented by a swain to the girl he was courting.

COVE A quarter-circle, concave, downward curve from the ceiling to a wall, or from the wall down to the floor. Also a large concave molding often used in a cornice or under the eaves of a roof.

COVE BASE See *Skirting.*

COVE LIGHTING A form of indirect lighting. The lighting source in the room or area is concealed from below by a recess, cove, or cornice, and the light is directed upon a reflecting surface.

COVED CEILING A ceiling into which the supporting walls flow in a curve, rather than meeting at a sharp right angle. A curved joining between walls and ceiling.

COVED CUPBOARD An early American cupboard design with a hoodlike projection on top.

COVED SKIRTING An applied cove-shaped strip used to cover the joint of the wall and the floor. Wooden, rubber, asphalt, and vinyl coves are used as flooring finishes between the floor and the wall, replacing flat floorboards.

COX, JOSEPH A mid-18th-century American cabinetmaker and upholsterer who worked in New York City.

COYPEL, NOËL (1628–1707) A French painter and decorator. As a member of the Gobelins group, he painted furniture panels and designed tapestries. Coypel also worked on the decorations at Versailles.

CRADLE A baby's bed usually set on a swinging device or on curved rocker supports. Many styles and variations are made.

CRAMOISY A crimson-colored cloth used in medieval and Renaissance England.

CRAMP A thin piece of metal with both ends turned back at right angles, used to bind together blocks of masonry or timber.

CRANE, WALTER (1845–1915) An English craftsman-designer. A disciple of William Morris and the Arts and Crafts movement. He said, "The true root of all art lies in the handicrafts."

CRAQUELURE The network of fine cracks on the surface of an old painting. It may be caused by shrinkages, movement of paint film and/or varnish.

CRASH Cotton, jute, or linen fabrics having coarse, uneven yarns and a rough texture. Can be hand-blocked or printed. Used for draperies.

CRÉDENCE A serving table and sideboard of the French Gothic period which may have evolved from a church piece. It was a chest mounted on a stand, or a display cabinet for plates, or for preparing and carving meats. See *Buffet* and *Desserte*.

CREDENZA The Italian form of the *Crédence.*

CRÉMAILLÈRE A swinging crane on a fireplace hearth.

CREMER An 18th-century French cabinetmaker who specialized in artificially colored Louis XV marquetry work.

CREMO An Italian marble with a creamy white ground and a network of golden veins.

CREPE A large group of fabrics characterized by a crinkled surface obtained by hard twisting of the yarns, chemical treatment, the weave, or embossing. Crepe can be made of many natural or synthetic fibers.

CRESCENT STRETCHER

CHARLES CRESCENT

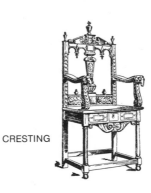

CRESTING

CRÉDENCE

CRIB

CRESCENT STRETCHER An arched or hooped stretcher, sometimes used between the legs of 18th-century furniture. It is often used as a reinforcing element on American Windsor chairs.

CRESLAN A trademark name for an acrylic fiber manufactured by the American Cyanamid Company, similar to orlon and Acrilan. A soft, bulky fiber with a wool-like hand. The name is applied to fabrics which meet the performance standards set by American Cyanamid.

CRESSENT, CHARLES (1685–1768) A leading French cabinetmaker of the Régence and Louis XV periods, noted more for his ormolu trim and chased metalwork than for marquetry. Cressent was a student of Boulle and designed clocks and wall decorations. Used floral forms, cupids, lovers, garlands, and roses as well as monkeys and grotesques for his metal enrichments. Illustrated is a Louis XV commode attributed to Cressent.

CREST RAIL The uppermost or top rail of a chair back. In the 16th and 17th centuries, this element was usually elaborately shaped and carved.

CRESTING Elaborate carving on the top rail of a chair back or settee, often centered on the top rail. The crown-and-cherubs was a favorite English Restoration cresting motif. See *Brattishing.*

CRETONNE An unglazed chintz, printed with larger designs than usual for chintz. A common slip-covering fabric, and may be made of cotton or linen.

CREWELWORK Embroidery done with loosely twisted worsted yarn and a large-eyed needle on unbleached cotton or linen, a popular fabric decoration in the 16th and 17th centuries in England. In the Jacobean period, often used in winding floral designs like the East Indian "tree-of-life" motif.

CRIB An infant's bed with enclosed sides, usually raised off the ground on tall legs.

CRICKET An archaic name for a low wooden footstool. An English and early American design.

CRICKET TABLE A small, three legged, polygonal or roundtop table of the Jacobean period in England. The straight legs were supported on a triangular frame with high stretchers between the legs.

CRINOLINE STRETCHER A common device of Chippendale's Windsor chairs. The stretcher is concave in form and separates and reinforces the two front legs. Two short arms extend from the back legs to support the crinoline stretcher. See *Crescent Stretcher.*

CRIOSPHINX An ancient Egyptian carved representation of an animal with a lion's body and a ram's head. See *Androsphinx* and *Sphinx.*

CRISS-CROSS CURTAINS See *Priscilla Curtains.*

CROCKET A projecting carved ornament used on the side of pinnacles and spires. The ornament is often bud- or leaf-shaped, and appears in Gothic art and architecture. In the 19th-century English Gothic revival furniture, this motif was sometimes carved on architecturally inspired cabinets, bookcases, and thronelike chair posts.

CROCKING The tendency of excess dye to rub off a printed or dyed fabric. It is most apt to happen in deep-colored pile or napped fabrics.

CROMWELLIAN CHAIR A severe, unadorned chair of the English Commonwealth period (1649–1660). It usually had knob or bobbin turnings, a low back, leather seat and back, and nailhead trim.

CROMWELLIAN PERIOD See *Commonwealth.*

CROQUET CHAIR A mid- to late-19th-century woven wicker or rattan barrel chair. The base resembles an inverted woven basket. The arms and back make a continuous line which seems partially to encircle the seated person. The back and seat are usually equipped with button-tufted upholstery. See *Peacock Chair.*

CROQUIS A preliminary sketch or rough draft. Illustrated is a rough drawing for a Grecian-type bracket.

CROSS BANDING A narrow band of wood veneer used as a frame or border design on a panel, door, tabletop, etc. The grain of the veneer wood of the band is at right angles to the grain of the panel itself. See *Banding.*

CROSS FIRE A vivid, mottled effect across the grain of some mahoganies, walnuts, and satinwoods that creates a striking pattern. The effect created is an uneven, corrugated, transverse pattern which appears as highlights on the wood.

CROSS RAIL OR MEMBER See *Slat.* A horizontal element which joins two verticals or two sides. In a chair back, the connecting element between the back posts. An Adam armchair is shown.

CROSS SECTION A view of an object with an imaginary cut through it, represent-

CROCKET

CROMWELLIAN CHAIR

CROWN GLASS

CROQUIS

C.R.T.
(CATHODE RAY TUBE)

CROSS RAIL

CROSS SECTION

ing a side view with the constructional elements, projections, and recesses from the straight elevation.

CROSS STRETCHERS See *Saltire* and *X-shaped Stretchers.*

CROSS VAULT A roof or ceiling formed by two vaults intersecting at right angles.

CROTCH The part of the tree from which the limbs and branches develop. It always produces a highly figured V-grain of an extremely decorative character.

CROTCH VENEER A thin sheet of wood cut at the crotch of the tree, used for veneer. The graining is often featherlike in appearance, or curly in effect, and always decorative.

CROWN The top point of an arch. As a decorative motif, the symbol of royalty, it appears in carved, painted, and embroidered form.

CROWN BED A simple canopy bed of the late-18th and early 19th centuries. The canopy is suspended over the bed, or extends partially out over the bed from the wall behind. See *Baldaquin Bed.*

CROWN GLASS An early form of window glass made with a blowpipe. The glass is formed as a flat dish with a button or bull's-eye center. Illustrated is a 16th-century French interior with crown glass set into leaded windows. See *Bull's-Eye.*

CROWN MOLDING The topmost molding, particularly the fillets and cymas placed above the fascia in a classical cornice.

CROW'S BILL A Gothic architectural enrichment like a *Bird's Beak* trim.

C.R.T. (CATHODE RAY TUBE) The video terminal with its cathode ray tube and the keyboard element that constitute the two basic components of the computer found in many offices and work areas —secretarial as well as executive—which must be provided for in the work space design.

CRUNDEN, JOHN An 18th-century English designer (he died in 1828), who created furniture frets, allegorical centers for ceilings, railings, and chimneypieces. In association with Thomas Milton and Placido Columbani, he prepared *A Treasury of New Designs for Chimney Pieces.* Crunden also published *Designs for Ceilings, The Carpenter's Compositions for Chinese Railings, Gates, etc.,* and *Convenient and Ornamental Architecture.*

CRYSTAL A clear, transparent quartz which resembles ice. It is usually cut and faceted to sparkle and reflect light. Crystal is often imitated in glass.

C-SCROLL An ornamental motif, painted, applied, or carved, which resembles the letter C or various combinations of the letter C. The C's may be inverted, touching back to back, top to bottom, or set askew of each other. Found in Spanish and French Gothic furniture. Used extensively in the Baroque, Rococo, Queen Anne, and Chippendale periods.

CUBE FOOT See *Block Foot.*

CUBICULUM A bedroom in an ancient Roman house.

CUBISM The parent of abstract art, the analysis of forms and their relationships to each other and space. It sometimes combines several views of the object more or less superimposed on one another, expressing the idea of the object rather than one view of it. Picasso and Braque were major exponents of cubism.

CUCCI, DOMENICO A great French cabinetmaker of the 17th century who designed in the Louis XIV style. He specialized in decorations of gold bronze, colored stones, ornaments, and figures, Cucci was a rival of Boulle and Caffieri.

CUIVRE French for copper.

CUIVRE DORÉ French for gilded copper, also called pomponne, after the Hôtel de Pomponne, where this plated ware was originally made.

CUIVRE-JAUNE French for brass.

CUL-DE-LAMP A pendant, either of wood, metal, or stone, used as a bracket for a lamp. These brackets were highly decorated with carving or painting. Illustrated is a 17th-century cul-de-lamp.

CUNEIFORM Wedge-shaped. The wedge-shaped characters used by the Assyrians and Babylonians in writing on clay.

CUP A metal sheath for a head of a screw in countersunk work. See *Countersink.*

CUP CASTER A brass cup with a roller below which fits on the bottom of a furniture leg. A Sheraton book cabinet is illustrated.

CUP AND COVER TURNING A popular Elizabethan and Jacobean turning used for furniture supports. It resembles a cup topped with a lid or an inverted saucer form. A late-16th-century Elizabethan oak four-poster bed is illustrated.

CUP-TURNED LEG The prominent cuplike feature in a turning popular in the late 17th and early 18th centuries. It was a

C-SCROLL

CUPID'S BOW

CUPBOARD

CUL-DE-LAMP

CUP CASTER

CUP AND COVER TURNING

development of a Portuguese bulb shape, and was also known as the bell and trumpet leg. In England the cup-turned leg is characteristic of the William and Mary style.

CUPBOARD A storage cabinet with doors. It may be raised up on high legs, or be set low. The cabinet may have drawers or another cabinet below. The style and design varies with type and use. A 19th-century German design of late Gothic influence is illustrated.

CUPID'S BOW A Chippendale-style top rail of a chair back shaped like a bow, with compound curves, and often with spiral volutes on the ends. The cupid's bow with arrows also appeared as a decorative motif in the Louis XV and Louis XVI periods.

CUPRAMA A cuprammonium-type rayon fiber produced in Germany by Farbenfabriken Bayer. It has a wool-like hand, resists soiling, and dyes somewhat darker than regular rayon.

CURL The markings or figure of a wood. The appearance of the grain of certain woods when they are sliced against the grain.

CURLED HAIR Animal hair used as a filler with stuffing on upholstered pieces under the muslin and the upholstery fabric, to add more resiliency. Horsehair is more desirable than the hair of hogs or cattle.

CURON A trademark name for a multicellular plastic material. Made by the B.F. Goodrich Company, it has a fine spongelike appearance, and is produced in many colors. Curon may be used for wall or ceiling installations, and will serve as an insulating or acoustical material.

CURRICULE CHAIR A late-18th-century, early-19th-century Sheraton chair with a semicircular back and splayed legs which, according to Sheraton, resembles an open carriage of the period.

CURTAIL STEP The bottom step of a flight of stairs which has a curved end that goes partially around the newel post.

CURTAIN A movable covering of lightweight fabrics for windows, doors, or alcoves. It was originally used to screen beds and bed areas.

CURTAIN WALL In contemporary architecture, a large surfaced façade of glass and metal, made possible by advances in the metal and plastics industries in overcoming problems of waterproofing, insulation, expansion, and contraction. Lever House, in New York City, completed in 1952, has an early, dynamic example: a green glass and aluminum trim curtain wall.

CURULE CHAIR A 17th-century chair. The arm supports and the back rails are semicircular in shape. The legs are also semicircular. The general appearance is an X created by the two intersecting S curves, or one C resting on an inverted C. A leather strip usually provides the back rest, and the seat is also a piece of leather. The design is based on a classic Roman prototype, the sella curulis of the Roman magistrate. Another version of the curule chair became popular in the early-19th-century Empire and Regency periods. A Sheraton design is illustrated. See *Dante Chair*.

CURULE LEGS X-shaped legs such as were used on classic Greek and Roman folding stools. They became popular again in the Renaissance period, and continued in favor up through the Regency and French Empire periods. A Chippendale design is illustrated. See *Curule Chair*.

CURVILINEAR Created within curved or arced lines. Some Gothic tracery was curvilinear in concept. A German Rococo console table, here illustrated, shows the curvilinear line quality prevalent during the Rococo period.

CUSHION A shaped, flexible bag of fabric or leather, filled with feathers or other filling materials. A pillow. Added to an upholstered platform and back for extra softness and comfort. Illustrated is a Louis XVI sofa with a separate cushion seat.

CUSHION FRIEZE A Renaissance convex or cushion-shaped frieze. Sometimes used on cabinets of the late 17th and early 18th centuries. Illustrated is the top of a chest of the latter part of the 17th century.

CUSPS The pointed endings of a trefoil or quatrefoil in Gothic architecture. The meeting points are the pendants between the arcs. Chippendale and Sheraton used cusping as a carved decorative trim on some of their chair backs. See *Quatrefoil* and *Trefoil*.

CUSSEY, DOMENICO A French 17th-century cabinetmaker to Richelieu, the chief minister to Louis XIII.

CUT PILE Fabric woven with an extra set of warp or filler yarns. These threads form the loop pile which is later cut. Velvet and plush are cut pile fabrics.

CUTOUT BORDERS Wallpaper designs usually applied below the ceiling line

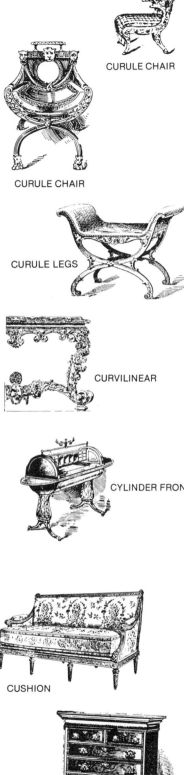

CURULE CHAIR

CURULE CHAIR

CURULE LEGS

CURVILINEAR

CYLINDER FRONT

CUSHION

CUSHIONED FRIEZE

or molding and used as a dado decoration, or around doors, windows, arches, etc. Designs are often architectural motifs combined with swags, garlands of flowers, fruits, etc. The lower edge of the design is cut out to conform to the outline of the artwork. When the paper is applied, it appears to be part of the wall. Also called a "scalloped border."

CUTTING A swatch or clipping of a piece of carpet or fabric. A small representation or sample of a larger whole.

CUVILLIÉS, FRANÇOIS DE (1698–1767) A great French furniture maker of the Louis XV period. He was an architect and engraver in the extreme Rococo style and favored the Chinese style in applied decoration.

CUVILLIÉS THE YOUNGER (Jean François) (1731–1805) A designer of ornaments and decorations influenced by Germanic styles.

CYLINDER FRONT A quarter-round front of a desk or secretary mounted so that it can be pivoted. Illustrated is a late-18th-century Sheraton desk design.

CYLINDER TOP A rolltop cover to a bureau or desk. It differs from the tambour top in that it does not roll up on itself. See *Gouthière, Pierre*, for an illustration of a Louis XVI cylinder secrétaire.

CYMA CURVE An S-shaped curve.

CYMA RECTA An S-shaped curve that starts and ends in a horizontal plane. An ogree molding.

CYMA REVERSA An S-shaped curve that starts and ends in a vertical plane.

CYMATIUM A cyma molding which forms the uppermost member of a cornice.

CYPRESS A native American, light-brown wood, adapted to all types of finishes. It is generally free from warping and twisting but is considered too weak for structural timber or flooring. In the Tudor period it was used for storage chests. "Pecky cypress" is popular today for paneling and wall finishes.

CYPRESS CHESTS Early Renaissance chests made to hold tapestries, robes, and such. Cedar came to be used because its aroma is repellent to moths. The cypress chest was a prototype of current cedar chests.

D

DACRON A trademark name for a polyester fiber obtained from a polymer with 85 percent or more of the polyester of ethylene glycol and terephthalic acid. A crisp, strong, resilient fiber manufactured by Dupont. Dacron combines well with cotton, linen, and wool.

DADA French for hobbyhorse. A period from about 1915 to 1922 when a group of artists emphasized shock rather than understanding. Marcel Duchamp was an outstanding exponent of this art movement, a predecessor of surrealism.

DADO The lower portion of the wall when treated differently or separated from the rest of the wall by a molding strip. A wainscot. In classic styles the dado had a base, shaft, and cap molding, and was often paneled or ornamented.

DADO CAP The crown or cap molding of a dado. Also called a *Chair Rail*.

DADO JOINT A joining technique for supporting shelving or drawer bottoms in vertical units. It is used to stiffen or reinforce the vertical member. The edge of the vertical piece of wood fits into a groove in the horizontal piece. Also called a rabbet joint.

DAGLEY A 17th-century French craftsman who introduced the secret of Japanese lacquer into France. The technique was used at the Gobelins and called *Vernis de Gobelins*.

DAGLIGSTUE A Danish word for a family room, a comfortable general-purpose recreation room.

DAGOBERT CHAIR A famous 7th-century folding chair, originally made of

DAIS

DADO

DADO JOINT

DAGOBERT CHAIR

gilt bronze, supposedly by St. Eloi. The back and arms were added in the 12th century by Abbé Suger. One of the very few pieces of furniture remaining from this period.

DAGUERREOTYPE First photographic process, invented in 1839 by Louis Daguerre. A faint image was produced, which had to be viewed from an angle for clarity.

DAIS A low raised platform usually located at the end or side of a room. Illustrated is a bench on a dais in a 10th-century interior.

DALBURGIA "Black wood." An Indian wood used for small carved decorative elements like boxes, gong stands, etc.

DALLAGE A French term for a pavement or floor of stone, marble, or tile.

DAMASCENE WORK (Damascening) See *Damascus Work*.

DAMASCUS WORK A type of metal inlay work in patterns or arabesques. The design is incised in metal and then inlaid with other metals or wires cut to fit.

DAMASK A firm, glossy, patterned fabric with a jacquard weave, introduced into Europe by Marco Polo, and named for the city of Damascus. Similar to brocade, but flatter and reversible and can be in one- or two-color designs. On the reverse side, the pattern changes in color or may appear shiny (the pattern is matte on the face side). Damask was originally made of silk but is now woven in cotton, rayon, linen, silk, wool, or a combination.

DAMASSÉ French for *Damask*.

58

DAN-DAY CHAIR   A form of the Windsor chair produced in Suffolk in the early 19th century. It was named for its maker. Norwegian copies were made of this chair, with slight variations on the design of the underframe.

DANISH MODERN   See *Scandinavian Modern.*

DANTE CHAIR   An X-shaped chair of the Italian Renaissance period, usually heavily carved and upholstered in leather. The X curved up from the floor and became the arms. Variations appeared in French, Spanish, English, and Teutonic early Renaissance furniture. See *Curule Chair* for another version.

DANTESCA CHAIR   See *Dante Chair.*

DARBY AND JOAN CHAIR   A mid-18th-century English chair with a double or triple chair back and a wide seat to accommodate several persons. A settee named for characters in a poem, "The Joys of Love Never Forgot," published in 1735.

DARLEY, MATHIAS   An 18th-century English architect, designer, engraver, and publisher. Darley engraved plates for Chippendale's *Director* and may have assisted him with his designs. He also published *A Compleat Body of Architecture, Embellished with a Great Variety of Ornaments* and, with George Edwards, *A New Book of Chinese Designs.* See *Fire Irons* for Edwards designs.

DARNICK   An 18th-century coarse damask fabric.

DAUPHINE   A matte-finish silk fabric popular in the late Louis XVI period.

DAVENPORT   An early-19th-century small kneehole desk with a lift top writing slope, and drawers at the side, named after a Captain Davenport. In contemporary usage, an overstuffed upholstered sofa with padded arms and back, named after a Mr. Davenport of Boston who originally made these sofas. Illustrated is a Sheraton late-18th-century design with a loose pillow back.

DAVENPORT BED   A sofa which converts into a bed.

DAVID   See *Roentgen, David.*

DAVID, JACQUES LOUIS (1748–1825)   A French painter, considered the dictator of the *Empire* style. Classic in technique as well as in subject matter, he was Court painter to Louis XVI. David joined in the French Revolution, was a friend of Robespierre, and was imprisoned for a while. Later, he became court painter to Napoleon I.

DANTE CHAIR

DAYBED

DARBY AND JOAN CHAIR

DAVENPORT

DECANTER

DAVILIER   A 17th-century French designer and architect under Louis XIV. He created many interior-detail designs.

DAVIS, JOHN   An early-18th-century American cabinetmaker who worked in Lynn, Massachusetts.

DAY, LEWIS F. (1845–1910)   An English industrial designer. A pioneer in the modern movement, he recognized the inevitable influence of machinery on decorative art. "Whether we like it or not, machinery and steam power, and electricity for all we know, will have something to say concerning the ornament of the future."

DAYBED   A studio couch, rest bed, or narrow bed, usually placed lengthwise along a wall. May have equally tall head and foot boards, or none at all. The daybed was introduced as a seating unit in the 17th century. It is related to chaise longues and couches. Illustrated is a caned daybed of the second half of the 17th century. The scrollwork on the stretchers and head-rails is typical of the time. See *Studio Couch.*

DE STIJL   A Dutch magazine published from 1917 to 1928 which fostered Mondrian and neoplasticism. Its ideas had a great influence on the Bauhaus movement, as well as German commercial art, posters, packages, etc.

DEAL   In the United States, southern yellow pine. In England, Scotch fir is called yellow deal. In Canada, deal refers to the northern soft pine. Deal also refers to pinewood cut into planks and the furniture made from these planks. It is also used for the *carcase* of veneered furniture.

DECALCOMANIA   A form of decoration based on a transfer technique. Designs are printed on thin paper in reverse, then transferred onto a piece of furniture or decorative accessory. An inexpensive method of decorating furniture.

DECANTER   From the French for to pour from the one vessel to another. A crystal, glass, or metal container which holds wine or other liquids. A serving piece. A rock crystal decanter of the French Renaissance is shown here.

DECEPTION BED   A concealed or partially concealed bed unit in 18th-century American cabinetwork. The term also refers to a bed which converts from a chest, chair, table, etc.

DECK   The cabinet, open or closed, with a grill or glass covering that is set on top of a buffet or credenza to make a hutch or breakfront for use in a dining area. See *Buffet, Credenza, Hutch* and *Breakfront.*

DECKLE EDGE A rippled, irregular edge with a torn appearance, usually associated with handmade paper.

DÉCOR The mode of decoration of an interior or of a theatre stage. The word often implies a "fashion trend" and may suggest something gay, whimsical, fanciful, and changeable.

DECORATED PERIOD The English Gothic architecture of the 14th century, noted for geometric and flowing tracery, enlarged clerestories, and star-shaped, or stellar, vaulting. It is also called the Geometrical, Curvilinear, Middle Pointed, Edwardian, and Later Plantagenet period. Illustrated is a window from the Cloisters at Westminister Abbey, A.D. 1360.

DECORATED QUEEN ANNE PERIOD The English furniture style prevalent about 1710 to 1730, also called the Early Georgian period. It was a continuation of the Queen Anne style, with cabriole legs, claw-and-ball feet, carved and shaped splats, but more ornate and heavily carved than the previous period.

DÉCOUPAGE An art form created by cutting and pasting down assorted materials in interesting new patterns and arrangements. It became popular in the 18th century as the "poor man's" method of embellishing wood furniture. The technique was also employed to decorate boxes, screens, trays, etc. Découpage is similar to *Arte Povera, Collage,* and *Montage.*

DELANOIS, LOUIS (1731–1792) A French master cabinetmaker under Louis XV, a protégé of Mme Du Barry, who designed much of the furniture at Versailles.

DELFT Brilliant blue-colored, heavily glazed pottery produced in Delft, Holland. The rich blue designs are on a white field, either scenic or provincial patterns. Ceramic tiles are also made in this particular blue and white. Used to face fireplaces and walls and on floors.

DELLA ROBBIA See *Robbia, Della.*

DEMARCY, GASPARD AND BALTHAZAR 17th-century French craftsmen who worked in stucco and wood and also did metalwork. Charles Le Brun employed them during the period of Louis XIV.

DEMIDOME A half dome topping cupboards, bookcases, and other architectural furniture of the early and mid-18th century. The demidome was often interpreted as a shell-shaped niche in Georgian furniture and interiors. Illustrated is the Lord Mayor's stall in St. Paul's Cathedral in London designed by Sir Christopher Wren at the end of the 17th century.

DEMILUNE

DEMI-PATERA

DECORATED PERIOD

DECORATED QUEEN ANNE PERIOD

DENTIL COURSE

DERIVATIVE

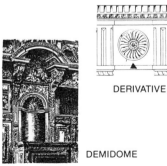

DEMIDOME

DEMILUNE A half of a circle or half-round plan. A semicircular commode, console, or sideboard. A late 18th-century Sheraton design with tambour doors is illustrated. See *Doe's-Foot Leg* for a Hepplewhite demilune table.

DEMI-PATERA A half-patera or rosette, a decoration often found in mid- and late-18th-century pier tables, consoles, or demilune commodes. An 18th-century Hepplewhite pier table is shown. See *Demilune.*

DEMOISELLE See *Wig Stand.*

DEMOISELLE À ATOURNER A Gothic wig-stand which also served as a dressing table. It was usually a round tabletop on a shaft base with a carved wooden head placed in the center to hold the wig. See *Wig Stand.*

DEN A retreat or informal library. (Formerly, a small, comfortable room equipped for the man of the house.) It may also serve as a small family room or guest room.

DENIER The size or number of filaments of silk or man-made fibers in a yarn or thread. The higher the denier, the coarser and heavier the yarn.

DENIM A firm, heavy twill-weave cotton fabric originally called serge de Nîmes; hence the name. The filler yarns are usually white with colored warp yarns. The filler yarns give the fabric its traditional whitish cast.

DENTIL One of a series of small projecting rectangular blocks in a cornice. It appears in Ionic and Corinthian cornices, and was also used as a furniture and interior detail by Adam, Hepplewhite and other classic and neoclassic designers.

DENTIL COURSE A series of dentils in a row. Illustrated is a design for an Ionic entablature designed by the Adam brothers in the mid-18th century in England.

DERBYSHIRE CHAIR A provincial Jacobean chair. The straight upright ends have inward scrolls on top. The top rail and crossrail are often archshaped.

DERIVED Drawn from or based upon. As the Renaissance style was derived from those of the classic Greek and Roman periods. Illustrated is an Adam entablature based upon a Greek prototype.

DESK A writing surface, with or without drawers and/or cabinets. See *Bureau, Cylinder Top, Drop Lid* or *Dropfront, Escritoire, Kneehole Desk, Pedestal Desk, Scritoire, Secrétarire,* and *Secretary.*

DESK BOX See *Bible Box.*

DESMALTER, JACOB An important cabinetmaker of the early 19th-century French Empire period. He executed designs created by Charles Percier. Illustrated is a piece of furniture of the type made by Desmalter in mahogany embellished with bronze and gilt.

DESORNAMENTADO Spanish for without ornament. A severe style of architecture and decoration developed by the Spanish Renaissance architect Juan de Herrera under Phillip II in the mid-16th century. An example of his work is the Escorial near Madrid.

DESSERTE A small serving table or sideboard with one or more under shelves, similar to a dumbwaiter. It appears in the Louis XVI period. See *Buffet* and *Crédence*.

DEU-DARN A two tiered *Tri-Darn* or a court cupboard without the dresser.

DHURRIES Flat, lightly woven wool carpets from India with overall geometric or very stylized animal designs.

DIAMETER A straight line drawn through the center of a circle and touching the perimeter in two places; also, the length of such a line. In classic orders the proportions are based on the diameter of the shaft at the base of the column.

DIAMOND MATCH VENEER Four pieces of straight-grained wood veneer are cut diagonally and are joined to meet in a central diamond shape. Increasingly larger diamond shapes emanate from the central point.

DIAMOND ORNAMENT See *Lozenge.* A favorite late-Tudor ornament used to enrich carved chest fronts, bedsteads, cabinets, etc.

DIAPER PATTERN An allover or repeating pattern without definite limits, applied as a decoration to a plain surface. Often the area is latticed and floral, or geometric designs are set into boxes. Used on walls, wallpapers, cabinet enrichments, etc.

DIE The space between the cap and base of a pedestal. Also, a rectangular block on the top of a leg. Illustrated is a Sheraton furniture leg. See *Patera.*

DIFFUSER or DIFFUSING SHIELD A baffle or screen set over a source of illumination to soften and disperse the light in a pleasant manner, and cut down on sharp glare.

DIFFUSING GLASS Rolled glass with assorted patterns or textures which tend to reduce the transparency of the glass.

DIMITY A double- or multiple-thread, sheer cotton fabric usually woven in a corded, striped, or checkered pattern. Used for bedspreads and curtains.

DIMMER A mechanism for varying the intensity of light in a given area by reducing the amount of electric current allowed to pass through the wires to the light bulbs. The "resistance dimmer" is the only type that will work on direct current (D.C.), while "autotransformer," "electronic resistance," "electronic and magnetic amplifier" dimmers will work on alternating currents (A.C.). Can be used to reduce the heat generated in a particular area, as well as the amount of power consumed and the maintenance required for the lamps.

DINANDERIE A 15th-century metal alloy of copper, tin, and lead. A forerunner of pewter. Used to make ornamental figures in Dinant in Belguim. Also called bell metal.

DINETTE TABLE A small dining table, usually used in kitchens, kitchenettes, foyers, or small dining areas. Seldom intended to accommodate more than four persons, but may be designed to open up to seat more.

DIORAMA A representation of a scene, showing small three-dimensional figures against an illuminated background, or a peepshow of a semitranslucent painted scene.

DIORITE A dark-colored hard stone sometimes used in Egyptian and Assyrian sculpture.

DIP SEAT A chair seat which is lower in the center than at the sides. It is also curved (concave) to accommodate the body of the sitter. Illustrated is a mid-18th-century Chippendale chair. See *Dropped or Dipped Seat.*

DIPTERAL Surrounded by a double row of columns.

DIPTYCH A small, two-panel, hinged screen, either painted or carved, which may be made of wood, metal, ivory, etc.

DIRECTORY The Directoire period in France (1799–1804). Antique Greek and Roman decorations found even greater favor and were superimposed on the already classic lines of the Louis XVI style. The Directory period led into the Empire. See also *French Directoire.*

DISHED A term applied to the sunken areas in the top surface of card tables, used to hold money or candles. A dished-top table has a raised edge or rim which makes the entire table surface appear to be sunken.

JACOB DESMALTER

DESSERTE

DIE

DIE

DIP SEAT

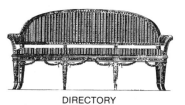

DIRECTORY

DISK FOOT A small, flattened ball foot or pad on a cabriole leg in the Queen Anne style.

DISK TURNING Flat circular turnings used to ornament furniture.

DISTANT COLORS Colors that appear to recede, creating a spacious effect. Light, airy, cool, open colors: blues, aquas, violets.

DISTEMPER An art medium: opaque water color paints, similar to tempera, consisting of pigments, water, and white of egg, size, or emulsion of egg yolk.

DISTRESSED Term for old pieces of wood furniture which show small scratches or holes, the result of age and use. In new furniture, these holes and scratches may be deliberately simulated in paint or spatter. "Fly-specked."

DIVAN A long armless and backless upholstered settee. Originally a Turkish or Persian court or council, or a room where such gatherings take place. The French adapted this cushion-like seat into the upholstered bench. See *Bench*. In current usage, a divan is a couch.

DIVIDER A piece of furniture, screen, pole arrangement, or the like, that separates one area of a room from the rest. May artificially create an entry foyer, a dining area, a music area, etc.

DOBBY WEAVE A cloth with a small geometric woven pattern. A special attachment is required on the loom to weave in this manner.

DOCUMENT BOX or DRAWER A small vertical drawer in 18th-century English and American secretaries and cabinet desks. It is usually ornamented with colonnettes, and is found on either side of the central compartment in the interior.

DOCUMENTARIES Fabrics or wallpapers based on, or derived from, authentic period designs.

DOE'S-FOOT LEG An elongated S-shaped leg typical of the Louis XV period. It originally terminated in a deer's cleft hoof. A Hepplewhite demilune table is illustrated.

DOG GRATE A fireplace accessory. A movable fire grate.

DOGLEGGED STAIRCASE A staircase in which the outer string of the upper flight lies vertically above that of the lower flight.

DOG'S TOOTH A form of ornamentation used in Early English Gothic architecture. It resembles a row of teeth.

DISK FOOT

DISK TURNING

DOLPHIN

DOME BED

DORMER WINDOW

DOE'S-FOOT LEG

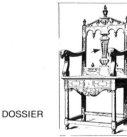

DOSSIER

DOLPHIN A sea mammal, a mid-16th-century decoration and symbol for the Dauphin, eldest son of the king of France. It was also the symbol for love and swiftness. The dolphin again appears in the Louis XVI period. The dolphin here illustrated decorates a keystone in the Fountain of Innocents in Paris, designed by Pierre Lescot and Jean Goujon in 1548–1549.

DOME BED An 18th-century canopied bed with a dome-shaped tester. Usually heavily draped and swagged, it was also called a Polish Bed. A Chippendale design is illustrated.

DOMED TOP See *Hooded Tops*.

DOMESTIC Manufactured or grown in the country where the label is applied, domestic products in the United States are items produced in the United States.

DOMESTIC ORIENTAL RUG See *Sheen Rugs*.

DOMINANT The leading or most prominent part of a design or scheme.

DOMINO PAPERS Marbleized squares of wallpaper, originally produced in Italy in the late 16th and early 17th centuries.

DOMINOTIERS Producers of domino papers in France in the late 16th century.

DORATURA Italian for gilding.

DOREUR The French word for one who gilds or applies a gilt finish to wood, metal, etc.

DORIC ORDER The oldest and simplest of the Greek classic orders of architecture. In the Roman version, the column was eight times the diameter of the shaft, and the entablature was two diameters high. See *Classic* and *Diameter*.

DORMER WINDOW A projecting upright window which breaks the surface of a sloping roof. Illustrated is a dormer window of the French Renaissance Château de Graves.

DORURE French for gilding.

DOS-À-DOS French for back to back. A seating device which consists of two attached seats facing in opposite directions. In order to converse, the seated persons must turn around in their seats and look over their shoulders. See *Conversation Chair* and *Vis-à-Vis*.

DOSSER A medieval or Gothic fabric hanging behind thrones or on walls behind benches, etc.

DOSSIER French for chair back or splat. A 16th-century French armchair or fauteuil (illustrated). Also a high-backed, canopied, wooden bench built into the wainscot of an English Gothic building. It was usually made to hold four, and it served as a seat for dining. In French interiors the term could also refer to the headboard or footboard of a bed.

DOSSIER PLAT A flat back. A French term used to describe the back of a chair. A late German Renaissance armchair is shown.

DOTTED SWISS A crisp cotton, usually sheer, which is woven, embroidered, or printed with tiny regularly spaced dots. It is a plain weave fabric.

DOUBLE BED A standard-size double-bed is usually 53″ wide × 75″ long. It may be made longer on special order.

DOUBLE CHAIR See *Courting Chair.*

DOUBLE CHEST A chest-on-chest unit. The lower chest is usually slightly wider and deeper, and the second set of drawers is set on top of it.

DOUBLE STRETCHER FLEMISH BOND In masonry, two stretchers alternate with a single header in a course. The header in the next course is centered over the join between the two stretchers. See *Bond, Flemish Bond,* and *Flemish Cross Bond.*

DOUBLE-ACTING HINGE A special hinge which allows a door to swing 180° on its jamb.

DOUBLE-DECKER BED Two single beds superimposed one over the other, with four uprights holding the upper bed aloft. See *Bunk Bed.*

DOUBLE-HUNG SASH A standard window made up of two sliding framed glass sections; one is lowered from the top, and the other is raised from the bottom. The raising and lowering on the frames is controlled by pulleys and weights.

DOUBLET In ornament, the term refers to a pair of the same design.

DOUGLAS FIR A very handsome, curly, grained wood that resembles white pine or soft pine, used extensively for plywood or laminated sheets. Douglas fir takes a natural or stained finish and is relatively inexpensive.

DOUPPIONI or DUPPION Silk fibers that are reeled from two silkworms that have spun a single cocoon. The yarns that are thus reeled are rough and slubby such as those found in shantung or pongee fabrics. Also fabric made from such fibers. Also rayon or acetate fibers of a slubby, uneven texture.

DOSSIER PLAT

DOVETAIL

DOWEL

DRAGON'S CLAW FOOT

DRAGON'S HEAD

DOVETAIL In cabinetry, a type of joint used to join the front and sides of a drawer. Wedge-shaped projections on one piece of wood interlock with alternating grooves in the other piece to produce a tight, secure joint.

DOWEL A headless wooden peg or metal pin to hold two pieces of wood together. A dowel is used in joints to prevent slipping and also to join the side rails or stretchers to the legs of chairs.

DOWEL JOINT See *Dowel.*

DOWER CHEST See *Cassone, Connecticut Chest,* and *Hope Chest.*

DOWN Soft, fluffy feathers from very young birds, or from under the ordinary feathers of older birds or fowls. Down is used for stuffing pillows, cushions, and upholstered chair backs. See *Eiderdown.*

DOWNING, ANDREW JACKSON A mid-19th-century American landscape architect and "tastemaker" of the period. He came from Newburgh, New York, and published *The Architecture of Country Houses* in 1850. The book had a great impact on the period, and the trend toward "Italian-style" villas. Downing also advocated "Gothic cottages" because they were not only "picturesque, but their floor plans are well suited to our informal world."

DRAFT A line drawing, often geometrically or mechanically projected, of a proposed structure or design. A preliminary sketch or drawing. A smooth strip on the face of a stone made by one line of following strokes with a chisel. When stones are left with a rough face, but the edges are made smooth, the edges are called drafted edges.

DRAGON'S CLAW FOOT See *Ball-and-Claw Foot.* An 18th-century furniture leg end which was a carved representation of a dragon's scaly claws, often grasping a ball or pearl.

DRAGON'S HEAD An Oriental motif, often found on heavily carved oriental furniture. The dragon is also the symbol of Wales, and the dragon's head appears as an ornamental carved motif on English *Tudor* and *Jacobean* chests. Illustrated is an 18th-century dragon from George Edwards and Mathias *Darley's A New Book of Chinese Designs* (1754).

DRAKE FOOT An 18th-century English furniture foot with three toes which resembles the contracted foot of a male duck.

DRAPE A term used to describe the way a fabric hangs or falls. The ability of the fabric naturally to shape well when pleated, shirred, or pinched.

DRAPER, DOROTHY A noted 20th-century American interior designer.

DRAPERY Fabric hangings on either side of a window, or covering a window or door, or an entire wall of windows. The fabric may be shirred, pleated, or pinched, and may be made of natural or man-made fibers. The choice of fabric, color, pattern, texture, and type of treatment depends upon the period of decoration and the scale of the opening to be draped. Regular vertical falling drapery may be enhanced with swags, jabots, lambrequins, and cornices. Also the fabric treatment on 16th-, 17th- and 18th-century beds.

DRAUGHT CHAIR An 18th-century upholstered wing chair with or without closed sides, which was constructed to protect one from draughts, similar to a *Porter Chair*.

DRAW CURTAIN A curtain that may be drawn along a rod or rail by means of a traverse arrangement of cords and pulleys.

DRAW LEAF TABLE See *Draw Table*.

DRAW RUNNER A supporting device for the drop-lid or fall-front surface of a secretary or desk, a small strip of wood inserted into a slot immediately below the surface to be supported.

DRAW SLIP A *Draw Runner*.

DRAW TABLE A three-leaved, refectory-like table. The two end leaves rest under the center one. When these two end pieces are drawn out from under the large central table surface, the center leaf falls down into the opening thus created, and the two end leaves make a large, continuous flush surface with the central leaf. The forerunner of the telescope dining table. The illustrated example is of late-17th-century England and shows the Dutch influence. Also called a "draw-leaf-table."

DRAWING The art of representing images, shapes, patterns, or three-dimensional elements on a two-dimensional surface.

DRAWING BOOK CHAIR BACK A popular Sheraton design for a chair back which was widely copied by American cabinetmakers from Sheraton's book *The Cabinet-Maker and Upholsterer's Drawing Book*.

DRAWING ROOM An abbreviated form of the term, withdrawing room. A comfortable sitting room to which people withdrew after dinner. In contemporary usage, a living room.

DRAWING TABLE A late-18th-century worktable designed by Sheraton for artists or designers. The top of the table

DRAPERY

DRAUGHT CHAIR

DRESSER

DRAW TABLE

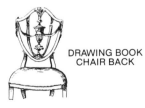

DRESSING TABLE

DRAWING BOOK
CHAIR BACK

rises on a double horse and is adjustable so that the artist may stand or sit to work. A small flap draws out of the top to hold a "still life" or the small model being painted. The sliders at each end hold drawing instruments and lamps. See *Architect's Table*.

DRAWN WORK An openwork pattern or design created by drawing or pulling out weft or warp threads from a fabric.

DRESS To smooth or finish the surface of stones or to plane the surface of wood.

DRESSER Originally a sideboard or buffet with storage space for plates, etc., or a cabinet with drawers and/or shelves. Illustrated is a Queen Anne oak dresser of the early 18th century. In contemporary usage, a long chest of drawers about 36" tall and 6' long or longer, usually part of a bedroom suite. Designed in both traditional and modern styles.

DRESSING MIRROR A small standing portable mirror, or a mirror on a stand, sometimes with drawers, which was set on a table, low chest, or cabinet and used as an adjunct to dressing. Also called a toilet mirror.

DRESSING ROOM A small room or area with a closet and/or drawer space, usually adjacent to a bedroom. It sometimes has a dressing table and mirror arrangement.

DRESSING TABLE A kneehole type of table with large and small drawers surrounding the central knee area. A mirror is usually attached to the table surface. In its present form it is based on a 19th century innovation. For an earlier type of dressing table, see *Poudreuse*.

DRESSOIR DE SALLE À MANGER French for a dining-room dresser or buffet. A 16th-century, large dresser-top cupboard unit like this French Renaissance piece of the period of François I. See *Buffet, Crédence, Dresser*, and *Welsh Dresser*.

DRILL A denim-like, heavy twill fabric, rough and durable.

DRINKING TABLE See *Wine Table*.

DROP FRONT See *Drop Lid*.

DROP HANDLE A pendant-like piece of hardware that functions as a drawer pull.

DROP LID A top or front of a desk hinged to cover an inner compartment of drawers, boxes, pigeonholes, etc. When the front is dropped down, the inner surface of the desk front makes a flat writing surface flush with the inner compartment. There are usually drawers below the enclosed top area. See *Slope-Front Desk*.

DROP ORNAMENT A carved, shaped, or pierced ornament which extends below the underframe of a chair or cabinet, but does not extend across the whole width of the underframe. When it extends across the whole length it is called an apron, front, or skirt.

DROP-LEAF TABLE See *Flap Table.*

DROPPED CEILING A ceiling partially or completely lowered from its original height to a lower and more intimate height. Often the dropped ceiling will hide exposed pipes and ducts that run close to the original ceiling. A hung or suspended ceiling. See *Hung Ceiling.*

DROPPED OR DIPPED SEAT A seat with a concave surface between the two side rails. A depressed center area in a chair seat, also called a "scoop seat." A late-18th-century Sheraton design is illustrated. See *Dip Seat.*

DRUGGET See *Numdahs.*

DRUM TABLE A round table with a deep apron, sometimes made with drawers set in all around the apron. The table usually presents a squat, drum-like appearance.

DRUNKARD'S CHAIR Also called a lover's chair. A Queen-Anne-period vogue which lasted through the 18th century. The seats were up to 33″ wide, and allowed one person to sprawl comfortably, or two to nestle closely. In current usage, sometimes referred to as a "chair and a half."

DRY CLEANING A process for cleaning fabrics which are not washable. Carbon tetrachloride mineral spirits are used to remove dirt and stains. Special types of stains may require other special cleaning agents.

DRY SINKS 19th-century low kitchen cabinets usually of pine, made to hold a pitcher and washbasin on the top surface, usually with closed cabinet space below. The top of the sink was sometimes covered with slate or marble. "Water benches" served the same purpose as the sinks.

DRYPOINT ENGRAVING The simplest of all etching techniques. It consists of drawing with a hard steel "pencil" on a metal plate. The burr that results from scratching the surface gives the "dry point" its ability to catch the ink, and it prints with a depth which adds sharpness to the design. Not many impressions or printings can be made from a plate. Drypoint engraving is a form of intaglio engraving.

DU CERCEAU, JACQUES ANDROUET A 16th-century French Renaissance architect, draftsman, and furniture designer who studied in Italy under Bramante. In 1550 he published *Recueil Grave de Muebles* which set forth rules of propor-

DUAL-PURPOSE UNIT

DROPPED SEAT

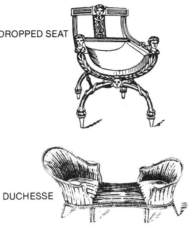
DUCHESSE

DUCHESSE BED

JACQUES ANDROUET
DU CERCEAU

DUMBWAITER

tion and ornamentation to be used on furniture based on antique forms. Du Cerceau originated the use of long columns on buffets and cupboards, which rose from the base to the top of the unit. Illustrated is a bench made from a design by Du Cerceau.

DUAL BED See *Hollywood Bed.*

DUAL-PURPOSE UNIT Something designed to serve more than one purpose, like a convertible couch. See *Library Armchair, Library Press Bedstead,* and *Library Steps.* A Sheraton design is illustrated.

DUBOIS, JACQUES (c. 1693–1763) Cabinetmaker of the French Régence and Louis XV periods. Twisted fishtails or mermaid appendages appear in several of his pieces as terminal ends for his mounts.

DUBOIS, RENE An 18th-century French cabinetmaker for Louis XV and Louis XVI.

DUCHESS A once-popular curtain fabric with an appliqué design.

DUCHESSE A chaise longue in one piece. It is described by Sheraton as two bergères with a footstool in the middle. A Sheraton design is illustrated.

DUCHESSE BED A canopy bed without posts. The tester is attached to the wall above the bed, and extends over the bed. The draperies from the tester are pulled back to either side of the bed, and they usually extend down to the floor. It was originally an 18th-century French design.

DUCHESSE BRISÉE A chaise longue with a separate foot piece.

DUCHESSE LACE See *Valenciennes Lace.*

DUCK A tightly woven cotton or linen fabric with plain or rib weaves. It is similar to canvas, and stripes may be woven in, or painted or printed on one side.

DUCK FOOT A webbed furniture foot of the late-17th- early-18th-centuries, found in Flemish and English furniture.

DUGOURC An 18th-century French designer of the Louis XVI period. He was especially partial to the quiver and arrows as a decorative motif, and he faithfully produced Pompeii-inspired furniture. His masterpiece was the Grand Salon à Coupola at Bagatelle.

DUMBWAITER A three-tiered, tripod, circular table, dating from the 18th century. Sheraton designed many elaborate dumbwaiters with drawers, shelves, and trays. See *Rafraîchissoir.* In the Victorian period, a dumbwaiter was a lift for bringing up food from the basement kitchen to the dining room.

DUMMY BOARD FIGURES   Also called picture-board dummies. See *Fireside Figures*.

DUNCAN PHYFE   See *Phyfe, Duncan*.

DUPPION   See *Douppioni or Duppion*.

DUPRE, PIERRE (1723–1799)   A noted furniture maker during the periods of Louis XV and Louis XVI.

DUST BOTTOM OR BOARD   A thin wood separator between drawers to keep out the dust that might enter through the open spaces.

DUST RUFFLE   A shirred, pleated, or tailored fabric piece which extends, usually, from under the mattress of a bed down to the floor. It covers the legs of the bed frame, and supposedly sets up a barrier to keep the dust from getting under the bed. Examples of dust ruffles are seen from the Elizabethan period to the present. A mid-18th-century Chippendale bedstead is illustrated.

DUTCH DOOR   A door horizontally divided into an upper and lower section. Each section is independently hinged, and either or both can be opened.

DUTCH DRESSER   A hutch cabinet. A two-section unit with a closed cupboard or drawer unit and open shelves above. See *Welsh Dresser*.

DUTCH FOOT   A pad foot or spoon foot on a cabriole furniture leg, especially

DUTCH LEG

DUST RUFFLE

DUTCH FOOT

popular in late-17th-century and early-18th-century furniture. See *Pad Foot*. See *Easy Chair* illustration.

DUTCH LEG   A wood turned leg consisting of rounded forms spaced with flattened oval discs. It usually ends in a squared-off form, and rests on a flat, oval foot.

DUTCH SETTLE   A wooden settle with a hinged tabletop surface behind. When flipped up on the settle top, the unit becomes a table.

DWARF WALL   A partition or wall which does not extend up to the ceiling; also an interior wall between the top ceiling level and the finished roof level.

DYEING   A process for coloring yarns or fabrics with either natural or synthetic dyes. Dyes differ in their ability to resist sun fading, laundering, perspiration, etc. See *Colorfast* and *Yarn Dyed*.

DYMAXION   A term created by designer-architect-inventor Richard Buckminster Fuller for industrial designs which give maximum performance at maximum economy.

DYNEL   A synthetic fiber made from acrylonitrile and vinyl chloride. A trademark of Union Carbide Corporation. The fiber is characterized by resilience, strength, and resistance to chemicals. Dynel fibers are used in upholstery and drapery fabrics as well as for carpeting.

E

EAGLE A favorite decorative motif used by the ancient Persians, Assyrians, Egyptians, and up into our present-day civilization. The Greeks considered the eagle the companion of Zeus, and the Romans used a representation of the eagle as a military standard. In ecclesiastical art, the eagle is the symbol of St. John the Evangelist. The Byzantines used a double-headed eagle, and in heraldry the eagle appears in all colors but blue. It made its appearance again in the Renaissance and bloomed as a mythological symbol in 18th-century decoration. Napoleon and the Empire used the eagle to its fullest as a motif on furniture, on fabrics, in carvings, paintings, etc. The American Revolution took on the eagle as its emblem, and again it was a popular enrichment on furniture, mirror frames, fabrics, and buildings.

EAGLE

EAMES CHAIR A new concept of completely separating a chair's back and seat within its supporting frame.

EAMES, CHARLES A 20th-century American architect and designer. He invented a process for molding laminated plywood into compound curves, and electronically joining the plywood to other plywood or steel members with rubber discs between for resilience. Eames has produced exquisite forms and proportions, including wire frame chairs for Herman Miller that can be covered with snap-on upholstery. Many of his designs are done in conjunction with his wife, Ray.

EAMES

EAMES LOUNGE CHAIR A contemporary classic lounge chair designed by Charles Eames in 1956. The shell is made of molded plywood and rests on a metal, star shaped pedestal base. The head rest is separated by an air space from the back support and the whole wooden frame is upholstered in soft leather. The cushions and arm rests are designed to snap off for easy replacement. A low, wide ottoman or footstool (also with a metal pedestal base) is designed to complement the chair. Many copies or variations on this wide, comfortable, relaxer-chair are available.

EARLY AMERICAN The period in American art, architecture and furniture from about 1650 to about 1720. The designs are basically Jacobean, Carolean, and William and Mary, but executed simply and provincially in native woods. Dutch influences were strongly felt in New York.

EARLY ENGLISH PERIOD The earliest Gothic architecture in England, dating from 1189 to 1307. It is also known as "Lancet," "First Pointed," and "Early Plantagenet" period. The architecture is marked by tall lancet openings, projecting buttresses, pinnacles, and steep-pitched roofs.

EARPIECE A scroll or volute springing from the knee of a cabriole leg and ending in the underframing of the piece of furniture. Especially popular in 18th-century English and French furniture.

EARS

EARS In architecture, moldings or cornices over doors or windows which overlap the uprights of the door or window frame. They were used as a cornice decoration in the 18th century in England and America. In furniture, the extended parts of the top rail beyond the upright supports of the chair back.

EARTHENWARE Pottery made of coarse clay. Heavy, soft, porous, and opaque like a common red flowerpot. May also be glazed.

EASTLAKE, CHARLES L., JR. (1793–1865) An advocate of the Gothic revival in England during the 19th century. A painter, scholar, and designer who combined Gothic and Japanese ornaments, and a widely used ornamental device of incising drawings of conventionalized flower, leaf, and linear abstract forms on wood and on stone surfaces such as lintels. Using machine methods, arranged to produce assorted pieces of furniture embellished with heavy hardware, metal, and tile panel inserts. Cherrywood was the principal wood employed. Illustrated is a chair from *Eastlake's Hints on Household Taste*. Oak furniture influenced by him enjoyed enormous popularity in the U.S.

EASY CHAIR A roomy, comfortable, upholstered chair of any style or period, which is made for ease and relaxation. It is usually based on the bergère and wing chair. An 18th-century easy chair is shown.

EAVES The lowest part of a roof which overhangs the top of a wall.

ÉBÉNISTE French for ebony worker. In the early French Renaissance (15th and 16th centuries), furniture was often made of ebony glued onto blackened pearwood for strength and size. The cabinetmakers who worked on these pieces were called ébénistes or joiners and carpenters on ebony. *Maître ébéniste* was the official title of the king's cabinetmaker. Illustrated is a French cabinet of the period of Henri II (mid-16th century). See *Stabre, Laurent.*

EBONY A tropical, hard, dense, heavy brown-black wood with a fine grain, popular in France during the Louis XIV period, and again in the Empire and mid-19th century. True ebony comes from Ceylon, and black ebony is found in North India and the Himalayas.

EBONY, GABOON An African rusty brown-black wood, expensive and available in relatively small pieces, therefore mainly used for veneering, musical instruments, and inlay work. See *Ebony, Macassar.*

EBONY, MACASSAR A very hard, dense wood, named for the city exporting it. Has an intense, black-brown stripe on a reddish ground, and takes a brilliant polish. Also called "coromandel." Usually figured in strong contrasting stripes.

ECHINUS An oval-shaped molding. It is part of a classical capital, located between the shaft and the abacus. In furniture ornament, the egg-and-dart, egg-and-tongue, or egg-and-anchor motif carved on the ovolo molding of furniture.

CHARLES L. EASTLAKE, JR.

EASY CHAIR

ECLECTICISM

ÉBÉNISTE

ÉCRAN

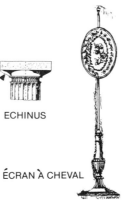

ECHINUS

ÉCRAN À CHEVAL

ECKHARDT, ANTHONY GEORGE An 18th-century English manufacturer of printed fabrics and wallpapers who had a patent for printing designs on silk, cotton, muslin, calicos, and wallpaper. He worked in association with his brother Frederick, and they employed the talented French designers Boileau, Feuglet, and Joinot. The wallpaper designs were produced with wood blocks or copper plates. Often hand details were added, as well as silver and gold leaf embellishments.

ECLECTICISM The borrowing and combining of art forms and motifs from past periods and adapting them to contemporary uses. The Victorian 19th century was an era of eclecticism. Older patterns and styles were borrowed and adapted to the new mechanized processes of the times. Illustrated is a German mid-19th-century chair which strongly resembles Early Renaissance prototypes.

ÉCOLE DES BEAUX ARTS The leading French art institute of the 19th century. It tended to give unity and consistency to the architecture and art of France, and it had a great influence on maintaining standards of taste, refinement, and correctness of style. It also delayed the advancement of new ideas and styles.

ÉCRAN A fire screen, or a small screen set on a table to shield one from the firelight. A small shade on a candlestick. Illustrated is a design by Antoine Watteau (18th-century France.)

ÉCRAN À CHEVAL A frame with a sliding panel, used as a fire screen. See *Banner Screen, Cheval Screen* and *Horse Screen.*

ÉCRAN À COULISSE A French term for a cheval or fire screen.

ÉCRAN À ÉCLISSE See *Pole Screen.*

EDWARDIAN PERIOD See *Decorated Period.*

EGG CRATE A metal or plastic unit which resembles a cardboard egg separator, used to diffuse ceiling light, usually over fluorescent light strips.

EGG AND DART A molding decoration which resembles a continuous string of egg or ovoid forms separated by dartlike or arrowhead points. "Egg and tongue" and "egg and anchor" moldings are almost identical. See *Echinus.*

EGGSHELL FINISH A semiflat paint. A painted finish with a soft, dull, low luster.

ÉGLOMISÉ An art form in which the painting is done on the reverse side of glass, and often embellished with gold leaf.

ÉGOUTTOIR A piece of French provincial furniture with open rack shelves for drying or storing dishes.

EGYPT The land of the Pharohs. One of the earliest developed civilizations of the world. The art and architecture of Ancient Egypt preceded the classic Greek and Roman civilizations. From the Egyptians we inherited such motifs and decorations as the sphinx, the lotus column, lion's paw, and palmetto leaf, cross-legged chairs with leather seats, tables, stools, sarcophagi, mother-of-pearl inlays, veneering methods, etc. With Napoleon's successful campaigns in Egypt and the discovery of the Rosetta Stone at the close of the 18th century, Egyptiana became the vogue, and Egyptian-type motifs were an important part of the Empire style in the early 19th century.

EIDERDOWN The soft fluffy feathers obtained from large sea ducks, used for luxurious stuffing of pillows and cushions.

EIGHT-LEGGED TABLE An 18th century English form of the gateleg table. It was usually made of mahogany. See *Gateleg Table* and *Thousand-Leg Table.*

EINGELEGATE ARBEIT German for inlaid or boulle work.

ELBOW CHAIR A chair with arms upon which one may rest one's elbows.

ELECTRIC RACEWAY See *Power Raceway.*

ELECTROPLATING An electrical process for covering one base metal with a very thin layer of a more expensive or desirable metal.

ELEVATION A drawing of a flat, two-dimensional view of a room or building, usually to scale, to show relative size of architectural and decorative details. Illustrated is a side of a room drawn by Michelangelo Pergolesi, a late-18th-century English designer.

ELIZABETHAN The reign of Elizabeth I of England, 1558–1603. Illustrated is the Great Bed of Ware, a state bed. Renaissance motifs are here intermingled with the remnants of the Gothic tradition. See *Chest* for an Elizabethan chest, *Center Table* for an Elizabethan interior, and *Alcove* for an Elizabethan *oriel* window.

ELL See *Three-Quarter Width.*

ELLIOTT, JOHN An 18th-century American cabinetmaker who worked in Philadelphia. Noted for wall mirrors and dressing cases.

ELM A strong, tough wood which looks well when stained and polished. It is a light, brownish red with dark-brown ring marks

EGYPTIAN

EMBOSSING

EMBROIDERY

ELEVATION

ELIZABETHAN

EMPIRE BED

and a strong figure. The northern elm has a finer, more uniform texture than the southern elm.

ÉMAUX DE NIELLURE A French term for an enameling process like niello. Lines are cut into the metal and then filled with enamel.

EMBLEM A decorative symbol or device used in heraldry. It appears in carvings, embroideries, and painted panels. Examples are Napoleon's bee and the salamander of François I.

EMBOSSED Decorated with a raised design produced on a surface by hammering, stamping, or molding.

EMBOSSING In fabrics, a process for pressing a design onto a fabric by passing the fabric through hot engraved rollers. A piece of embossed velvet is shown. See *Cut Pile.*

EMBROIDERY The art of decorating a fabric with a raised design or pattern worked out with a needle and thread, either by hand or machine. The design may be of one or more colors, and a great variety of stitches or combinations of stitches may be employed. A 16th-century example of Spanish Renaissance embroidery is illustrated.

EMPAISTIC Sculpture or structual elements made of, or covered with sheet metal which has been hammered in decorative patterns. It was a forerunner of boulle work. See *Boulle, André Charles.*

EMPIRE The Napoleonic period in France and the great classic revival style of architecture, art, and decoration, roughly from 1804 to 1820. It is a period which combines the grandeur and martial symbols of Rome with Ancient Egyptian motifs and the elements of Greek architecture. The furniture of the period is massive, architectural in concept, and lavishly trimmed in bronze and brass on rosewood, mahogany, and ebony. Charles Percier and Pierre Fontaine were the great designers of furniture and interiors of the period, and Jacques Louis David was the major art force of the time. The style spread into England where Thomas Hope and Thomas Sheraton become leading exponents of the Empire style. Duncan Phyfe in America developed a style along the lines of the Empire, and in Germany and Austria, the Biedermeier style evolved. See *Biedermeir; David, Jacques Louis; Empire Drape; Fontaine, Pierre François Léonard; Normand, Charles P.T.;* and *Percier, Charles.*

EMPIRE BED A typical bed of the early 19th century in France, low and usually set against a wall or in an alcove, with only one major side exposed. Curved sweeping ends form the headboard and footboard. The Empire bed is similar to the boat bed and the gondola bed, and was a forerunner of the American sleigh bed. Illustrated is Napoleon's bed at the Grand Trianon, Versailles.

EMPIRE DRAPE A simple, classic drapery treatment. The fabric is caught at the top hem at equidistant points, and the valleys, formed between these points, fall freely. A formal pattern is created of fairly rigid verticals from the caught points to the floor, alternating with draped billows. Very popular in the early 19th century. Illustrated is a wall treatment in the Royal Palace in Venice in 1834.

EMPREINTES VELOUTÉES French for flocked prints or wallpaper. See *Flock Paper*.

EN CAS or EN CASE A small table of the Louis XV period similar to a night table (table de chevet). It was usually marble-topped and had a drawer and a cupboard below.

EN CHARRETTE From the French for "on the cart." Last minute work. Derived from the practice of 19th-century artists working on their paintings as they were being carted to the Beaux Arts for judgment. Doing last minute touch-ups.

EN RESSAUT Engaged to a wall or projecting from it. Illustrated is an English corbel table of the 11th century.

EN SUITE Of a set. See *Set*.

EN TABLEAU An upholstery technique of the late 18th century. A sharp ridge, outlined in gimp, braid, or cord, defined the straight lines of the sofa or chair. Illustrated is a late Sheraton sofa.

EN TAILLE D'ÉPARGNE Another French term for Champlevé enamel.

ENAMEL A colored glaze used to decorate metal or ceramics. After firing it becomes hard and permanent. It is applied to *pottery* or *porcelain* after a preliminary glaze. The piece is then fired again to fuse the enamel to the original glaze. Enamel is also a generic name for a paint which dries with a hard, shiny surface. A 12th-century enameled reliquary is illustrated.

ENCARPUS A fruit or flower festoon used to enhance flat surfaces. It was employed extensively in the Italian Renaissance and in the Louis XV and Louis XVI periods.

ENCLOSING WALL An exterior, nonbearing wall in skeletal frame construc-

EMPIRE DRAPE

ENCOIGNURE

END TABLE

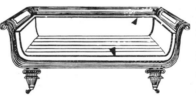

EN RESSAUT

EN TABLEAU

ENAMEL

ENRICHMENT

tion which is anchored to columns, piers, or floors, but not necessarily built between columns or piers as a curtain wall. See *Curtain Wall*.

ENCOIGNURE A corner cabinet or table, often built in as part of the architecture of the room. See *Coin*.

ENCRIER French for *Inkwell*.

END TABLE A small table placed at the end of a sofa, settee, or couch, or at the side of a chair to hold a lamp, ashtray, etc. A modern device that can be styled to suit any period of furnishing. See *Side Table*.

ENDIVE MARQUETRY A Queen Anne style of fine flowing-line marquetry similar to seaweed marquetry. The flowing lines resemble the leaves of the endive plant. See *Seaweed Marquetry*.

ENDS The lengthwise yarns in cloth. See *Count of Cloth* and *Warp*.

ENIFLADE French term for a set or suite of rooms. The term also describes a low provincial buffet with four or more cupboard doors.

ENGAGED COLUMN A column, partially attached to a wall and projecting from it 1/3 to 3/4 of the extent of its diameter. See *Pilaster*.

ENGLISH BOND In masonry, bricks laid in alternate courses of headers and stretchers (the header is the end of the brick, the stretcher is the side of the brick). The headers are centered on the stretchers, which lie in horizontal lines.

ENGLISH CROSS BOND A masonry method similar to English bond in that it consists of alternate courses of headers and stretchers. Instead of the stretchers lying one directly above the other in alternate courses, they break joints evenly in the successive stretcher courses. See *Bond* and *English Bond*.

ENGRAVING A generic term covering many methods of multiplying prints. In general, a design is cut in a hard material such as copper, steel, or wood. The artist may incise his design; or he may remove the areas around it. The design is inked, and impressions are taken. Some engraving techniques are: woodcut, linocut, line engraving, drypoint, etching, mezzotint, aquatint, wood engraving, intaglio engraving.

ENGRAVING ROOM See *Print Room*.

ENRICHMENT A painted or carved repeated design on moldings, such as the guilloche, egg and dart, honeysuckle, chevron, etc. Illustrated is a section of a French Romanesque portal showing a series of enriched moldings.

ENTABLATURE In architecture, the upper portion of a classic order which consists of an architrave, frieze, and cornice. The entablature rests upon the column. See *Architrave, Classic,* and *Cornice.*

ENTASIS A slight curve on the shaft of a column, to correct an optical illusion and make a column appear straight. The slight swelling makes the column appear straight-lined.

ENTRELAC A Louis XVI decorative carved interlacing motif which is similar to a *Guilloche.*

ENTRESOL French for mezzanine. The low story over the ground floor or a low story between two high ones.

ENVELOPE TABLE A square table top with four "envelope flap" hinged sections which, when flipped back, increase the tabletop surface. A late-18th-century design, also found in the French Directoire period. It is often used for card table designs, and is similar in concept to the triangular *Handkerchief Table.*

ÉPERGNE A French word for an ornamental stand with a dish on top. May have candelabra branches extending out from the stand, below the dish, or a trumpet-like container rising above the dish. The bell-like opening is used as a flower container. The épergne is usually used as a table centerpiece.

EPISTYLE A beam that spans the space between two columns or piers, or between a column or pier and a wall. It is also called an architrave.

ÉPOQUE ROMANTIQUE See *Romantic Epoch.*

EPOXY An extremely strong adhesive or sealant available in kit form. Also available as a liquid resin which must be catalyzed to become effective as a coating or cement. Used in molding, casting, laminating and as a means of encapsulating other materials. The epoxy resins are thermosetting and are widely used in reinforced plastics since they adhere well to glass fibers.

ERGONOMIC DESIGN Design based on the needs of the human being in relationship to machines or mechanical devices. As biotechnology, it takes into consideration the psychological and physiological problems inherent in the performance of specific tasks using a mechanism. An increasingly important approach to the planning of offices and work spaces which use computers.

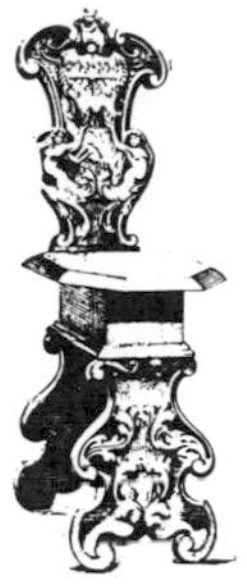
ESCABELLE

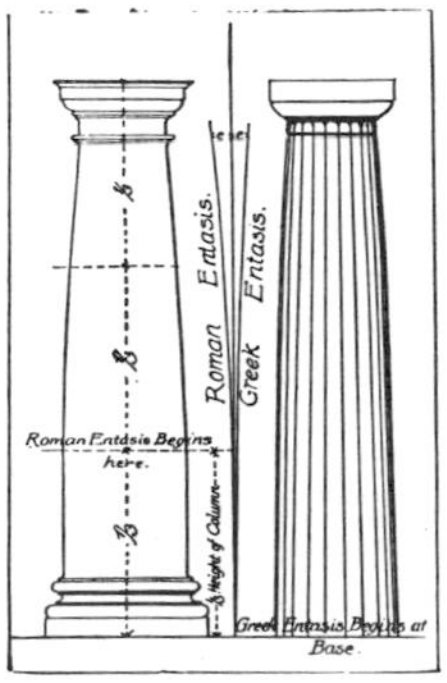

ENTASIS

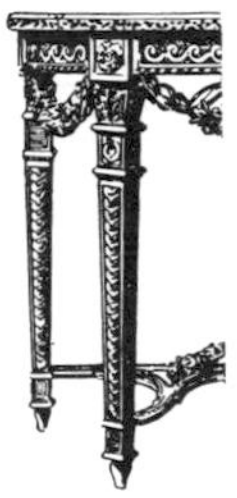
ENTRELAC

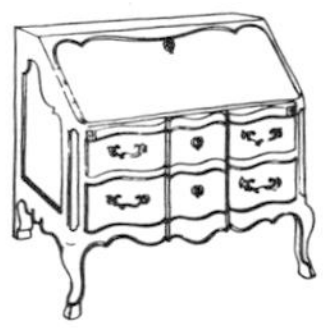
ESCRITOIRE

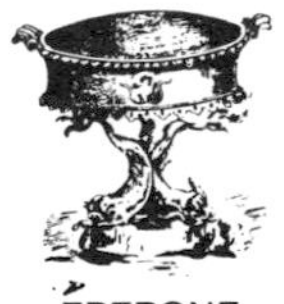
ÉPERGNE

ÉTAGÈRE

ESCABEAU See *Escabelle.*

ESCABELLE An early French Renaissance stool or chair supported on trestles. It is similar to the Italian sgabello.

ESCALLOP See *Cockleshell* and *Scallop Shell.*

ESCRITOIRE A French term for a small desk with drawers and compartments. A secretary.

ESCUTCHEON A shield with a heraldic device. In hardware, a decoratively shaped plate for a keyhole, knob, pull, or doorknob backing.

ESPAGNOLETTE A terminal ornament popular in 16th- and 17th-century French furniture. It is a female bust used as part of a support, or the ending of a volute. In the French Régence period it is a female head with a tall, stiff lace collar or ruff that gives a generally Spanish flavor. The ornate head was a popular decorative motif for wood carvings and bronze mounts.

ESPALIER A latticework of wood upon which fruit trees or ornamental shrubs are trained to assume decorative patterns. The branches are tied to grow in a set direction and make an overall preconceived pattern. The "educated," stylized trees are referred to as espalier.

ESTAGNIE A French provincial open hanging shelf unit used to hold pewter utensils. The piece sometimes had a drawer under the shelves.

ESTRADE The French version of the Spanish estrado, a drawing room. The word also refers to an elevated part of the floor or room, a platform placed at one end. It originally meant a couch area or bed area in an alcove. A feature in 17th-century Spanish architecture. See *Alcove.*

ESTRON A trademark name for a natural, uncolored *acetate* fiber produced by the Eastman Company. A heavy-denier yarn is especially designed for home-furnishing uses.

ÉTAGÈRE Hanging or standing open shelves. A light, elegant unit for displaying books, bric-a-brac, etc. A whatnot unit. Illustrated is a hanging étagère designed by Chippendale. In the 19th century applied to worktables with several shelves.

ETCHED GLASS Sandblasted glass which has a milky, opaque quality. Also called frosted glass.

ETCHING A form of intaglio engraving. A copper plate is covered with a resinous ground impervious to acid, and the artist or etcher than draws on this surface with a needle. The plate is bathed in acid, which bites into the scratched lines, engraving the design. The design is inked and impressions are taken. Rembrandt was a famous etcher, and the 17th century was a noteworthy period in the production of etchings.

ETRUSCAN ORDER Also called the Tuscan order. A Roman variation of the simple Doric order. A heavy, massive column, seven diameters high. See *Diameter* and *Doric Order.*

ÉTUI French for box or container.

EUCALYPTUS See *Walnut, Oriental.*

ÉVENTAIL French for fan

EVOLUTE A continuous wave or Vitruvian scroll. A classic motif used in the

EXTENSION TABLE

EVOLUTE

18th century as a decoration on bands, cornices, friezes, etc. See *Vitruvian Scroll.*

EXEDRA A public room in a Pompeiian or Roman home. A semicircular or rectangular recess for seating. An apse or niche in a church.

EXPANDED VINYL A stretch upholstery fabric made of vinyl plastic with an elastic knit backing. Its capacity to stretch and shape against curved contours makes it ideal for covering irregular shaped forms and furniture.

EXTENSION TABLE A tabletop which separates in the center, and extends outward in both directions. Additional leaves are then added in the open space created. Illustrated is an early-19th-century Duncan Phyfe extension table.

EXTRADOS See *Arch.*

EYE The center of an Ionic volute.

F

FABRILITE A trademark for vinyl-coated fabric and sheeting manufactured by Dupont, used as an upholstery material and as a durable wall covering.

FAÇADE The front or face of a structure. The main view. Also the front of an architecturally designed piece of furniture. Illustrated is the façade of Notre-Dame in Paris.

FAÇADE D'HONNEUR French for the main face of a building. Illustrated is the cathedral of Laon. See *Postern*.

FACCIATA Italian for façade or front.

FACE The exposed surface of a wall or structure.

FACE BRICK Bricks which have been selected for their better color, texture, etc., and are used to face or surface the exposed walls or fireplaces, etc. Cheaper bricks or baser materials are used behind the face brick.

FACED WALL Wall where the facing and backing are bonded and tied together to work together under the common load.

FACETTES The French word for the flat projections between the flutes of a column shaft.

FACIA The flat vertical face in the architrave of an entablature. See *Fascia*.

FACING The finishing material (stone, brick, stucco, wood, etc.) which is applied to the façade of a building or wall.

FAÇONNÉ A Jacquard type of fabric made of silk or rayon. Façonné is French for fancy weave. A brocaded velvet.

FAÏENCE French for pottery. Terra-cotta. A peasant type of glazed pottery

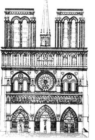

FAÇADE

FAÇADE D'HONNEUR

FALL FRONT

FAN DESIGN

originally made at Faenza, Italy. A glazed bisquit ware. Used as a facing for buildings or walls in the form of tiles or blocks. Also used as a flooring material. See *Terra-Cotta*.

FAILLE A soft, slightly glossy silk, rayon, or cotton fabric in a rib weave. The filler yarns are heavier than the warp yarns; thus they cause a flat cross-grain rib or cord.

FAKE A counterfeit reproduction of an object made to pass as the original. Usually artificially aged or patinaed.

FALDISTORIUM A late Italian Renaissance curule chair made of wrought iron and brass, with a leather or velvet seat. See *Curule Chair*.

FALDSTOOL A folding or portable stool of the Gothic period.

FALL FRONT See *Drop Lid*. Illustrated is a Queen Anne toilet chest.

FAMILLE NOIRE, VERTE, JAUNE, ROSE, ETC. French names for Chinese pottery having a background of a certain color. Literally black family, green family, yellow family, rose family, etc.

FAN DESIGN A semicircular, fanlike ornament used in late-18th-century furniture in England and America.

FAN VAULTING Also called palm vaulting. A collection of ribs springing from a point and spreading out in a fan shape, peculiar to the Perpendicular Period in Gothic architecture.

FANBACK CHAIR A chair or settee with a fanlike motif, either upright or reversed, for the chair back. Originally an 18th-century French design.

FANCY CHAIR   A Sheraton-designed small-scaled, elegant side chair. A late-18th-century favorite.

FANLIGHT   A window set above a door or entranceway. In Georgian buildings, the fanlight is often semicircular in shape, and the panes are separated by bars radiating from the center in a fanlike arrangement.

FARTHINGALE CHAIR   A wide-seated chair, without arms, made to accommodate the voluminous skirts (farthingales) of the Elizabethan costume.

FASCES   A Roman symbol of power. A bundle of rods enclosing an axe. Appeared most recently as the symbol of the 20th-century Italian Fascists.

FASCIA   The projecting crown molding of a cornice. A molding with a flat vertical plane in section. Also spelled *facia*.

FASHION   A vogue or style. A present trend or fad.

FAUDESTEUIL   A Romanesque bench or seating stool with curved X-shaped supports. This type of stool usually had a leather sling for a seat, and the piece was collapsible. In the Gothic period, the legs are fixed and the chair does not usually fold. Illustrated is a 14th-century French Gothic faudesteuil made of iron with brass finials and a leather strap for a seat. See *Pliant*.

FAUN   A creature from classical myth, half-man, half-goat, a decorative element in the French and Italian Renaissance period. Also appears in the Adam brothers' designs. The faun is sometimes used as a support.

FAUTEUIL   French for armchair. An upholstered armchair with open sides, usually with upholstered arm or elbow pads. Popularized in the Louis XIV period; the arms originally were placed directly over the front legs. In the Régence and Louis XV periods, the arms were set farther back, and the legs were shortened. The early Renaissance armchairs were not usually upholstered. See *Caquetoire*.

FAUTEUIL À CHÂSSIS   Armchair constructed by a French method devised in the Louis XIV period (also used to make upholstered sofas). A secondary wood framework was covered with fabric, then slipped into the prime wood frame of the piece of furniture. This technique made changes of upholstery relatively simple; the upholsterer merely put a new framed upholstered seat or back into the ornate carved frame. See *Slip Seat*.

FAUTEUIL DE BUREAU   A desk chair of the Régence and Louis XV periods. Usually had one leg centered in the front, one centered in the back, and one at

FANCY CHAIR

FANLIGHT

FARTHINGALE CHAIR

FAUDESTEUIL

FAUTEUIL

FENDER

either side of the seat. The curved sloping back was either caned or upholstered in leather. Similar to the English roundabout chair of the 18th century.

FAUVE   French for wild beast. An early-20th-century art movement by artists who used bright, strong colors, flat patterns, and wild distortions. Henri Matisse, Albert Marquet, André Derain, Maurice de Vlamenck, and Georges Rouault are grouped in this school.

FAUX ROSE   A French rosewood or Madagascar rosewood. A pinkish-brown wood with striped markings.

FAUX SATINE   An amber to golden-brown cypress crotch wood found largely in the southeastern part of the United States. A soft, oily wood, easy to work is used as a veneer treatment on furniture and for paneling. Similar in appearance to satinwood.

FAVAS   A Louis XVI decoration which resembles a honeycomb.

FAVRILE   A late-19th-century iridescent glass, made by Louis C. Tiffany in a variety of delicate and decorative patterns, many in the Art Nouveau style.

FAY, JEAN BAPTISTE   A famous 18th-century French textile and wallpaper designer. His work captured the spirit and quality of the Louis XVI period.

FAYARD or FOYARD   French for beech.

FEATHERED EDGE   A chamfered or beveled effect in which the edge is thinner than the thickness of the board. A thinning off of the edge of a piece of wood.

FEATHERING   Tracery, in the Gothic style, formed by an arrangement of cusps and foils. Also called foliation.

FEDERAL   American period of architecture, art, furniture, and decoration from about 1790 to 1820. A classic period greatly influenced by the Adam brothers, Hepplewhite, Sheraton, and the English Regency. Duncan Phyfe is the leading American furniture designer of this period.

FELT   A material made by matting and interlocking, under heat and pressure, woolen and other fibers. It has no weave or pattern.

FELT BASE RUG   An inexpensive floor covering material which has an enameled design printed, and sometimes an embossed pattern pressed, on the felt-based material. Like linoleum but not as durable; the wearing surface does not go through to the backing.

FENDER   A low, metal guard made of iron and/or brass, used to protect the rug or floor from flying embers or sparks from the fire. A hearth or fireplace accessory.

FENESTRATION The window and door arrangement of a building, and the relative proportions of the openings in the facade. Illustrated is the Italian Renaissance Farnese Palace in Rome.

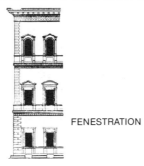

FENESTRATION

FENÊTRE À BATTANTS French term for a pair of door-like windows. See *French Window*.

FENSTER ROSE German for rose window.

FERAGHAN RUGS Persian-style rugs that usually have a deep blue background and a rich overall pattern of small stylized flowers in rows.

FERRONERIE VELVET An antique Venetian velvet with a delicate wrought-iron-like pattern.

FERRULE Formerly "verrel" from the French "virole," a metal ring holding an object fixed to the end of another object. In current usage, a metal cup (usually of brass) placed on the bottom of a wood furniture leg for protection and as a reinforcement. Also the metal section of a paintbrush which holds the hairs or bristles to the wood stem.

FERRULE   FIDDLEBACK CHAIR

FESTOON A string or chain of any kind of material suspended between two points to form a curved or inverted arc drop. A sculptured garland of leaves, flowers, fruits, etc., suspended between two points. A favorite Renaissance motif. In furniture, usually a carved or painted arced design of leaves, flowers, fruits, etc.

FESTOON

FÊTE GALANTE A French 18th-century romantic version of a picnic with ladies and their escorts, in rich court apparel, gaily flirting and playing musical instruments and games. This theme appears in murals, tapestries, designs, and painting.

FIBER RUG A reversible rug woven of kraft or sisal fibers, sometimes combined with wool or other fibers. Available in assorted sizes, colors, patterns, and shapes for use as area rugs or to cover a complete floor.

FIBERBOARD A pulped wood panel, usually 4′ × 8′, compressed under great pressure to form a rigid, strong, no-grain construction unit. Many trademarked types available: Masonite, Beaverboard, Homosote, etc. Used for partitions, ceilings, and the interior construction of inexpensive furniture.

FIBERGLAS A trademark name for fine filaments of pure glass and the textiles woven from them. The fiber is strong, soft, and pliable, and resists heat, chemicals, and

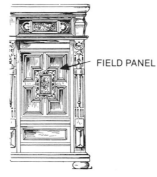

FIELD PANEL

FIELD BED

soil. Manufactured by the Owens-Corning Fiberglas Corporation. Glass fibers are also manufactured by the Pittsburgh Plate Glass Company (PPG) and Johns-Manville Corporation (J-M).

FIBERGLASS SHELLS, PLANTERS, ETC. Planters, shaped seats and other dimensional forms made of fine filaments of glass saturated with polyester plastics which are then poured into and formed in molds of the desired shape and size. Excellent for outdoor use and in contract design.

FIDDLE BRACE BACK See *Braced Back*.

FIDDLEBACK A wood grain effect having a fine, even ripple running at right angles to the direction of the grain of the wood. Used for fiddleback veneers. Often appears in maple and mahogany.

FIDDLEBACK CHAIR A Queen Anne style, American colonial chair. The back splat is shaped like a fiddle or a vase and the seat is usually made of rush. The chair has cabriole or bandy legs. A similar chair appears in Louis XV-period furniture.

FIDDLE-STRING BACK or STICK-BACK A name sometimes applied to a Windsor chair or any chair which has a back made up of many rods or thin turnings which resemble the strings of a fiddle.

F.I.D.E.R. See *Foundation of Interior Design Education Research*.

FIELD or FIELDED PANEL The surface of a panel on the same level as the surrounding woodwork and defined or outlined by a sunk bevel or applied molding.

FIELD BED A small-scaled, arched canopy bed originally intended to be moved from place to place; used in the field by army officers. In 18th-century design, a bed with smaller tester and less imposing bedposts. A Chippendale design is illustrated.

FIGURE The highlights or cross graining in a piece of wood or veneer. Also, shapes created by the abnormal growth of a tree. See *Burl*. The vertical graining of a piece of wood is described as the pattern.

FIL D'ARGENT French for silver thread. See *Fil d'Or*.

FIL DE BOIS Veneer used in a full, uninterrupted length on a piece of furniture.

FIL DE CHYPRE French for Cyprus thread. See *Fil d'Or*.

FIL D'OR French for gold thread. A gilded silver thread originally made in Genoa and used in tapestries from the Middle Ages up to the 18th century.

FILAMENT A term for a yarn (usually acetate, rayon, and other synthetic) made up of a number of fine continuous strands lightly twisted together. It is sold by the *Denier* size.

FILET A square-meshed, net fabric.

FILET LACE A type of lace in which the design is created by embroidering on net with a thread similar to that used in making the net. See *Lace.*

FILIGREE Decorative openwork. Usually fine, lacelike work done in gold or silver wire.

FILLER Threads that run across the width of the fabric from selvage to selvage. Another term for the weft. In weaving, the filler is the thread carried by the shuttle. In woodwork, a liquid or paste composition, often pigmented, used to fill the pores or irregularities in coarse or open-grained woods. After using the filler, the wood can be finished and polished.

FILLET A molding with a small, flat, vertical surface as seen in section view, usually used above and below a curved molding. The fillet is also the upright band between the flutings of a column. The term is also applied to the uppermost member of a cornice.

FILLING The weft or woof yarns. Used in the shuttle that moves back and forth across the lengthwise threads of a loom. Also, the pick threads. In carpetmaking, the fillings are the threads that cross the warp and fill up the spaces between the knots or tufts. See *Pick, Weave,* and *Weft.*

FILMS Synthetic "fabrics" made from liquids, which adhere to backing materials. The liquid is applied directly to a formed or molded piece of plastic furniture. The applied film actually supplies a fabric-like surface texture to the piece, and thus substitutes for a cover of fabric on the unit.

FIN DE SIÈCLE French for end of the century. The end of the 19th century and the *Art Nouveau* style are described by this phrase.

FINGER JOINT A movable, interlocking joint mainly used between the movable and fixed parts of a bracket or fly rail, such as one used to support the leaves of a dropleaf table in a horizontal position. See *Knuckle Joint.*

FINIAL The terminating ornament on a post, pediment, or intersection. A pineapple, urn, knob, or a cluster of foliage are among the shapes chosen.

FINISH In fabrics, the treatment given to produce a desired surface effect; nap-

FIRE DOGS

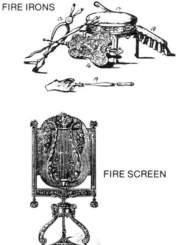

FIRE IRONS

FIRE SCREEN

FIREBACKS

FINIAL

FIRESIDE CHAIR

ping, embossing, glazing, waterproofing, wrinkle resistance, etc. The finish sometimes contributes to the "feel" or "hand" of the fabric. In cabinetry, a treatment applied to wood to protect the surface, to make it more durable and resistant to stains and burns, to accentuate the natural grain, to lighten or deepen the color, to make a dull or glossy surface appearance, or to change the color completely, as by painting, lacquering, antiquing, distressing, etc.

FIR A soft, textured wood used for commercial plywood and interior trims. Not usually used for solid work in furniture.

FIRE DIVISION WALL A wall which subdivides the building and is used to resist the spread of fire, but does not go continuously through the building as a fire wall does.

FIRE DOGS See *Andirons.*

FIRE IRONS Hearth accessories: the poker, tongs, and shovel used to tend a fire. Illustrated is a collection of fire irons and bellows from George Edwards and Mathias, Darley's 18th-century ornaments in the Chinese style.

FIRE SCREEN An ornamental screen set in front of an open fireplace to keep sparks from flying into the room, or to provide protection from intense heat. The screen shown served the latter purpose.

FIRE WALL A wall constructed of fire-retarding material which starts at the foundation and extends up to and above the roof of a building, completely dividing it, designed to hinder the spread of fire for a defined period of time.

FIREBACKS Metal liners or screens, often decorative, placed behind a fire in a fireplace. They served to reflect the heat back into the room and also to protect the masonry. These pieces, which were popular in the 17th and 18th centuries, were usually made of cast iron.

FIRECLAY A clay, resistant to heat, used to make firebricks for lining fireplaces.

FIRE-RETARDANT WIRED GLASS Sheet glass with a wire mesh, chromium-dipped to ensure clean wire and a firm adhesion which is embedded, as closely as possible, in its center. Produced by a continuous rolling process, and made in many patterns, types, and finishes. Also used as a decorative material, as on the curtain wall of the Time and Life Building in New York City.

FIRESIDE CHAIR An upholstered chair, usually skirted, with a high roll-over back which flares out as it rises up. The arms sweep away from the chair back and scroll around. The pillow seat is often T-shaped. A 20th-century design. Illustrated is a Jacobean prototype.

FIRESIDE FIGURES Fire screens made of wood and/or canvas, representing contemporary figures in just under life size. Often these figures were female and dressed in exotic Oriental costumes. The fireside figures were also called "picture board dummies" and were popular in the late 17th century.

FIRING The heating of clay in a kiln to harden it. A term used in pottery making.

FIRST PLANTAGENET PERIOD See *Early English Period.*

FIRST POINTED PERIOD See *Early English Period.*

FISH TAIL A carved detail in the shape of a fish's tail which sometimes appeared on the top rail of spindled or banister-back chairs of 18th- and 19th-century American design.

FITMENTS An English expression for units (bookcases, cabinets, etc.) designed and built to fit the walls of a room. Illustrated is a mid-19th-century chimneypiece with built-in bookcases, cabinets, etc. The doors are perforated brass; the units are carved walnut with colored marble decorations.

FITTINGS Metal hardware, mounts, escutcheons, etc.

FLACHBILDWERK German for low or bas-relief work.

FLAG A long grass which is twisted and woven into provincial-type seats. See *Rush.*

FLAGSTONE Large, flat stones, square or irregular in shape, used as flooring or pavement material. Slate is often used for flagstone floors.

FLAKED A wood figure or grain of oak which has been quarter-cut. Horizontal highlights streak across the grain of the wood. A breaking or loosening of the flake is called "broken flake."

FLAMBEAU A flame or flaming torch used as a decorative motif. Popular in the 18th and early 19th centuries in England and France.

FLAMBOYANT French for flaming. The late Gothic style in French architecture (14th and 15th centuries). The window tracery was designed in conventionalized flamelike forms with reversed curved lines. See *Tracery.*

FLAME CARVING A finial carved in a swirling, spiral effect to simulate a flame.

FLAP TABLE

FLARE

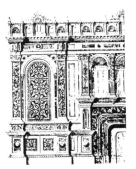
FITMENTS

FITTINGS

FLEMISH CHAIR AND FOOT

Used to decorate urns in the late 17th and early 18th centuries.

FLAMMENSTIL German for "flamboyant style."

FLÂNEUSE From the French *flâner* which means to lounge. A garden-type lounge chair with a footrest, similar to the current deck chair. The flâneuse usually had a caned seat, back, and footrest.

FLAP STRAPPING See *Strapwork.*

FLAP TABLE An early-17th-century table with a fixed center slab and two side flaps which can be lowered by folding back the legs which support them. These legs fold back under the central table surface. The flap table is a form of gateleg or eight-legged table. An American Jacobean Thousand-leg Table is illustrated.

FLARE An outward spread, as in a chair seat which is wider at the front than at the back. Illustrated is an early-19th-century Sheraton design.

FLAT A dull, nonglossy paint finish.

FLAT-CUT VENEER A combination straight-grain and heart-figure veneer produced by slicing half of a log directly through the center or heart.

FLATTED A term used to describe painted furniture, such as was popular in the Louis XV and Louis XVI periods.

FLATTING AGENT A substance added to varnishes, paints, and other coating materials to reduce the gloss on the dried painted surface.

FLAX The fiber from the inner bark of the flax plant, used in the manufacture of linen. More expensive than cotton, but more absorbent, has a crisper, firmer hand; generally more resistant to mildew.

FLEMISH Referring to Flanders, the old name for the area now Belgium, Holland, and parts of northern France.

FLEMISH BOND In masonry, an arrangement of brick in which the headers and stretchers are used alternately in the same course. In the next course the arrangement is alternated so that the header is centered over the stretchers below. A single Flemish bond is used for facing only. See *Double Stretcher Flemish Bond.*

FLEMISH CHAIR A late-17th-century English high-backed chair, with or without arms. The splat was a panel of cane, upholstery, laths, or balusters surmounted with an elaborate carved cresting. The legs had straight backs with bold curves in front, and were supported by scroll feet. The stretcher consisted of two concave curves joined by a convex curve in the center. See *Flemish Scroll.*

FLEMISH CROSS BOND In masonry, alternating Flemish and stretcher courses, with the headers in vertical lines and the stretcher courses crossed. See *Bond* and *Flemish Bond.*

FLEMISH EAR A late French Renaissance and Baroque furniture foot, similar to the Flemish scroll foot, except that the design (the S or C) is inverted. Appears on some furniture of the Louis XIV period. See *Flemish Foot* and *Flemish Scroll.*

FLEMISH FOOT A scroll-like ending to an S or C curved leg, popular in 17th-century styles in Flanders, England, and France.

FLEMISH SCROLL An S or C curved ornamental form in which a scroll is broken by an angle, used in Flemish Renaissance furniture and also in the English Carolean and William and Mary styles.

FLEMISH SPIRAL BOND In masonry, Flemish courses laid out so that the headers break joint over each other and form diagonal bands on the face of the wall. See *Bond* and *Flemish Bond.*

FLEUR DE LIS or FLEUR DE LYS A decorative, conventionalized iris flower which has symbolized royalty and the French Bourbon kings.

FLEURETTE French for small flower. A motif carved on Louis XVI furniture and accessories.

FLEURETTED TREILLAGE Anglicized French for beflowered trellis. A popular decorative motif in carved and painted form in French and German Rococo and Louis XV furniture and accessories. Illustrated is the back of a sofa designed by François Peyrotte.

FLEURON A small, flower-like decoration set on the abacus on the Corinthian capital. It appears to spring from a small bud above the middle leaf in the capital. An Italian Renaissance example is illustrated.

FLIERS In plan, rectangular steps in staircase construction.

FLIGHT A series of steps uninterrupted by a landing.

FLIP TOP TABLE A contemporary expansion table with two leaves, one set on top of the other. When the top leaf is raised and set down even with the plane of the lower leaf, the surface is doubled in area. This construction device can be used on many periods and styles of furniture. See *Chess Table* illustration.

FLITCH

FLEMISH SCROLL

FLEUR DE LIS

FLEURETTED TREILLAGE

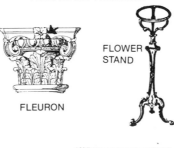

FLEURON

FLOWER STAND

FLOREATED

FLITCH Any part of the log which is sliced into veneer.

FLOATING FURNITURE Modern furniture hung or suspended from the walls. The case pieces do not have legs, and are usually bracketed off stiles or upright wall standards bolted to the wall.

FLOCK Finely powdered wool or other short clipped fibers glued onto paper, fabric, wood, etc., to provide an allover suede or velvet finish, or applied in a design to create a cut velvet effect. See *Flocking.*

FLOCK PAPER A wallpaper with a velvet-like or suede surface.

FLOCKING A technique for applying flock. Originally, the finely powdered wool was scattered over the entire surface to be decorated, but the particles adhered only to that part of the surface which was treated with glue. The rest of the flock, which did not stick to the fabric, leather, canvas, or paper, was blown or brushed off. A technique developed during the Middle Ages, and first applied to paper during the 17th century. Paper subjected to this treatment was called "velvet paper." The design was painted, stenciled or printed on the paper with a slow drying adhesive or varnish. When powdered color was sprinkled on in place of flock, the paper was called a counterfeit flock. In 1634, Jerome Lanyer was granted a patent for flocking.

FLOKATI (FLOKATES) Greek rugs loomed from long fibers of sheep wool into a thick shag, usually left in its natural creamy, off-white color. See *Shag Rug.*

FLOOR PLAN See *Plan.*

FLOORCLOTH An early-18th-century rug made of heavy linen or canvas heavily sized and coated and then painted or ornamented. Similar to *Wachstuch-tapete.*

FLOREATED A term for Gothic tracery and ornaments which used floral and leaf motifs in flowing, rhythmic lines.

FLORENTINE ARCH A Renaissance architectural feature. A semicircular arch springing directly from a column, pier, or capital, and trimmed with an architrave. The outer arch or extrados is pointed, while the inner arch or intrados is semi-circular. These arches are frequently used in a series. See *Arcade.*

FLOWER STAND A stand for holding a plant or pot of flowers. Adam designed flower stands with sloping legs, rams' heads, and garland enrichments. A Chippendale design is illustrated. See *Jardinière.*

FLUE The enclosed portion of a chimney stack which carries the smoke up and out.

FLUORESCENT LIGHTING   A lighting device consisting of a glass tube coated on its inner surface with a substance that glows when a gas-conducted current is induced in the presence of mercury.

FLUSH   Said of a surface which is even, or at the same level, with adjoining surfaces.

FLUSH BEAD   A molding in which the sunk bead is even with the surface adjacent to it.

FLUTING   Continous parallel hollows or channels, usually cut perpendicularly, as in a column, pilaster shaft, or furniture leg. It is like narrow concave moldings used in parallel lines. Spiral fluting is sometimes used on columns and furniture supports. Short flutings are often used on friezes as ornamentation.

FLY BRACKET   A bracket, similar to a fly rail, used to support a drop-leaf on a Pembroke or library table. The bracket sometimes had shaped or diagonally cut ends. See *Loper*.

FLY RAIL   The folding bracket support for the flap or drop leaf of a table.

FOAM RUBBER   Latex, the sap of the rubber tree, whipped with air to create a light, porous rubber composition. The firmness of the foam rubber depends upon the air content. Used for mattresses, pillows, upholstery filling, etc.

FOILS   The small arcs which make up Gothic tracery. The foils are separated by the cusps. See *Multifoil*.

FOLD OVER   A desk or table with a "desk leaf" which folds over the upper surface, used in the late 18th century in France and England, and particularly by Sheraton.

FOLDING FURNITURE   Collapsible furniture which can fold into a compact unit: a folding stool, folding chair, table, bed, etc. This principle was employed by the ancient Egyptians, Greeks, and Romans, and has continued popularity up to our current bridge sets. In the mid- and late 18th century, Shearer, Hepplewhite, and Sheraton designed many folding and convertible pieces of furniture (e.g., library steps).

FOLDING TABLE   An early English Renaissance multilegged table. Often had from twelve to as many as twenty legs, and the entire table could be folded to about one-third of its full size. The forerunner of the gateleg table, and worked on the same principle of expansion. Illustrated is a later 17th-century example (Stuart or Restoration period).

FOLIAGE

FOLLY

FLUTING

FONDEUR

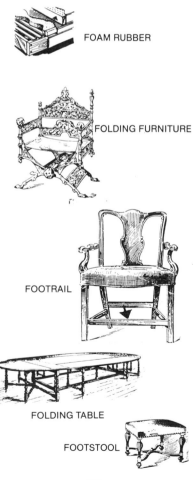

FOLDING FURNITURE

FOOTRAIL

FOAM RUBBER

FOLDING TABLE

FOOTSTOOL

FOLIAGE   In decoration or ornament, plant and leaf forms carved, painted, or otherwise decoratively interpreted. A carved 13th-century frieze (from Notre-Dame) is illustrated.

FOLIATION   See *Feathering*.

FOLLY   A garden or park structure resembling a classic or Gothic ruin, specially built to create a view or a charming effect. Popular in 18th-century France. The Chippendale frame shown illustrates the classic "folly" as a decorative carved design.

FOLWELL, JOHN   See *Philadelphia Chippendale*.

FONDEUR   French for metal caster. One who makes metal mounts, hardware, furniture embellishments, and accessories.

FONTAINE, PIERRE FRANÇOIS LÉONARD (1762–1853)   A French architect-designer who, with Charles Percier, created the architectural and interior style known as Empire for Napoleon at the start of the 19th century. Together they designed interiors and furniture for Malmaison, St.-Cloud, the Tuileries, and the Louvre. Their creed was: "simple lines, pure contours, correct shapes replacing . . . the curving and the irregular." See *Empire*.

FONTAINEBLEAU   A French Renaissance château begun in the reign of François I in the early 16th century. The rooms that were created at this time had Italian Renaissance style paneling with classic order details and Vitruvian motifs. Raphael-like arabesques made of modeled plaster and fresco paintings were also used. Additions were made to the château, and variations in periods and styles of decoration are clearly discernible.

FOOTBOARD   A supporting wooden piece at the lower end of a bed which connects with the two side rails. It can be an important decorative feature, carved and ornamented, or simply a horizontal rail, depending upon style or period. In the Hollywood bed, the footboard is omitted.

FOOTCANDLE   A unit of measurement of light, based on the amount of light produced by a standard candle one foot distant.

FOOTMAN   See *Trivet*.

FOOTRAIL   The lower supporting stretcher between two legs of a chair or table. An early-18th-century English chair illustrates the footrail.

FOOTSTOOL   Originally an accompanying step for high throne seats; currently used as a stool or bench. A small, low hassock.

FORGED   A term applied to metals which have been heated and then hammered or beaten into a shape.

FORM   A long, backless bench or seat of the Jacobean period, often furnished with loose pillows.

FORMAL   Regular, symmetrical, traditional in effect. Usually describes an arrangement or placement of furniture or decoration which is stately and carefully balanced. Not haphazard or whimsical. Illustrated is a late-18th-century Sheraton elevation with a chinoiserie influence.

FORTISAN   A trademark name for a strong regenerated cellulose yarn produced by the Celanese Corporation of America. The yarn is often combined with silk, cotton, or linen to make sheer fabrics used for curtains. Fortisan fabrics are strong, drapable, and not much affected by changes in humidity.

FORTREL   A polyester fiber produced by Fiber Industries, Inc. It has properties similar to Dupont's Dacron: wrinkle resistance, quick drying, and good wash-and-wear performance. The trademark Fortrel may be used on those fabrics which use the polyester and meet the performance standards set by Fiber Industries.

FORTY, JEAN FRANÇOIS   An 18th-century French designer, engraver, and metal carver. He published eight volumes on design, and created some of the most beautiful metal accessories and furniture mounts of the Louis XVI period.

FORTY WINK CHAIR   See *Wing Chair.*

FOUNDATION OF INTERIOR DESIGN EDUCATION RESEARCH (F.I.D.E.R)   An arm of the American Society of Interior Designers which is concerned with acrediting educational programs in Interior Design. Works closely with schools to promote better and more relevant courses of study. Funded primarily by the A.S.I.D. membership and chapters, industry, students and fees paid by the schools. Sends teams to educational institutions which request evaluation of their Interior Design programs. Publishes evaluations as a nationwide guide to students and guidance counselors.

FOUNTAIN   Usually a decorative, sculptured or carved unit made of marble, stone, bronze, concrete, etc., which pumps water up and out in a spouting or cascading manner. The fountain may be in a street, square, park, or garden, inside a courtyard, or in the interior of a public building or a home. It may be set in a pool area or have a small basin which catches the water.

FORGED

FORMAL

FOUR-WAY CENTER
AND BUTT MATCH

FRAME

FOUNTAIN

Many home fountains are worked electrically with a recirculating pump arrangement. A French Renaissance fountain is illustrated.

FOUR-POSTER BEDSTEAD   A bed with two posts in front and two in the back, or posts rising from carved or paneled foot and head boards. It was sometimes made to support a tester and drapery, or a fabric canopy. Designs vary with the changing periods and styles.

FOUR-WAY CENTER AND BUTT MATCH   A veneer like the *Diamond Match Veneer*, usually using butt, crotch, or stump slices. Brings out the full interest of the graining.

FOYER   An area between the entrance and a main room of a home, apartment, or public building.

FRACTUR (or fraktur) PAINTING   Decorative birth and marriage certificates of the 18th- and 19th-century Pennsylvania Dutch.

FRAGONARD, JEAN-HONORÉ   (1732–1806)   A French painter and designer of the Louis XV and Louis XVI periods. He decorated many dainty boudoirs with murals and other wall decorations. Among his charming paintings are "The Swing" and "Progress of Love," originally created for Mme. Du Barry's home. (She rejected the painting.)

FRAILERO   A Spanish Renaissance monk's chair, usually made of walnut, with plain legs and a broad front stretcher. Decorative nailheads secured the leather seat to the two side rails and the back panel between the two uprights. These were usually capped with finials. The arms were wide and simple. The frailero was probably the most typical chair of the Spanish Renaissance. See *Mission.*

FRAME   The skeleton or basic structure of a piece of furniture later filled in with webbing, stuffing, muslin, upholstery, etc. The unfinished framework illustrated is the frame of a Louis XV wing chair. See *Carcase* or *Carcass.*

FRAME   A surrounding case or structure for the protection and enhancement of drawings, paintings, mirrors, etc. Can be carved of wood, trimmed with moldings, or embellished with gesso composition. Metal frames are also used.

FRANÇOIS I (1494–1547)   King of France from 1515 in the early French Renaissance period. He was a great patron of the building arts and the châteaux at Chambord, Blois, and Fontainebleau were built during his reign. In his time, the flamboyant Gothic motifs were combined with the advancing Italian Renaissance style.

FRANKLIN STOVE Originally called a Pennsylvania stove. A combination stove and fireplace invented by Benjamin Franklin in the mid-18th century. It burned wood set on andirons, and it had a decorative front. Illustrated is an "improved" 19th-century version, the open-grate coal stove.

FREE FORM An irregular, flowing abstract shape as used in modern cocktail tabletops, accent area rugs, wall decorations, etc. Free forms may also be used in paintings, gardens, etc.

FREESTANDING COLUMN A column with clear or open space all around it. In Sheraton sofas and settees it was usually a vase-shaped extension of the front corner legs. A Sheraton Regency chair is illustrated.

FREESTANDING POLES Metal or wood poles with sleeve connections to make them longer or shorter. The principle is the use of the pressure of the adjustable sleeve insert set in the bottom of the pole and resting on the floor, and the one set on top with its disk pressing up against the ceiling. The pole remains erect because pressure is exerted up against the ceiling and down against the floor. Modern designer George Nelson's "Omni" system is based on use of these poles. Also used for pole lights, traveling display units, etc.

FRENCH BED An early-19th-century Empire bed with high rolling S-scrolled head and foot boards. Elegant versions were made of rosewood, had carved legs (dolphin- or cornucopia-shaped), and were splendidly embellished with ormolu designs or medallions. See *Sleigh Bed.*

FRENCH BRACKET FOOT A bracket foot with a concave curve down the mitred edge which gives a splayed effect. Almost always combined with a valanced skirt or apron. Both the inner and outer edges of the leg are curved, giving the appearance of a stunted cabriole leg. Also called "French foot." Popular in 18th-century English and American furniture.

FRENCH BURL A Persian walnut wood with an interesting curly grain favored for inserts in cabinetwork.

FRENCH CHAIR A general name for upholstered chairs used in England in the mid-18th century. It did not apply to a particular style or decoration but to the general type of rococo chair like the bergère. A Chippendale design is illustrated.

FRENCH DIRECTOIRE The period in France from 1789 to 1804. It followed

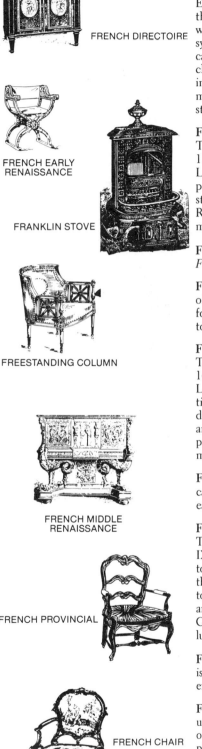

FRENCH DIRECTOIRE

FRENCH EARLY RENAISSANCE

FRANKLIN STOVE

FREESTANDING COLUMN

FRENCH MIDDLE RENAISSANCE

FRENCH PROVINCIAL

FRENCH CHAIR

the Louis XVI period and was the transition from the Greek styles of Louis XVI to the Egyptian and Roman qualities of the Empire style. Essentially a continuation of the classic tradition of the Louis XVI style with the addition of Revolutionary motifs: symbols of liberty, triumphal arches, liberty caps, spirit levels, pikes, oak boughs, clasped hands. Egyptian motifs were also introduced as well as martial Roman elements like spearheads, drums serving as stools, etc.

FRENCH EARLY RENAISSANCE The period from approximately 1484 to 1547, covering the reigns of Charles VIII, Louis XII, and François I. A transitional period which blended outgoing Gothic structural forms with the incoming Italian Renaissance architectural details and ornaments.

FRENCH FOOT See *French Bracket Foot.*

FRENCH HEADING The gathering of a drapery or valance into regularly spaced folds. The folds are usually stitched in place to give a more set appearance.

FRENCH LATE RENAISSANCE The period from approximately 1589 to 1643, covering the reigns of Henri IV and Louis XIII. The Italian Renaissance continued to dominate the architecture and decorations of the period along with Dutch and Flemish influences. In interiors, wall paneling became more important, and formality appeared to be the keynote.

FRENCH LEG A scrolled leg, often carved and ornamented, used in 17th- and early-18th-century furniture designs.

FRENCH MIDDLE RENAISSANCE The reigns of Henri II, François II, Charles IX, and Henry III, covering the years 1547 to 1589. Catherine de Medici dominated the period, and local variations were added to the dominant use of Italian ornament and Renaissance architectural details. The Gothic forms were gradually eliminated. Illustrated is a walnut dresser of the period.

FRENCH POLISH A high, glossy finish on wood obtained by adding several layers of shellac to the wood surface.

FRENCH PROVINCIAL The term usually associated with simplified furniture of the Louis XV or Rococo style. However, plain furniture was made in the provinces in all times and styles, usually of walnut, oak, or fruitwood. *Provincial furniture* is simpler in line than the prevailing high fashion and rarely veneered or decorated with marquetry or ornate carving.

FRENCH RÉGENCE or REGENCY

The transitional period (1700 to 1730) between the grandiose formality of the Louis XIV Baroque period and the frivolous, asymetrical quality of the Louis XV Rococo period. Philippe, Duc d'Orléans, was Regent of France. Flat curved paneling was used for ornament with curves at the corners. Foliage and ribbon ornament was used for embellishment, and curved or cabriole legs began to replace the straight ones. Slight curves, like a crossbow, appeared on the upper parts of cabinets and bookcases. The bombé commode made its appearance at this time, and ebony was replaced as the favored wood by polished walnut, mahogany, and rosewood *veneers*. Illustrated is a great clock of the period made of bois de rose and bois de violette marquetry with bronze doré trim.

FRENCH RESTORATION PERIOD

(1830–1870)   After the French monarchy was restored, the period included the reigns of Louis XVIII, Charles X, Louis-Philippe, and Napoleon III. Eclectic designs, cheaper machine production, and a general decline in taste marked this Second Empire period. See also, *Second Empire* or *Late Empire*.

FRENCH SEAM   An especially fine finish in tailoring and upholstering in which the raw edges of the fabric being sewn are folded inside two rows of stitching and completely covered.

FRENCH WHORL FOOT   A furniture foot that swirled or curled forward and often rested on a shoe. It most often appeared as the termination of a cabriole leg in the Régence and Louis XV periods.

FRENCH WINDOWS   A pair of multipaned doorlike windows which extend down to the floor, and, like hinged doors, are used for access to, or egress from, a room. They usually lead out onto a terrace, a balcony or other platform; or into a garden. A Louis XV interior with French windows is illustrated.

FRESCO   The Italian for fresh. A wall painting in a watercolor-like medium (tempera) on wet plaster. The cartoon (full-sized sketch) is drawn on the plaster surface. The damp plaster is painted with pigments mixed with water or lime water. The color dries lighter and becomes integrated into the wall or ceiling itself. Frescos were made in Italy in the 14th century, and perfected in the 16th century. Raphael's decoration in the Stanza of the Vatican is a fine fresco. Illustrated is the ceiling fresco by Raphael in the Farnesina in Rome.

FRESQUERA   A Spanish latticework or spindle-decorated hanging food cupboard.

FRENCH RÉGENCE

FRETWORK

FRIEZE

FRENCH WINDOWS

FRIEZE RAIL

FRESCO

FRINGE

The openwork on part of the cupboard door was for ventilation.

FRET   A border motif or geometric band of Greek origin. It is made up of interfacing and interlocking lines and forms. Also called "Chinese key" pattern or "meander."

FRETWORK   Ornamental woodwork cut to represent small interlacing fillets or trellis work. It is usually made in a complicated, repeating, geometric pattern. A favored technique of Chippendale in his Chinese period (mid-18th century).

FRETWORK MIRROR   See *Silhouette Mirror*.

FRIAR'S CHAIR   See *Frailero*.

FRIESIAN   A simple technique for carving with a chisel, usually used to create basic geometric forms. A popular technique in Colonial American woodwork. Also called Frisian.

FRIESLAND   A province in the Netherlands noted for its carved furniture in the baroque style in the 17th century.

FRIEZE   The central portion of the classic architectural entablature, located above the architrave and below the cornice. It usually has a flat surface embellished with decorative sculpture or carving. Also a painted or sculptured horizontal motif. Illustrated is the frieze of the monument of Lysicrates at Athens. In furniture, the underframing of a table between the top surface and the legs. See *Apron*.

FRIEZÉ or FRISÉ   A pile fabric with uncut loops which is sometimes patterned by shearing the loops at different levels. Usually made of wool, mohair, or heavy cotton. The term is from the French *frisé*, which means curled, and the fabric was originally made in Friesland, Holland. In carpet manufacture, rugs made of hardtwist, heavy, brushed wool yarns.

FRIEZE DRAWER   The top drawer of a chest which extends forward over the main body of the chest. It is usually supported by columns or pilasters. An Empire or Biedermeier early-19th-century design.

FRIEZE RAIL   In a door made up of three horizontal rows of panels, the horizontal rail between the middle and top set of panels. Illustrated is a doorway designed by Inigo Jones (early 17th century). See also *Picture Molding* or *Rail*.

FRINGE   An ornamental edging used to finish or trim drapery, upholstery, etc. A continuous band or ribbon with hanging twisted threads, loops, and tassels. It may be cut, looped, tassel, or Bullion fringe.

FRISÉ   See *Friezé or Frisé.*

FRISIAN   See *Friesian.*

FRONT   The front surface of a piece of furniture. The front may be a flat rectangle, or consist of several planes, bombé or bulging, serpentine, block or breakfront.

FROSTED GLASS   See *Etched Glass.*

FRUCHTGEHÄNGE   German for a painted or sculptured festoon of fruit.

FRUIT FESTOON   Garland of fruit, leaves, and flowers, tied with ribbons and usually draped between two rosettes to form a downward curve. A popular Roman motif, revived in the Renaissance.

FRUITWOOD   Wood from fruit-bearing trees like cherry, apple, pear, etc., largely used in provincial furniture. An 18th-century favorite which is having a revival currently in provincial and country-style furniture.

FRUITWOOD FINISH   A light, honey-brown finish applied to soft woods to simulate a fruitwood. The natural grain of the wood shows through this finish. The wood is often distressed.

FUMED OAK   A furniture finish of the late 19th and early 20th centuries. The oak wood was stained by ammonia fumes, and the graining became more pronounced and

FRUIT FESTOON

FUMED OAK

deeper in color. Much of the mission furniture was produced in fumed oak as well as late English Victorian pieces.

FUMEUSE   A smoking chair. An 18th-century variation on the Voyeuse. The broad crest rail on the narrow, shaped back of the chair often had compartments to hold tobacco, pipes, flints, etc., and the person straddled the chair, facing the chair back and the equipped rail. See *Cockfight Chair.*

FUNCTIONAL FURNITURE   Utilitarian furniture in which the function is most important and the aesthetics secondary.

FUR   The pelts or hairy skins of animals used for furniture and/or floor coverings.

FURRING   A method of finishing the inside of a masonry wall by either applying plaster directly to clay tiles or attaching metal or wood strips to a lathed wall. The purpose is to provide an air space for insulation, or to level the irregularities in the wall surface. It also prevents the transfer of moisture.

FUSTIAN   A sturdy cotton fabric with a suede or velvet-like pile. A twill-weave fabric.

FUSTIC   A light yellow wood from the West Indies. In the 17th and 18th centuries it was used for marquetry and inlay.

G

GABARDINE A hard-finished twill fabric with a steep diagonal effect to the twill. Produced of wool, cotton, rayon, or mixed fibers. The term is from the Spanish for protection against the elements.

GABLE The triangular space of wall enclosed at the end of a building by a sharply pitched roof.

GABOON A soft, straight-grained wood, golden to pinkish brown in color, used in Europe for plywood, furniture, and interior work. Light in weight and fairly strong. Native to the African west coast. See *Samara*.

GADROON From the French godron. A series of elongated egg or ovoid forms in a band. It is similar to a bead molding in that it projects above the surface it ornaments. When this type of decoration is used around a circular object, the oval form of ornament is called splayed gadroon. See *Nulling*.

GAINE A square post or pedestal which narrows and tapers toward the bottom. The gaine may be supported by human or animal feet. It is used as a decorative support or ornament, and is often topped with a head or bust. Illustrated is a Sheraton bookcase design of the early 19th century in the Regency style. Note the use of gaines for free columns to support the frieze, and on the front ends of the base.

GALLERIES The metal rods and supports at the back of sideboards of the late 18th century in England. Also the raised metal or carved rims around tabletops or servers.

GALLERY A wide corridor walled in on one side only, and usually located on the upper story. In furniture, the miniature

GAME TABLE

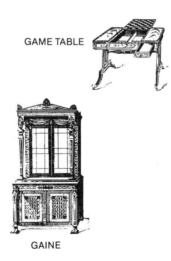

GAINE

metal or wood railing along the edge of a shelf or tabletop, as in gallery-top tables.

GALLOON or GALON A narrow, closely woven braid used for trimming draperies and upholstery. Frequently used in the early 18th century to finish off rough upholstery work. A lace or embroidered band with a scalloped edge on two sides is also called a galloon. See *Guimpe*.

GALVANIZED IRON A zinc-coated iron. The coating process makes the iron rust-resistant.

GAME TABLE Table devised for particular card games, chess, etc. Also called a card table, or by the specific name of the game to be played, like "bridge table." A Sheraton chess table is illustrated

GARDE DU VIN A Hepplewhite term for a cellarette. See *Cellarette*.

GARDE-MANGER A French term for a food cupboard; a larder or cupboard.

GARDEN APARTMENT A multiple dwelling, usually two stories high, and set in a landscaped area in a suburban residential area.

GARDEN SEAT An Oriental or Chinese outdoor seat made in the shape of a small keg, barrel, or drum. Originally these pieces were carved of stone, and then they were produced in porcelain. Still later they were made with a lattice-like wooden center part but with a solid top and bottom

GARDE-ROBE A wardrobe or armoire. Illustrated is a 16th-century Flemish garde-robe.

GARGOYLE In Gothic architecture, a rainspout which often was decoratively

GARDE-ROBE

carved as a fantastic human or animal head, and ornamentally placed along the top of a parapet or roof. The term is from the Old French for throat. Also, an ornament in the shape of such a head.

GARLAND A wreath or circlet of leaves, flowers, and/or fruit with ribbon ties, used as a carved or painted decoration on furniture.

GARNITURE Any motif used for enriching a surface or area. The embellishing or decorating may be painted, carved, inlaid, applied, etc.

GARRETING A surface finish of small stones or pebbles pressed into a mortar joint while it is still soft.

GARRETT From the Old French for place of refuge or lookout. A room constructed in the roof of a building. An attic.

GATCH An Oriental term for decorative elements made in molded plaster. See *Anaglypta* and *Carton-Pierre*.

GATELEG TABLE A drop-leaf table with oval or rounded ends. The leaves are supported by single or double wing legs or gates. It was introduced in mid-17th-century Jacobean furniture and was popular in Colonial America. See *Eight-Legged Table, Folding Table,* and *Thousand-Leg Table.*

GAUDÍ i CORNET, ANTONIO (1852–1926) A noted Spanish architect who created unique architectural forms in keeping with the "Art-Nouveau" or "modernismo" style of the times. In some of his sculpture-type architecture he introduced color and odd bits of materials which achieved effects similar to abstract expressionism and surrealism. Gaudí was a spirited innovator, and favored the hyperbolic paraboloid form. The Expiatory Church of the Holy Family (1882–1930) represents the culmination of his techniques and ideals. Other works by Gaudí are: structures in the Park Güel, the undulating façades of the Casa Battló, and the Casa Milá.

GAUDREAUX An 18th-century French furniture maker in the Louis XV style. His pieces were often designed by the Slodtz brothers, and lavishly embellished with gilt bronze trim. Oval medallions with gilt bronze bas-reliefs on blue enamel grounds were sometimes used for ornamenting Gaudreaux's furniture.

GAUGE The thickness of a material.

GAUZE Thin, transparent fabric made of a netlike or plain weave, or combination of the two, originated in Gaza, Palestine. Gauze can be made of silk, cotton, linen, wool, synthetic fibers, or combinations. It is often used for *Glass Curtains.*

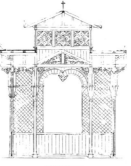

GAZEBO

GATELEG TABLE

GEORGIAN

GRINLING GIBBONS

GAUZE, THEATRICAL A semitransparent loosely woven cotton or linen fabric with a shimmering appearance.

GAZEBO The turret on the roof of a lattice-constructed garden house, or the entire structure. An ornamental, open summerhouse.

GELOSIA Italian for Venetian blind. See *Jalousies.*

GENERAL LIGHTING The overall lighting plan that is used to create a virtually shadowless interior, covering area with an even level of illumination. See *Secondary Lighting.*

GENOA VELVET A multicolored patterned velvet on a satin ground.

GEOMETRIC DESIGNS Designs or ornaments based on the repeated use of mechanically drawn forms like circles, squares, and triangles.

GEORGIAN The reigns of the Georges in England (1714 to the Regency, approximately 1811). The golden period of furniture design and architecture: Adam brothers, Chippendale, Shearer, Hepplewhite, Sheraton, etc. An early Georgian chair of the first part of the 18th century is illustrated. It has the typical pierced urn splat, cabriole legs with shell carvings on the knees, and ball-and-claw feet. Usually divided into three separate periods: Early Georgian, 1714–1750; Middle Georgian, 1750–1770; and Late Georgian, 1770–1810.

GERMAN SILVER An alloy of copper, nickel, and zinc.

GESSO A dense and brilliant white coating of gypsum or plaster with a high degree of absorbency used as a ground for tempera painting. The panels to be painted are treated with several coats of gesso and size. Also, a plaster-like composition molded to form a raised or bas-relief applied ornament on walls, furniture, frames, moldings, etc., often painted and gilded. See *Anaglypta, Carton-Pierre,* and *Composition Ornament.*

GEWIRKTER TEPPICH or TAPETE German for tapestry or arras.

GHIORDES KNOT One of the two traditional knots used for hand-tying pile yarn in Oriental Rugs, over two warp threads and up between them. Also called the *Turkish Knot.* See also *Sehna Knot.*

GIBBONS, GRINLING (1648–1721) An English master woodcarver and sculptor. He worked in close association with Sir Christopher Wren, and he created many famous carved trophy panels and mantels.

Gibbons did much of the sculptured embellishment for the choir in St. Paul's Cathedral, as well as the dimensional foliage and festoons of the stalls. He worked mainly in limewoods, used oak for church panels and moldings, and occasionally cedar for architraves. Medallion portraits were sometimes carved of pearwood or boxwood. Gibbons sculptured realistically in high relief, with deep undercuts, and his motifs included fruit, vegetables, game, fish, leaves, and flowers created into swags, festoons, draperies, and frames.

GIBBS, JAMES (1683–1754) An English architect and furniture designer in the tradition of Sir Christopher Wren. He created, in the first part of the 18th century, many interior features such as mantels, as well as furniture. Gibbs is probably most known for St. Martin's-in-the-Fields in London (1721–1726), which is here illustrated.

GIGLIO An Italian word for a decorative element similar to a fleur de lis, usually associated with Florence, Italy.

GILDED or GILT FURNITURE Furniture finished by gilding, an early-17th-century finish adopted in England during the early Queen Anne period, and also in France. William Kent was a leading designer of English gilt furniture. Illustrated is a Louis XV carved gilt console table. See also *Gilding*.

GILDED LEATHER A popular treatment for leather hangings from the 16th through the 18th centuries. The leather was sized, then covered with gold or silver leaf. Areas of the leather were then colored in lacquer. Sometimes the surface was tooled or embossed with chisels or patterned punches called irons. Tiny roses, rosettes, squares, circles, arabesques and heraldic motifs were popular designs. The Dutch during the 17th century often used colored grounds, and bronzed or gilded fruits and cherubs in bold relief. The English favored chinoiserie motifs. See also *Cordovan Leather*, *Guadamicil*, and *Moroccan (Maroquin) Tapestries*.

GILDING The art of ornamenting furniture, accessories, and architectural details with gold leaf or gold dust. Illustrated is a mid-18th-century gilded frame (English).

GILLINGHAM, JAMES A Philadelphia cabinetmaker of the mid-18th century.

GILLOT, CLAUDE (1673–1722) A French painter and designer of fauns, satyrs, and grotesques during the period of Louis XIV. He was the teacher of Watteau.

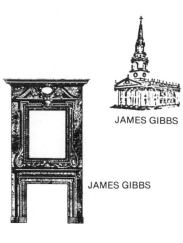

JAMES GIBBS

JAMES GIBBS

GILDED FURNITURE

FRANÇOIS GIRARDON

GILDING

GIRDER

GILLOW, RICHARD and ROBERT Furniture makers in the first half of the 18th century in England. Much of the furniture and cabinetwork produced by the Gillows was exported to the West Indies.

GIMP or GUIMPE Originally a woven silk braid of assorted designs. A binding material used on the outer edges of upholstered furniture to cover fabric joins or upholstery tacks, or as an enrichment. Gimp is also used as a trim on draperies, bedspreads, etc.

GINGHAM A lightweight, yarn-dyed, cotton material woven in checks or stripes.

GIOTTO DI BONDONE (c. 1270–1337) A Florentine painter who broke with the stereotyped forms of Italo-Byzantine art. He brought humanism into his work, as well as a degree of naturalism. Giotto is also known as an architect. His "Bell Tower" is particularly well known. He greatly influenced not only his contemporaries (the Giotteschi school of painting) but also Masaccio and Michelangelo.

GIRANDOLE A multibranched wall sconce to hold candles, which is often mirrored. A late-17th- and 18th-century accessory and lighting device. When lit, it seemed to have the sparkle and shimmer of fireworks. In the 19th century, the term described a circular mirror, often convex, with or without a candle sconce. In American designs, the mirror was often capped with an eagle. In the mid-19th century, a girandole was a Bohemian glass, prism-hung candlestick, often used in pairs on mantels. See *Applique* and *Bull's Eye Mirror*. Also any branched candlestick.

GIRARDON, FRANÇOIS (1628–1715) A French sculptor whose work was used to enhance the Louvre, Grand Trianon, and Versailles. Illustrated is a war trophy by Girardon, now in the park at Versailles.

GIRDER A heavy beam used over wide spans, and supporting small beams or concentrated weights. Illustrated is a late-19th-century interior showing iron girders and columns which were designed to support a vaulted ceiling.

GLASS BRICK A hollow block, composed of two halves of molded soda-lime glass. The pieces are sealed together with a vacuum between, and can then be mortared together into wall units.

GLASS CURTAINS Curtains made of sheer, semitransparent fabrics which hang against a windowpane or glass surface. They may be used with blinds or shades, or be overhung with draperies.

GLASTONBURY CHAIR A 16th-century ecclesiastic chair with X-shaped legs and sloping arms and back.

GLAZE In pottery, a thin coating of glass fired on pottery to give it a glossy appearance, or to color it.

GLAZED CHINTZ A chintz or plain colored fabric given a crisp feel and a sheen by means of calendering or by being paraffin-treated. See *Calendering.*

GLAZED DOOR A door made up of panes of glass framed in wood molding strips, similar to a French door. In furniture, cabinet, secretary, bookcase, etc., doors made of glass panes held together in a decorative framework of wood strips. A Chippendale mahogany bookcase is shown.

GLAZING In fabrics, a method of giving a smooth, high-polished finish to fabrics like chintz or tarletan. The fabrics can be treated with starch, glue, shellac, or parafin, and then run between hot friction rollers. The finish will not withstand washings unless synthetic resin or something similar is baked in at high temperatures.

GLAZING BARS The wood or metal strips which form the framework around individual panes of glass in a window or door. Also called *Muntins.*

GLOBE STAND A favored 18th-century accessory. It was usually a carved tripod made to hold a rotating globe of the world. Smaller stands were made to stand on tables or desks, and larger units were made to stand on the floor.

GLYPH A shallow, vertical groove, cut into a flat or carved surface. A form of fluting. Glyphs are often found in classic Doric architecture. See *Triglyphs.*

GOBELINS A tapestry factory started in Paris in the 16th century by a family of dyers named Gobelin. Louis XIV, in 1662, purchased the factory, and Charles Le Brun was made chief designer and director of the art-producing plant which now turned out textiles, metalwork, silverwork, wood carvings and frescoes, as well as tapestries. During this period the Savonnerie rug factory was combined with the Gobelins. Among the famous artists and artisans who worked at the Manufacture Nationale des Gobelins are the following: Marc de Coomans, François Delaplanche, Laurent Guyot, Guillaume Dumée, Antoine Caron, Simon Vouet, Michel Corneille, Eustache Le Sueur, Nicholas Poussin, Philippe de Champaigne, Louis and Charles Le Brun, Antoine and Charles Coypel, Pierre Mignard, Jean-François de Troy, Louis de Boulogne, François Desportes, several members of the Audran family, and the Anguiers.

GLASTONBURY CHAIR

GLAZED DOOR

JOHN GODDARD

GLAZING BAR

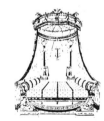

GONDOLA BED

GOBELINS

GODDARD, JOHN (1724–1785) An American designer and cabinetmaker in Newport, Rhode Island. He produced, in association with his son-in-law John Townsend, a particular type of blockfront desk, secretary, and cabinet, usually with ogee bracket feet and shell ornaments. See *Blockfront.*

GODROON See *Gadroon.*

GOING The horizontal distance between one riser face and the next, in stairway construction.

GOLD LEAF Also called mosaic gold or Dutch gold. Originally, it was made in Germany, and was an amalgam of tin and copper. The bright, shiny, thin sheet is laid over the surface which has been made tacky by a shellac, adhesive, or gold size. The sheet adheres to the sized surface. See *Gilding.*

GOLD PLATING A process whereby particles of gold are made to coat a baser metal unit, usually accomplished electrolitically.

GOLDEN OAK Very early 20th-century furniture similar to the Mission Style. It is basically heavy, rather clumsy and Empire inspired with many of the pieces resembling the designs of Charles L. Eastlake, Jr. Large round, massive pedestal tables are typical. See *Eastlake and Mission Style.*

GONÇALO ALVES Also called bossona. A Brazilian wood with a decided black and brown streak on a red-brown ground. It is hard and horny and sometimes develops surface cracks.

GONDOLA BED A 19th-century Empire bed with foot and head boards which appear to scroll or roll over like the ends of a gondola. See *Boat Bed* and *Sleigh Bed.*

GONDOLA CHAIR A low chair for a writing desk, or a sofa whose back curves downward to form the arms. The sweeping, curving line resembles an 18th-century gondola.

GOODISON, BENJAMIN An 18th-century furniture maker to the English royalty from 1727 to 1767.

GOOSENECK A double-curved pediment popular in 18th-century English and American furniture. It is also referred to as broken arch or swan neck. See *Swan Neck Pediment.*

GOOSENECK LAMP A light fixture with a metal pipe shaft constructed to be flexible and bendable. It is possible to alter the direction of the beam of light by twisting the corrugated pipe right or left, up or down.

GOSTELOWE, JONATHAN (1744–1806) An American cabinet-maker who worked in Philadelphia, Pennsylvania, in the Chippendale style. He produced many fine mahogany pieces.

GOTHIC PERIOD The period from approximately 1150 to 1500 in Europe. The only European architectural style not based on classical forms, it is an outstanding period of ecclesiastic architecture and art. Named by the Italians, who preferred Greek and Roman architecture, and assumed that only German barbarians (the Goths) could admire such a style. The Gothic period is also referred to as the Middle Ages.

GOTHIC REVIVAL See *Romantic Epoch*. The renewed interest in Gothic architecture and art forms during the early 19th century in England and on the Continent. John Britton's *The Architectural Antiquities and Cathedrals of Britain* and Sir Walter Scott's novels helped foster this interest in the medieval period. Augustus Welby Pugin was the great architect and advocate of the Gothic revival in England. He erected 65 churches in the Gothic Style. He decorated the interior and exterior of the Houses of Parliament, London, which was influential in popularizing this revival.

GOTICO Italian for Gothic.

GOUACHE An opaque watercolor paint like poster paint. It dries much lighter than it appears when wet. Gouache is an art medium, as well as a technique for making studies for oil paintings. It was a popular painting technique in the 18th century. *Tempera* is the Italian term for gouache.

GOUJON, JEAN (1510–1566) A French architect and sculptor. He did reliefs in the Louvre, including some on the exterior and some figures, and the caryatids of the gallery "Salle des Caryatides." He created elongated, elegant figures, somewhat influenced by classic forms. Attributed to him is "Diana the Huntress," made for the courtyard of the Château of Diane de Poitiers. Illustrated is a bas-relief by Goujon for the Hôtel Carnavalet in Paris. See *Bas-Relief* for panels designed by Goujon.

GOUT CHAIR An 18th-century chair devised for sufferers from the gout. The footstool could be pulled out from below the seat, so that the affected leg could rest on it in an extended, straight-out position. When not in use, the trundle-like footrest could be pushed back into the sea-trail.

PIERRE GOUTHIÈRE

GOUTY STOOL

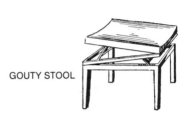
GOVERNOR WINTHROP DESK

JEAN GOUJON

GRAND MIRROR À LA PSYCHÉ

GRANDFATHER CHAIR

GOUTHIÈRE, PIERRE (1740–1806) A notable French designer of exquisite ormolu mounts for Louis XVI period furniture. He also created mountings of great refinement and delicacy for vases of jasper, Sèvres, and Oriental porcelains, as well as designs for clocks and candelabras. Illustrated is a cylinder secrétaire of the Louis XVI period with ormolu mountings by Gouthière. See *Bureau Plat*.

GOUTY STOOL A leg rest with an adjustable top for the support of gout-afflicted legs. An 18th-century English design.

GOVERNOR WINTHROP DESK A typical fall-front desk of Colonial America (c. 1750), concurrent with Chippendale's designs in England. The piece has two to four graduated drawers running the width of the desk with bat-wing or willow brasses. Usually supported by bracket feet. The interior was an arrangement of arcaded pigeonholes, with a single or double tier of small drawers beneath. The assorted governors called Winthrop, and there were several, actually lived in the 17th century, so the name is confusing.

GRADIN See *Table à Gradin*.

GRAFFITO WARE Heavy pottery decorated with a primitively scratched or scribed design. See *Sgraffito*.

GRAIN In wood, the fiber lines. The figure or pattern inherent in the wood, the product of annual growth rings. The cells and pores of the tree.

GRAINED FURNITURE Late-19th-century cheap furniture, dark in color, which was painted and artificially grained to simulate oak wood. See *Graining*.

GRAINING A painted imitation of the grain of wood. Often the grain of an expensive or rare wood is simulated on a less expensive or plain painted surface.

GRAND MIROIR À LA PSYCHÉ Also called a psyche. A tall Empire pier mirror which stood on the floor and could be tilted forward or back. A German Empire version with candle brackets is illustrated. See *Pier Glasses*.

GRAND RAPIDS, MICHIGAN A furniture-manufacturing city for over a century. Popularly priced furniture is mass-produced in this area.

GRANDFATHER CHAIR A large, roomy, upholstered chair developed from the 17th-century wing chair. It was particularly popular in the Queen Anne period.

GRANDFATHER (long case) CLOCK A floor-standing clock with a wood case which consists of a hood, a waist, and a base. The pendulum and the weights are protected inside the clock which usually stands over six feet high. It was introduced into England after the Restoration, and became extremely popular during the 18th century.

GRANDMOTHER CLOCK A smaller-scaled and more refined version of the grandfather clock. See *Grandfather (long case) Clock.*

GRANITE The hardest and most durable of building stones. A granular crystalline rock of quartz, feldspar, and mica.

GRAPHIC ARTS The arts of drawing, engraving, etching, block-printing, and painting.

GRASS CLOTH A wall-covering material glued onto a paper or fabric backing. It is woven of coarse vegetable fibers creating a strong horizontal effect and a nubby, irregular texture. Grass cloth may be simulated as a printed, embossed paper cloth, or vinyl material.

GRASS MATS Rugs of assorted shapes and sizes made of long blades of grass braided and/or woven into either lacy openwork patterns or close weaves. Produced in geometric patterns or florals in assorted natural colors or trimmed with especially dyed grasses.

GRATING See *Grille.*

GRAY GOODS Cloths as they come from the loom without either wet or dry finishing, before dyeing is begun. In the silk and rayon industries, this material is called "greige goods."

GREAT HALL In the medieval castle, the large, two-storied central hall used for dining and entertainment.

GREAT MONAD or OVUM MUNDI A circle with a horizontal S shape dividing it into two equal areas which represent the union of basic principles: the material and the spiritual, or the feminine and the masculine. Similar to the Chinese symbol for Yin and Yang.

GRECIAN SOFA Another name for an Empire couch. Illustrated is an early-19th-century Sheraton design. The head part is higher. It rolls over, as does the lower or foot end. See *Récamier.*

GRECO, EL (Domenikos Theotocopoulos) (c. 1541–1614) A Greek artist who worked in Spain. His work has an ecstatic and passionate quality, a personal blending of the traditions of Titian, Michelangelo, Dürer, and his own Byzantine background. His very personal relation to his work and his mysticism are recorded in

GRANDFATHER CLOCK

GREEK REVIVAL

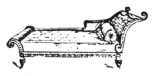

GRECIAN SOFA

GRIFFIN

GRILLE

the elongation of the limbs, the tense figures, the sharp color contrasts, and the draperies that seem to have a movement of their own. Among his best known works is "A View of Toledo."

GRECO-ROMAN The classic style from about 200 B.C. to A.D. 200. Its Romanized Greek forms such as were unearthed in Pompeii and Herculaneum are the basis of the 18th-century classic style of the Adam brothers and the Louis XVI period.

GREEK CROSS Two lines of equal length bisecting each other at their centers.

GREEK KEY A fret design. A continuous band decoration of interlacing, hooked squares.

GREEK REVIVAL A renewed interest in Greek art and architecture in the 18th and 19th centuries. It affected the Directoire, English Regency, and Empire styles.

GREER, MICHAEL A 20th-century interior designer.

GREIGE A neutral grayish-beige color.

GREIGE GOODS See *Gray Goods.*

GRENADINE A leno-weave fabric like marquisette, but finer in texture. It is either plain, or woven with dots or figures, and is made of silk and cotton, silk and wool, or all cotton.

GRENDEY, GILES (1693–1780) An English furniture maker and exporter of simple, domestic Georgian furniture, much of which was japanned.

GRENFELL CLOTH A closely woven, waterproof, windproof fabric. A sturdy twill weave.

GRESE, GRECE, GRYCE Medieval terms for "step."

GREYWOOD Artificially dyed English harewood, or, in America, dyed maple wood.

GRIFFIN A decorative device in the shape of a monster with the body of a lion and the head and wings of an eagle. In antiquity, the griffin was associated with fire, and thus often appears on friezes with candelabras. In heraldry, the griffin represents wisdom and watchfulness. Popular in Gothic architecture. The Adam brothers and later Empire-style designers also used it.

GRILLE A metal, usually brass, lattice or trellis used in place of glass on cabinet doors, etc. Adam and Hepplewhite made extensive use of this textural device. Often rosettes and other ornaments were added on the intersections of the crisscrossing wires or rods. A late-18th-century Sheraton design is illustrated.

GRIS TRIANON A soft, grayish, off-white color found on late 18th-century French painted furniture. See *Blanc de Plomb.*

GRISAILLE A monochromatic painting in neutral grays or beiges only, which gives the effect of a sculptured relief panel. Popular as a trompe l'oeil painting technique for overdoors or overmantels in the Louis XVI period. Piat Joseph Sauvage was an outstanding painter of the time in that technique. The grisaille may also serve as a first stage for an oil painting, or it may serve as a model for an engraver. Adam, Sheraton, and Hepplewhite used grisaille medallions and plaques to enhance their furniture. Angelica Kauffmann and Giovanni Battista Cipriani painted in this style.

GROIN The curved, sharp edge which is formed by the meeting of two vaulted surfaces.

GROIN RIB An exposed rib which follows the line of the groin on a vaulted surface. See *Rib.*

GROOVE AND RABBET JOINT See *Barefaced Tongue Joint.*

GROPIUS, WALTER Born in 1883. A 20th-century architect and founder of the Bauhaus in Weimar. In 1909, Gropius worked out a memorandum on standardization and mass production of small houses. He became the head of the Staatliches Bauhaus in 1919, an Academy of Art, which became the creative center of Europe at that time. It was a community of architects, painters, and craftsmen working in a new spirit in this combination school-workshop. Gropius, along with *Marcel Lajos Breuer,* is responsible for a distinct modern New England style of domestic architecture which blends white wood frames and fieldstone fireplaces with sophisticated German details of the 1920's. His great influence as an architect and educator has been in the field of medium-priced private homes.

GROS POINT A coarse tapestry effect produced by using cross-stitching through net, canvas, or coarse linen. The embroidery threads are usually woolen and there are approximately twelve stitches to the lineal inch.

GROSGRAIN Ribbed or rep silk. The cords are close together and rounder than those of faille. It is used for draperies and ribbon decorations.

GROTESQUES (GROTTESQUES) Decorations in antiquity like sphinxes, masks, or fantastic monsters which com-

GRISAILLE

GROIN RIB

GUADAMICIL

GUÉRIDON

bined human with plant and animal forms in a free manner: winged females, mermaids, etc. These classic ornaments were rediscovered in grottos, hence the name. Raphael was one of the first Renaissance artists to make use of them.

GROTTO A cave or recess, natural or artificial.

GROUND The rough wood framing on or in a wall, upon which paneling is applied.

GROUND COLOR The background color of a fabric, wallpaper, carpet, etc., upon which other colors (the top colors) are applied. In screened or printed materials, the background color is the ground color, and the design may be produced in one or more top colors.

GROUT A liquid-like mortar or concrete which dries hard and solid, and is used as a filler or fixing agent for tiles and mosaics, and between blocks of stones, etc.

GROUTITE A finer mortar than grout, used for small mosaic work like contemporary tabletops, plaques, decorative accessories, etc.

GUADAMICIL A leather "tapestry" or decorated hanging. The technique was introduced into Europe in the 11th century by the Arabs from Morocco. Leather decorated in this way was first produced in Guadamicileria, Spain, in the 16th century. In the 17th and 18th centuries, leather tapestries were produced in France, the Netherlands, England, Germany, and Italy under such names as Cordovan or Moroccan (Maroquin) tapestries. Illustrated is an early-17th-century Spanish chair of carved walnut with embossed leather covering. See *Gilded Leather.*

GUANACASTE A tropical hardwood. See *Kelobra.*

GUÉRIDON A small ornamental stand or pedestal. A little round table popular in the late Queen Anne period, adopted from France, where it appeared during the reign of Louis XIII. In the Chippendale design shown, it is also used as a candlestand. See *Torchère.*

GUÉRIDON À CRÉMAILLIÈRE A small round table or candleholder of the Louis XVI period. Its main feature was that it could be adjusted to various heights by means of a toothed (crémaillière) support which set into three supporting feet. The table usually was made of mahogany and had a marble top and a gilt brass gallery.

GUERITE The French word for sentry box. A high-backed, hooded armchair which enveloped the seated person and also kept out the draughts. In the 18th century it was interpreted in wicker, and the design became a popular piece of garden furniture. Today this piece of wicker furniture is seen on the beaches of French and Italian resorts.

GUILLOCHE   A geometric classic band or border pattern of overlapping or interlacing circular forms. The circles are sometimes filled with ornamental designs. Much used in Renaissance and Victorian Renaissance furniture.

GUIMARD, HECTOR (1867–1942)   A French architect and furniture designer. Greatly influenced by Victor Horta, he became the French interpreter of the art nouveau style. One of his most noted pieces in this style is the entrance gate to the Métro stations in Paris. The cast iron has been shaped into elegant, twisted, curving, flowerlike forms. In 1938, Guimard moved to New York. See *Horta, (Baron) Victor.*

GUIMPE   See *Gimp* or *Guimpe.*

GUINEA HOLES or POCKETS
Dished or scooped-out areas in a gaming table to hold money or chips, an 18th-century English device. See *Dished.*

GUMWOOD   A pink to reddish-brown wood of a heavy, strong texture. It has a wild figure with pleasing contrasts. It is possible to get a ribbon stripe veneer if the wood is quarter-cut. The heartwood, or red

GUILLOCHE

GUILLOCHE

GUNSTON HALL

GUINEA HOLES

gum, is used for cabinetmaking, and architecturally inside and outside the house. The sapwood is called "sap gum" and is not as durable; it is used for plywood and furniture lumber, and for woodwork that gets a painted finish.

GUNSTON HALL   Built in 1755, near Mount Vernon, for George Mason. William Buckland was brought from England to create and supervise the magnificent woodwork for this house. The Chippendale dining room was the first in the Colonies done in the "Chinese style." The drawing room is Palladian in concept. See *Buckland, William.*

GUSSET   A triangular insert between two pieces of fabric, to enlarge or strengthen the whole structure.

GYPSUM   Hydrous calcium sulfate which is used in making plaster of Paris.

GYPSUM BOARD   A wallboard material with a core of processed gypsum rock, encased in a tough, heavyweight paper. The smooth paper surface can then be treated with paint, wallpaper, etc., after it has been primed with a primer sealer or varnish. Comes in various thicknesses (¼″ to ½″) and can be obtained with square, tapered or beveled edges. The panels are usually 4′ to 8′ tall.

GYRO CHAIR   See *Aarnio, Eero.*

H

H HINGE An H-shaped hinge with one upright attached to the jamb, and the other upright attached to the door. The horizontal piece works as a pivot. It is similar to an HL hinge.

H STRETCHER A reinforcing element for chair, table, and case furniture legs. A wooden piece, or turning, connects each front leg with the leg immediately behind it. A crosspiece from one of these connecting pieces to the other forms an H. A Chinese Chippendale chair is illustrated.

HABILLÉE An art appliqué form in which actual pieces of fabric, lace, etc., are pasted onto a picture. These textures and materials are used to represent clothing, drapery, upholstery, etc.

HACKBERRY A native American wood which resembles the elm. Its light, natural yellowish color stains and finishes well.

HADLEY CHEST An early American (c. 1700), New England chest on four legs. The chest had one, two, or three drawers, and would vary in height (according to the number of drawers) from 32″ to 46″. These units were decorated with simple incised carvings, and stained red, mulberry, or black. The owner's initials were often carved on the central panel. The top, body of drawers, and back were usually made of pinewood.

HAIG, THOMAS An 18th-century English cabinetmaker, and partner of Thomas Chippendale II.

HAIRCLOTH A stiff, wiry fabric made of cotton with a horsehair, mohair, or human hair filling, woven plain, striped, or with small patterns. Very durable, but is usually woven in narrow widths. Popular for upholstery in mid-19th-century England

H STRETCHER

HALF TIMBER

HALF-HEADED BED

HALL CHAIR

and America and used today for interlining and stiffening.

HALF COLUMN A rounded pilaster or a column partially engaged in a wall. See *Engaged Column*.

HALF TIMBER A form of Gothic house construction in which the heavy beams and posts form the visible skeleton on the interior as well as the exterior. The areas between the wood construction were filled with wattle and daub, plaster, stone or brick. Illustrated is a 15th-century dwelling in Rouen. See *Pane* for an illustration of a 13th century example.

HALF TURNING See *Split Spindle*.

HALF-HEADED BED A bed with short posts at the four ends and no canopy.

HALFPENNY, WILLIAM An 18th-century English carpenter and architect who helped popularize the Chinese trend in architecture and decoration. In collaboration with his son, he published many books during the early part of the 18th century, including *The Modern Builder's Assistant* and *New Design for Chinese Temples, Triumphal Arches, Garden Seats, Railings, etc.* A pig-tailed Chinese mandarin, with umbrella, often was crowded into his ceilings, over chimneypieces, etc.

HALF-ROUND SLICING VENEER A method similar to the rotary method for cutting veneers from the log. The slicing goes slightly across the annual growth rings, producing a wavy look.

HALFTONE A color halfway between white and black in tonal value.

HALL CHAIRS 18th-century English formal chairs, usually with decorative backs, originated by Manwaring and also designed by Chippendale and Sheraton. A late-18th-century Sheraton design is illustrated. See *Light Chair* and *Side Chair*.

HALL CLOCK See *Grandfather (long case) Clock*. A Sheraton-style case clock of the 18th century is illustrated.

HALL TREE. A hat and/or coat rack made of metal or wood turnings. It is a floor-standing unit with upturned arms at the top to hold hats and coats.

HALLET, WILLIAM (1707–1781) A cabinetmaker under *George II*.

HALLMARK The mark or stamp of official approval of a standard of purity, originally from the Goldsmith's Company of London. Now a mark of quality or genuineness that usually appears on metalwork.

HALVED JOINT A joint formed by two pieces of wood, the end of each sunk to half its depth. They are placed at right angles to each other; thus the projection of one fits into the sinking or groove of the other. This method is called "halving in."

HAMMER BRACE The curved vertical member which supports a hammer beam. See *B* on *Hammer-Beam Roof* illustration.

HAMMER-BEAM ROOF A Gothic form of roof construction in which the rafters are supported by a horizontal beam which projects from the wall but does not join up with the corresponding projections from the opposite wall. The hammer beam is marked A.

HAMMER-BEAM TRUSS An early English Renaissance form of roof support. A Tudor arch form in wood, each end of which rested on a large wooden bracket which was usually carved.

HAND The "feel" of the fabric, the resilience, flexibility, and drapability of the fabric. The finish of the goods affects the hand. See *Finish*.

HAND BLOCKING A method of printing a design on a surface. A design is carved or incised on a wood, linoleum, or other type of block. The flat surface is the design; the gouged-out areas will not print. Paint or dye is rolled on the surface of the block, and then pressure is exerted on the block as it makes its imprint.

HAND PRINTS Wallpapers, murals, fabrics, accessories, etc., produced by a hand-screening rather than a machine process.

HAND SCREENING A silk-screen process for applying colored decorations, designs, or artwork to paper, fabrics, vinyls,

HALL CLOCK

HANDLE

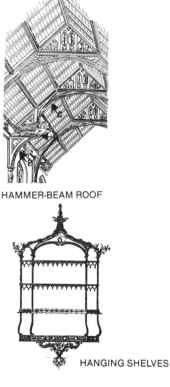

HALVED JOINT

HANDLE

HAMMER-BEAM ROOF

HANGING SHELVES

HANGING

wood, or other materials. The design is prepared on one or several (depending upon the number of colors in the design) fine silk screens in wood frames. The silk is covered with a fine, non-porous film, and the film is cut away in those areas where the design will be printed. A roller or squeegee is rolled in paint, and then rolled or spread over the screen which is set down on the material that is to be printed. The paint goes through only the fine silk mesh where the film has been cut away. Each color requires a separate screen. Each succeeding screen, as it is laid down, must be lined up true to the previous screens so that the various colored areas set in next to one another properly, and create the intended design.

HANDKERCHIEF TABLE A triangular table, designed to fit into the corner of a room. A second triangular top is hinged on so that when this second triangle is flipped back, a rectangular table surface results.

HANDLES Knobs or pulls used on furniture. In the Jacobean period in England, wood turnings and wrought iron were favored. Brass handles were introduced into England during the William and Mary period. In France, mounts and handles were chased and engraved and made of ormolu, and were often works of art. The ring hanging from the lion's mouth was one of Sheraton's favorite handle designs (see *Hardware*).

HANDRAIL The top rail into which the tops of the banisters are usually set. It follows the incline of the stairs, and serves as a support for persons walking up or down the stairs.

HANGING SHELVES Wall-attached units used for the display of books, plates, and china collections. Very popular in the late 17th and through the 18th century in France and England. Chippendale designed Chinese or Gothic types (see illustration). In the 19th-century Victorian period, hanging whatnots or knickknack shelves were the vogue.

HANGINGS Draperies on tester beds or window curtains and draperies. Also wall tapestries or arras. The fabric embellishment may be made of damask, brocade, cotton, linen, wool, leather, etc. A 16th-century wall hanging from the Palace of Fontainebleau is illustrated. See *Arras*, *Guadamicil*, and *Wachstuch-Tapete*.

HARD CORE A rubble filling placed under a concrete ground floor and directly over the ground. It prevents the damp or moisture from rising.

HARD PASTE   True porcelain made of kaolin or China clay.

HARDOUIN-MANSART, JULES (1646–1708) French architect who took over from Louis Le Vau the work on Versailles after 1679. He is credited with creating the Hall of Mirrors.

HARDOY CHAIR   A 20th-century version of the folding wood and canvas Italian officer's chair. Made of metal (noncollapsible) and canvas and originally manufactured and sold by Knoll Associates, Inc., in 1947, designed by Hardoy.

HARDWARE   In cabinetry, metal handles, pulls, escutcheons, hinges, decorative push plates, etc. Also called mounts.

HARDWOOD   A general term for the lumber of broad-leafed trees, in contrast to the conifers, which are termed softwoods. The name has no real connection with the hardness of the wood. The furniture hardwoods are porous, and include oak, walnut, mahogany, beech, maple, and gum.

HAREWOOD   A creamy white wood (English sycamore) which dyes a silvery gray. It has a close, curly figure and a dense grain with a tendency to lose the dye on exposure to strong light. Plain, curly, fiddleback, finger roll, or heavy crossfire figures are all possible in Harewood veneer depending upon the slicing method. Harewood is used in cabinetwork, and will turn a grayish green when stained with oxide of iron.

HARICOT   French for kidney bean. A small crescent- or bean-shaped Louis XV table with cabriole legs and small drawers set into the curved apron.

HARLEQUIN TABLE   A gadgety, complicated dressing-writing table, of the end of the 18th century. It was designed with hidden compartments, pigeonholes, small drawers, etc. Sheraton and Shearer both designed these pieces.

HARMONIUM   A small reed organ with one or two rows of keys or bellows controlled or pedaled by foot. A French early-19th-century invention ascribed to Alexander Debain.

HARP   A triangular instrument played by plucking its strings; stands on a heavy base with pedals that influence the tone. An Italian Renaissance example is illustrated. In furniture, the shaped metal piece which extends up from the lamp base, and to which the lampshade is affixed. The harp is usually bowed in the center to allow the bulb to be screwed inside the socket to which the harp is attached.

HARPSICHORD   A piano-like instrument which preceded the pianoforte of the

HARDWARE

HASP

HARLEQUIN TABLE

HARP

HATCHING

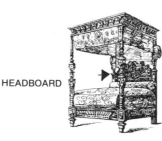

HEADBOARD

18th century. The strings are plucked by means of quills attached to levers. It works on the same principle as the spinet and virginal.

HARRATEEN   An 18th-century woven curtain material.

HARRISON, PETER (1716–1775) Harrison is considered the first American architect in that he prepared sketches for others to build from. His best known works are in Newport, Rhode Island, and he made it the center of architectural art in colonial New England. His masterpiece, the Synagogue of the Congregation Jeshuat Israel (known as Touro Synagogue), was begun in 1759 and is the oldest synagogue in the United States. Harrison was probably the American master of the British version of Renaissance design.

HARVARD CHAIR   An early American (17th-century) version of a Gothic-type three-cornered chair made of wood turnings.

HARVARD FRAME   A trademark name for a steel bed frame. See *Bed Frame.*

HARVEST TABLE   A long, narrow, drop-leaf table. The legs may be straight or turned, and the flaps have either squared ends, or they are gently rounded. The design is usually associated with 18th-century American furniture.

HASP   In a hinge lock, the hinged part which swings over the pin. In Spanish Gothic chests, the hasp was usually an ornate piece of metalwork.

HASSOCK   A heavy cushion or thick mat used as a footstool or ottoman.

HATCHING   In drawing, a method of shading by means of close parallel lines. "Cross-hatching" is criss-crossed sets of parallel lines.

HAUSMALEREI   Homemade and amateurish German pottery. The pieces were partially fired, then decorated and returned to the kiln for glazing and further firing. See *Firing.*

HAUT BOY   See *High Boy.*

HAUT RELIEF   In sculpture and ornament, high relief as opposed to bas-relief. See *High Relief.*

HAUTELISSE   The French for high warp. A tapestry woven with an upright warp.

HEADBOARD   The board or panel which rises above the mattress at the head of the bed. It can be made of wood or metal, upholstered, or inset with cane or leather panels, etc., simple or ornate, modern or traditional in style. A back support when a person is sitting up in bed. See *Footboard*.

HEADER   The end of a brick usually laid perpendicular to the face of the wall. It is used to tie two thicknesses of masonry together.

HEADER BOND   In masonry, a brick pattern made up of headers only. See *Header*.

HEART AND CROWN   A pierced motif carved on the cresting of a baluster chair of the late 17th century in England.

HEARTH   The brick, stone, or tile pavement beneath the opening in a chimney and inside the fireplace, where the fire is made.

HEART-SHAPED CHAIR BACK   A typical 18th-century Hepplewhite shield chair back which resembles a heart.

HELIX   A small spiral element beneath the abacus of a Corinthian capital.

HELLENISTIC   Greek art under Alexander in the third century B.C. It is a realistic and emotional form of art with the Roman influence interpreting the Greek forms.

HEMLOCK   A wood which resembles white pine. It is strong, lightweight, and easy to work.

HENRI II and III   The rulers of France during the 16th century whose reigns form part of the mid-French-Renaissance period. The period was noteworthy for its carvings and interlaced strapwork.

HEPPLEWHITE, GEORGE   An 18th-century English furniture designer who worked in the classic style. In 1788, he published *Cabinet-Maker and Upholsterers Guide*. His work was characterized by lightness of construction, elegant curvilinear forms, and perfection of workmanship. Hepplewhite used heart-shaped and shield chair backs carved with wheat ears, fern leaves, honeysuckle, swags, and Prince of Wales feathers. He designed *japanned* furniture with fruit and flowers on a black ground, as well as satinwood and inlaid pieces. Hepplewhite favored the spade foot for his delicately grooved and fluted chair legs.

HERCULANEUM   A historic Roman city which was excavated about the middle of the 18th century, and became a source of inspiration for the classic designers of the 18th century in France and England. The influence of Herculaneum is found in the architecture and interior designs of the Adam brothers in England and is the basis

HEARTH

HEART-SHAPED
CHAIR BACK

HERMA

HERCULANEUM

HERCULANEUM

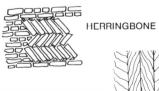

GEORGE HEPPLEWHITE

HERRINGBONE

HERRINGBONE MATCH

of the Louis XVI style in France. Herculaneum also refers to an antique Roman-type chair designed by Sheraton in the late 18th century. Also shown is a bronze stand excavated at Herculaneum. See *Pompeii*.

HERCULON   An olefin fiber produced by Hercules, Inc., used for indoor-outdoor carpeting, contract carpeting and upholstery fabrics. Has a waxy feel and fair soil- and stain-repellancy. Highly heat-sensitive, and can "melt" in temperatures over 200° F.

HEREKE RUG   An extremely fine Oriental rug made of silk yarns and metallic threads hand-knotted into an intricate overall design.

HERMA   A stone pillar, usually square, which tapers downward and is topped by a bust of Hermes. The Romans used it as a boundary marker, and also as an outdoor decoration. Similar to a *Term*. Illustrated is a Hermes figure at the Dauphine Gate of the Fountainebleau Palace.

HERMES or HERMS   See *Term*.

HERRERA, JUAN DE (1530–1597)   A Spanish architect who was responsible for the desornamentado style. He worked under Phillip II, and his work was simple, severe and almost harsh in relation to the Plateresque period which preceded him and the Baroque (or Churrigueresco) which followed. Herrera was a pupil of Michelangelo. His greatest achievement is the Escorial, about 30 miles from Madrid. He also added the southern portion of the Alcazar in Toledo.

HERRINGBONE   Woodwork, brickwork, or stonework in which the material is laid at angles, so that the alternate courses point in opposite directions. Inlay, marquetry, and parquetry are sometimes done in a herringbone pattern.

HERRINGBONE MATCH   Two V-match veneer or wood panels butted together to form a series of horizontal valleys and peaks.

HETRE   French for beechwood. A popular wood for fine 18th-century chairs.

HEURTAUT, NICOLAUS (1720–1771)   A French furniture-maker who specialized in the Rococo style popular during the reign of Louis XV.

HEX SIGN   A Pennsylvania Dutch motif for good luck, or to ward off evil spirits, usually a variation on a circle with a six-pointed star or another geometric motif enclosed in the circle. Painted on barns and houses, and on chests, furniture, etc., usually in bright, pure colors.

HICKORY A hard, tough and heavy wood of the walnut family. It is not usually used decoratively, but it is elastic and bonds easily. Effective where thinness and strength are required, therefore often used for bent and molded plywood.

H.I.D. LIGHTING Lighting from a high-intensity discharge lamp, in which the electric current passes through a gas, usually mercury, metal halide, or high-pressure sodium. Provides illumination at reduced energy costs. See *Mercury Halide Lamp, Sodium Vapor Lamp.*

HIDEAWAY BED See *Murphy Bed* and *Trundle Bed.*

HIERACOSPHINX A sculptured Egyptian lion's form with the head of a hawk.

HIERATIC An abridged form of hieroglyphics used for religious writings.

HIEROGLYPHICS A system of picture writing and phonetic indications used by the ancient Egyptians.

HIGH DADDY An 18th-century American tall chest unit of six or more drawers, graduated in size.

HIGH RELIEF Sculpture, the figures of which are carved out from the background to the extent of at least half their total mass, so that they appear almost detached or full round. See *Haut Relief.*

HIGHBOY A tall chest of four or five drawers, on legs, with a cornice or pediment crown. It was originally mounted on a dressing table. Introduced from Holland into England during the William and Mary period, and popular in America through the 18th century. Illustrated is a mid-18th-century flattop New England highboy. The name may be derived from the French *hautbois* (high wood).

HIGH-RISER An armless and backless couch, usually 75″ long by 30″ to 36″ wide, with another slightly shorter and narrower mattress on a collapsed frame beneath it. The under-unit can be pulled out and raised level with the upper mattress to sleep two people. When the under-unit is not in use, the high-riser takes up the space of an ordinary couch.

HIGH-TECH A term describing furniture and furnishings that are, or appear to be, constructed of factory or industrial parts and pieces: grids, pipes, metal stampings, expanded metals, vacuum-formed elements, etc. The design and its elements suggest commercial or heavy-duty use, although adapted to the home, office or retail-store.

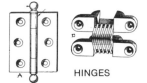

HINGES

HIERACOSPHINX

HIGH RELIEF

HIP

HISTORIATED

HIGHBOY

LAMBERT HITCHCOCK

HOCK LEG

HINGE A metal device consisting of two plates joined by a pin in such a manner that they can pivot or swing on it.

Butt Hinge: The two plates are fixed inside the door or chest unit, and only the pivot with pin is visible. Invisible Hinge: Almost completely concealed when in use. Double-acting Hinge: Makes it possible to swing a door or panel in either direction and almost a full 360°. Sometimes hinges are very decorative, and both plates are exposed for their beauty as well as their use.

HIP In architecture, the angle formed by the meeting of two sloping roof surfaces. In furniture, the "knee" of the cabriole leg. The extensions above the chair rail in early-18th-century English cabriole-legged chairs were called hips.

HISPANO MAURESQUE Spanish art influenced by Moorish designs. It was a part of the Gothic or Medieval period in Spain, and lasted for several hundred years. Typical of the Moorish craftsman's influence on Spanish architecture: horseshoe arches, pierced stonework, tracery, and rich surface decoration.

HISTORIATED Ornamented with figures, animals, etc., which are representational or symbolic. Historiated initials were a popular ornament in medieval manuscripts.

HITCHCOCK CHAIRS See *Hitchcock, Lambert*

HITCHCOCK, LAMBERT (1795–1852) An American designer working in Connecticut, the designer of the "Hitchcock chair," derived from the Sheraton pillow back or oval-turned top rail chair. The chair usually was painted black, and had a rush or cane seat, turned, splayed front legs, and gold stenciled fruit and flower decoration on the wide top rail.

HL HINGE A provincial hinge usually made of forged or wrought iron. The design resembles an uppercase I attached by a short crosspiece to an uppercase L. The hinge or pivot joint between the I and the L creates the H in the name. See *H Hinge.*

HOCHRELIEF German for high relief.

HOCK LEG Also called broken cabriole leg. The curve is broken below the knee on the inner side. The sides of the knees are sometimes ornamented with carved spiral scrolls called ears. See *Cabriole Leg.*

HOFFMAN, JOSEPH (1870–1956) An Austrian decorator and architect who was the taste and pace setter for Austrian decor in the first three decades of the 20th century. The Palais Stoclet in Brussels (1905–1911) is probably his masterpiece, and in it one can see his subtle compositions based on simple rectangles and squares with delicately handled trims. Hoffman was a student of *Otto Wagner.*

HOGARTH CHAIR A decorated Queen Anne chair with heavy knees and modified cabriole legs. The hoop back is usually hollow-crested and has a pierced splat.

HOGARTH, WILLIAM (1697–1764) A noted painter and illustrator of the life in 18th-century England. He did many series of famous etchings. Illustrated is "Temple Bar."

HOLLAND, HENRY (1740–1806) An English architect-decorator.

HOLLAND SHADE CLOTH A plain cotton or linen cloth finished with sizing or starch and oil to make it opaque, used to make window shades.

HOLLOW WALL A wall containing an air space, the facing and backing bonded together with masonry units. See *Cavity Wall.*

HOLLY, WHITE A native American wood. The whitest and least grained wood available, used for marquetry, inlays, and stringing and banding. It turns brown with age and exposure.

HOLLYWOOD BED A bed without a footboard, the spring and mattress set on a metal bed-frame unit, often equipped with casters. A headboard can be attached to the frame, or the headboard can be attached to the wall, and the frame then hooked on to it. The size varies from twin to king size. Period and style are determined by the choice of headboard. See *Harvard Frame.*

HOM The Assyrian "tree of life" pattern.

HOMESPUN Originally a fabric loomed by hand at home, but now the name of a loose, rough fabric with a tweedy look which is obtained by using unevenly spun fibers of cotton, rayon, or wool. Used for curtains and upholstery.

HONEYSUCKLE A Greek decoration resembling a conventionalized fanlike arrangement of petals. Often called the anthemion. It appears on Renaissance furniture as a carved enrichment, and Hepplewhite used it for a chair back design. Adam created a swag of honeysuckles to decorate panels, girandoles, furniture, etc.

HOOD In furniture, the case enclosing the dial and works of a grandfather or long case clock. Also see *Hooded Tops.* In architecture, a sheltering overhang.

HOOF FOOT

WILLIAM HOGARTH

HOOPBACK CHAIR

HORSE

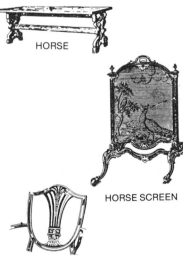

HORSE SCREEN

HONEYSUCKLE

HOODED TOPS The rounded tops of cabinets, especially those of the early Queen Anne period (early 18th century England). Also called domed, curved, rounded, or semicircular tops.

HOOF FOOT See *Cloven Foot, Does'-Foot Leg,* and *Pied de Biche.* Illustrated is a Queen Anne chair with hoof feet.

HOOKED RUG A pile-surfaced rug made of loops of yarn or strips of cloth pushed through a canvas backing. Color and patterns are unlimited. Now made by machine as well as by hand. See *Braided Rugs.*

HOOPBACK CHAIR A chair in which the uprights and top rail of the back form a continuous curve or hoop. Appears in the Queen Anne period; also prominent in the Hepplewhite period.

HOPE CHEST See *Cassone* and *Cedar Chest.*

HOPE, THOMAS (1770–1831) The leading furniture designer in the Empire style in England, which is correctly termed English Regency. His book of furniture designs, *Household Furniture and Interior Decorations,* published in 1807, moderated the extravagant pseudoclassical style. See *Regency (English).*

HOPPER LIGHT The upper section of a casement window which is hinged at the bottom and opens inward.

HOPPER WINDOW A casement window which is hinged along its bottom edge so that it opens out and backward, usually part of a larger window unit.

HORSE A simple support for a trestle table. It may be an inverted V or a shaped piece as illustrated in this Tudor period table (early 16th century).

HORSE SCREEN An English term for a cheval screen. A fire screen with two bracketed feet. A Chippendale design is illustrated. See *Cheval Screen.*

HORSEHAIR A furniture covering woven from the hair of a horse's tail and mane. Hepplewhite used it as an upholstery material, and it was most prominent in the Victorian period. Stiff, sturdy, and generally quite dark in color.

HORSESHOE ARCH An arch with a curve greater than a semicircle or 180°, prominent in Moorish and Spanish architecture.

HORSESHOE TABLE A horseshoe-shaped table, about 30″ wide, and popular in the late 18th century. See *Hunt Table* and *Wine Table.*

HORTA, (BARON) VICTOR (1861–1947) A Belgian architect who created in the Art Nouveau style. Two of his most noted works are the home of Baron von Eetveldes (1895) and the "Maison du Peuple" (1896). The interior architecture in both structures is significant for the irregularly shaped rooms which open freely onto one another at different levels. The iron balustrades are typically Art Nouveau in their twisted, plantlike elements, as is the curving sweep of mosaic floors, plaster walls, etc. His later works are more traditional.

HOT TUBS Originally, large vats or tubs made of redwood or other closely grained woods that were filled with steaming water and used out of doors by one or several persons together. The hot tub now may have "seats" inside and be made large enough to accommodate a small party. Some are equipped with Jacuzzi-like attachments which circulate strong streams of hot water around the inside of the tub, like a whirlpool. Also available in molded plastics or metal with porcelain finishes. Can be used indoors as well as out. See *Jacuzzi*.

HOTHOUSE A greenhouse. See *Conservatory* and *Orangery* or *Orangerie*.

HOUNDSTOOTH A fabric and wallpaper design. A medium-sized broken check motif often used in tweeds.

HOURGLASS BASE A typically Regency base for stools, benches, and sometimes chairs. Made up of two curved elements, one set on top of the other to create a rounded X shape. Examples can be seen in earlier 18th-century stools and chairs by Chippendale, Adam, and Sheraton.

HOUSED JOINT A socketed joint as opposed to a butt joint. One piece is grooved out to fit into the grooved part of the other. The joint illustrated is also called a gain joint.

HOUSSE The French term for slipcover.

HUCHIERS - MENUISIERS The French term for furniture makers of the early Renaissance period. Literally the term means hutch carpenters. Illustrated is a crédence of the late 16th century (period of Henri II).

HUDSON RIVER SCHOOL (1825–1870) A 19th-century American school of romantic landscape painters who glorified nature. Washington Allston and Thomas Cole were major artists of the group, as were Frederick Edwin Church and Albert Bierstadt.

HOURGLASS BASE

HOUSED JOINT

HUCHIERS-MENUISIERS

HUE A color. A tint is a color with white added. A shade is a color with black added.

HUET, CHRISTOPHE French artist during the reign of Louis XV. He created many chinoiserie-rococo designs: mandarins, pagodas, parasols, monkeys, ladders and fantastic foliage.

HUET, JEAN-BAPTISTE (1745–1811) A French designer of toiles de Jouy for Christophe-Philippe Oberkampf, and wallpapers for Réveillon. His designs were full of grace, charm, animation, and a touch of humor. After the French Revolution, he created architectural and geometric backgrounds against which were set medallions, classic figures, and arabesques, usually printed by a cylinder machine.

HUETEX, BLUE RIDGE A trademark of American Saint Gobain for a tempered glass 5/16" thick, with ceramic enamel fused to the back, and aluminum welded to the enamel. The aluminum protects the enamel, reflects heat, and insulates. It was developed as a spandrel material, and is also used as a decorative ceiling paneling. The glass is textured on the weathering side to subdue bright reflections.

HUEWHITE A trademark of American Saint Gobain for a translucent white, light-diffusing glass with the added strength of embedded wire mesh.

HUNG CEILING A ceiling installed below another by setting a new series of cross strips of wood or metal lower than the existing ceiling, then sheathing this framework with acoustic tiles, plasterboard, plastic panels, special light units, etc. Also called a suspended ceiling. See *Dropped Ceiling*.

HUNT TABLE A popular 18th-century English table with a horseshoe-shaped top surface. Often had drop leaves at the two ends of the horseshoe. A swinging decanter stand (which followed the inner edge) was sometimes added.

HUNTING CHAIR An 18th-century Sheraton chair design with a special wood strip or footrest in front.

HURRICANE LAMP A tall, glass cylinder shade set over a candlestick to protect the flame, introduced in the late 17th century and used through the 18th century. In current decorating, hurricane lamps are often used in pairs trimmed with prisms, and flame-shaped bulbs have replaced the candles. Similar to the 19th-century *Girandole* or *Lustre*.

HUSHALON A wool felt material used for wall covering, with acoustical and thermal insulating properties. Also moth and flame proof, soil resistant, and colorfast. A trademark name.

HUSK ORNAMENT   A decorative representation of the husks of oats when ripe. The spreading of the husk into two halves makes it possible to create a chainlike pattern by having husk drooping from husk. This motif was very popular in England in the Adam and Sheraton periods. It was used as an inlay design, as a composition ornament of walls and ceilings in painted decoration, and also by Wedgwood on his Jasper ware. A section of an Adam mantel is illustrated. See *Bellflower Ornament*.

HUTCH

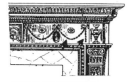

HUSK ORNAMENT

HUTCH or HUCHE   *Huche* is Old French for bin or chest. Originally a Gothic chest. In current usage, a cabinet or cupboard placed over a buffet unit. The cupboard part may be left completely open, or have doors on two sides with an open shelving area in the middle. See *Ménagère*.

HUYGENS   A 17th-century Hollander who was brought to France during the reign of Louis XIV by Charles Le Brun. He was a furniture designer especially noted for his lacquerwork.

HYDRIA   A Greek three-handled water jar.

I

I BEAM A rolled steel beam shaped like a capital letter I with a pronounced top and bottom stroke.

I.B.D. *Institute of Business Designers.*

IBERIAN Referring to the Iberian Peninsula (Spain and/or Portugal).

ICHTHUS The Greek word for fish. The word and the symbol were used in early Christian art to represent Jesus Christ. The initial letters of "Jesus Christ, God's Son, Saviour," in Greek, formed the word ichthus.

ICON or IKON Greek for image. A religious painting of Christ, Mary, or a saint, painted on a panel.

ICONOCLASTIC MOVEMENT
Decorative style of the early 8th century, when sculptural representations of humans or animals were prohibited by the Eastern Emperor Leo III, who feared that statues might foster paganism and idolatry. The resultant typically Byzantine and near-Eastern decoration was dependent upon floral and geometric patterns in rich color and texture.

ICONOGRAPH A ground plan.

IDEOGRAPH The illustration of an idea, word, or object. See *Rebus*.

I.D.S.A. *Industrial Designers Society of America.*

ILLUMINATION The medieval art of hand-decorating manuscripts with scrolls, arabesques, foliage, etc., in rich color and gold and silver. Religious manuscripts were often greatly enriched with colored illumination. See *Historiated*.

I BEAMS

IMBRICATE

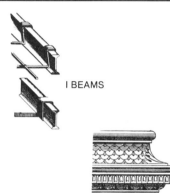

ICONOCLASTIC MOVEMENT

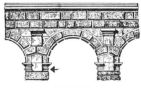

IMPOST

ILLUSIONISM See *Trompe l'Oeil*.

I.M. The inner measurement of a unit as opposed to the O.M. or outer measurement. The I.M. of a hollow pipe is the diameter measured between opposite points on the inside surface; the O.M. is the diameter measured between opposite points on the outside surface. See *O.M.*

IMAGINE D'ÉPINAL A simple wood block.

IMBRICATE To place in overlapping tiers or to give a fish-scale-like appearance. A technique used for tile roofs and also on columns, walls, etc.

IMBUYA Brazilian walnut. The wood varies in color from olive to a deep, rich, red-brown color, and is used for veneering fine-grade furniture. It is fine-grained and moderately hard and heavy.

IMPASTO An oil painting technique developed by Titian. Thin layers of opaque pigment and oil glazes are used to create a depth of color. When so many layers are applied as make the paint appear thick or lumpy, and the brush strokes are clearly evident, the painting is said to be "heavily impasted."

IMPOST The member just below the springing line of an arch, where the arch rests.

IMPRESSIONISM One of the first of the modern art movements in the 19th century. The aim was to achieve greater naturalism by analysis of tone and color, and the rendering of light on surfaces. Paint was often dabbed on in bright colors, even in the shadows. There was a lack of firm outline. Major Impressionists were

Claude Monet, Camille Pissaro, and Alfred Sisley.

IN SITU Latin for in place. Work done directly on the locale of the job and not made in a workshop for later installation.

INCANDESCENT LIGHT A sealed glass bulb with a filament which produces a glow and a light when an electric current passes through it.

INCARNADINE A 17th-century English term to describe a light crimson to a pale fleshy pink color.

INCE, WILLIAM An 18th-century English cabinetmaker, and follower of Chippendale. With Thomas Mayhew, he published *The Universal System of Household Furniture*, from 1762–1763. It contained designs for lanthorns, sideboard tables, bookcases, beds, etc. Ince used fretwork, combined with Chinese and Gothic motifs, and chair backs carved with ribbons and scrolls and patterned with brass nails. See *Mayhew, Thomas*.

INCISED The opposite of relief carving. The pattern is produced by cutting or etching into the material. The design is engraved below the surface. See *Intaglio*, and *Eastlake*.

INCISED LACQUER Several coats of lacquer are applied to create a certain thickness. A design is then cut or carved into this thickness. This form of decoration was used on Chinese-style lacquered furniture and screens.

INCROSTARE Italian for inlay.

INDIA PAPERS (Also called Japan papers.) Chinese papers imported into Europe in the mid-17th century by means of the Dutch, French, and English East India companies; hence the name "India papers." See *Chinese Wallpaper*.

INDIA PRINT A printed cotton fabric with a Persian or Indian pattern hand-blocked in bright colors on a white or natural ground. It is used for draperies, bed throws, wall hangings, etc.

INDIAN RED A soft reddish-brown or terra-cotta color, often used on American provincial pine furniture in the 18th century.

INDIENNE FABRICS The French interpretation of India print cottons made during the late 17th and the 18th centuries. See *Toiles d'Indy*.

INDIRECT LIGHTING Lighting arrangement in which the light is directed up to the ceiling or another reflective surface, from which it is bounced back to illuminate the general area.

INGLENOOK

WILLIAM INCE

INLAY

INSET PILASTER

INDOOR-OUTDOOR CARPETS See *Herculon* and *Polypropylene-Olefin Carpets*.

INDUSTRIAL DESIGNERS' INSTITUTE A professional organization for industrial designers, but it also includes members of the interior design field, like Jens Risom and Edward Wormley.

INGLENOOK A wide, recessed chimney opening usually furnished with benches at either side. A Scottish term for chimney corner.

INGRAIN A reversible, flat woven wool or wool and cotton carpet made on a Jacquard loom. The ground color on one side becomes the top or design color on the reverse side. Ingrain is also a woven, multicolored fabric with a flat weave. The threads are dyed before they are woven.

INLAY A technique in which a design is cut out of the surface to be decorated and then filled in with other contrasting materials cut to fit exactly into these openings. The contrast of color or materials creates the decoration. The inserts may be of wood veneer, metals, shells, ivory, etc. Illustrated is a Hepplewhite tabletop. See *Boulle Work*, *Certosina*, *Intarsia or Tarsia*, and *Marquetry*.

INLAY, IMITATION A painted decoration or decalcomania which simulates inlay work, but is recognizable by its smooth, uninterrupted surface.

INNERSPRING MATTRESS A fairly recent (around 1924) innovation. The mattress has a center core of springs for buoyancy and resilience, with a protective pad on either side of it, sometimes made of sisal. This pad keeps the felted cotton, short-fiber cotton, curled hair, or other soft material from getting twisted in the coils. A tough fabric, like ticking, encases the whole unit. The construction, methods of tying or casing the coils, the quilting material, etc., vary with the manufacturer and with the price.

INSET PILASTER A flat half column set against a flush surface, usually at the front corners of a chest, cabinet, or other case piece. Illustrated is a late 16th-century chest.

INSTITUTE OF BUSINESS DESIGNERS (I.B.D.) A professional organization of architects and interior designers working in contract and commercial interior design rather than residential interior design.

INSULATION The application of materials which keep in warmth, keep down sound vibration, or generally protect a structure from the outside elements. May be built into the building, or added as facing materials to the inside surfaces of the rooms.

INTAGLIO Designs cut out of a surface, leaving a relief in reverse. The finished design is below the plane which has been worked upon.

INTAGLIO ENGRAVING Distinguished from other metal plate engraving techniques by the printing process used. The ink lies in the engraved furrows, rather than on the smooth surface. A piece of paper is dampened and laid on the plate, and both are rolled through a mangle-like heavy press. The damp paper is forced into the furrows, and picks up the ink. When the paper is dry, the engraved inked lines stand up in relief. See *Aquatint, Drypoint Engraving, Etching, Line Engraving,* and *Mezzotint.*

INTAILLE French for intaglio.

INTARSIA or TARSIA Incised work inlaid with contrasting materials. A type of mosaic. Italian designers in the early Renaissance period used shell, bone, and ivory inserts. Illustrated is intarsia work from a stall in Santa Maria Novella in Florence. See *Certosina, Inlay, Intarsio,* and *Nonsuch Furniture.*

INTARSIATURA Italian for marquetry.

INTARSIO Pictures executed in wood veneers and inlays. A highly sophisticated form of inlay.

INTERLACED CHAIR BACKS An interlaced strap or ribbon-back chair similar in character to fretwork. It was used in late-18th-century French furniture, and in the Chippendale and Hepplewhite styles.

INTERPENETRATIONS In Gothic vaulting, moldings intersecting each other and appearing to run through one another.

INTERRUPTED ARCH An arched pediment top for cabinets and chests of the 18th century. The apex or top central segment of the arch is missing. See *Broken Pediment.*

INTONACO The final layer of wet plaster upon which the fresco artist actually works. The final coat is applied to just that area which the painter will be able to cover before the plaster dries. See *Arricciato* and *Fresco.*

INTRADOS The inner curve or surface of an arch. The soffit of an arch. See *Extrados.*

INVERTED CUP A detail in the wood-turned shaped legs of the William and

IONIC ORDER

INTARSIA

INTERLACED CHAIR BACK

ISLAND BED

INVERTED CUP

Mary period in England resembling an inverted cup.

IONIC ORDER A classical order of architecture and decoration. The spiral-shaped volute or scroll is characteristic of the capital. The Romans proportioned the columns at 9 diameters high. For an illustration of the Ionic capital, architrave, frieze, and cornice see *Zoophorus.*

IREME Also called African teak or black afara. It is native to Ghana. A pale yellow to light brown, faintly ribbon-striped wood. It has noticeable rays and an intermediate grain.

IRIDESCENT FABRICS Fabrics with contrasting colored warps and filling yarns. A changeable colored effect is produced, as in tafetta.

IRISH CHIPPENDALE Mahogany furniture made in Ireland in the mid-18th century, based on Chippendale drawings. The furniture lacked the refinement and lightness of the original Chippendale pieces. Lion masks and paw feet are often found on Irish Chippendale furniture.

IRISH POINT A net curtain material with an appliqué design similar to *Duchess.*

IROKO An African wood sometimes mislabeled African oak or teak. It bleaches on exposure, though the natural color ranges from light yellow-brown to deep reddish-brown. Iroko is used as a veneer wood, and is also called *kambala.*

IRONWOOD The olive wood of South America, an exceptionally hard wood. American ironwood is a brown-gray wood which is hard, heavy, and strong.

ISABELLINA The Spanish term for the Gothic phase of minute, detailed, patterned design. The Renaissance phase was termed plateresco. Manuelino is the Portuguese counterpart of Isabellina.

ISINGLASS Thin, translucent sheets of mica which were sometimes used for fenestration in 18th- and 19th-century homes.

ISLAND Any unit which stands free and independent, away from walls, and can be approached from any direction.

ISLAND BED A bed placed in the middle of a room or not in contact with any of the perimeter walls. A designer may back the head of the bed with a screen or "wall" of cabinets or shelves, making it somewhat less of an island bed.

ISLON A trademark name for an all-nylon fabric with the soft look of velvet. It has body, and is drapable, soil resistant, durable, and color stable.

ISOMETRIC PROJECTION A three-dimensional schematic view of an object. The lines are set at a 45° angle to the horizontal, and the vertical lines are projected from it in scale. The diagonal and curved lines are distorted, but the general appearance of the projection is more natural.

ISPAHAN RUGS Persian rugs usually recognized by an intricate, allover floral pattern which stands out from a deep red background.

ITALIAN NEOCLASSIC STYLE A late-18th-century furniture style inspired by Greek and Roman antique designs. The rediscovery of Pompeii and the neoclassic styling that became the Louis XVI style in France and was interpreted in England by the Adam Brothers, Hepplewhite, and Sheraton, interpreted with Italian flair.

IVORY

IVY

ITALIAN PROVINCIAL STYLE A misnomer for modern Italian versions of the late-18th- and early-19th-century popular Directoire and Empire styles, as updated and adapted to contemporary tastes and mass production techniques. Popular in the United States in the 1950's and 60's. Also called the Palladian style. See *Palladian*.

IVORY The tusks of elephants used for decorative inlay work and carving. It is a rare material but has been imitated in plastics. Illustrated is a 15th-century French 9½"-tall statue.

IVY A decorative leaf design, the symbol of friendship. It was also sacred to Bacchus, and therefore appears on many ancient vases. Usually broad, five-lobed, and appears at the end of long shoots in lancelike forms.

J

JABOT A ruffle or frill. The cascading side pieces of a swag.

JACARANDA See *Rosewood, Brazilian.*

JACKKNIFE SOFA BED See *Sofa Bed.*

JACOB, FRANÇOIS HONORÉ GEORGES A French cabinetmaker of the Louis XVI and Directoire periods. He also made and designed furniture for Napoleon.

JACOB, GEORGES The father of the equally famous François Honoré Georges Jacob. A noted cabinetmaker of the Louis XVI period.

JACOBEAN The period (1603–1649) in English architecture and art which extends over the reigns of James I and Charles I. It is a term which covers the merging of English Tudor designs and motifs with the Renaissance in England.

JACOBEAN ORNAMENT Bands of molding applied to furniture in geometric patterns to create a paneled effect. Popular decoration on furniture made in England in the 17th century. A table (c. 1630) is illustrated.

JACOBSON, ARNE A modern Scandinavian designer of a laminated plywood-and-steel chair similar to the Eames chair. He also created an egg chair, which is in the tradition of Saarinen's womb chair.

JACQUARD In carpeting, the pattern-control device on the Wilton loom. It was invented by Joseph-Marie Jacquard in Brussels, Belgium, and adapted to the Wilton loom in 1825.

JABOT

JALEE

JACOBEAN ORNAMENT

JALOUSIE WINDOW

JACQUARD, JOSEPH-MARIE (1752–1834) The Frenchman who, in 1801, created the Jacquard loom, which revolutionized the production of figured woven textiles. The loom made it possible to produce certain multicolored designs inexpensively. In 1825, the loom was adapted for the carpet industry.

JACQUARD WEAVE A weave with intricate, multicolored patterns produced on the type of loom created by Joseph-Marie Jacquard in the early 19th century. Damasks, tapestries, and brocades are all Jacquard weaves.

JACQUEMART AND BENARD French wallpaper manufacturers from 1791 to 1840. They were successors to Réveillon.

JACUZZI A trademark name for a plumbing system to produce strong jets of water that circulate through a tub or vat. It is used to set up a powerful circulating movement in a hot-water bath to relax tired or aching muscles or encourage blood circulation to injured parts of the body. Sometimes called a Whirlpool Bath.

JALEE In India, the decorated pierced marble or stone work such as was used in the Taj Mahal. Illustrated is an open-work stone window arch. See *Stone, Edward Durrel.*

JALOUSIE A French word for louvers, similar to Venetian blinds. A jalousied room is constructed of louvered windows or panels.

JALOUSIE WINDOW A window with numerous horizontal slats of glass which can be tilted to any desired angle, in the manner of a Venetian blind. The multitude of panels, break up the visibility through the window and make it difficult to clean and weatherproof. See *Awning Window*.

JAMB The interior side of a door or window frame.

JAPANNING An 18th-century finishing process. Furniture and metalwork were enameled with colored shellac, the decoration shaped in relief and painted in color and gilt. The technique was an imitation of the brilliant lacquered colors of the Japanese work imported by the Dutch into Europe during the 17th century. See *Lacquer* and *Martin Brothers*.

JARDINIÈRE A plant container or stand made of wood, metal, or porcelain. The jardinière reached the height of elegance during the latter part of the 18th century in France and England. A Chippendale design is illustrated.

JARDINIÈRE VELVET A silk velvet having several depths of uncut loops set against a damask or silk background. It is usually a multicolored pattern resembling a flower arrangement against a light satin background. Originally produced in Genoa.

JASPÉ In carpeting, irregular warp stripes of two hues of a color in a surface yarn, in either a patterned or plain fabric. In fabric, a streaked or mottled effect produced by an uneven dyeing of warp threads. It resembles the stone jasper.

JASPER An opaque quartz, red, yellow, or brown.

JASPER WARE An 18th-century type of hard bisquit ware (pottery) introduced by Wedgwood in England.

JEANNERET, CHARLES ÉDOUARD See *Le Corbusier*.

JEFFERSON, THOMAS (1743–1826) The third President of the United States, and a great political philosopher. He was interested in architecture, and besides designing his own home, Monticello, and its furnishings, he was active in the planning of Washington D.C. Impressed by Roman architecture, he designed the Capitol in Richmond, Virginia (1785–1792) based on the Maison Carrée at Nîmes. The rotunda of the University of Virginia in Charlottesville, Virginia (1822–1826), was planned by Jefferson in association with Benjamin Henry Latrobe.

JENNY LIND BED A spool-turned bed named for Jenny Lind, the "Swedish Nightingale," who was visiting America at the time it was designed (1850–1852).

JESTING BEAM

JAMB

JEWELING

JARDINIÈRE

JIGSAW MIRROR

It had a low headboard and modest bedposts.

JESTING BEAM A decorative or ornamental beam, not necessarily a structural member.

JEWELING Any small, ornamental feature carved on furniture or a building, either above or below the surface, to resemble a polished or cut jewel. Illustrated is an ornamental detail from a 16th-century English building.

JIB DOOR A flush door which is painted or papered over to make it as inconspicuous as possible.

JIGSAW DETAIL A cutout or fretwork design made with a jigsaw, an early power-operated tool. Used for the enhancement of buildings of the mid and late 19th century. The bargework was often made with a jigsaw. The "gingerbread" or "steamboat Gothic," late Victorian period was jigsaw work in its most extreme form.

JIGSAW MIRROR A framed mirror popular in the 18th and 19th centuries in America and England. The earlier examples were hand cut, and had detailed scrolls, while 19th-century pieces were cut on a jigsaw, one of the first of the power-operated tools. Shown here is a Queen Anne type of mirror of the early 18th century.

JOHNSON, PHILIP An American architect and designer born in Cleveland, Ohio, in 1906. One of his most famous buildings is his own glass home in New Canaan, Connecticut. Johnson was associated with Mies van der Rohe in the Seagram Building in New York City and the Four Seasons restaurant in that building.

JOHNSON, PHILIP: "GLASS HOUSE," NEW CANAAN, CONNECTICUT An all-glass house with a brick guesthouse pavilion designed by Philip Johnson. The architecture and furnishings show the influence of Mies van der Rohe's work of the 1920's. Low partitions inside the glass structure separate the work and sleeping areas from the dining and living areas. A brick cylinder, repeating the flooring material, houses the bathroom. The brick guesthouse has a noteworthy vaultlike ceiling with strip lighting which increases the sense of space.

JOHNSON, THOMAS A mid-18th-century English carver of fanciful and eccentric girandoles, sconces, etc. He was a contemporary of Chippendale, and used a mixture of Gothic, Chinese, and Louis XV Rococo styles.

JOINER An artisan or draftsman skilled in joining woods together by means of joints, glue, nails, etc. See *Joinery*.

JOINERY The craft of assembling woodwork by means of mortise and tenons, dovetails, tongue and grooves, dowels, etc. A dovetailed joint is illustrated. See *Dovetail, Mortise and Tenon Joint,* and *Tongue and Groove.*

JOINT The junction at which two pieces of lumber unite to form a support or make a closure. Illustrated is a mortise and tenon joint.

JOINT STOOL A 17th- and 18th-century simple stool made of turnings, and joined together. An oak stool of the Jacobean period (17th century) is shown.

JOIST A horizontal construction member used to support a floor or ceiling.

JONES, INIGO (1572–1653) A famous English Renaissance architect who introduced the classic Palladian style into England. Besides designing assorted public buildings, and the Queen's House, Greenwich, he created fanciful and imaginative masques and balls for royalty. Jones has been called the English Palladio. Illustrated is the Banquet Hall at Whitehall. See *Palladio, Andrea.*

JONES, WILLIAM An 18th-century English architect in 1739, he published

JOINT   JOINERY

JOINT STOOL

INIGO JONES

The Gentleman's or Builder's Companion with plates of chimneypieces, slab tables, pier glasses, tabernacle frames, ceilings, etc.

JOUY See *Toile de Jouy.*

JUDGE'S CHAIR An 18th-century high-back chair. The upholstered back is raised up from the seat, and curved to cradle the head and shoulders. The upholstered arms curve around at the same level as the bottom of the chair back. The arm stumps and back chair rails are exposed. The legs are squarish, and bracket out at the seat. Box stretchers connect the four legs.

JUGENDSTIL German for youth style. The period in German design contemporary with the Art Nouveau of France (1895–1912).

JUHL, FINN A 20th-century Danish architect and furniture designer. The legs, arms, backs, etc., of his furniture designs are beautiful and subtly sculptured wood elements.

JUTE The fibrous skin between the bark and the stalk of a tiliaceous plant grown in India. The long, tough fibers are carded and spun into strong, durable yarns used as stuffer warps, and binding and filling wefts. The jute yarns add strength, weight, and stiffness to carpets.

K

KAHANE, MELANIE A 20th-century interior designer and member of the *American Society of Interior Designers* (A.S.I.D.).

KAKEMONO An unframed Chinese or Japanese painting mounted on brocade, usually equipped with bamboo rods, top and bottom. Used as a wall hanging.

KAKIEMON, SAKAIDA A 17th-century Japanese pottery artist who developed the use of colored enamel designs on porcelain. Decorations done in this manner bear the name of this artist, or are sometimes referred to as Korean Decoration.

KAMBALA See *Iroko.*

KAOLIN A white clay used in making true porcelain. Also called china clay. Hard paste is made of this clay. See also *China.*

KAPOK Silky fibers, obtained from the seed pods of the kapok tree. Used as a stuffing material for mattresses, cushions, etc. Also called *Silk Floss.*

KAPPA SHELL A trademark name for fine sheets of real ocean pearl nacre shell, iridescent in color. Available in assorted sizes and thicknesses, and can be used for walls, furniture tops, lamps, lighting fixtures, screen inserts, etc. The material is similar to mother of pearl in appearance.

KARABAGH RUGS Geometric patterned rugs from the Caucasus. Typically, woven in bold color combinations and with a coarse primitive texture. Also produced in long, narrow shapes for use as runners.

KARL JOHANS STYLE The Empire style in Sweden (early 19th century).

KAS Dutch term for chest or cupboard. A tall, upright cabinet, clothespress, or

KEEL ARCH

WILLIAM KENT

KAS

wardrobe. It usually had ball feet, a plain heavy cornice, and two doors that opened outward. It was the proud possession of the Dutch colonist in America. See *Armoire.*

KAUFFMANN, ANGELICA (1741–1807) A painter born in Switzerland, but who did most of her work in England, where she decorated and painted plaques, panels, and medallions for Adam, Hepplewhite, and Sheraton. See *Grisaille.*

K.D. See *Knocked Down (K.D.)*

KEEL ARCH A curved arch that rises to a point. An ogee arch.

KEEL MOLDING See *Ogee.*

KELOBRA A wood native to Central America and Mexico, and primarily used as a veneer. It is a neutral brown color and is also called guanacaste and genisero.

KEMP Short, wavy, coarse wool or hair fiber, not usable for dyeing or spinning. It is often used as carpet wool.

KENT, WILLIAM (1684–1748) An English architect, furniture designer, painter, and landscape designer in the tradition of Inigo Jones. His furniture designs were in the heavy Venetian style with classical detailing, and they served as a link between the Queen Anne style and the Chippendale designs. Kent's furniture was usually produced in mahogany and gilt, and trimmed with ornately carved scrolls, swags of fruit and flowers, and often an eagle's head terminating in a scroll. In association with the Earl of Burlington, he designed the Palladian Chiswick House.

KERF A saw cut. Several adjacent saw cuts, when made against the grain of a wood plank, sometimes make it possible to bend the wood into a curve or arc.

KERMAN RUGS Gentle, pastel-toned, fine wool rugs from Iran. Usually have a central medallion on a soft ground color, surrounded by a border design. The border may be straight-lined or convoluted. The most favored background colors are cream, rose, and light blue.

KETTLE BASE A bombé base. A piece of furniture which has an outward swelling front and sides similar to a kettle. This shape appears in English and American furniture in the mid- and late-18th century. Illustrated is a unit found in Salem, Massachusetts. See *Bombé.*

KETTLE FRONT See *Swell Front.*

KEY A wall or ceiling surface which has been scratched or gouged so that plaster will adhere. Any roughened surface which aids in adhesion.

KEY CORNERED A rectangular panel whose corners are broken by right angles. Paterae or rosettes are sometimes used to decorate these "opened" corners. Adam used this type of paneling, and it was also used in the Louis XVI, Directoire, and Empire periods.

KEY PATTERN A Greek geometric band or border design. See *Fret.*

KEYING A method of closing securely by means of interlocking. Dovetailing is one method of closing by keying. A half-lap, multiple, dovetail joint, such as is used on drawers, is illustrated.

KEYSTONE The central wedge-shaped stone at the top of the curve of an arch. Illustrated is an arch at the Palais du Louvre in Paris. See *Voussoir.*

KHILIMS Handwoven Oriental tapestries, without pile, lightweight enough to be hung on the wall, though durable enough to be used as rugs.

KICKPLATE A plate, usually of metal or plastic, placed on the lower rail of a door to prevent the scuffing of this area.

KIDNEY DESK or TABLE An ornamental kidney-shaped table with the concave side toward the sitter, who is therefore semisurrounded by the curved front. The shape was used as a kneehole-type desk or dressing table by Sheraton and as a poudreuse in the Louis XV period. See *Writing Table* for an illustration of a Sheraton desk.

KILN-DRIED Lumber which has been artificially dried in heated chambers, rather than air-dried in the open. In the kiln-drying method, the lumber is less subject to warping or checking since the moisture

KETTLE BASE

KINGWOOD

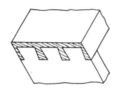

KEYING

KEYSTONE

KIDNEY DESK

KNEEHOLE DESK

content of the wood can be more easily controlled. See *Checks.*

KING-SIZE BED A double bed which can be made up of two twin-sized box springs and mattresses pushed together, or one oversized spring and mattress. Usually 72" to 78" wide by 76" to 84" long and has one wide headboard. Though a comparatively modern concept, it can be used in traditional or period rooms, depending upon the style and decoration of the headboard.

KINGWOOD A dark, purplish-brown wood with black and golden-yellow streaks. It is a fine cabinet wood native to Sumatra and Brazil, also called "bois de violette." Popular in the Louis XV and Louis XVI periods. An early Louis XVI secrétaire in kingwood and tulipwood is illustrated. It was decorated with Sèvres plaques and ormolu mounts.

KIOSK From the French kiosque, a small shelter or pavilion. The word is usually associated with a French newsstand.

KIRMAN RUGS See *Kerman Rugs.*

KITCHENETTE A small kitchen or service area, usually equipped with a stove, sink, and refrigerator.

KJAERHOLM, POUL A modern Danish furniture designer.

KLINE A multipurpose ancient Greek piece of furniture which served as a sofa, dining couch, and bed. It resembles an oversized bed with a sweeping curved back at one end. The front legs curved forward, and the rear legs curved out behind. The back of the unit resembles the *Klismos.*

KLISMOS A classic Greek type of chair with a concave curved back rail and curved legs that splay out front and back. This design appears again in the Directoire, Empire, Regency, and Duncan Phyfe styles.

KNEE The upper convex curve of the cabriole leg, sometimes embellished with carved decorations like a shell, lion's head, etc. Also called the hip. See *Cabriole Leg* and *Hip.*

KNEEHOLE DESK A desk with a central open space below the writing surface for legroom. Either side of the opening is solid or filled in with drawers which may continue down to the floor. See *Reverse Serpentine* for a kneehole table by Sheraton.

KNEEHOLE PANEL See *Modesty Panel.*

KNIFE BOX A decorative wooden chest, with vertical slots for knives. Usually used in pairs on top of sideboards, it was extremely popular in 18th-century England. Chippendale and others designed beautiful inlaid knife boxes.

KNIFE URNS Ornamental vaselike forms resting on top of pedestals set at either end of an Adam side table. The urns were used to hold knives, forks, and spoons, or hot or iced water. These urns were later replaced by knife boxes.

KNOB TURNING A turning resembling a series of knobs or balls, used for furniture legs and stretchers during the 17th century.

KNOCKED DOWN (K.D.) The practice of shipping furniture unassembled, or in several parts which must be put together at the point of use. An economy of space, labor, and shipping costs is effected when a unit is shipped "K.D."

KNOP An archaic spelling for knob. A handle or holding device to open doors, drawers, etc. An 18th-century Adam brass door knop is shown. The term is also used to describe a small bouquet of leaves or flowers.

KNORPELWERK German for rinceau or Renaissance scrollwork.

KNOT or KNOB A cluster or nosegay of flowers and/or leaves used as a boss or pendant at the intersection of vaulting ribs (see *Boss*). A knot is also a dark round or oval interruption in the grain of wood. It marks where a branch grew on the tree.

KNOTTED RUG An Oriental rug with a pile surface formed by the ends of threads knotted around the warps. The weft threads serve merely as spacers.

KNOTTY PINE Pinewood showing knots or dark oval shapes, often accentuated by pickling the pinewood (whiting the wood). Used for Early American reproductions and for paneling informal rooms. The wood grows in Idaho, Washington, and Montana.

KNUBSTOL A Norwegian provincial tree-trunk chair.

KNUCKLE CARVING The shaping often found on the outer edges of the arms of Chippendale chairs. It resembles the knuckles of the human hand.

KNUCKLE JOINT The hinged joint of a drop-leaf table. Functions in the same

KNIFE URN

KNOB TURNING

KNOP

KNUCKLE CARVING

way that the knuckle joint of the finger does. See *Finger Joint* and *Pembroke Table*.

KOA A showy Hawaiian wood used for decorative effects. It takes a fine, lustrous finish. Koa has a reddish stripe on a yellow-brown ground with a decided cross ripple or curl, which gives it a plaid effect. It is used on fine furniture, for art objects, and for musical instruments.

KODEL The trademark name for a polyester fiber manufactured by Eastman. It is not as strong as Dacron, and has less abrasion resistance, but it dyes well, dries quickly, resists wrinkling, and is considered more stable and heat-resistant than many other polyesters.

KORAI Votive statues of women in early Greek art, usually heroic in scale.

KOREAN DECORATION See *Kakiemon, Sakaida*.

KORINA A trademark name for limba, a light, golden blond wood that resembles primavera. It is available in long, wide panels uniform in color and satin-like in appearance. A stripe or crossfire figured veneer is also available. Also called *afara*.

KOROSEAL A trademark name for flexible synthetic fabrics or wall coverings derived from coal, limestone, and salt. Like leatherette or Naugahyde. They are produced by The B.F. Goodrich Company.

KOUROI Early Greek life-sized statues of nude youths which were made between c. 650 B.C. and 480 B.C., probably dedicated to young athletes in the Olympic games.

KOYLON The trademark name for latex-rubber foam produced by United States Rubber Company.

KRAGSTEIN German for bracket or console.

KRATER An ancient Greek two-handled bowl used for mixing wine and water.

KYANIZE A process to make wood decay-resistant. The lumber is impregnated with mercuric chloride.

KYLIN A fantastic dragon-like beast sometimes used in Chinese decorations.

KYLIX An ancient Greek drinking cup. It is usually flat, two-handled and set on a slender foot or stem.

L

LABEL See *Ribbons.*

LABRUM A stone bath of ancient Rome.

LABURNUM A hard yellow to reddish-brown wood, native to southern Europe. Takes a fine polish; used in Queen Anne period for inlay and veneer.

LABYRINTH A complicated, intricate maze. In the classic Greek period, an edifice composed of complicated passageways which twisted, turned, and intersected one another, e.g., the Labyrinth of Crete.

LAC A resinous material deposited on trees by an insect *(Coccas lacca)*. This material is treated and converted into shellac and also used in fine varnishes.

LACE An openwork fabric consisting of a network of threads formed into a design made by hand bobbins, needles, or hooks. Lace is also made by machine. See *Filet Lace, Nottingham Lace, Reticella,* and *Valenciennes Lace.*

LACEWOOD An Australian decorative veneer wood with a lacy, pockmarked, flaked surface effect. It is pink to light brown in color, and has a silky sheen. Lacewood is used in small decorative areas for borders, inlays, etc.

LACQUER A colored or opaque varnish made of shellac dissolved in alcohol, sometimes with pigment added. Chinese and Japanese lacquer is a hard varnish made from the sap of the lacquer tree. It has a shiny, lustrous quality. See *Huygens, Japanning,* and *Vernis Martin.*

LACQUERWORK Articles covered with a lacquer surface on which flat or relief

LABEL

LADDER-BACK

RICHARD LALONDE

LACQUERWORK

designs are drawn. A fashionable furniture finish and form of decoration in Europe from the mid-17th to the late-18th century. Illustrated is a Chinese Chippendale style four-poster bed of about 1760.

LACUNARIA See *Caissons* and *Coffered Panel*

LADDER-BACK A chair back which resembles a multirung ladder. A series of horizontal rails is contained by the two vertical chair-back stiles, replacing the usual vertical splat. Often found in provincial furniture. Chippendale chairs sometimes had ladder-backs. See *Slat-Back.*

LAGYNOS A Greek wine jug which has a broad bottom and a tall narrow neck as well as a loop handle. See *Aryballos* and *Oinochoe.*

LALLY COLUMN A trade name for a supporting unit which is a cylinder of stainless steel filled with concrete.

LALONDE, RICHARD An 18th-century French court designer of furniture and interiors in the classic Louis XVI style. Illustrated is a chased door lock by Lalonde.

LAMBELLE A lightweight, damask, textured fabric with coarser contrasting weft threads. The warp is usually fine, mercerized threads.

LAMBREQUIN A valance board for draperies. Usually a horizontal stiff covering for curtain or drapery headings, as well as the rods, hooks, and other hardware. It is also called a pelmet or palmette. Originally the lambrequin was a fabric unit, but it was often reproduced in carved wood panels with applied moldings, or metal work decorations. See *Cantonnière* and *Pentes.*

LAMBRIS D'APPUI A French term for paneling that reaches to waist or elbow height.

LAMBRIS DE HAUTEUR A French term for paneling that reaches up to the cornice or picture rail.

LAMINATION A bonding or gluing together of various layers of wood, often with a veneer on top to form a permanent unit. See *Plywood*. Fabric may be laminated on other materials.

LAMPADAIRE A classic pedestal designed to hold a lamp or candlestick. Illustrated is a Thomas Hope English Regency or Empire design.

LAMPAS A patterned textile with two warps and two or more fillers. The pattern is always twill or plain weave, and the background is a plain or satin weave. Lampas is similar to a two-colored damask, and was extremely popular during the 18th and 19th centuries. The patterns, even today, are usually classic in style. Originally lampas was an East Indian printed silk.

LAMPSHADE A covering or shield for a light bulb set in a lamp base. Usually a metal frame of the shade, which is cylindrical, oval, or bell-shaped, is covered with silk, rayon, polyplastex, parchment, or opaque board. Used to diffuse the light, cut down the glare of the bulb and/or direct the stream of light. Metal lampshades are also used. See *Bouillotte Shade*, *Harp*, and *Tole Shade*.

LANAI A Hawaiian term for an outdoor patio, terrace or veranda.

LANCASHIRE SPINDLE-BACK CHAIR A country-style spindle-back chair of early-18th-century England. The uprights are turnings connected with a top rail embellished with a shell-like ornament in the middle. One or two rows of four or five spindles are contained by one or two horizontal rails and the top rail. The seat is made of rush, and the front stretcher is turned with a knoblike centerpiece.

LANCASTRIAN PERIOD See *Perpendicular Style*. Illustrated is the Church of Fotheringhay, Northamptonshire, England.

LANCET ARCH A narrow pointed arch. A feature of early Gothic architecture and furniture.

LANCET WINDOW A narrow pointed window, lancet-shaped.

LANCRET, NICHOLAS (1690–1743) A French decorative painter in the style and tradition of Watteau.

LAMINATION

LAMPADAIRE

LANCASHIRE SPINDLE-BACK CHAIR

LANTERN

LANCASTRIAN PERIOD

LANTHORN

LAP JOINT

LANDING A flat platform between two flights of stairs.

LANDSCAPE An outdoor scene depicted in art. A planting arrangement. A painting, mirror, or panel which is wider than it is tall.

LANDSCAPE OFFICE SCREENS Modular panels and screens, often made of soundproofing materials, that can be combined to differentiate work spaces in an open-office plan. Available from many manufacturers and in an infinite variety of size modules, fabric coverings, and colors. Relatively simple to join together, and may include raceways for power and communication in their construction. Some panels are designed with slotted vertical uprights at their ends which makes it possible not only to create a cubicle or work station but furnish it with hook-on shelves, desk tops, files, task lights, etc. See *Open Planning*.

LANGLEY, BATTY (1695–1751) An English architect and designer who frequently used ogee or cyma curves for moldings around doors and drawers. Langley's *Gothic Architecture Improved by Rules and Proportion* helped bring in the Gothic Revival. He also compiled *Ancient Masonry*, which provided inspiration for the Colonial American 18th-century builders.

LANGLOIS, PETER A late-18th-century French immigrant craftsman in England who worked in the technique of Boulle. See *Boulle Work*.

LANNUIER, CHARLES-HONORÉ A late-18th- and early-19th-century French cabinetmaker and designer. He worked in America in the Louis XVI classic style, and influenced the work of Duncan Phyfe.

LANTERN In furniture, a case with a metal or wood framework furnished with panes of glass or other translucent materials. A lighted candle was originally inserted inside the framework. Today lanterns are also electrified. See *Lanthorn*.

LANTERN CLOCK A lantern-shaped shelf clock of the late 17th century. It was usually made of brass, and was also called a birdcage clock.

LANTERN LIGHT A raised, vertical skylight which is set above the roof of a building. The panes of glass are vertical rather than arranged in the more usual horizontal framework.

LANTHORN An archaic term for lantern. Horn was used instead of glass panes in the wood or metal framework. Illustrated is a German Renaissance wrought-iron lanthorn.

LAP JOINT Two pieces of wood with exactly grooved out areas laid one up and one down, so that they make a flush X arrangement when they are notched into each other at right angles. A form of joinery.

LAPIS LAZULI A semiprecious, azure stone of a rich blue color. It is an aluminous mineral resembling the blue carbonate of copper. Used in inlay work and on decorative hardware.

LAQUÉ French for lacquered.

LARSEN, JACK LENOR A 20th-century architect/interior designer specializing in the design and manufacture of textiles that combine style, texture and the finest hand craftsmanship with the best technical production techniques. Founded the Jack Lenor Larsen, Inc. Textile House in 1952.

L'ART DEL POVERO An Italian form of Découpage.

L'ART MODERNE A weekly periodical founded in Belgium in 1884. Its major premise was "art is the eternally spontaneous and free action of man on his environment, for the purpose of transforming it and making it conform to a new idea." The periodical was published until 1893, and brought together a group of avant-garde young Belgian artists known as "Les XX." The group included James Ensor, Ferdinand Knopff, Alfred William ("Willy") Finch, and Maus. See *Art Nouveau*.

LASALLE, PHILIPPE DE (1720–1803) A French designer and manufacturer of textiles, as well as the inventor of special weaving devices. During the *Louis XVI* period he was especially noted for his floral patterns and *lampas*. His artistry earned him the title, "the painter of textiles."

LATERAL FILE An office file in which letters, forms, etc. are stored from side to side, rather than from front to back as in the traditional upright file. Available in widths of 30″–36″–42″ up to 48″ and may be several tiers high. The traditional vertical (upright) file is usually 15″ or 18″ wide, may also be several tiers tall—but it is usually deeper than the lateral file. See *Vertical File*.

LATEX A product made from the sap of the rubber tree. It is a rubber coating on carpet backings, or to hold the yarn ends of tufted fabric on to the backing. See *Foam Rubber*.

LATEX PAINT A popular interior paint which uses a synthetic resin, latex, as a vehicle to carry the pigment. The fine latex disperse in water, and as the water evaporates, they create a strong and durable film. Latex paint dries quickly, is odorless and has good covering powers. When

LATH

LATTEN

LATTICEWORK

LATERAL FILE

LAUREL

thoroughly dried, it is water resistant and scrubbable.

LATH A thin strip of flat wood used for understructures or as a support of a framework for finishing materials. Illustrated is a lath framework for stucco in a wall.

LATHE In cabinetry, an instrument for holding a rotating piece of wood or dowel against a tool that shapes it to make a wood turning.

LATIN CROSS A cross form with the vertical line longer than the horizontal one.

LATROBE, BENJAMIN HENRY (1766–1820) An American architect who worked in the Greek Revival style, greatly influenced by classic Greek and Roman architecture. Latrobe also designed in the Gothic Revival style, and designed a popular stove for heating interiors.

LATTEN German for laths or thin plates. A mixed metal of copper and zinc which resembles brass, used during the Gothic period for engraved panels and cast statues. Illustrated is an engraved 14th-century latten panel.

LATTICE An openwork crisscross or fretwork made of wood laths or thin metal strips.

LATTICE WINDOW A window with leaded glazing bars forming a lattice pattern. The panes are usually diamond- or lozenge-shaped.

LATTICEWORK A chair-back design by *Sheraton* and *Manwaring* which consisted of wooden or metal strips crossing over each other diagonally. This name also applies to tracery on the doors of cabinets and bookcases. Fretwork is usually much smaller in scale than latticework. See *Trelliswork*.

LAUAN A reddish-brown Philippine hardwood that resembles mahogany. It is sometimes called Philippine mahogany. A handsome ribbon figure is produced when the lauan log is quarter-sawed. See *Almon*.

LAUBGEHÄNGE German for a festoon of foliage.

LAUREL An ornamental motif used as a symbol for glory. Singers and heroes in ancient times were crowned with laurels. It was used in the classic Greek and Roman periods for decoration, and also in the Louis XVI, English 18th-century, and early 19th-century European styles as an architectural or furniture decoration on friezes and in bands.

LAUREL WOOD An East Indian walnut, gray or brown, coarse-grained, hard and brittle, used as a veneer on fine cabinetry. The pattern may be striped, fiddle-backed, figured, or have indistinct rays.

LAVABO   French for washstand. A table and washstand, or a washbowl with a fountain, cistern, or water supply. The lavabo is now often used as a planter in a decorative wall arrangement.

LAVORO A SBALZO   Italian for repoussé work.

LAWN   Originally a lightweight, fine linen fabric. Now also made of highly polished cotton yarn.

LAWSON COUCH   A simple, usually skirted, sofa or loveseat, with rollover arms which are usually mid-height between the seat and the top of the sofa back. A Lawson chair is similar in general line, but seats only one person.

LAYLIGHT   A glass or translucent panel set flush into a ceiling to admit natural or artificial light.

LAZY SUSAN   A revolving tabletop or tray for serving relishes and condiments. An American adaptation of the dumbwaiter of late 18th-century England. A Sheraton design is illustrated.

LAZY SUSAN

LE BRUN, CHARLES (1619–1690)   Le Brun was King Louis XIV's favorite painter and decorator. He created tall, stiff, pompous, heroic-scaled furniture. Among his achievements was the semicircular vaulted arch in the Hall of Mirrors (Galérie des Glaces) in Versailles, designed by Jules Hardouin-Mansart. Le Brun was the Director and chief designer of the Gobelins Factory. He was the embodiment of the soul and spirit of the decoration of the Louis XIV period. An armoire, designed by Le Brun and executed by Charles-André Boulle, is illustrated.

CHARLES LE BRUN

LE CLERC, SÉBASTIAN (1637–1714)   French engraver.

LE COMPTE, LOUIS (1639–1694)   A French sculptor of the Louis XIV period. He did decorative carvings at Versailles.

LE CORBUSIER   (pseudonym of Charles Édouard Jeanneret or Édouard Jeanneret-Gris) Born in Switzerland in 1887, he was an architect, painter, writer, and architectural critic. One of the most influential architects and city planners of this century, he also designed chairs.

LE LARGE, JEAN-BAPTISTE   A late-18th-century French furniture designer and manufacturer. He created many bergères and fauteuils for the Palais de Versailles.

LE LEU, FRANÇOIS (1729–1807)   A French cabinetmaker noted for his exquis-

LEADED GLAZING

LEAFWORK

LEATHER

ite marquetry. He worked under Jean-François Oeben at Versailles, and also created pieces for Mme Du Barry. Le Leu worked in the Louis XV and Louis XVI styles.

LE MAIRE, ELEANOR   A 20th-century designer-decorator.

LE MÉDAILLON   An oval back chair of the Louis XVI period. The chair had straight legs, and the arms were brought forward and fastened directly above the front legs. See *Cameo Back* and *Oval Back*.

LE NÔTRE, ANDRÉ (1613–1700)   A French architect-designer of the parks and gardens at Versailles, the Trianon, and Vaux-le-Vicomte.

LE ROI SOLEIL   "The Sun King," sobriquet of Louis XIV of France (1643–1715) who loved pomp, splendor and magnificence. A most regal and extravagant king. The flaming sunburst with radiating gilt rays appeared as a carved, painted, and embroidered decoration during this French Baroque period.

LE SUEUR, EUSTACHE (1617–1655)   A late French Renaissance painter and decorator, who was associated with the Gobelins works.

LE VASSEUR, ÉTIENNE (1721–1798)   A furniture designer and cabinetmaker in the styles of Louis XV and Louis XVI. He created furniture for the Petit Trianon.

LEADED GLAZING   Lead strips soldered together into a pattern, with small pieces of glass are set in and held by the lead strips. Clear, colored, patterned, or textured glass can be used. Religious and educational institutions often have leaded glass windows with pictorial representations composed of colored glass. Illustrated is the leaded glazing of Little Moreton Hall in Cheshire, England. See *Stained Glass*.

LEAF SCROLL FOOT   A variation of the scroll foot. There is foliage carved on the face of the leg, and it sometimes hips out in front of the ankle.

LEAFWORK   Small collections of carved leaves used as decorative details on legs, splats, and cabinets during the last quarter of the 18th century in England. A Sheraton chair leg is illustrated.

LEATHER   Animal hide used as an upholstery material, a wall hanging, a tabletop finish, a material to cover accessories, books, etc. Usually the hide of a steer is used, sliced or split five times. The three middle slices are used for upholstery. A leather-upholstered 17th-century Jacobean chair is illustrated.

LEATHERETTE (artificial leather) A nitrocellulose material with a heavy cotton backing. The top surface may be embossed or carved to simulate leather grainings. The material comes in a wide range of colors, textures, and weights, and is used for upholstery and wall covering. See *Naugahyde*.

LEAVES Additional flat panels which can be added to extend or increase the surface of a tabletop. Some leaves are hinged to the table surface and must be raised to a horizontal position, as in the Pembroke or gateleg table. Other leaves are drawn out from beneath the table surface, as in the draw table (a late-16th-century English Renaissance table here illustrated). In other tables the framework is extended and the leaves put into the space so made. See *Draw Table, Extension Table, Folding Table, Gateleg Table* and *Pembroke Table*.

LECTERN A reading desk. A carved or turned pedestal support for a Bible or a large book like a dictionary. A Hepplewhite design is illustrated.

LECTUS A Roman bed or couch. The bed was sometimes equipped with a reading desk and cubicles to contain necessities.

LEDGE A simple horizontal structure, usually fixed across two vertical supports. A mantel is a ledge. Illustrated is a 15th-century early Italian Renaissance mantel.

LEG A furniture support. The leg of a chair usually starts at the seat rail and ends in a foot. Leg designs vary with periods and styles of decoration. Illustrated are some typical turned legs of the late 17th century in England.

L'ENFANT, PIERRE-CHARLES (1754–1825) A French engineer-architect who redesigned the old City Hall in New York into the First National Capitol. He created the pediment over the balcony and entrance with a crouching eagle emerging from the clouds. Thirteen stars fill the metope of the frieze, and the pilaster capitals are composed of rays and stars. L'Enfant is probably best known for his layout of Washington, D.C., which is reminiscent of Versailles; the Capitol represents the Palace, the White House is in a position similar to that of the Grand Trianon, and the Mall is the equivalent of the Park. He also laid out the gridiron of radial avenues.

LEKYTHOS The Greek word for oil flask. It is named after the shape of seed vessels. It is also spelled *lecythis*.

LENO WEAVE A weave in which pairs of warp yarns are wound around each other between picks or filler yarns, and a netlike effect results.

LEONINE BASE

LEAVES

JEAN LEPAUTRE

LECTERN

PIERRE LESCOT

LEDGE

LIBRARY

LEGS

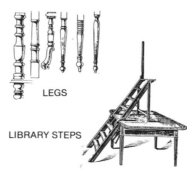

LIBRARY STEPS

LEONINE BASE A table, chair, or other furniture support carved to resemble the legs and paws of a lion. Illustrated is a German 19th-century Néo-Grec wine cooler by Ruhl.

LEPAUTRE, JEAN (1617–1682) An interior designer and clockmaker for Louis XIII and Louis XIV. He published several works on decorative furniture which had a great influence on Flemish and English styles. Louis XIV named Lepautre the Royal Architect. A frieze designed by Lepautre is shown here.

LESCOT, PIERRE (1510–1578) A French Renaissance architect under François I and Henri II. He designed the original section of the present Louvre. Illustrated is a door in the Henri II room of the Louvre.

LETTERWOOD A wood native to Guiana which is also called snakewood. The reddish-brown wood is distinguished by an irregular darker pattern.

LETTO Italian for bed.

LETTO CON BALDACCHINO Italian for a bed with a tester.

LEWAN In Oriental houses, a room with an open side which lets out into an inner court.

LIBRARY A reading room, sometimes equipped with bookcases on all four walls. The room usually has a desk or writing table and some comfortable chairs. Illustrated is an elevation of the elegant 18th-century Adam library in Syon House, Middlesex, England.

LIBRARY ARMCHAIR A late-18th-century convertible chair with steps under the seat. The seat flips over and becomes a small step unit.

LIBRARY CASE A late-18th-Century Hepplewhite term for a bookcase.

LIBRARY PRESS BEDSTEAD A convertible bed which folded up into a cupboard, bureau, or pseudobookcase. Popular in the 18th-century Sheraton, Shearer, and Hepplewhite periods for a sitting room that could double as a bedroom.

LIBRARY STEPS Many stepladder devices were used in the 18th-century for getting at the uppermost shelves of the high built-in bookcases which often covered all the walls of the library. Illustrated is a Sheraton unit which converted into a library table, or, as shown, opened into a stepladder.

LIBRARY TABLE Originally, the English term for a large pedestal or kneehole desk. Presently, a large table with drawers or a pedestal table. The kneehole desk has drawers on both sides of the opening. Illustrated is a Sheraton design. See *Partners' Desk.*

LIEBES, DOROTHY An outstanding 20th-century American interior and textile designer.

LIERNE A short rib which serves to connect ridges or intermediate ribs in ceiling vaulting. It does not rise from the same spring line as the ridge rib.

LIGHT CHAIR A lightweight, easily movable side chair. A Sheraton late-18th-century design with tapered legs and a carved vase back is shown here. See *Hall Chair* and *Side Chair.*

LIGHTING LOUVERS Plastic, metal, or glass filters set over electric bulbs to diffuse the light and soften the glare. They look like miniature circular or rectangular Venetian blinds.

LIGNEREAUX A noted, early-19th-century French cabinetmaker of the Empire period.

LIGNUM VITAE A hard, heavy, greenish-brown wood used by the Dutch and Flemish in the 17th century for linen chests and cupboards. Very durable, oily, and waxy, and has a fine interwoven grain texture. It is difficult to work. Lignum vitae was introduced into Europe at the beginning of the 16th century for its medicinal value; it's name means wood of life.

LIMBA The French name for korina wood. See *Afara* and *Korina.*

LIME Calcium oxide derived from burning limestone.

LIME MORTAR A mortar consisting of sand, water, and slaked lime, used to bind bricks or stone masonry.

LIMED OAK A special finish applied to oak to give it a frosted or silvery-gray appearance. A whitish filler or paint is rubbed into the grain of the wood and then wiped off. This process tends to accentuate the grain. Woods other than oak can be limed.

LIMESTONE A building stone, usually gray or beige, which is mainly carbonate of lime or carbonate of calcium.

LIMEWOOD An excellent carving material favored by Grinling Gibbons in the late 17th century. It is close-grained and light in color. Illustrated is a Grinling Gibbons carving from a choir stall in St. Paul's Cathedral, London.

LIMOSIN, LÉONARD (c. 1505–1577) A French artist who painted portraits on fine enameled copperware in Limoges.

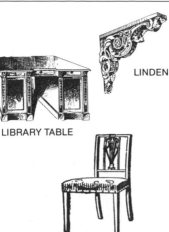

LIBRARY TABLE

LIGHT CHAIR

LINENFOLD

LINING

LIMEWOOD

LINDEN A fine, white-grained wood from the lime tree, excellent for carving. Many of Grinling Gibbons' mantels and trophies were carved in linden. The American basswood is sometimes referred to as a linden. See, *Gibbons, Grinling,* and *Limewood.*

LINE ENGRAVING A form of intaglio engraving used for reproducing works of art. Dürer is considered one of the greatest artists to use this technique, which demands great discipline and precision. A sharp graver is used to create V-shaped furrows on a copper plate.

LINEN A strong yarn made of smooth surfaced flax fibers. It can be woven in a plain or damask weave fabric. There are many types of linen: Belgian, English, Irish, handwoven, hand-blocked, hand-printed, homespun, satin, etc.

LINENFOLD A carved Gothic panel embellishment made to resemble folded linen or a scroll of linen. It was popular in England in the mid-Tudor period and was originally a Flemish motif. Another name for linenfold panels is parchment panels. See illustration for *Oak, Quartered.*

LINING In furniture, a fine line of inlaid veneer, the same as "stringing." Illustrated is a late-18th-century Sheraton dressing table with inlay banding around the drawers. See *Banding.* In drapery and upholstery, a fabric used to back up the fine face fabric. It gives additional weight and body to the drapery, and may also serve as an insulating agent or protect the face fabric from suns rays, etc.

LINING PAPER An inexpensive paper applied to a wall before the patterned or textured wallpaper is applied. It supplies a clean background for the wallpaper, and helps prevent cracking.

LINNELL, JOHN AND WILLIAM 18th-century English carvers, cabinetmakers, and upholsterers. They worked in the Rococo, Chinese, and Classic styles.

LINOCUT or LINOLEUM CUT A modern adaptation of the woodcut printing technique, using a piece of linoleum fastened to a wood block as a surface into which the design is cut.

LINOLEUM A manufactured floor-covering material cured by heating, and therefore fairly resistant to indentation and temperature changes. The wearing surface goes through to the backing, it is fairly resistant to grease and oil, and it has some resiliency underfoot. Linoleum will absorb moisture, and is not recommended for use where there is high humidity. Usually manufactured in 6′ widths, in a multitude of colors and patterns.

LINSEED OIL An oil processed from flaxseed, commonly used in house paints and furniture finishes.

LINTEL A horizontal piece of wood or stone over a door, window, or other opening to support the weight above. Illustrated is the rock-cut façade of the Egyptian tomb of Beni Hassan.

LINTERS The short cotton fibers which stick to the cotton seed after the first ginning. They are used for upholstery stuffing, mattresses, and for producing cellulose sheets used in making rayon.

LION The "king of the beasts," and always a favorite animal symbol in furniture, interiors, art, and architecture. In ancient Egypt, the lion was associated with water and was usually shown at rest, carved with a formalized rufflike mane. In the Greek and Roman periods, the lion was the symbol of the fallen hero, and was also used as the guardian of gates, temples, and public buildings. Christian art used the lion to represent the Redeemer, and in medieval heraldry and in current seals, flags, shields, etc., the lion often is used as a symbol of strength, courage, and royalty.

LION HEAD A carved representation of a lion's head used on furniture and in architecture. The head served as a gargoyle on ancient classic temples, and was often used as a knocker or handle on Gothic and Renaissance doors and cabinets. It also functioned as a holder at the end of a swag or festoon. Sometimes the lion head was combined with a leg and paw, and used as part of a furniture support. Illustrated is an Empire bureau designed by Charles Percier. See *Lion Period*.

LION PERIOD The period from 1720 to 1735 in England when carved lions' masks on the knees of cabriole legs and the arms of chairs and settees, and lion's paws on furniture feet were the most popular motif.

LION'S PAW FOOT The carved representation of a furry paw at the end of a furniture leg. Appeared in early Greek and Roman furniture, and found in French, English, and Italian Renaissance designs. A prime decorating motif in 18th-century English furniture. An Italian Renaissance bed is illustrated. See *Lion Period*.

LIP MOLDING A small convex molding found in Queen Anne and Chippendale chests and cabinets. Usually the molding was set around doors and drawers to act as a dust stop.

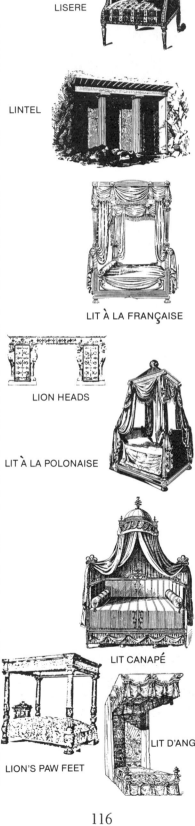

LISERE

LINTEL

LIT À LA FRANÇAISE

LION HEADS

LIT À LA POLONAISE

LIT CANAPÉ

LIT D'ANGE

LION'S PAW FEET

LISERE A typically French fabric of the late 18th century which became popular in England, a silk with a warp of Jacquard designs and a weft of brocaded flowers. Illustrated is a Louis XVI winged armchair upholstered in a lisere fabric.

LISEUSE A Louis XVI reading table. A collapsible bookrest was set into the center top panel of the rectangular desklike table. Often several small drawers were set into the apron of the table.

LISIÈRE The French word for selvage; the outer woven edge of a textile or tapestry. See *Selvage*.

LISTEL or LIST A border fillet molding.

LIT The French word for bed.

LIT À LA FRANÇAISE "French bed," a bed with a canopy over it placed sideways against a wall. A late-18th-century design. Illustrated is an early-19th-century Sheraton variation.

LIT À LA POLONAISE "Polish bed," a late-18th-century bed with a pointed crown canopy. A Sheraton design is illustrated.

LIT À TRAVERS A sofa bed.

LIT CANAPÉ A sofa bed. An 18th-century Sheraton design is illustrated.

LIT CLOS A bed with wood panels to enclose the sleeping area, often built against the wall, could be completely screened in. Often found in French country estates from the 17th through the 19th century. See *Built-in Furniture*.

LIT D'ANGE "Angel bed," an 18th-century French bed with a small canopy supported by the back bedposts only. There are no front pillars, and the canopy extends only partially over the bed. A Daniel Marot design (early 18th century) is illustrated.

LIT DE REPOS A daybed.

LIT DE REPOS À CROSSE A daybed with outward, rollover scrolled ends. See *Chaise Longue*.

LIT DUCHESSE A bed of Louis XIV design with a large canopy supported by the four bedposts.

LIT EN BATEAU A 19th-century French boat-shaped bed, similar to the *Sleigh Bed*.

LITHOGRAPH A drawing or design done with a grease pencil or crayon on a special type of stone. A limited number of printed impressions are possible with this technique.

LITS JUMEAUX French for twin beds. See *Summer Bed*.

LIVERY CUPBOARD A 17th-century hall cupboard consisting of several open shelves for the display of plate. The lower chest or cupboard part was originally the receptacle for unused food. "Livery" is an old form of delivery, and referred to the taking of food during the night, and therefore the livery cupboard was often found in the bedchamber. In churches, the livery cupboard was called a dole cupboard, and held food set aside for distribution to the poor. Illustrated is a carved oak English livery cupboard made in 1674. (The pediment top was added toward the end of the 18th century.)

LOBBY CHEST Described by Sheraton in 1803 as a half chest of drawers about three feet tall, and with four rows of drawers. A pullout writing board sometimes was provided beneath the top surface. This small unit seemed most appropriate for small studies, lobbies, or bedchambers.

LOBE A foil in Gothic tracery. See *Foils*.

LOBING See *Gadroon*.

LOCK MATTHIAS A mid-18th-century English designer in the rococo style. He originally worked along the lines set by Chippendale, but later switched to the more classic style of the Adam brothers. He published books on foliage, ornaments, pier frames, girandoles, shields, and sconces.

LOCK RAIL The middle horizontal rail of a door, usually where the lock is fixed. Illustrated is a Sir Christopher Wren design executed by Grinling Gibbons.

LOCKER In 18th- and 19th-century furniture, a small central cupboard in the interior of a writing desk or secretary. A compartment or storage unit.

LOEWY, RAYMOND A 20th-century American industrial and interior designer.

LOGGIA An Italian word for a room or area with an open arcade or colonnade at one side. An arcaded gallery. Illustrated is the Loggia of the Vatican in Rome with frescoes by Raphael and Jean d'Udine.

LOIR, ALEXIS (1630–1713) A French painter and decorator of the Louis XIV period, noted for his decorations on furniture.

LOIR, NICHOLAS (1624–1679) A French painter, decorator, and member of the Gobelins Factory. He created many fine mural and tapestry designs; a ceiling design is illustrated.

LOMA-LOOM A trademark of Burlington Industries for a carpet of wool and nylon pile with a built-in sponge rubber cushion. The cushion is an integral part of

LIVERY CUPBOARD

LONG CLOCK

LOOKING GLASS

LOOP BACK

LOCK RAIL

LOPER

LOGGIA

LOUIS XIII STYLE

NICHOLAS LOIR

the carpet. It helps absorb shocks and friction, and gives the carpet extra resiliency.

LOMBARD STYLE Northern Italian version of the Romanesque.

LONG CLOCK An 18th-century hall or grandfather clock. A Chippendale design is illustrated.

LOOKING GLASS See *Mirror*. A mid-18th-century Chippendale example is illustrated.

LOOP BACK An oval chair back or a Windsor Bow Back without arms. A Hepplewhite design is illustrated.

LOOS, ADOLF (1870–1933) An Austrian architect and one of the leaders in the modern movement of the early 20th century. He recognized the impact of machinery on ornament and design and its ultimate effect on architecture. His strong, austere quality had a great influence on the development of the functional style in Austria.

LOOSE SEAT See *Slip Seat*.

LOPER The slide support under the drop front or lid of a desk. A Hepplewhite design is illustrated.

LORRAIN, CLAUDE (1600–1682) A great French landscape painter of the Louis XIII and Louis XIV periods. He decorated the Chapelle des Carmes at Nancy.

LOTUS A plant of the ancient Oriental and Egyptian civilizations which was used as a decorative motif. The Egyptians used the flower form for a column capital, household utensils, and as an embellishment on their wall decorations.

LOUIS XIII STYLE See *French Late Renaissance*. Illustrated is a chair in the Louis XIII style.

LOUIS XIV (1643–1715)—THE BAROQUE STYLE The Golden Age of the French Renaissance and the reign of the Sun King, Louis XIV. A native style based on the classic orders combined with the baroque, developed in splendor and magnificence. Rooms and furniture were enormous in scale. The ornamentation was rich and heavy, done in gilt and strong colors with sharp accents. Compass-formed curves relieved the rectangular wooden wall panels.

LOUIS XV (1715–1774)—THE ROCOCO PERIOD The reign of Louis XV in France. A period of gaiety and frivolity, effeminacy and sentimentality. Rooms and furniture were human-scaled for greater comfort, and the effect was more intimate. Curved free forms, S-shapes and asymmetry became the dominant. The classic orders were replaced by the exotic and Chinoiserie. Lacquered and painted furniture added to the effect of this "age of the boudoir," and Mme de Pompadour was a guiding influence.

LOUIS XVI (1774–1793)—THE NEO-CLASSIC STYLE The reign of Louis XVI in France and the return to naturalism, simplicity, and reason in the decorative forms. The classic architectural forms and orders were revived, with Pompeii, Herculaneum, Greece, and the Adam brothers of England as the dominant influences. Straight lines and compass curves returned, with symmetry and a more severe classic quality.

LOUIS-PHILIPPE PERIOD The reign in France of Louis-Philippe, 1830–1848, when the fashions and styles of the Louis XV period had a brief revival. The work was eclectic and lacked the grace and hand workmanship of the original period.

LOUNGE A late-19th-century sofa or couch. It was often designed with one arm higher than the other, to serve as a headrest. Also, a room for relaxing or resting. A large sitting room, often in a public building.

LOUNGE CHAIR A deep, full upholstered chair designed to envelop and relax the seated individual, a comfortable chair into which one settles. May be of any style or period.

LOUVER An opening in a wall or ceiling, covered with slats placed at an angle. Also, one of the slats.

LOUVERED DOORS Doors with panels of overlapping horizontal slats which can be adjusted to be open, closed, or in a position in between.

LOUVRE (PALAIS DU) (1546–1878) The full range of Renaissance art and architecture encompassed in one structure which was begun in the time of François I and worked on till the reign of Napoleon III. Jean Goujon added sculpture details to the two-story façade of Corinthian and composite pilasters and an attic story above. Jacques Du Cerceau in 1600 added a gallery. Many famous artists and craftsmen worked on the magnificent interiors.

LOVE SEAT An upholstered settee for two persons. It first became popular in the Louis XIV period in France and in the Queen Anne period in England. The double seat is also called a "courting chair." Illustrated is a Louis XVI love seat.

LOVER'S CHAIR See *Drunkard's Chair.*

LOVOA A tropical African wood that is yellow-brown to dark-brown. Though it

LOW-BACK CHAIR

LOWBOY

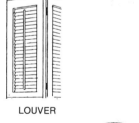

LOZENGE

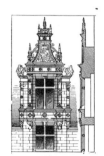

LUCARNE

LOUVER

LUNETTE

LOVE SEAT

resembles Circassian walnut, it actually belongs to the mahogany family. In the veneer resulting from slicing a quartered log there is a straight stripe with sharp color contrasts.

LOW-BACK CHAIR A mid-17th-century term for the small side chairs with backs which replaced the stools and benches in middle-class homes. The Cromwellian chair is one example. The illustrated Farthingale chair is another.

LOWBOY A serving table or low chest of drawers. A late-17th-century English example is shown.

LOZENGE A conventional diamond-shaped motif. The Normans used the diamond shape in lozenge and billet molding. A Jacobean settle with lozenge carving on the paneled back is illustrated. A product of the first part of the 17th century, the lozenge also appears in the French Directoire period.

LUCARNE French for a dormer window. Illustrated is an early French Renaissance example from the Château de Chambord.

LUG A small projecting element on a building material, which makes fixing the material into place easier and the resultant setting more secure. On ceramic tiles, this projection is called a nib. It supplies an extra surface to glue or cement in place, and therefore an extra surface for adhesion.

LUMINOSITY The quality of reflecting or giving light.

LUNETTE In architecture, a semicircular window area. Also, a subsidiary vault intersecting with a main vault or dome, and, having its crown at a lower level, causing a crescent-shaped groin to be formed. The crescent shape is a lunette. In furniture, a crescent or half-moon shape. It may be used in a repeated decorative band design or, as in the Jacobean period, as a carved or inlaid motif. In the 18th century, tables sometimes had lunette designs painted or inlaid on them. A Hepplewhite commode tabletop is illustrated.

LUNNING, FREDERICK A 20th-century Scandinavian furniture producer and designer.

LUREX A trademark name for a nontarnishing, aluminum-base metallic yarn often incorporated into upholstery, drapery, or curtain fabrics. Produced in various metallic colors by the Dobeckmun Company.

LUSS, GERALD A 20th-century American designer of Designs for Business, Inc. He is a pioneer in space planning for offices and commercial installations. Luss has devised many modular systems for office interiors.

LUSTER   A thin metallic glaze applied to pottery to produce an iridescent color. Used on Persian ceramics, Majolica ware, and also on antique English and American ware.

LUSTRAGRAY   A trademark of American Saint Gobain for gray-tinted window glass which reduces glare by approximately 50 percent but does not obscure vision. The exterior opacity contributes to privacy, and the neutral color places no restrictions on interior decor. Manufactured in several thicknesses.

LUSTRE   A table light or wall sconce in crystal, or enriched with crystal drops or pendants.

LUSTRE FABRIC   In carpets, any pile-cut fabric woven with surface yarns spun from soft types of staple and chemically washed to give a bright sheen. The term also means a glossy finish achieved by

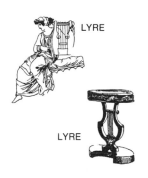

LYRE

LYRE

LYRE-BACK CHAIR

means of heat or pressure. Handwoven Oriental fabrics are also washed in this way.

LUSTRE RUGS   See *Sheen Rugs.*

LUTHERN   In a classic building, a window (bull's-eye, square, arched, or semicircular) above the cornice, vertically in line with the front exterior of the structure.

LYRE   A stringed instrument which appears in Greek decoration and was adapted in the Renaissance period, and in various forms in the 17th through the 19th century in France, England, and Germany. A popular motif in the Empire period, and a particular favorite of the 19th-century American designer Duncan Phyfe. Illustrated are a German Empire table and a classic Greek lyre.

LYRE-BACK CHAIR   A Duncan Phyfe early-19th-century American chair. The splat was an open-carved lyre design. The lyre was previously used by Adam, Sheraton, and Hepplewhite in 18th-century English furniture. A Sheraton design is illustrated.

M

MACAROON or MACARON A decorative rosette carving used to ornament Louis XVI furniture, named after the cake called in French macaron and in English macaroon. It is usually an eight-petaled flower with a central bud, and resembles a cookie or patera. The macaroon usually was carved on the upper block of the chair leg or in the corners of the front seat-rail. A Louis XVI fauteuil is illustrated. See *Patera*.

MACKINTOSH, CHARLES RENNIE (1868–1928) A Scottish artist, architect, and furniture designer who designed and created in the Art Nouveau style.

MACRAME A technique used to produce wall hangings and decorative trimmings with knotted cotton yarns and twine. Usually conceived in a geometric pattern and executed by knotting or tying strands together to form a lacy intricate openwork design.

MADAME JUMEL CHAIR An early-19th-century Empire chair, without back stiles. The top rail of the chair back curves and sweeps forward to meet the front legs. The splat (central upright of the chair back) is often lyre- or vase-shaped. Similar to the Regency spoon-back chair. See *Spoon-Back*.

MADIO A 16th-century Italian Renaissance sideboard.

MADOU See *Maidou* or *Madou* and *Padouk*.

MAGASIN AU BON MARCHÉ The first complete modern glass-and-iron department store with natural light throughout, built in Paris in 1876. It was designed by Louis Auguste Boileau and the engineer

MACAROON

MACAROON

MAHOGANY

MADAME JUMEL CHAIR

Alexandre Gustave Eiffel. The corner of the store is built out in a pavilion-like affair. The interior is a combination of glass skylights, aerial bridges in iron, and ornamental thin iron columns. The ground floor consists of a continuous line of show windows.

MAGNOLIA A straight-grained and generally uniformly textured wood similar to yellow poplar, but harder and heavier. Native to the southern United States, especially the Appalachians.

MAHOGANY A longtime favorite furniture and interior wood with a beautiful reddish color and a handsome grain. It works easily, is wormproof, and takes a high polish. Figured mahogany may be plain or broken stripe, mottled, fiddlebacked, or swirled. Available in wide widths and long lengths. Among the true mahoganies are: African, Cuban, Peruvian, Brazilian, and tropical American mahogany. A wardrobe of the early Georgian period (1725) is illustrated. It was built during the Age of Mahogany. See *Acajou, Age of Mahogany,* and *Primavera*.

MAHOGANY, HONDURAS A yellowish-white to salmon-pink to rich golden-brown wood, figured in a rich mottle or with a straight-grained moderate crossfire. See *Baywood*.

MAHOGANY, SPANISH One of the finest mahoganies grown. It is imported from Santo Domingo.

MAHOGANY, WHITE See *Primavera*.

MAIDOU or MADOU A decorative veneer-wood from the East Indies and Indo-China, found in a long grain, or an amboyna-like, fine burled figure. The color varies from pale straw yellow to red. Padouk burl wood is sold under the name of maidou.

MAÎTRE-ÉBÉNISTE Master cabinetmaker. A title bestowed on favored royal furniture designers and cabinetmakers by the French kings. See *Ébéniste*. Illustrated is a buffet with copper ornaments by Jean Berain (17th century).

MAÎTRE-ÉBÉNISTE

MAJOLICA Italian and Spanish pottery coated with a tin enamel, and decorated with bright colors. The name is derived from the island of Majorca. See *Luster*.

MAKIMONO An Oriental painting in the form of a long scroll. See *Kakemono*.

MAKORE or MAKORI African cherrywood, pale pinkish brown to dark red or purplish brown in color, with a fine, smooth-surfaced texture, sometimes a mottled figure. Resembles American cherrywood. Used for furniture, cabinetry, and interior finishes.

MALACHITE A sea-green to dark green stone with intricate patterned scalloping whorls. Takes a high polish, and was used in ancient Egypt for amulets. In Italy, known as the "Peacock Stone."

MALTESE CROSS A cross consisting of four equal arms; each is wedge-shaped, and the points meet in the center.

MANCHETTE The French term for a padded arm cushion. See *Arm Pads*.

MANDORLA Italian for almond. An almond-shaped halo. See *Aureole*.

MAN-MADE FIBERS Synthetic fibers. Manufactured fibers not of natural plant or animal origin.

MANNERISM or THE MANNERIST SCHOOL A term coined in this century to describe the chief painting style, especially in Italy, from 1520 to 1600. It broke the rules of classic art. The human figure was set into distorted, elongated, and tortured positions with strained and bulging muscles. Compositions were strained and lopsided; perspective and scale were violently manipulated. The Mannerist artist usually used bright, harsh colors which were intended to heighten the emotional effect: reds blending into orange, and greens running into yellow. Tintoretto and El Greco are among the most famous of the Mannerist artists.

MANSARD ROOF A hipped roof with two slopes on each side. The first or lower slope is very steep, and the upper angle is less extreme. A mansard roof that is not hipped is also called a gambrel roof. The

MANTELPIECE

MANTELSHELF

MANCHETTE

MARBLE

mansard roof is named for François Mansart, the late French Renaissance architect who popularized its use.

MANSART, JULES HARDOUIN- See *Hardouin-Mansart, Jules*.

MANSONIA An African wood which greatly resembles walnut, often used as a walnut substitute in England. Sometimes called African black walnut. Usually straight-grained and fine-textured. It works and glues well and takes an excellent finish.

MANTEL A shelf projecting above a fireplace. See *Chimney Piece* and *Ledge* for illustrations.

MANTELPIECE The stonework, brickwork, or woodwork surrounding a fireplace opening. It is usually treated in a decorative manner. An 18th-century example by the English designer Abraham Swan is illustrated.

MANTELSHELF A shelf placed over a fireplace opening. Illustrated is a late-18th-century Adam design. A Mantel.

MANUELINO See *Isabellina*

MANWARING, ROBERT An 18th-century English furniture maker, a contemporary of Chippendale, noted for his chairs, usually characterized by a small bracket between the square leg and the front seat rail, and a latticework splat.

MAPLE A hard, strong, light-colored wood similar to birch. Straight-grained maple is excellent for interior finishes. Bird's-eye maple is curly-grained, swirled, blistered, and/or quilted. It is used as a decorative veneering material. Maple was used for marquetry and veneer in 17th- and 18th-century English furniture.

MAQUETTE French for a small-scale model. See *Bozzetto*.

MARBLE A calcerous stone of compact texture which is found in most countries. The color, pattern, and textural effects are unlimited, and the material is used architecturally and decoratively. Marble was popular for furniture decoration in the late 17th and 18th centuries in France and in the Architects' period in England. Illustrated is a marble mantelpiece designed by Robert and James Adam for the great salon of the Queen's House (mid-18th century).

MARBLING A painted imitation of the veining and texture of marble.

MARILLIER, CLÉMENT-PIERRE (1740–1808) A designer of flowers, trophies, and metal trimmings for furniture during the Louis XVI period. Also a notable illustrator of books.

MARLBOROUGH LEG A straight, grooved leg with a block as a foot that was used in mid-18th-century English and American furniture. It was especially favored by Chippendale. Illustrated is an American colonial sideboard. See *Block Foot.*

MARLBOROUGH LEG

MARMO Italian for marble.

MAROT, DANIEL A French 17th-century designer of the Louis XIV period. Because of the religious persecution, he fled from France to Holland, and then to England and became the chief designer to William III. In his designs he blends Louis XIV and Dutch styles. His position at court enabled him to direct a large group of refugee artisans into England. He designed mantels, sidewalls, cabinets, clocks, beds, and draperies.

DANIEL MAROT

MAROT, JEAN (c. 1617–1679) French architect, designer, and engraver.

MAROUFLAGE A support or backing for a mural or a second canvas or wood panel behind a painting. A reinforcing element.

MARQUEE See *Marquise*

MARQUETRY Pattern made by setting contrasting materials into a veneered surface. The resultant decoration is flush and level. Usually, the material set in is finely grained, interestingly colored woods, but tortoiseshell, horn, metal, and mother-of-pearl are also used. Popular in the Renaissance period and also in 18th-century France and England. Marquetry can be imitated with lithographed transfers. See *Boulle Work, Inlay, Intarsia* or *Tarsia,* and *Parquet.*

MARQUETRY

MARQUISE A projection or canopy over an entrance which is often decorative and made of metal and glass. It is sometimes referred to as a marquee.

MARQUISE CHAIR A completely upholstered small sofa, prototype of the love seat, comparable to an overly wide bergère. It was introduced in the Louis XV period in France, and was designed to accommodate the wide skirts and panniers of the period.

MASCARON

MARQUISETTE A lightweight open-mesh fabric in a leno weave. It is similar to gauze in appearance, and is made of cotton, silk, rayon, synthetics, or a combination of fibers. It is often used for glass curtains.

MARQUISE CHAIR

MARRIAGE CHEST A cassone. An elaborately carved or painted Italian Renaissance long chest, used for storing household linens, etc. Illustrated is a 16th-century carved walnut cassone.

MASHREBEEYAH

MARRIAGE CHEST

MARTHA WASHINGTON CHAIR A Sheraton or Hepplewhite type of chair, with open arms and a high, fully upholstered back and seat. The legs were usually slender and tapered and often inlaid, though some chairs were made with turned or reeded legs. See *Reeding.*

MARTHA WASHINGTON SEWING TABLE An oval-shaped table with deep semicircular end pockets that flank the legs of the unit. The top was hinged to allow access to the two rounded ends and the fitted central tray. The front, back, and sides of the pockets were either finely reeded to look like tambour work, or covered with pleated fabric. The legs were usually turned or reeded. A late-18th-century, early-19th-century American design. See *Reeding.*

MARTIN BROTHERS 18th-century French artisans (Guillaume, Simon, Étienne, Julien, and Robert) distinguished for their lacquer finishing in the Chinese manner. Their technique, called Vernis Martin, employed a clear lacquer speckled with gold, and some forty other lacquers in the Oriental style, but the Martin brothers were best known for their green varnish finish. Snuffboxes, furniture, and even complete rooms were finished in this technique.

MASCARON A grotesque mask or head used as a painted or carved ornament. It is usually distinguished from a masque by being a grinning deformed caricature, distorted and sometimes terminating in foliage, the masque was often an idealized portrayal of nature. In the Gothic period, mascarons were usually caricatures. In the Renaissance and Baroque styles, the mascaron was used to accentuate a keystone in an arch, or used on the backs of chairs, on carved furniture, shields, cartouches, or consoles. The illustrated design is from the Louvre in Paris. See *Grotesques (Grottesques).*

MASCHERONE The Italian word for a painted or carved mask or gargoyle.

MASHREBEEYAH A latticed window. See *Qamariyyah.*

MASKS See *Masques.*

MASLAND DURAN A trademark of Masland Duraleather Company for a vinyl fabric with elastic backing, used for upholstery, produced in a wide range of colors, textures, and patterns.

MASONITE A compressed, rigid compo or building board. It may be tempered for extra strength. It is difficult to drive nails into Masonite.

MASONRY The construction of stones, tiles, bricks, etc., fitted together with mortar.

MASQUES Exaggerated representations of the human face to suggest emotions or ideas such as those of comedy and tragedy. Used in antique classic architecture and decoration, and very popular during the Renaissance. Masques were often used as ornaments on the keystone of door or window arches. See *Mascarons*. Also, magnificently produced entertainments with splendid costumes, scenery and floats. Inigo Jones was a master designer of such masques. See *Jones, Inigo*.

MASSWERK German for tracery.

MASTIC An adhesive for fixing tiles, glass, asbestos, and vinyl tiles, etc. Also a gum or resin used in the manufacturing of varnish.

MATCH BOARDS or MATCHED BOARDS Boards tongued and grooved together. The joint is either beaded or chamfered.

MATELASSÉ From the French for padded, or cushioned. A fabric with an embossed pattern which resembles quilting or a raised quilted design. Matelassé can be imitated by stitching or embossing.

MATTE A dull, nonshiny finish.

MATTED A term used to describe the rough, flat, sunk background of carving on oak furniture. This background was often pitted with small dents or gouge marks.

MATTRESS A fully filled pillow or pad placed over the springs or slats of a bed frame for comfort and softness. Filled with any or a combination of some of the following: down, feathers, hair, cotton batting, foam rubber, etc.

MAURESQUE See *Moresque*. Moorish. Illustrated is the cornice impost of the central arch of the Court of Lions in the Alhambra, Granada, Spain.

MAYHEW, THOMAS An 18th-century English cabinetmaker who worked with William *Ince*. Together they published a book of designs, *The Universal System of Household Furniture*. He was a contemporary of Chippendale.

McCOBB, PAUL A 20th-century American furniture designer (died in 1969) who had a great influence on American furniture during the 1950's and 1960's. He was especially active in creating modular furniture and coordinated groups which combined good design and craftsmanship with mass production techniques.

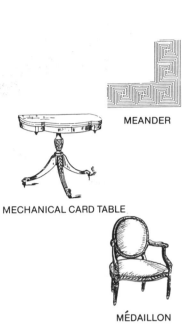

MEANDER

MECHANICAL CARD TABLE

MÉDAILLON

MEDIEVAL

MAURESQUE

THOMAS MAYHEW

McINTYRE, SAMUEL (1757–1811) An American wood-carver of Salem, Massachusetts, who created many mantelpieces and overdoors as well as carvings on furniture. Greatly influenced by Sheraton's later designs, he, like Duncan Phyfe, was a leading designer of the American Federal period.

MEANDER A decorative, geometric, repeating band. A Greek band. See *Fret*.

MECHANICAL CARD TABLE An early-19th-century tripod card table created by American furniture designer Duncan Phyfe. A steel rod is concealed in the turned, foliage-carved, hollow, urn-shaped support. It moves the rear legs and leaf brackets into a supporting position when the top leaf, which lies on top of the fixed leaf, is turned back to provide extra surface. The lower leaf is attached directly to the column. This table was usually made in pairs, of mahogany, and they were used as console tables when not used for gaming.

MÉDAILLIER A French 18th-century small cabinet or display case for medals or decorations.

MÉDAILLON See *Le Médaillon*.

MEDALLION A circular or oval tablet or panel, usually with an ornamental motif enclosed in a frame.

MEDIEVAL See *Gothic Period*. Illustrated is the interior of a 12th-century château according to Eugène Emmanuel Violet-le-Duc, a 19th-century Gothic Revival authority. See *Tapet* illustration.

MEDIUM The liquid or vehicle in which pigments are mixed: water, oil, wax, egg, etc. The word is also used for a technique of creating or rendering a work of art: oils, tempera, marble, wood, bronze, etc.

MEISSEN A factory established at Dresden, then in 1710 removed to Meissen, by Augustus, the King of Saxony. It used a process of copying Chinese porcelain credited to Johann Friedrich Böttger. The French Rococo period began to affect the designs by the middle of the 18th century, and copies of scenes by Jean Antoine Watteau and Nicolas Lancret appeared on the china. The factory produces toleware, vases, statuettes, and other decorative pieces, with the trademark of crossed swords.

MEISSONIER, JUSTE (or JUST) AURÈLE (1695–1750) The father of the Rococo style. An Italian designer who produced a book of engravings using the shell motif which captured the fancy of the French craftsmen. They adapted and incorporated his designs into the Rococo French period woodwork (boiserie) and furniture. Meissonier became designer to Louis XV in 1725, and personally as a painter, goldsmith, architect, and interior designer carried the rococo style to its most extravagant limit. He balanced masses rather than shapes, and used asymmetrical balance as the basis of his designs.

MELON BULB A thick, bulbous turning retained from the Gothic period and used to support and embellish Elizabethan and Jacobean furniture. See *Leaves* for an illustration of a late Elizabethan draw table with melon bulb turned legs.

MELON BULB TABLE A table of the Tudor period (early 16th-century England) with conspicuous globular turned legs. The "melon bulb" turning appeared as a support on other pieces of furniture as well. See *Melon Bulb.*

MELON BULB TABLE

MELON TURNING See *Cup* and *Cover Turning* and *Melon Bulb.*

MÉNAGÈRE A low dresser with open shelves for crockery. The open shelves were usually equipped with racks and guardrails. It was also called a vaisselier. See *Hutch* or *Huche.*

MENDLESHAM CHAIR An early-19th-century variation of the Windsor chair made in Mendlesham, England, by Daniel Day. The back had a narrow splat and a series of turned wood balls between the straight top rail and the lower cross rail. The seat and legs were like those of the usual Windsor chair. See *Dan-Day Chair.*

MEUBLE

MENUISIER The French term for a craftsman who made chairs, beds, sofas, stools, and other pieces out of solid woods rather than with veneer. These pieces could be carved and painted and/or stained. A French Renaissance table of the mid-16th century is illustrated.

MENUISIER

MERCERIZING A process for treating cotton fibers or fabrics with a solution of caustic soda at a low temperature. The process makes the cotton stronger, more lustrous, more susceptible to dye, and more absorbent.

MERCURY HALIDE LAMP A high-intensity discharge light source. Light is produced by the radiation from mercury combined with the halides of metals such as sodium, thalium, and indium. More efficient than the mercury lamp and has generally acceptable color properties. The lamp has a life range from 7,500 to 15,000 hours.

MÉRIDIENNE A short sofa with one arm higher than the other. It was possible to recline in a half-sitting position on this

MEZZO-RILIEVO

MÉRIDIENNE

particular sofa, which was popular at the end of the 18th and the early 19th centuries, especially in the Empire period. A late Sheraton design is illustrated.

MERINO The fine, cashmere-like wool obtained from the Spanish merino sheep.

MERISIER The French for wild cherry-wood, or for a light fruitwood finish.

MESH FABRICS Open loose-weave fabrics of any fiber content.

MESHERABIJEH An Arabic term for a latticework window or shutters of a latticed effect.

MESOPOTAMIA. The "Cradle of Civilization." The fertile plain area around the Lower Tigris and the Lower Euphrates in western Asia. It is now known as Iraq. Early civilizations and cultures flourished in this area. The Babylonians or Chaldeans controlled Mesopotamia from 4000 to 1275 B.C. From 1275 to 538 B.C., the Assyrians ruled over Mesopotamia, and the conquering Persians held sway from 538 to 333 B.C.

MESSALINE A lightweight silk satin fabric.

METAL MOUNTS See *Mounts.*

METOCHE The space between the dentils in the classic Ionic order.

METOPE The space between the triglyphs in the classic Doric entablature. It is usually square (may be oblong) and is generally decorated with designs or groups of figures.

MEUBLES French for movable furniture as opposed to architectural furniture or built-ins. Illustrated is an early-19th-century French Empire chair.

MEUBLES À HAUTEUR D'APPUI French low secretaries, cupboards, or bookcases against which one could comfortably lean or rest.

MEUBLES À TRANSFORMATIONS Mechanically designed convertible furniture of the late Louis XV period. This trend for double-duty furniture was also prevalent in the late-18th-century English designs of Sheraton and others.

MEZZANINE A low-ceilinged story, usually above the ground floor. An entresol.

MEZZO-RILIEVO An Italian term for a relief sculpture which is more than a bas-relief but not as deep as high relief.

MEZZOTINT The art reproduction process of the 18th century. It was especially popular in England where portraits by Sir Joshua Reynolds and Thomas Gainsborough were reproduced in this technique which can produce halftones and highlights. A form of *Intaglio Engraving.*

MICARTA The trademark of the United States Plywood Corporation for vinyl sheet material used for lamination onto wood or walls, for tops and fronts of contemporary furniture, counters, service tables, etc. Available in a wide range of colors and patterns.

MICHELANGELO BUONARROTI (1474–1564) "The Father of Baroque." A great painter, sculptor, architect, and poet of the High Renaissance

MIDDLE AGES See *Gothic Period.*

MIDDLE POINTED PERIOD See *Decorated Period.*

MIGNATURES Small-scaled sprig patterns for fabric created by Christophe-Philippe Oberkampf at his factory in Jouy during the latter part of the 18th century. Machine-made prints with small repeats printed on cotton.

MIGNONNETTES Small, sometimes egg-shaped patterns found on the background of fabrics (toiles) produced in the early 19th century. These small shapes filled the spaces between the framed or paneled elements of the design.

MILD STEEL Steel which contains some carbon, and is not easily tempered.

MILIUM A trademark name for a metalized fabric used for drapery linings. A metal in a resinous binder is sprayed on the fabric to give it a silvery look and a high reflectivity of high radiant heat. Produced by Deering, Milliken, Inc.

MILK or PIE SAFES 19th-century American cupboards found in Pennsylvania and the Midwest, the early "refrigerators." The doors had tin panels pierced in a decorative pattern to allow air to circulate through. Illustrated is a very early 16th-century Tudor-Gothic oak cupboard, a forerunner of the milk or pie safe. Note the pierced openings for ventilation.

MILL ENDS Mill remnants or short ends remaining from a run of fabric.

MILLE-FLEURS French for thousand flowers. A 15th-century Gothic tapestry pattern which contained a multitude of plants, leaves, and flowers. Also later multiple flower designs.

MILTON, THOMAS An 18th-century English designer noted for his chimneypieces. See *Crunden, John.*

MINIATURE Any very small painting, sculpture, or objet d'art. Illustrated are two miniature portraits by Antonio Bencini

MIROIR

MIRROR

MISERICORD

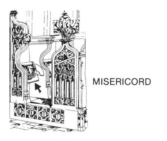

MISSION

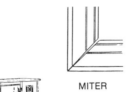

MITER

MILK SAFE

MINIATURE

(c. 1760) which were set into a golden box.

MIRADOR A Spanish term for a balcony with a view, a loggia, or a window overlooking a vista. See *Belvedere.*

MIROIR French for mirror. Illustrated is a Louis XVI table mirror.

MIRROR Looking glass. A highly polished smooth surface which reflects back an image. The earliest were the polished silver mirrors of ancient Egypt. Metal mirrors were also used during the Gothic period. The first silvered-glass mirrors were made in Venice in the early 14th century. A Renaissance example is illustrated.

MISERERE See *Misericord.*

MISERICORD A bracket on the underside of a hinged stall seat which is arranged to support a person when standing, after the seat has been raised. It is also called a miserere.

MISSION A briefly popular style of the late 19th to early 20th century, based on the crude, massive furniture made by the priests and Indians for the missions in the southwest United States. Generally made of oak, with leather upholstery, and trimmed with oversized nailheads. The dark stain and massive clumsy appearance soon ended its popularity. Gustav Stickley, who designed bungalows, also designed mission furniture.

MISSION CHAIR An early-20th-century cheap adaptation of the Spanish Renaissance frailero chair. See *Mission.*

MITER or MITRE The corner junction of two pieces of wood cut at a similar angle, as in the corner of a picture frame. Usually the two pieces form a right angle.

MOBILE A form of moving sculpture originated by the American artist, Alexander Calder. It is usually a collection of shapes connected by wires in such a manner that the entire unit can revolve and create a new arrangement of planes and solids in a three-dimensional movement.

MODACRYLIC FIBERS Synthetic fibers which are bulky and soft to touch and used to make "fake fur" fabrics and carpets. They are chemical-resistant and non-flammable, but their resistance to heat is poor. The fibers can also be blended with cotton to produce a cashmere-like fabric. Modacrylics are produced under the registered trademarks Dynel (Union Carbide) and Verel (Tennessee Eastman). See *Acrylics.*

MODEL A three-dimensional small-scale representation of a piece of furniture, a sculpture or a building.

MODERN The architecture, furniture, and furnishings of today. Hence a constantly changing style influenced by various countries, new inventions, new materials, etc. Generally in the 20th century, modern can be described as clean, straight lines with simple refined curves and a recognizably, functional quality. Ornament is used sparingly and is usually well integrated into the design. See *Oriental Modern, Scandinavian Modern,* and *Shaker Modern.*

MODERNE Term now used for a style of furniture which appeared after World War I (around the mid-1920's). It was based mainly on straight and angular lines with grained woods used for contrasting effects. There was some painting and inlay work. A "moderne" chest is illustrated.

MODESTY PANEL A panel of metal, wood, plastic, or cane set into the exposed end of a pedestal or kneehole-type contemporary desk. The seated person's knees are shielded from view, and the desk has a more enclosed appearance. Also called a knee-hole panel.

MODIGLIONE Italian for a bracket or corbel; also called a *modillion.*

MODILLION The projecting decorated bracket used in a series to support the Corinthian cornice. It is one of the modillion band. Also called a *console.*

MODULAR FURNITURE A 20th-century concept in furniture design. Correlated pieces are designed to a given set of dimensions (module) and also to fractions of that module. The fractions and modules can be stacked or butted together, and units can be added or taken away as needed. Connecting devices are usually designed to combine these units: modular case goods, modular seating, modular lighting panels, etc. See *Module.*

MODULAR HOUSING Dwellings erected of compact, self-contained units prefabricated in a factory, transported to a building site, and combined with other prefabricated units to form a complex of individual homes or a high-rise structure of apartments. The individual unit, built as a module, is designed to combine with other such modules into vertical or horizontal arrangements. See *Pre-fabricated Houses, Module.*

MODULAR SEATING Sectional seating, updated. Seating for conversational areas or larger groups, made up of pieces designed to fit together to satisfy the space and physical requirements. Modular seating may consist of seats without arms, seats with a right or left arm, corner seats, or

MODERNE

MODESTY PANEL

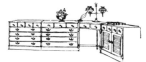

MODULAR FURNITURE

MOLDED BASE

MOLDING

MODULAR SEATING

backless seats. Each seating unit is of a shape and size that will combine with other elements in the collection. See *Module.*

MODULE A measuring unit for an architectural order. See *Diameter.* Basic units of the same size which can be used interchangeably, added to, or subtracted from. In office planning, makes for greater flexibility and mobility. It is possible to make adjustments and changes as new needs arise. Modules of lighting units can be of the same size as the ceiling panels, and thus interchangeable. Glass partitions, walls, doors, etc., when based on the same module, may be rearranged into spacial arrangements. Most important in a modular system are the dimensions, the detailing of the connections, and the possibilities for different visual effects.

MOHAIR A cloth made from the fleece of the angora goat, now woven in combination with cotton and linen. A resilient fiber; adds body to other fabrics. Mohair is also a pile fabric of cut or uncut loops similar to frieze. It is strong and durable, and was a popular upholstery fabric in 18th-century France.

MOIRÉ A waved or watered effect on fabric, especially rep or corded silks and synthetics. The fabric is pressed between engraved cylinders which emboss the grained design onto the material. The pattern is believed to hold better on the synthetic fabrics. See *Tabby.*

MOLDED BASE The base of a piece of case furniture, made up of molding strips or carved into a decorative molding. Illustrated is a Chippendale writing table.

MOLDING or MOULDING A shaped strip (concave, convex, half round, quarter round, ogee, cyma, etc.) used on projecting or receding features of buildings, walls, or furniture. It produces interesting patterns of light and shade. Illustrated are the moldings at the base of an ancient Roman column.

MOLESKIN A heavy cotton fabric with a soft napped surface, used as a lining for synthetic leathers, oilcloths, vinyls, etc.

MOMIE CLOTH A rough, pebbly-surfaced fabric of cotton, rayon, or silk warp, usually with a woolen filling, used for draperies and upholstery.

MONDRIAN, PIET A 20th-century abstract artist whose interesting designs of rectangular patterns made a great impression on the wallpaper and fabric designers of the 1940's and 1950's. In current usage his name is applied to an abstract arrangement of rectangles in an allover design.

MONEL A trademark name for a metal alloy made of nickel and copper. Its main attribute is its great resistance to corrosion.

MONEY MOTIF A series of overlapping disks (like coins) which forms an imbricated pattern or continuous border design.

MONIAL See *Mullion.*

MONK'S CHAIR See *Frailero.*

MONK'S CLOTH Also called friar's cloth. A heavy, coarsely woven cotton fabric. Groups of warp and weft threads are interlaced in a plain or basket weave.

MONK'S SEAT See *Table Chair.*

MONNOYER, JEAN-BAPTISTE (1634–1699) A French decorator and painter of floral decorations in the Louis XIV period.

MONOCHROME or MONOTONE Tints or shades of one color. A complete range of one color from very light to very dark. See *Grisaille.*

MONTAGE The placing of one layer over another or their juxtaposition. A design created by the overlapping or superimposing of decorative elements. See *Collage.*

MONTANT A French word for stile, or a vertical element in a frame, door, chair, etc. See *Stile.*

MONTGOLFIER CHAIR A Louis XVI chair with a balloon back designed to honor the Montgolfier brothers and their successful balloon ascension made in 1783. The slat simulates the lines of an ascension balloon. The original was designed by Georges Jacob, noted French designer of the late 18th century.

MONTICELLO Thomas Jefferson's home in Charlottesville, Virginia, from 1770 to 1809. It was designed by Jefferson and based on Palladian concepts, especially Palladio's Villa Rotonda with octagonal projections on either side of the domed central block. The interior is filled with many marvelous inventions and devices which reflect Jefferson's ingenuity and sharp intellect.

MOORISH ARCH A horseshoe arch. The curve of the arch is approximately three-quarters of a circle, and springs from the column's capitals. Illustrated is the gate of Las Palmas in Spain.

MOQUETTE An uncut pile fabric similar to frieze, with set patterns of assorted colors. It is made of mohair and wool, or heavy cotton, and is used as an *upholstery* fabric. During the 16th and 17th centuries, in France, it was made of wool in multicol-

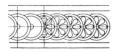

MONEY MOTIF

MONTANT

MOORISH ARCH

MOQUETTE

MOQUETTE

ored designs. The Dutch version was called *velours d'Utrecht.* In France today, the term is used to describe a wool Wilton carpet. A 27″ wide carpet woven on a loom similar to the English Wilton. Used by the French during the mid to late 18th century and into the early 19th century. The modern Axminster rug is woven on concepts which evolved from the Moquette loom.

MORAND, P. DE V. A 17th-century French cabinetmaker noted for his clock cases in the Louis XIV style.

MOREEN See *Morine*

MORESQUE Decoration in the Moorish style. The Moors possessed a large part of Spain during the early Gothic period, and thus greatly influenced the style of Spanish and Portuguese art, architecture, and decoration. In carpet construction, the tweed or pepper-and-salt effect produced by twisting two different colored yarns together in the weaving process.

MORINE A thick wool upholstery material of the 17th and 18th centuries. Usually the warp was woolen, and the fillers were of linen, cotton, or wool. The material was either plain or figured. In the 19th century it was called moreen.

MORNING ROOM A sitting or writing room in English architecture with a sunny exposure, used for a lady's morning activities: correspondence, etc.

MOROCCAN (MAROQUIN) TAPESTRIES Decorated leather hangings. See *Guadamicil.*

MORRIS CHAIR A large overstuffed 19th-century easy chair designed by William Morris, with loose cushions and an adjustable back. The seated person could lean back, after lifting the front edges of the chair's arms, and the chair back would decline to permit a semireclining position. See *Morris, William.*

MORRIS, WILLIAM (1834–1896) English producer and designer of wallpapers, furniture, tapestries, carpets, stained glass windows, and home accessories in the Art Nouveau style, with dark, heavy colors. Greatly influenced by Dante Gabriel Rossetti and Burne-Jones, Morris revolted against the eclecticism of the late 19th century. He created and designed the furnishings for his Red House at Upton in Kent. Morris said, "I don't want art for a few, any more than education for a few, or freedom for a few. What business have we with art at all unless all can share it?" He attempted to bring art back to the common man, in his home and its furnishings, but unfortunately his beautiful products were too costly for the common man. See *Pre-*

Raphaelite Brotherhood and *Webb, Phillip Speakman.*

MORTAR A bonding material used in bricklaying and masonry for bedding and pointing the various members. It is usually made of cement or lime mixed with sand and water. It dries hard and firm.

MORTISE A hole cut in a piece of wood which receives a tenon projecting from another piece of wood. It is used in cabinet joinery. See *Joinery, Mortise and Tenon Joint,* and *Tenon.*

MORTISE AND TENON JOINT A method of joining two pieces of wood. The projecting tenon of one piece fits into the open shape (mortise) of the other. Often used to join stretchers to leg posts or seats to the back posts of chairs, as a glued joint.

MORTLAKE TAPESTRIES Early-17th-century English silk tapestries woven at Mortlake factory. They did not compare in technique or color with products of the Gobelins Factory.

MOSAIC Small cubes (tesserae) of colored stones, marble, glass, etc., stuck into cement to form a pattern or design. The irregular surface quality catches light and reflects it at various angles. Much favored as a form of decoration in the Early Christian and Byzantine churches. Currently having a revival as a decorative art, in table and counter tops, on splashboards, etc. See *Pietra Dura.*

MOSHEE An 18th-century term for decorative borders.

MOSS A chenille-like edging to a braid, used to finish and decorate pieces of upholstery and drapery. Illustrated is an early-18th-century stool or bench with rollover sides.

MOTHER-OF-PEARL The iridescent lining of the pearl oyster and other shells, used for inlay work as well as small decorative items. See *Boulle Work, Intarsia* or *Tarsia,* and *Nacre.*

MOTIF or MOTIVE The theme or distinctive feature of a design, period, or style. See *Lion Period* as an example. Illustrated is an early-16th-century English oak armoire with pierced work resembling the architectural tracery of the same Tudor Gothic period. The tracery motif appears in the architecture and furnishings of the period.

MOTTLE A wood grain effect produced by short irregular wavy fibers across the face of the wood as cut.

MOUNTINGS The base and harp used to make an electrified lamp.

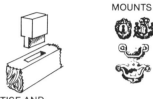

MOUNTS

MORTISE AND TENON JOINT

MOZARABIC

MUDEJAR

MULE CHEST

MOSS

MOTIF

MOUNTS Ornamental and/or useful metalwork on cabinets or drawer units: handles, escutcheons, drawer pulls, etc. Cabinet hardware. Illustrated are some 18th-century brass escutcheons and handles.

MOYEN ÂGE French for Middle Ages.

MOZARABIC The arts and designs of Moorish Spain in which Christian and Gothic elements were also used. Illustrated is a painting on leather from the Hall of Judgment in the Alhambra.

MUDEJAR A transitional art style of the 13th to 17th centuries in Spain, in which Moorish and Christian details were often used together. It was the style of the Christianized Moor, and was superimposed first over Gothic, and later over Renaissance forms. Illustrated is the façade of the College of S. Gregorio, Valladolid (1488). It is embellished with statues, heraldic devices, canopied niches, and pinnacles. The inner courtyard is done in the Plateresco style. See *Plateresco.*

MUFFIN STAND A small tiered table to hold plates, used for teas and for other genteel entertaining. It was popular in 18th- and 19th-century England and America.

MULE CHEST In Chippendale's style, a massive chest which resembles two chests set side by side and sharing a single centered bracket foot. It was a forerunner of today's double dressers. The chest often had handles on the sides, probably for moving it around. It evolved from the coffer or chest of the 17th century which had a drawer or two under the lid portion. Illustrated is an early-17th-century design (Jacobean).

MULLION A slender vertical or horizontal bar between windows or glass panels. See also *Muntin.*

MULTIFOIL A pattern having many lobed or leaflike forms. An arch having more than five foils or arcuate divisions. A scalloped arch.

MUMMY CLOTH A silk or cotton fabric with an irregular warp figure. It has a light, fine texture.

MUNSELL SYSTEM Albert F. Munsell's color system which designates and classifies colors, and is widely used as a standard for color and color matching. Published as the *Munsell Book of Color* by the Munsell Color Company, Baltimore, Maryland.

MUNTIN or MUNTING The central vertical part of a door which divides the panels above and below the middle or lock rail. A vertical strip between two panels. The horizontal strip is called the lock rail. Also used to identify the wood strips that hold the panes of glass in a glazed door or window.

MURAL Any kind of wall painting, ei ther painted directly on the wall, or printed on paper or canvas and then applied to the wall. It is not the same as a fresco, which becomes an integral part of the material of the wall. See *Fresco*. Illustrated is an 18th-century mural decoration designed by Giambattista Piranesi.

MURAL

MURANO GLASS Fine colored glass produced in the Murano glassworks in Venice. Much of what is called Venetian glass is produced on the nearby island of Murano. A 17th-century Venetian glass ewer is illustrated.

MURANO GLASS

MURPHY BED Originally, a fall-down bed hidden away in a closet or in a covered recess in a wall. Later, the term for many sophisticated space-saving beds consisting of a rigid frame with a mattress that fits into a closet, bookcase, or architectural setback when not in use. Also called a *Cabinet Bed*, *Wall Bed*, or a *Hideaway*. Murphy Bed is a trademark name for a particular manufacturer of these hideaway beds, rather than a generic name.

MURPHY BED

MURRHINE Ancient Roman glassware, fragile and opalescent.

MUSHREBEEYEH An Arabic term for a balcony enclosed with lattice screens.

MUSHROOM TURNED KNOBS Wooden turned knobs with flat carved tops that resemble mushroom caps.

MUSLIN A plain-weave fabric which may be bleached or unbleached. It is used as undercovering on upholstered pieces to tie in the stuffing and padding materials prior to putting on the final upholstery fabric. Muslin may also be dyed or printed and used for curtains, bedspreads, etc.

MUTED Of colors, soft, restrained, dulled-down.

MUTULE Any projection from the surface of a wall. It describes especially the square block, like the end of a beam, which appears at regular intervals above the frieze of a Doric building.

MYLAR A trademark name for a polyester film made into metallic yarns. The polyester film is metalized by aluminum deposited on its surface, and then the entire fiber is sandwiched in clear film. It is usually used with Nylomar Fortisan since Mylar is a weak yarn and stretches easily. Nontarnishing and soft in hand. Also used to decorate upholstery and drapery fabrics.

MYRTLE BURL A highly figured, very blond to golden-brown wood of widely varying designs, native to the western United States. Hard and strong and used for cabinetwork, inlay, and veneer.

N

N Napoleon I's initial, which appeared as an important decorative motif in the First French Empire style (early 19th century). The monogram was carved, inlaid, painted, woven, and embroidered. Illustrated is the motif in Napoleon's throne room which was designed by Charles Percier and Pierre Fontaine.

NACRE The lustrous, iridescent material which lines some seashells. Called mother-of-pearl, long popular as an inlay material on tabletops, chair frames, cabinets, barometers, and small accessories. The Victorians found nacre irresistible as an inlay decoration on their papier-mâché trays, ornaments, and whatnots.

NAILHEADS Nails or brads with plain or decorated oversized heads made of brass, copper, or other metals, used to secure leather or fabric upholstery. They may also be used to embellish leather panels, or create a tufted effect, over wood panels and doors. The nailheads are exposed and spaced to create a definite line or pattern. Originally a Spanish and Italian Gothic ornamentation. An early Italian Renaissance chair with nail-head trim is illustrated. See *Stud*.

NAKORA A trademark name for a Japanese blond hardwood. It is extremely light in color, and has a definite grain pattern when rotary-cut.

NANMU A Chinese aromatic wood which turns rich brown in color as it ages. Also called Persian cedar.

NAP Fibers raised on the surface of a fabric to create a downy or fuzzy appearance. Differs from pile on a fabric. See *Pile*. Moleskin and flannel are napped fabrics.

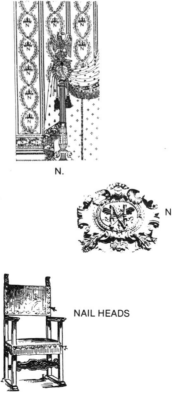

N.

N.

NAIL HEADS

NATTES

NARRAWOOD A Philippine hardwood which varies from light golden tones to brown, and also from light to dark red. Narrawood may resemble mahogany or satinwood because it has ripples and also a fine mottled effect. Excellent for furniture production and interior veneer.

NATIONAL COUNCIL FOR INTERIOR DESIGN QUALIFICATION (NCIDQ) A group formed by the A.S.I.D. to prepare and administer examinations for basic competence to qualify an individual to practice Interior Design. The A.S.I.D. has established testing criteria and accreditation apparatus.

NATOIRE, CHARLES-JOSEPH (1700–1777) A French painter of voluptuous nudes in the style of Boucher. Many of his paintings were integrated into the decorating schemes of salons and boudoirs, being set permanently into the boiserie panels, overdoors, or overmantels.

NATTES A surface texture or decoration that resembles a plaited, basket-weave design.

NAUGAHYDE A trademark name for vinyl upholstery and wall-covering fabrics produced by the United States Rubber Company.

NAUGAWEAVE United States Rubber's trademark name for "breathable" vinyl upholstery fabrics.

NAVAHO RUGS Rugs handwoven by the American Navaho Indians, traditionally characterized by bold geometric patterns in black, gray, and white with strong accents of bright red. Other strong colors have been added in some newer pieces.

NAVE The main or central part of a cruciform church. It is usually flanked by aisles, and terminates in an apse. See *Apse* and *Transept.*

N.C.I.D.Q. See *National Council for Interior Design Qualification.*

NEBULE ORNAMENT A Norman form of ornament which consisted of a continuous wavy line, used to enrich moldings.

NÉCESSAIRE A French term for a small writing or toilet accessory case.

NECESSARY STOOL See *Close Chair* or *Stool.*

NECKING See *Collar.*

NEEDLEPOINT A dense cross-stitch embroidery done on net, heavy canvas, or coarse linen. It resembles a coarse tapestry. From the 15th century on, used as an upholstery covering for chairs, sofas, etc. A Louis XVI chair with needlepoint covering is illustrated. See *Gros Point* and *Petit Point.*

NELSON, GEORGE A 20th-century American furniture and interior designer with a simple, direct style. He introduced the slat bench, the adjustable headboard bed, and case furniture built on steel frames and finished in a wide range of woods or lacquered colors. Nelson is also the innovator of the "basic storage component system." OMNI office furniture composed of interchangeable parts (see *Modular Furniture*), the swagged-leg desk and chair, clocks, steel-framed chairs, and elastic webbing daybeds.

NEOCLASSIC See *Neoclassicism.*

NEOCLASSICISM A movement which originated in Rome in the mid-18th century as a reaction against the excesses of the baroque and rococo styles. The discoveries at Herculaneum and Pompeii gave impetus to a return to the art and architecture of classic Greece and Rome. The Louis XVI style in France and the Adam style in England were part of this trend. An Adam wall candelabrum is illustrated.

NÉO-GREC The French form of new Greek style during the Louis XVI period, influenced by the discoveries at Herculaneum and Pompeii. Greek motifs became popular for furniture and interior decorations. A Louis XVI table is illustrated. Note the caryatid-type figures used on the legs, and the classic motif on the decorative inlaid drawer fronts.

NÉO-GREEK A rarely used term for the American period of art and architecture (from 1815 to 1845), which was heavily flavored with classic Greek motifs.

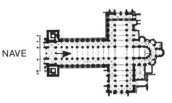

NAVE

NEBULE ORNAMENT

NEEDLEPOINT

NEW COLONIAL PERIOD

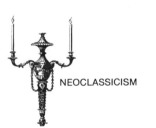

NEOCLASSICISM

NÉO-GREC

NESTED TABLES A series of small tables, graduated in size, so that one can be set inside the other. They may serve as sofa or end tables, and are made in a variety of styles, traditional or contemporary. See *Quartette Tables.*

NET An open-weave, meshlike fabric used for glass curtains. May be made of cotton, linen, or synthetic fibers.

NEUTRA, RICHARD A 20th-century American architect born in Vienna in 1892. In the late 1920's he produced the D. R. Lovell house which was a combination of Californian skeletal pavilions and European cubist designs. It was made of light steel framing with balconies and horizontal strip walls cantilevered out. He believes "constructed human environment should be an entity, and not split up by specialists."

NEUTRAL In colors, one of no definite character or personality. A neutral color usually blends well with most true colors. White, black, gray, and beige are considered neutrals.

NEW COLONIAL PERIOD or MODERN COLONIAL An early 20th-century style of furniture. The classic features from both the colonial era and the later Federal and American Empire styles were retained, but the ormolu and brass mounts were omitted. The S-shaped scroll, scroll foot, lion's paw foot and classic columns were often in evidence. Mass-produced in Grand Rapids, Michigan. Better pieces were often made in mahogany. Illustrated is a typical china closet of the New Colonial style.

NEWEL or NEWEL POST A heavy upright post or turning at the end of a handrail of a stairway.

NIB See *Lug.*

NICHE A recessed or hollowed-out space in a wall, usually designed to hold a statue, vase, or ornament.

NICKING A notched or gouged ornamenting technique used on 17th-century English oak furniture.

NIELLO A method of decorating metal surfaces by engraving lines on them and filling them with a black composition which makes the design stand out in sharp contrast.

NIGHT STOOL See *Close Chair* or *Stool.*

NIGHT TABLE A bedside table, usually small, with or without a drawer or shelf, used to hold a lamp, ashtray, clock, etc. Sometimes small commodes are used in period rooms in place of night tables. See *Chevet*.

NIMBUS A circular halo, a ring of gold, around a painted or carved representation of the head of Christ, the Madonna, or a saint.

NINON A smooth, very sheer, closely woven voile, usually of rayon, sometimes called triple voile, used for *Glass Curtains*.

NO-FINES A concrete composed of cement and coarse aggregate.

NOGGING In the construction of a partition, the placing of a horizontal piece between two vertical studs.

NOGUCHI, ISAMU A 20th-century American sculptor-designer who created sculptural free-form glass-topped tables which rest on intricately shaped abstract bases, a curving, armless sofa with a small backrest, and exquisite folding-paper akari lanterns. Noguchi has also designed stage sets, costumes, and landscapes.

NOIL Short fibers combed from wool, cotton, or silk in making high-quality yarns. Used for yarns of lower quality or for padding and stuffing.

NONBEARING Describing a wall or partition which does not support a load or resist a force or thrust from above. A filler section.

NONSUCH FURNITURE Trompe l'oeil decorated furniture of the 16th and 17th centuries in England. The term refers especially to perspective views of Nonsuch Palace, which was built for Henry VIII. Designs of the palace were executed on flat-surfaced chests in inlay work. Illustrated is the Palace of Nonsuch. See *Intarsia*.

NORMAN PERIOD The period in England under the Norman kings, dating approximately from 1066 to 1189. The architecture is characterized by massive constructions, rough, thick-jointed masonry, rounded arches, projecting parapets carried on a corbel table, wide buttresses of slight projection, and assorted carved capitals. The prominent motifs in decoration were

CHARLES PIERRE
JOSEPH NORMAND

NOSING

NOYER

NONSUCH FURNITURE

the chevron, star, billet, zigzag, and bird-beak moldings. Romanesque is the Continental name for Norman.

NORMAND, CHARLES PIERRE JOSEPH (1765–1840) A noted architect and publisher of Empire style designs. He favored the Roman models as standards for his works and collections.

NORMANDY A province of France which produced a charming, simple, country-style, furniture in the 18th century. It was similar to the colonial New England designs of the same time.

NOSING The curved or shaped front edge of a stair tread.

NOTCHING See *Nicking*.

NOTTINGHAM LACE A general name given to machine-made flat lace, particularly lace tablecloths or curtains which are made in one piece. Originally a hand-made product.

NOYER French for walnut. Illustrated is a 16th-century French crédence made of walnut.

NUB YARN See *Slub Yarn*.

NULLING A Jacobean wood-carving technique which produced an effect similar to repoussé or chased metalwork. The patterns were created by a series of small projections or recessions from the surface (like a boss or bead) of the wood.

NUMDAHS Felted rugs made in India, usually from cow's hair, also known as Druggets. On them, allover designs of vines and blossoms are embroidered in brightly colored wool yarns.

NURSING CHAIR An English term for a chair with a low seat. See *Chauffeuse*.

NYLON A protein-like chemical which can be manufactured as fibers, in sheet form, or as bristles. Tough, elastic, and strong, it is often used in fabrics which were originally produced from silk or rayon yarns. Also used as a carpet fiber. It provides a high degree of abrasion resistance, dries quickly, and is easy to care for.

O

OAK A hard, durable wood of a red or whitish color which lends itself to carving or paneling. Because it is so porous, it must be treated with a filler before it is stained. French and English oaks are finer-grained than the American varieties.

OAK, POLLARD English brown oak, nut-brown to deep brown in color, and spotted in black. The figure is often tortoiseshell in effect. The wood has a medium hard texture.

OAK, QUARTERED Planks of wood sawed toward or through the center of the tree trunk, resulting in a more decorative plank or veneer. The wood has a "flake" pattern which is caused by the wide rays that reflect the light. Generally, oak is heavy, hard, and strong, and has prominent pores in springcut wood. A carved oak cupboard of the early 16th century is illustrated. Note the linenfold pattern carved on the panels.

OBELISK A tall, tapering column or structure, square or rectangular in section, with a pyramid-shaped top. It is often used as a commemorative monument, or in a small version as a decorative object.

OBERKAMPF, CHRISTOPHE-PHILIPPE (1738–1815) The founder of the fabric factory at Jouy near Versailles, and the creator of "toile de Jouy," a particular type of printed cotton fabric. See *Mignonettes, Picoté* and *Toile de Jouy.*

OBJET D'ART A small art object: miniature painting, sculpture, vase, snuffbox, etc. See *Bibelots.* Illustrated is a vase of the Sung dynasty.

OBLIQUE ARCH See *Skew Arch*

OBVERSE

QUARTERED OAK

OCCASIONAL TABLE

OBJET D'ART

OBSCURE GLASS A translucent rather than transparent glass. It allows in light but does not permit a clear, uninterrupted view.

OBVERSE The main face of a medal, ornament, coin, etc. The opposite side is the "reverse" side. A Roman coin is shown.

O.C. An abbreviation for "on center." When dimensions or measurements are given in relating one structural element to another, the distance is sometimes given from the center point of one to the center point of the other. In this case, the letters O.C. appear next to the measurement.

OCCASIONAL CHAIR A small, pull-up chair of any style or period usually used in a living or sitting room. See *Pull-up Chair.*

OCCASIONAL TABLE A general term for a small odd table that can have one or several purposes: end table, sofa table, coffee table, lamp table, cocktail table. Usually to add comfort and convenience to a room. A mid-18th-century English whatnot table is illustrated.

OCCHIO DI BUE Italian for bull's-eye. See *Bull's Eye.*

OCULUS A circular opening such as might appear in the crown of a dome. A round window.

ODALISQUE A female slave or concubine in a seraglio. Because of its exotic connotation, the odalisque was a popular decorative motif in the erotic period of Louis XV.

ODEUM A small ancient Greek and Roman theatre where public music and poetry competitions took place.

ODIST, J.B.C. A French 19th-century metalworker and creator of mounts for Empire furniture.

OEBEN, JEAN FRANÇOIS An 18th-century master cabinetmaker to King Louis XV. He created many beautiful pieces decorated with fine marquetry in colored woods. Oeben designed furniture for the Marquise de Pompadour, who preferred simpler pieces to the then current rococo style. Illustrated is the famous desk (bureau á cylindre) created for Louis XV. It was begun by Oeben and completed by Riesener.

OEIL-DE-BOEUF French for bull's-eye. A round or oval window in Renaissance architecture. See *Bull's-Eye.*

OFFSET A small projection, ledge, or lip.

OFF-WHITE White that is tinted with a color: bluish-white, yellowish-white, etc.

OGEE A molding made up of a concave and a convex curve. Also called an ogive or keel molding. In architecture, an arch consisting of two opposed ogee curves meeting in a point at the top. It was popularly used in the English Decorated Gothic Period. It is also called a *Keel Arch.*

OGEE BRACKET FOOT See *Chinese Bracket Foot* or *Chinese Foot.* Illustrated is a Chippendale press.

OGIVE See *Ogee.*

OIL FINISH A wood finish accomplished by repeated polishing with boiled linseed oil. A low, satin-like luster is achieved, and the wood is made fairly resistant to stains from heat and water. A popular finish on walnut and teak.

OIL PAINTING An art technique for which pigment is ground in oil and applied to a slightly absorbent surface or to a primed canvas. It is traditionally the usual technique for large and important pictures. The Eycks are credited with "inventing" oil painting for pictures, though the use of oil mixtures for house and/or decorative painting dates back to antiquity. Illustrated is the "Madonna of Canon van der Paele" by Jan van Eyck.

OILED SILK A sheer silk fabric waterproofed by being oil-soaked and then dried.

OINOCHOE A Greek wine jug. The word is from the Greek for "to pour out wine." The spout was shaped in a triangular form which made pouring easy and accurate.

OLEFIN An extremely light synthetic fiber, soil resistant and an excellent insulator, used to produce outdoor carpets and

JEAN FRANÇOIS OEBEN

OGEE BRACKET FOOT

ONION FOOT

OIL PAINTING

OPEN BACK

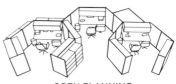

OPEN PLANNING

sturdy upholstery fabrics resistant to abrasion, pilling, and aging. Sensitive to heat and susceptible to shrinkage. Some of its trademark names are: Fibergrass, Polycrest, Durel PP, and Murress III.

OLIVE WOOD Wood from a small Italian tree that, as a veneer, can be used only in small, closely matched patterns. It can also be used as a decorative inlay wood. Light yellow with greenish-yellow figures, somewhat like English ash.

O.M. An abbreviation for "outside measurement." A measurement of distance between outer surfaces of a hollow object, rather than of distance between inner surfaces (inner measurement or I.M.). Outside measurement includes the thickness of the shell.

OMBRÉ A shaded or graduated one-color pattern, usually in a striped effect. The term is derived from the French for shadowed. It is a range of tints to shades of a single color.

ON-THE-GLAZE A colored design applied over glazed biscuit pottery, as in Majolica pottery.

ONION FOOT An onion-shaped turned foot of the Early Renaissance not very much used after the William and Mary Period. Illustrated is a 17th-century Jacobean cupboard.

ONLAY A decorative overlay or facing like a sheathing or a veneer.

ONYX A semiprecious gem, chalcedony, with two or more layers of strongly contrasting colors or marked with white and stratified with opaque and translucent lines. An agate stone used for cameos and inlay work.

OPALESCENT Showing an iridescent reflection of light, opal-like in its play of color; having a rainbow-like or pearly appearance.

OPEN BACK A chair back which has an unupholstered opening between the rails and side splats, or a decorative open frame back. Illustrated is a Hepplewhite shield-back chair.

OPEN PLAN OFFICE See *Open Planning.*

OPEN PLANNING A concept in store and office layout without constructed walls or partitions. Large, open flexible areas are created, which can be divided, as needed, with movable panels, screens, or with fixtures and case furniture.

OPEN STOCK Furniture which is regularly kept in stock and is usually available for immediate delivery. Not custom-made or specially finished. It is possible to buy parts of suites rather than complete groups from open stock.

OPEN-WELL STAIR   A stairway of two or more flights surrounding an open space.

OPERA GAUZE   See *Theatrical Gauze.*

OPPENORD (or OPPENORT), GILLES MARIE (1672–1742)   A French designer of interiors, furniture, and metalwork. He was the director of styles during the French Régence period, and was partially responsible for introducing the Rococo period. His painted panels resembled the works of Watteau and Gillot in style. See *Baseboard* for an Oppenord interior.

OPPENORD, JEAN   A 17th-century French cabinetmaker of the Louis XIV period.

OPUS ALEXANDRINUM   The mosaic work used on floors in Byzantine and Romanesque churches.

OPUS SECTILE   Roman mosaics made up of large pieces of stone or tile set into geometric patterns.

OPUS SPICATUM   A Roman method of facing a wall with stones diagonally set to form a herringbone design.

OPUS TESSELATUM   Latin term for a mosaic pavement which has tesserae laid into patterns or pictures. Tesselated pavements or floors.

OPUS VERMICULATUM   A type of Roman mosaic work which employed diamond-shaped or long, irregularly shaped stones. It was especially adapted for pictorial designs: hair, drapery folds, features, etc.

ORANGERY or ORANGERIE   A hothouse for growing orange trees. A glassed-in house for plants.

ORCHESTRA   In the ancient Greek theatre, the space in front of the stage where the chorus sang and danced. In present-day auditoriums, the main floor which is usually pitched so that the level of the front row is just below the surface of the stage and the rows behind are placed progressively higher.

ORDERS OF ARCHITECTURE   The classic orders consisted of the pedestal, the column, and the entablature. The Greek orders were Doric, Ionic, and Corinthian. The Roman orders included the three plus the Tuscan and the Composite. See *Classic* and *Vignola, Giacomo Barozzi da.*

GILLES MARIE
OPPENORD

ORIEL WINDOW

ORIEL WINDOW

OPUS TESSELATUM

ORIENTAL

ORGANDY (ORGANDIE)   A very thin, translucent, stiff and wiry cotton muslin. It can be piece-dyed or printed. Swiss organdy is chemically treated to keep its crisp, sheer finish through many launderings.

ORGANIC ARCHITECTURE   Frank Lloyd Wright's term for architecture which has been conceived as an organic whole, with the various parts relating to one another and in harmony with the environment.

ORGANZINE   A two-ply silk yarn twisted in the opposite direction from the single yarn from which it is produced.

ORIEL WINDOW   A large projecting window supported by a corbelled brick or stone construction. Illustrated is the oriel window of a German Renaissance structure. See *Alcove* for the interior view of an Elizabethan oriel window.

ORIENTAL   Far Eastern or Asiatic. Referring to things Chinese, Japanese, etc. A Chinese black lacquer panel with a raised design in gold is shown.

ORIENTAL MODERN   A popular furniture and interior trend since the mid-1950's. The basic Japanese and Chinese lines and geometric designs combine well with the low, sleek uncluttered modern concepts. Teak and bamboo are used with walnut and rosewood. Heroic bronze, brass, and pewter hardware is used for decorative accents.

ORIENTAL RUGS   Hand loomed rugs made from natural materials (wool, camel's hair, silk, finely spun cotton) produced in countries of the East, including Iran, Afganistan, India, China, Pakistan, Turkey, Tibet, the Caucasian regions of Russia, and Rumania. Handcrafted with pile made of yarns tied into knots of two distinct types: Ghiordes (Turkish) or Sehna (Persian). The finest antique examples have as many as 500 knots to the square inch, compared to about 200 for a modern rug of good quality. Designs may be geometric; mystical or mythical; shapes of plants, foliage, and flowers; animals; or rarely, human figures. With or without borders. See: *Ardabil Rug, Caucasian Rugs, Chinese Rugs, Dhurries, Feraghan Rugs, Ispahan Rugs, Karabagh Rugs, Kerman Rugs, Khilims, Oushak, Persian Rugs, Prayer Rugs, Sarabend Rugs, Sarouk Rugs, Tabriz Rugs, Turkish Rugs, Turkoman Rugs.*

ORIENTAL WALNUT   See *Oriental Wood.*

ORIENTAL WOOD   A hard-textured Australian wood of brown to pink-gray color, sometimes with a pinkish cast or with pinkish streaks. A strong, distinctive striped figure. A member of the laurel family, also called Australian laurel, Australian walnut, and oriental walnut.

ORIENTATION The establishment of a relationship between the position of a wall or a piece of furniture to a point of the compass, a natural landmark, or another major element of an interior design.

ORLON A Dupont trademark for an acrylic fiber with at least 85 percent acrylonitrile. The fiber adds warmth without weight, and is resistant to sun fading and some chemical reactions. Orlon has a wool-like hand, and takes a brilliant dye.

ORME French for elm wood.

ORMOLU or ORMOULU Gilded bronze. A bright goldlike metallic alloy with a high percentage of copper plus zinc and tin. Also bronze ornaments, hand-chased and surfaced with gilt, particularly popular in France in the 17th and 18th centuries. Mounts, moldings, and medallions were used as applied decoration on furniture. Illustrated is an ormolu inkstand of the Louis XV period. See *Bronze Doré*.

ORNAMENT A decoration, trimming, enhancement, or embellishment.

ORNAMENTAL ENGLISH See *Decorated Period*.

OS DE MOUTON French for mutton bone. A carved motif popular in the period of Louis XIII in France, used for the legs and arms of chairs and sofas. The line is similar to that of a cabriole leg, but much heavier and stumpier in appearance.

OSNABURG The plain coarse cotton fabric from which cretonne is produced. See *Cretonne*.

OSTWALD SYSTEM A color system devised by Wilhelm Ostwald of Germany. See *Munsell System*.

OTTOMAN Originally a backless, long, cushioned seat, couch, or divan. In current usage, an oversized upholstered footrest, often designed to relate to a club or easy chair. The contemporary use and proportion developed during the Victorian period. A late-17th-century English ottoman is illustrated. See *Hassock*. Also, a heavy corded fabric like faille, but with heavier and rounder ribs.

OTTOMANE A French upholstered canapé or settee introduced in the Louis

OUTROUNDED CORNERS

ORMOLU

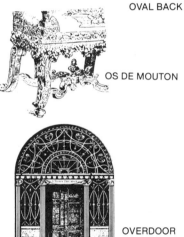
OS DE MOUTON

OVAL BACK

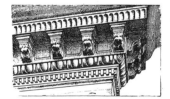
OVERDOOR

OVERSAILING

OTTOMAN

XV period. The curved enclosing side pieces are a continuation of the rounded back. A *canapé à corbeille*.

OUDRY, JEAN-BAPTISTE (1686–1755) A French court painter to Louis XV, and the superintendent of the Beauvais and Gobelin Factories, noted for his designs for a series of tapestries based on the fables of La Fontaine, as well as for his historical and animal paintings.

OUSHAK Oriental rug of near-East origin, now available largely in reproduction. Originals are rare collector's items. Characteristically made in beige, gold and soft orange and earth tones, with geometric designs contained by a wide border.

OUTDOOR FURNITURE Patio, terrace, or porch furniture made to withstand the elements. Metal, glass, and plastics are favorites for outdoor tables, chairs, and lounges, as well as redwood and cypress wood. Molded fiberglass and polyvinyl chloride are especially well suited to outdoor use.

OUTROUNDED CORNERS The corners of a square or rectangular tabletop, or panel, shaped into semicircular curves or quarter arcs. See *Segmental Cornered*.

OVAL BACK A Hepplewhite chair back similar to French chair backs of the Louis XVI period. Also referred to as *Le Médaillon*.

OVERDOOR An architectural design set over a front entrance door, usually made of wood or lead mullions, and paned with glass. In the 18th century in England, these windowed transoms were greatly admired, and Chippendale, Manwaring, Ince, Mayhew, as well as the Adam brothers designed many fine ones. The design illustrated is by J. Carter of the Georgian 18th century. See *Fanlight*.

OVERHEAD TRACK See *Track Lighting*.

OVERSAILING A continuous row of corbels which supports a load. See *Corbel Table*. The cornice of the Italian Renaissance Palazzo Riccardi is illustrated.

OVERSTUFFED Heavily upholstered pieces of furniture, usually with concealed frames; a word often associated with plump, fluffy pillow seats and backs, and tufting.

OVOLO A quarter-round convex molding, often decorated with an *Egg and Dart* motif.

OXBOW CHEST See *Yoke-Front Chest*.

OX-EYE A round or oval window. See *Oeil-de-Boeuf.*

OYSTER GRAIN A peculiarly figured walnut veneer which resembles the inside of an oyster shell. It is a busy, splotchy, swirly pattern that was popular in the Queen Anne period in England (early 18th century). See *Oystering.*

OYSTERING The process of veneering furniture with certain burr veneers during the early 18th century. See *Oysterpieces.*

OYSTERPIECES Transverse slices through the gnarled boughs or roots of walnut and other trees.

OYSTERWOOD See *Oystering.*

P

PABST, DANIEL A 19th century American cabinetmaker who produced excellent furniture and cabinets in his Philadelphia shop during the 1860's. His Victorian designs showed a distinct French Rococo influence; his work was mainly executed in black walnut.

PAD FOOT A flattened disklike foot often found under a cabriole leg. It is similar to a club foot. A late-17th-century English chair is illustrated.

PADDING (RUG) See *Carpet Padding*.

PADOUK A hard, firm-textured durable Burmese wood similar to rosewood. Varies from pinkish tones to a deep reddish brown, often with darker streaks, highly decorative. Also grows in Africa, Brazil, and the Andaman Islands and is sometimes sold under the name madou. See *Vermilion*.

PAFRAT, JEAN An 18th-century cabinetmaker for Louis XVI who specialized in mounting panels of old lacquerwork into small pieces of furniture.

PAGODA A Chinese tower having several stories, each with its own upswept roof. Each succeeding roof seems to umbrella out and graduate up from the one below—the roofs get smaller as they go up. The pagoda was adapted into an 18th-century decorative element during the chinoiserie vogue.

PAILLON The base coat for transparent lacquer, which is often a reflecting metallic surface or a gilded base, then treated with transparent coloring.

PAD FOOT

WILLIAM PAIN

JAMES PAINE

PAINTED FURNITURE

PAILOU In Chinese architecture, a gateway which was constructed of wood (or stone in imitation of wood) with a swooping curved tile roof.

PAIN, WILLIAM An 18th-century English architect-designer who wrote many books, including *The Practical Builder, The British Palladio, The Carpenter's Pocket Dictionary*, and *The Practical House Carpenter*. Pain designed in the classic Adam style, and his sons followed the same tradition in the homes they built in Ireland.

PAINE, JAMES (1725–1789) A classic 18th-century English architect who preceded the Adam brothers, but later used Adam-type stucco decorations in his work. Among his most noted designs were the ceilings and chimneys for Sir Joshua Reynolds' home in Leicester Square, London. A ceiling design by Paine for Doncaster Mansion House is illustrated. See the drawing for Bust for a wall interior design by Paine.

PAINTED FURNITURE Furniture which has been finished, usually in color, with enamel, lacquer, or some other type of paint. This finish covers the natural grain and color of the wood. Painted furniture is often enhanced with gilding, line work, painted medallions, stenciling, etc. The technique, an ancient one, reached its peak during the 18th century in the Venetian and French Rococo periods, and in the Adam style. A painted Adam commode is illustrated.

PAISLEY A printed or woven fabric design which imitates a Scottish shawl pattern created in the town of Paisley. The amoeba- and paramecium-shaped elements in the paisley design were originally Persian in concept.

PAKTONG A silvery alloy of copper, nickel, and zinc which was imported from China during the 18th century. It is hard and resonant, and was used for fire grates, fenders, fire irons, etc. Called "white copper."

PALAMPORES Printed East Indian cottons decorated with the tree of life motif, imported into England in the 17th and 18th centuries. Originally they imitated English papers, textiles, and crewel embroidery. The patterns usually contained interlacing branches and foliage with peacocks and other birds intermingled.

PALANQUIN A covered carriage for one person which was carried on the shoulders of four persons by means of poles which projected fore and aft on both sides with the carriage suspended between the poles. It was a form of conveyance, originally oriental, that was used in 17th- and 18th-century Europe.

PALDAO A Philippine wood of a variable tan ground with black to brown streaks. It has a hard texture and a striped or mottled figure.

PALETTE A board or tray for mixing paint colors; also a range of colors available in fabrics, papers, carpets, etc. Illustrated is an 18th-century French Renaissance trophy panel with a palette motif.

PALISADE CONSTRUCTION A wall construction of interlocking vertical planks of wood.

PALISANDER The French name for East Indian rosewood, dark brown with a violet cast and a definite combed grain stripe. The wood takes a high polish. See *Rosewood, Honduras.*

PALLADIAN Referring to the works or designs of Andrea Palladio and the classic Roman antiques he uncovered and recorded. It is also a generic term for the 18th-century classic architecture influenced by his research. See the entries that follow.

PALLADIAN MOTIF A typical architectural device designed by Palladio and illustrated in the Basilica Vicenza, twin columns support the arches in a rhythmic arcade. The Palladian window is based on the same motif.

PALLADIAN WINDOW A three-part window design usually consisting of four pilasters or columns marking off three tall window areas. The two outer windows have a straight cornice over each, the taller cen-

PALETTE

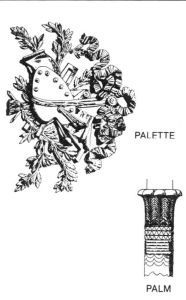
PALM

PALM VAULTING

PALMATED

PALLADIAN MOTIF

PALLADIAN WINDOW

tral window an arched semi-circular cornice. Very popular in 18th- and 19th-century architecture in England and the United States, the Palladian window was almost a trademark of the mid-18th-century New England house where it was centered to light up the stairway of the main central hallway. In the designs of William Sprat of Connecticut, it was often set over Ionic columned porticoes which decorated the main doorway, as in the Samuel Cowles House in Framington, Connecticut. The design illustrated here is by an 18th-century English designer, William Halfpenny.

PALLADIO, ANDREA (1518–1580) An Italian architect and excavator who, with Giacomo Barozzi da Vignola, rediscovered and standardized the proportions of the Roman architectural orders. His *I quattro libri dell'Architettura*, 1570, had great influence on architecture and design. Palladio also designed many buildings in the pure Italian Renaissance style.

PALM Palm leaves, branches, and the tree itself, used by early civilizations for decorative motifs. The palm was also used as a symbol of victory, triumph, and peace. The palm motif appeared in Egyptian, Greek, and Early Christian art. Illustrated is a palm capital from an ancient Egyptian temple.

PALM VAULTING See *Fan Vaulting.* Illustrated is the vaulting in Westminster Abbey in London. It is considered one of the most beautiful ceilings in European Gothic architecture.

PALMATED A decorative carved band of half circles with leaf designs enclosed, typically found on the oak furniture of the Stuart period in England. Note the lower bands of decoration on this mid-17th-century oak chest with drawers, here illustrated.

PALMETTE A conventionalized fanlike branch of the palm used as a decorative motif. It is similar to the anthemion and fan motifs. The term is also used to describe a pelmet or a lambrequin.

PAMPRE A French term for a decorative composition of grapes and vine leaves which was often used as a spiral element in the hollow areas of a twisting or twisted column.

PANCARPI A Greek term for swags, festoons, or garlands of fruits and/or flowers.

PANCHETTO An Italian Renaissance wooden chair with three splayed legs and a chip carved fan back. It was much like the sgabello, but less sophisticated or finished in decoration. See *Sgabelle* or *Sgabello*.

PANE A piece of glass set in a window or glazed door. (The term also refers to the space between two timbers in a half-timbered building.)

PANEL In drapery, a width of fabric with hemmed edges and a finished top and bottom. The actual width of a panel varies (usually 36″ to 52″), but in deciding how many panels are needed to cover a window or wall, one measures the finished pleated top. If the material is to be shirred or draped, depending upon the weight of the fabric, two or three unpleated panels usually make one finished or pleated panel. Also, a flat surface, usually enclosed by a frame. Panels can be decorated with moldings, carvings, painting, applied fabric, wallpapers, etc.

PANEL, BOLECTION A raised panel, one with the surface above and/or in front of the frame.

PANEL, SUNK A recessed panel, one with the surface below or behind the frame or molding.

PANEL WALL In building construction, a nonbearing wall built between columns and piers, completely supported at each story, and serving only to separate spaces.

PANEL-BACK CHAIR A massive, high-seated oak chair with heavy legs, stretchers, and a paneled back usually decorated with carving. An early English Renaissance design. Also called a *Wainscot Chair*.

PANELGLAS A trademark of the Johns-Manville Corporation for acoustic panels made of glass fibers. The panels (2′ × 2′ or 2′ × 4′) are mounted in simple overhead grids, and help to diffuse light as well as soak up sound.

PANETIÈRE A small hanging cupboard, originally used to store bread.

PANIER French for basket.

PANIER or PANNIER The French word for the corbel or angled element that fills the right angle between a pilaster and the beam which rests on it.

PANNE French for shag or plush. A pile fabric with a shiny or lustrous surface. The finish is produced by pressing back the pile, which is longer than that of velvet. It is usually a silk or synthetic satin.

PANNE VELVET A velvet with a lustrous finish produced by flattening the pile and making it all lie in the same direction.

PANNEAU

PAPER SCROLL

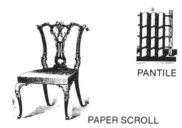
SUNK PANEL

PANTILE

PANEL-BACK CHAIR

PAPIER-MÂCHÉ

PANNEAU French for panel. The term may be used to describe a panel of paper, fabric, wood, etc. Illustrated is a bas-relief sculptured wood panel for a 16th-century French Renaissance coffer.

PANTILE A flattened S-shaped tile made of baked clay.

PANTON, VERNER A 20th-century furniture designer who pioneered in the use of molded plastics for lightweight colored portable chairs in interesting shapes and forms. His cantilevered, curved, and saddle-seated chair was designed to conform to the human body.

PANURGE A bed design of the Louis XVI period in France. French for a part of a harness.

PAPELERA A small Spanish cabinet with many compartments that held papers and writing materials. It was similar to the Vargueño, but it did not have the drop-lid front. Introduced in the late 16th and early 17th centuries.

PAPER SCROLL A scroll sometimes carved on the ends of the top rails of chairs, representing a rolled-up sheet of paper only slightly uncurled. Popular in the mid-18th century, as this Chippendale example shows. It is also called spiral whorl, spiral scroll, spiral volute, conical volute, and helicoidal volute.

PAPER STUCCO See *Papier-mâché*.

PAPIER PEINT The French term for early painted or printed wallpapers.

PAPIER-MÂCHÉ A technique for making three-dimensional units, originated in the Orient, and revived in the mid-18th century in France. Paper is pulped and mixed with whiting and glue. This semifirm material is shaped and molded, and as it dries it becomes strong, hard, and durable. In France, the original artisans in this technique were the paperhangers, and they made rococo mirror frames, girandoles, and fancy boxes. Later, moldings and ceiling designs were made in papier-mâché or "paper stucco," as it was called in late-18th-century England where it was used as a substitute for plaster ornament. In the Victorian period, pieces of furniture and accessories were made of papier-mâché, many painted black and inlaid with mother-of-pearl. A Victorian screen is illustrated.

PAPIERS COLLÉS A French term for a technique introduced in painting by Braque in 1909, and taken up by Picasso and other cubist artists. Bits of paper, wallpaper, assorted everyday cartons and boxes, and other materials were glued on the canvas or paint boards, incorporated in the composition.

PAPIERS D'ANGLETERRE An 18th-century French term for flocked papers made in England.

PAPIERS DÉCHIRÉS French for tattered papers. A montage of assorted twisted, torn, and otherwise manipulated papers which are assembled on a board in semblance to reality or an abstract design. The adaption of papiers collés was supposedly developed by Picasso. See *Papiers Collés*.

PAPILLON, JEAN A noted French wallpaper designer of the late 17th century. He was one of the first artists to specialize in wallpaper designs.

PAPYRUS A plant important in the ancient Chinese and Egyptian civilizations. Paper was made from the plant, and the flower was used as a decorative motif in the wall paintings, architecture, and domestic arts of the ancient Egyptians, and in later revivals of the style.

PARAVENT French for screen. A folding screen.

PARCEL GILDING A form of decorating in which only selected parts of a frame, carving, or surface are gilded. Practiced in the late 17th and early 18th centuries, it was particularly popular during the Decorated Queen Anne period for decorating mirror frames. Often accomplished by means of stencils. Illustrated is a pair of early-18th-century frames.

PARCHMENT A writing material of antiquity, made by separating the inner side of a sheepskin from the outer or woolly side. The peeled skin was then treated to make the surface suitable for writing. Also the warm beige-white color of parchment.

PARCHMENT PANEL Another name for *Linenfold* paneling.

PARGETRY See *Pargework*.

PARGEWORK Ornamental plaster or stuccowork applied to a flat surface to create a bas-relief design, a late-16th-century development which attempted to emulate the ribs in a complicated fan- or star-vaulted ceiling. The oriel window in the great hall of Crosby Hall in London is illustrated. The pargework on the ceiling is a decorative effect rather than a structural rib vaulting.

PARKER, GEORGE See *Stalker, John*.

PARLIAMENT CHAIR An 18th-century Queen Anne side chair made of mahogany in the British colony of Bermuda. It

PARQUET

PARCEL GILDING

PARSON'S TABLE

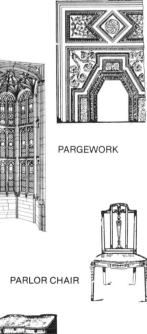

PARGEWORK

PARLOR CHAIR

PARTNERS' DESK

had a high back with a shaped splat. The front legs were cabrioled with club feet.

PARLOR LAMP A late-19th-century Victorian lamp on an ornate brass base, consisting of two bulbous globes set one on top of the other with the chimney projecting through the upper sphere. Both globes were usually painted or decorated with decals of lush, multicolored flowers.

PARLOR or PARLOUR From the French parloir, a room where company is received. It is the present-day living room or drawing room. In Johnson's *Dictionary* (1755), defined as "a room on the first floor, elegantly furnished for reception or entertainment." Illustrated is a parlor chair.

PARQUET An inlaid wood floor, or a mosaic wood floor, with a design created by strips of wood laid out in a definite pattern. Sometimes different colored woods are used. Illustrated is a Louis XVI salon with parquet floor. *Marquetry*, a similar technique, is used for furniture.

PARQUETRIE or PARQUETRY Furniture inlay work in geometric patterns like the checkerboard pattern, etc. See *Marquetry*.

PARSON'S TABLE A simple, squarish table design made famous by the Parson's School of Design in New York. The square legs blend in with the apron of the table top in a sharp, clean flow.

PARTERRE French term for a flat and planned garden. A garden landscaped in a formal set pattern. Also, the part of the theatre floor behind the orchestra.

PARTHENON It was erected in Athens on the Acropolis between 454 and 438 B.C. Ictinus and Callicrates were the architects, and Pheidias is credited as the major sculptor. The structure is surrounded by eight columns on the front entrance and seventeen on each of the sides. The Doric columns were about 6'2" in diameter at the base and 34'3" tall. The columns supported an entablature which was approximately eleven feet. Some of the finest classic Greek sculpture filled the tympana in the pediments. The Panathenaic frieze was carved along the top of the exterior of the naos wall. The sculptured metopes were done in high relief. Bright colors were originally used to decorate the sculptures in the pediments, metopes, and friezes.

PARTITION An interior wall of one story or less in height.

PARTNERS' DESK An 18th-century extra-wide keyhole or pedestal desk with drawers on both faces of the pedestal. It was therefore possible for two people to sit facing each other, one on either side of the desk, and for each to have his own set of drawers. There is no front or back to the desk. The unit probably evolved from the large library tables of the early 18th century. The endpieces were usually paneled, and the desk top was often made of tooled leather. A Hepplewhite design is illustrated.

PARTRIDGE WOOD A Brazilian wood with graining which resembles partridge feathers in its red and brown coloration. It was used in the 17th century as an inlay wood.

PARTY WALL A common wall between two structures, separating each from the other but belonging to both units.

PASSEMENTERIE From the French passement, a strip of lace. A trimming or edging of braid, gimp, beads, or cording.

PASSEPARTOUTE From the French for pass everywhere. A mat used in framing, a gummed paper, and also a form of picture mounting. In the mounting technique, the mat and the glass are taped together along the four edges with gummed tape.

PASTE The body of pottery. Soft paste is produced by a glass mixture, while hard paste is a mixture of kaolin and feldspar.

PASTEBOARD STUCCO See *Papier-Mâché.*

PASTELS Sticks of dry powdered color mixed with enough gum to bind the powder into a chalk. When the sticks are rubbed on paper, they disintegrate, and the colored powder remains on the paper's surface. Properly used, soft pastels can give the effect of a painting. Hard pastels are more closely related in effect to drawings. Quentin de La Tour and Jean-Baptiste Chardin were exponents of soft-pastel technique; Edgar Degas was perhaps the greatest of the pastelists.

PASTIGLIA A bas-relief design achieved by adding successive layers of thin plaster over a surface covered with a fine fabric. The finishing details were done with a knife, and often the design was gilded and burnished. Pastiglia was introduced in the Italian Renaissance. Also refers to molded plaster ornaments (gilded gesso work). The Queen Anne mirror of the early 18th century here illustrated has pastiglia decorations. See *Anaglypta, Carton-Pierre,* and *Composition Ornament.*

PATERA A round or oval disk usually decorated with a rosette or other ornament.

PATINA or PATINE A greenish coating on the surface of old bronze. Also the

PATIO

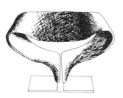

PIERRE PAULIN

PAW FOOT

PASTIGLIA

PAW-AND-BALL FOOT

mellowing of age on any object or material due to exposure, or repeated waxings and polishings. The patina is also the gloss on woodwork. See *Bronze.*

PATIO An inner court, open to the sky. Illustrated is a Spanish patio with Moorish horseshoe arches. See *Atrium.*

PATIO FURNITURE See *Outdoor Furniture.*

PATTERN The vertical graining of wood and veneer, as opposed to the highlights or cross grains which are called figures.

PATTERNED ROLLED GLASS See *Diffusing Glass.*

PAULIN, PIERRE A 20th-century French designer noted for his biomorphic furniture, usually made of chrome, foam, and stretch fabrics for a futuristic or 21st-century look. The units are sculptured in appearance, lightweight, and comfortable. His Ribbon Chair is illustrated.

PAVÉ DE MOSAÏQUE French for tesselated or mosaic pavement.

PAVEMENT Inside a building, a flooring of stone, marble, or tile.

PAVEMENT LIGHT A glass area set in a pavement to allow light to filter through to an area below.

PAVILION A separate but related building, an integral part of the design of a larger or main building. Derived from the Latin for butterfly, the pavilion was originally a tentlike affair spread out like the wings of a butterfly.

PAVIMENTO DI LEGNO LUCIDO Italian for parquet floor.

PAW FOOT Usually a carved representation of a lion's or bear's paw, decorated with foliage, and used as a furniture foot in the late-17th- to early-18th-century French and English furniture. The illustrated foot is from a Chippendale garden seat. See *Bear's Foot.*

PAW-AND-BALL FOOT A mid-18th-century replacement for the claw-and-ball foot. See *Ball-and-Claw Foot.*

PAYSAGES or PAYSAGES-DÉCORS An early-19th-century French term for wall murals featuring country landscapes, hunts, etc. These printed wallpaper designs were usually applied from the chair rail up to the cornice, and would form a continuous scene around the entire room. They were not "repeats" of a scene, but a series of scenes which formed a continuous panorama. The English had developed a similar art in tempera painted scenics on paper which they called perspectives.

PEACOCK CHAIR A large, sweeping fanback chair woven of rattan or wicker, and usually made in Hong Kong. A mid- to late-19th-century Victorian design which, with slight variations, is made today much as it was then. Usually has an hourglass pedestal base with supporting uprights. It is a light, lacy, openwork piece.

PEAR-DROP ORNAMENT An ornament usually decorating the upper section of a plain frieze. In Hepplewhite and Sheraton designs it appears as a crystal-like drop at the lower points of a series of Gothic arches in relief. Illustrated is a Sheraton cornice treated with the pear-drop ornament.

PEARLING A series of rounded forms of the same size, or graduated like a string of beads, used as a furniture embellishment, either in straight lines, arced, or swagged. A brass 18th-century mounting with pearling decoration is illustrated.

PEARLS A string of beads, either of the same size or graduated, used as an ornament on furniture or wall decor. It may be a painted or carved representation, and it is often used in a swaglike arrangement. Popular in mid- and late-18th-century French and English designs. A design by Michelangelo Pergolesi is shown.

PEARWOOD A pinkish brown, finely grained wood similar to boxwood, often used for inlay and fine cabinetwork. In the 16th and 17th centuries, it was used for country-made furniture; sometimes it was stained to simulate ebony in inlay.

PEASANT WEAVE See *Homespun.*

PEBBLE DASHING Stucco or mortar which is surfaced with partially embedded pebbles.

PECAN A South-Central United States wood of the hickory family. It resembles walnut with its strong grain pattern, and is often used in conjunction with walnut on exposed areas of furniture.

PÉCHÉ MORTEL French for deadly sin. A mid-18th-century term for a chaise longue which was sometimes made in two parts, an oversized easy chair with an upholstered stool, and joined in the middle. A Chippendale design, in one piece, is illustrated. See *Chaise Longue* and *Duchesse.*

PECKY CYPRESS A scarred, pitted, crumbly-textured cypress wood used for interior wood paneling. It is worm-eaten in appearance, and it is structurally weak, but due to its uneven surface quality, has a striking effect, in some interiors.

PEAR-DROP ORNAMENT

PEARLING

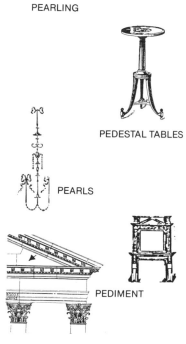

PEDESTAL TABLES

PEARLS

PEDIMENT

PEMBROKE TABLE

PÉCHÉ MORTEL

PEDESTAL A supporting base or block for a statue, vase, etc. In architecture, it is the lowest portion of a classic order, and it consists of a base, dado, and cornice.

PEDESTAL CHAIR A 20th-century chair design with the seat on a single support with a flaring base. The support is usually made of metal, wood, or plastic. Sometimes the seat is molded in one with the pedestal in a continuous sculptured design. See *Saarinen, Eero.*

PEDESTAL DESK See *Kneehole Desk.*

PEDESTAL TABLE Usually a round or an oval tabletop supported by a single member base. This support is often a column or turning which ends in a heavy base with spreading feet. It is found in 18th-century English furniture, as illustrated, as well as in 19th-century Regency and Duncan Phyfe designs. The pedestal table is also a popular modern design with the table surface resting on a thin support which flares outward as it reaches the floor.

PEDIMENT Originally, in Greek architecture, a triangular space at the roof line of Greek temples or other structures which was accentuated by the moldings of the entablature. In 18th-century furniture designs, the pediment is used as a cap or finishing design for case pieces, bookcases, chests, cabinets, secretaries, etc. The pediment may vary in design: swan, segmented, broken scroll, etc. A chimneypiece designed by Inigo Jones (early 17th century) is illustrated.

PEG A wooden pin, dowel, or spike used for fastening or joining furniture, wood panels, floors, etc., in place of a nail. A joint which is accomplished with pegs is referred to as a doweled joint.

PELLET ORNAMENT A Norman and Gothic ornament which resembles flattened balls or disks.

PELMET See *Lambrequin.*

PEMBROKE TABLE An 18th-century occasional table with two wide drop leaves, and a drawer set in the apron. The drop leaves are supported by brackets set into the table frame. The central, fixed table surface is usually twice as wide as one of the drop leaves. Believed to have been named for the tenth Earl of Pembroke. Illustrated is a Sheraton design. See *Table* illustration.

PENCIL AND PEARL Another name for bead and reel molding, made up of alternating round and elongated forms.

PENCIL STRIPE A wood-grain effect similar to a ribbon stripe. The stripes are much finer and much closer together. Sometimes found in walnut.

PENDANT A drop, or a hanging ornament, on furniture, lighting fixtures, etc. It may be a pendant sphere, pendant finial, or pendant husk. The term may also refer to a boss or projection hanging down from a vault or ceiling. See *Boss* and *Cul-de-Lampe.*

PENDULE French for pendulum clock.

PENDULE À GAINE A tall clock or grandfather clock. Illustrated is a Louis XIV design. See *Gaine.*

PENNE D'OISEAU French for bird's feather. A carved ornament on wooden furniture of the mid-French Renaissance period. Illustrated is the chair back of a 16th-century fauteuil.

PENNON A streamer, ribbon, or label, used as a decorative motif.

PENNSYLVANIA DUTCH Name given to German and Swiss Mennonites who settled in Pennsylvania near York, Lancaster, and Germantown at the end of the 17th century. "Deutsch" (German) became "Dutch," hence the misnomer. Using simple, functional lines as a basis, they decorated their furniture, homes, and utensils in bright, gay colors and designs. Among their favorite motifs were circular geometric hex signs, peacocks, hearts, tulips, rosettes, roosters, hens, reindeer, and leaves. Their furniture was similar in construction to other 18th-century Colonial American designs.

PENNSYLVANIA GERMAN See *Pennsylvania Dutch.*

PENNSYLVANIA STOVE See *Franklin Stove.*

PENTES A 15th-century term for lambrequins. Ornamental draperies, valances, or scalloped fabric treatments for use on the upper part of a window, across the top of a doorway, or on mantels. See *Lambrequin.*

PENTHOUSE A medieval term meaning a hanging roof, or a lean-to bracketed out from a wall. In present day usage, a dwelling on the uppermost story of a high building or an additional structure set on a roof. The penthouse is usually set back from the main building wall to allow for a terrace or walk area.

PERCALE A medium-weight cotton fabric made of carded yarns with a firm plain weave and a dull smooth finish, often printed.

PERCIER, CHARLES (1764–1834) French architect, decorator, and furniture designer to Napoleon I. With Pierre Fon-

PENDULE À GAINE

PENNE D'OISEAU

PENTES

CHARLES PERCIER

taine, he helped create the Empire style of the early 19th century. Percier worked on Malmaison, St.-Cloud, the Tuileries, and the Louvre. He designed furniture, textiles, ornaments, wallpapers, and accessories for these palaces. Illustrated is a wall decoration by Percier and Fontaine. See *Caryatid* for another example of their work. See *Empire Period.*

PERFORATED METAL A sheet of metal with dots, dashes, or other simple designs punched out, creating a canelike or regular lattice effect.

PERGOLA Italian for arbor. A balcony or lattice framework covered with vines or shrubs. A latticed structure used as a summerhouse or shade area. A bower. See *Gazebo*

PERGOLESI, MICHELANGELO An 18th-century decorative painter, architect, and furniture designer. He worked with Robert Adam, and painted ceilings, panels, and furniture for him. Pergolesi painted his designs on a flat tint, usually pale green or yellow, rather than on the natural wood itself. See *Elevation* for his rendering of an 18th-century room.

PERIOD A roughly defined time when a particular influence or style prevailed. These styles usually started before and lasted past the time of the designated period. Often there are transitional periods when the incoming and outgoing styles mix and blend.

PERIOD FURNITURE Newly made furniture of a style other than that of the present day. Such designs do not have to be authentic reproductions of historical styles, but they should have the scale, details, or motifs of a particular period. Examples of period furniture are: *Empire, Chippendale,* and *Queen Anne.*

PERIWIG CHAIR A tall-back chair of the late 17th century (William and Mary period in England) which had an elaborate pierced and/or carved cresting to accommodate and provide a setting for the elaborate wigs and headdresses of the time. Designed with turned walnut supports, and with or without arms. The back was usually caned.

PERLON A synthetic fiber, similar to nylon, manufactured in Germany.

PEROBA A pale rosewood of South America which is identified by its streaks. The streaks may fade under exposure to strong light.

PERPENDICULAR STYLE (1377–1485) The last phase of the Gothic period in England. It is noted for the large windowed spaces and the slender vertical lines that appear on the interiors in the tracery, and in the moldings and decoration. Also called rectilinear, late pointed, and Lancastrian.

PERRON A landing at the head of a flight of stairs and directly in front of an entrance door of a building.

PERSANE A French 18th-century printed fabric inspired by Persian originals; a pseudo-Oriental design.

PERSIAN CEDAR See *Nanmu.*

PERSIAN KNOT See *Sehna* Knot.

PERSIAN RUGS The most admired of the Oriental Rugs, noted for their magnificent designs, beautiful colors, and expert craftsmanship. Today, they are produced in Iran (formerly called Persia). Among the best known are: *Sarouk, Kerman, Sarabend, Ispahan,* and *Feaghan.* (See individual entries.) Each province produces its own traditional and characteristic style, theme, and type. Antique examples are especially prized. Rugs from neighboring countries are sometimes mistakenly called "Persians."

PERSIANA Venetian-blind-like elements used in Spain.

PERSIANS See *Atlantes.*

PERSIENNE A French word for an external Venetian blind. A shutter of thin laths in a wood frame. See *Persiana.*

PERSPECTIVE The representation of three-dimensional objects in spatial recession on a two dimensional surface. The basic assumption is that parallel lines never meet, but they appear to do so at a "vanishing point" on the horizon.

PERSPECTIVES See *Paysages* or *Paysages-décors.*

PETIT POINT See *Needlepoint.* A finer version of needlepoint with about twenty stitches to the lineal inch. Used for upholstery, wall hangings, and accessories. Illustrated is a Louis XIV fauteuil covered in a petit-point embroidered fabric.

PETITE COMMODE A small table, usually with three drawers set one under the other.

PETITOT An 18th-century French interior designer and creator of vases and urns in the pure Louis XVI style.

PETTICOAT MIRROR A console mirror set over a low console or pier table. It was an Empire style, and ladies could peek into the mirror to see if their petticoats were showing. See *Console Mirror.*

PETTICOAT VALANCE

PERSPECTIVE

PETIT POINT

PETTICOAT MIRROR

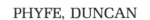

DUNCAN PHYFE

PETTICOAT VALANCE A fabric valance, very full and shirred, used below the mattress on a canopy or tester bed. A dust ruffle. Illustrated is a four-poster bed of the Hepplewhite period (latter half of the 18th century). The tester has a serpentine shape.

PEWTER A metal alloy of tin and lead, dull gray in appearance, originally used as a substitute for silver.

PHARMACIST'S LAMP A lightweight, floor-standing light fixture of brass or chrome with a semi-circular shield to cover the bulb. The shield can be turned or twisted to direct the light source and the device was used in pharmacies in the first quarter of the 20th century. The stem of the fixture is usually a narrow pipe. A modern adaptation is now available.

PHILADELPHIA CHAIR A Windsor-style chair manufactured in Philadelphia during the 18th century. Gilbert and Robert Gaw were important Philadelphia manufacturers of this American version of the Windsor chair. See *Windsor Chairs, American.*

PHILADELPHIA CHAIR CONSTRUCTION A term for the construction used on Queen Anne and Chippendale chairs made in Philadelphia in the latter part of the 18th century. The side rails of the chair seat were mortised into the rear uprights.

PHILADELPHIA CHIPPENDALE Chippendale-style furniture made of mahogany and produced in the Philadelphia area in the latter half of the 18th century. William Savery, Trotter, and John Folwell were craftsmen of the period who produced these highboys, lowboys, and chairs rich in carved details.

PHILADELPHIA PEANUT A bean-shaped cabochon ornament used as a decorative carved motif on 18th-century furniture made in the Philadelphia area.

PHILIPPINE MAHOGANY See *Lauan.*

PHOTOMURAL An enlarged photograph or montage of photographs used as a mural on a wall. See *Mural* and *Scenic.*

PHYFE, DUNCAN (1768–1854) A Scottish cabinetmaker who worked in America. His earliest works, while he resided in the Albany area, were in the classic Adam tradition. Today one associates Duncan Phyfe with the style of Sheraton and Hepplewhite and the Empire and Directory styles. Phyfe personified the American Regency period. The lyre and the plume are two motifs often found in his designs.

See *Mechanical Card Table* for another illustration of Phyfe's designs.

PIANO NOBILE The principal floor or main story of a building. In Renaissance structures the grand stairway usually led up to this main floor. In France, it is sometimes called the bel étage.

PIANO STOOL A round, square, or rectangular seat with a screw pivot below so that it can be raised or lowered. This unit dates back to the late 18th century. A late-19th-century German piece is illustrated.

PIANOFORTE A musical instrument invented by Cristofori in the early 18th century, a forerunner of the piano.

PICK The single filling thread that goes completely across the loom and interlaces with the warp threads to weave a fabric. In carpet manufacturing, the weft threads (across the loom) tie in the yarn that forms the tufts and loops on the carpet's surface. The number of picks per inch indicates the closeness of the weave. In Axminster weaving the word row means the same as pick. See *Count of Cloth* and *Weft.*

PICOT A purl on lace, or a small loop woven on the edge of ribbon.

PICOTAGE A printing technique used on toiles during the late 18th and early 19th centuries. Short metal wires were driven into the wood blocks used for printing, and these wires created a dotted background on the paper or fabric.

PICOTÉ A small-scale floral pattern created by Christophe-Philippe Oberkampf at his factory in Jouy during the latter part of the 18th century. A short-repeat pattern printed on cotton. The printed motif was usually surrounded by numerous dots which softened the silhouette.

PICTURE MOLDING or RAIL A grooved molding on a wall placed close to the ceiling line, or the lowest border of a frieze, originally to suspend pictures. Also called a frieze rail. Illustrated is a mid-18th-century English room designed by William and John Halfpenny.

"PICTURE" RUGS A modern Scandinavian development of woven abstract designs which may serve as dramatic area rugs, or may be mounted as wall decorations. They are modern floor tapestries or hand-knotted or hooked hangings. Some of the leading artists creating these rugs today are the Danes Franka Rasmussen and Tusta Welfing, and the Swedish weaver Brittan Valberg.

PICTURE WINDOW A large, single pane of glass similar to but somewhat smaller than the usual shop-front glass,

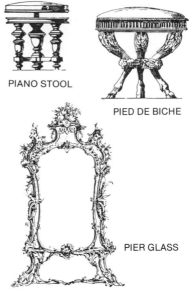

PIANO STOOL

PIED DE BICHE

PIER GLASS

PIER TABLE

PICTURE MOLDING

PIERCED SPLAT

PIERCED WORK

PIETRA DURA

used in an interior as a dramatic focal point of a room, usually a living-room, where the outside surroundings provide an interesting "picture" to be viewed from within.

PICTURE-BOARD DUMMY See *Fireside Figures.*

PIE SAFES See *Milk or Pie Safes.*

PIECE DYED Fabric dyed after it has been woven. The opposite of yarn dyed.

PIECRUST TABLE A round pedestal table with the raised edge of the top surface carved in scallops, like the crimped edge of a pie. A common design in 18th-century England and America, especially in Chippendale's mahogany tripod tables.

PIED DE BICHE French for hind's foot. A decorative cloven hoof-shaped foot for seating units, tables, etc., used in the late Renaissance periods in Italy, France, and England. Illustrated is an Italian Directory stool.

PIER An isolated, heavy, vertical masonry support like a column or pilaster, but lacking the proportions or details of either. The pier gives support to arches and beams, and it is attached to a wall at the point where a heavy load is imposed.

PIER GLASS Originally a mirror that stood on the floor against the wall, intended as a facing for piers or to cover the wall space between windows. The term is also used to describe wall mirrors set over console tables. A mid-18th-century design by Matthias Lock is illustrated. See *Cheval Glass* or *Mirror.*

PIER TABLE A console table usually used in conjunction with a pier glass or mirror. Originally intended to be used on the space (or pier) between two windows. A French Empire example is illustrated.

PIERCED SPLAT The splat or center vertical panel of a chair back decorated with an openwork design, usually cut out with a fretsaw. An early-18th-century English chair is illustrated. See *Fretwork.*

PIERCED WORK Ornamental woodwork in which portions of the background are cut or chiseled out, leaving an openwork design. It is similar in appearance to fretwork. Pierced work was a popular form of decoration for chair backs, as illustrated in Chippendale's Gothic-style chair with pierced splat. Pierced work has also been used for windows, etc., in Moorish or Mohammedan architecture. It is having a renaissance in the current works of American architect Edward Durell Stone.

PIETRA DURA or PIETRE-DURE An Italian Renaissance mosaic inlay of marbles and assorted stones. Fine stones and marbles are inlaid or laminated into a stone base. The colors and markings are intricately used to create a pattern or picture. The pietra-dura technique was used for tabletops, cabinet embellishments, etc. A 16th-century marble inlay is illustrated. See *Intarsia* or *Tarsia* and *Mosaic*.

PIETRE INTARSIATE   See *Pietra Dura.*

PIGEONHOLES Small compartments in a bureau or secretary, often found in late-17th- and 18th-century pieces. Illustrated is the interior arrangement of a secrétaire-writing table.

PIGMENT Powdered coloring matter for painting, dye, or ink, made from natural or synthetic materials.

PILASTER An engaged pier built as part of a wall and acting as a support for a cornice, pediment, etc. A flat-faced vertical projection from a wall, sometimes with the proportions, details, and capital and base of a classic column. Illustrated is the Italian Renaissance Cancelleria in Rome. In furniture, the pilaster is a carved representation of the architectural feature, usually at the vertical ends of a cabinet, chest, console table, etc., and it forms a support for an overhanging table surface, shelf drawer, or the like.

PILASTRO Italian for column, pier, or pillar.

PILE In carpet construction, the uncut or cut loop tufts of surface yarn that form the wearing surface. The nap or top surface, in fabrics, see *Frieze, Plush,* and *Velvet.*

PILLAR An upright member, usually a column. May not be cylindrical or have the proportions of a classic order. Also, a commemorative shaft. An ancient Indian pillar is illustrated.

PILLAR-AND-CLAW TABLE A pedestal table of the Chippendale style with a central column-like support terminating in splayed legs. The feet are usually carved lion or bear paws.

PILLAR-AND-SCROLL A mantel clock case designed by the American clock designer Eli Terry, of Plymouth, Connecticut, in the early 19th century. It resembled the upper portion of a grandfather clock. The case had a scrolled top and skirt with columns or pillars at either side. The dial was opaque and enameled. Often a picture was painted on the glass area below the dial.

PILLEMENT, JEAN (1728–1808) A French painter and textile designer of the Louis XV and Louis XVI periods. He

PILLOW CAPITAL

PIGEONHOLES

PILLOWBACK CHAIR

PILASTER

PILLAR

created textiles with winding stripes, interlacing ribbons, and chinoiserie patterns.

PILLOW CAPITAL A Romanesque, simplified version of the Corinthian capital. It is simply a square block, rounded at the corners, and decorated in bas-relief sculpture. An arcade from Canterbury Cathedral in England is illustrated.

PILLOW FURNITURE Chairs, couches, lounges, and ottomans almost entirely made up of oversized, plump pillows, retained in a minimal frame or on a pedestal or platform. An inexpensive home-furnishing idea that evolved in the 1970's. Reupholstery is as simple as recovering a cushion.

PILLOWBACK CHAIR A variety of 19th-century Hitchcock chair with the usual rush seat, decorated or stenciled rails, and turned front legs. The distinguishing characteristic is the pillow or block in the middle of the top rail with turned decorations on either side. A Sheraton motif.

PINACOTECA The Italian word for picture gallery.

PINCHED TRAILING See *Quillwork.*

PINCUSHION CHAIR See *Compass Seat.*

PINE The abundant and popular American wood, with an interesting grain. It is economical, easy to work with, and used for furniture as well as interior finishes.

PINE, PICKLED A finish for interior walls or furniture which is a whitish patina or rub on knotty pine. Probably developed from the custom of scraping paint off old English furniture. The residue paint which accented the graining gave the old furniture a mellow quality now emulated in new reproductions.

PINE, WHITE A soft pine. The grain is usually uninteresting, and the wood, which is generally used for structural and finishing purposes, is often painted rather than stained.

PINE, YELLOW Hard pine, stronger and heavier than white pine, and good for cheap flooring, trims, doors, and furniture. Usually painted rather than stained.

PINEAPPLE A decorative carved stylized finial resembling the fruit, often used as a terminal piece on bedposts, newel posts, in pediments over doorways, etc. In early-19th-century America it was the symbol of wealth, prosperity, and especially hospitality.

PINNACLE A cone-shaped or pyramidal turret used in Gothic architecture to top roofs or buttresses. The pointed termination of a spire is often decorated with *Crockets*. A pinnacle may be used decoratively as an ending or a finial at the crest or top of an architectural piece of furniture.

PINWALE   A narrow rib or ridge in a fabric, as in pinwale corduroy.

PIPING   A tubular edging used to trim and decorate upholstery, draperies, etc. The tube may sometimes have a cord filler which gives the piping more roundness and a firmer appearance.

PIPKIN   An 18th-century English term for a metal coal container used at the fireside.

PIQUA   An African satin-textured wood with a uniform pinkish-brown color. See *Bosse*.

PIQUÉ   A heavy cotton fabric with raised cords running lengthwise. The name is derived from the French word for quilted. Piqué is also called Bedford cloth. In inlaying, gold or silver, shell, mother-of-pearl, or ivory, set in points or strips. This inlay technique was popular in the 17th and 18th centuries in France for decorating small accessory pieces like snuffboxes, small cabinets, jewel boxes, etc.

PIRANESI, GIAMBATTISTA (1720–1778)   A Venetian architect-artist who made a record of Roman antiquities in a collection of magnificent etchings. His works had a great effect on the classic movement in the 18th century. A section of a room designed by Piranesi is illustrated. See *Mural*.

PITCH   In the manufacturing of carpets, the number of warp threads per inch, measured across the width of the loom. The closer the warp threads, the finer the weave. The pitch is considered in connection with the "pick" or "rows" per inch. See *Pick*.

PLACAGE   The French word for veneering or plating on metal.

PLAFOND   French for ceiling. A part of a 16th-century French Renaissance coffered ceiling is shown.

PLAIDS   Multicolored, checkered, or squared patterns created by bars of different colors and thicknesses crossing each other at right angles in the weaving process. This design may also be printed on fabric, paper, etc. Originally, the word meant the shawl worn by Scots, and the pattern was called the tartan; each Scottish clan had its own identifying Tartan.

PLAIN SLICING VENEER   Consecutive slices cut from the half log or flitch parallel to a line through the center of the log. A variagated figure is usually produced.

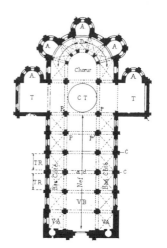

PLAN

PLANTED MOLDING

GIAMBATTISTA PIRANESI

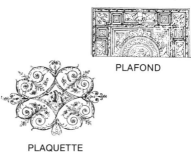

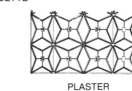

PLAQUETTE

PLAIN WEAVE   A basic weave in which the warp and weft are the same size, and alternate under and over each other in a regular manner. Used to make muslin, tafetta, etc.

PLAN   The horizontal projection of any object. A drawing which shows the arrangement and horizontal measurements of a building or room. Illustrated is a typical plan for a Romanesque church: nef=nave, T=transept, A=apse, choeur=choir, D =ambulatory, C=buttress, VB=barrel vault, VA=half vault, P=pillars, AD= double arch.

PLANCER or PLANCEER   The finished underside or soffit of a cornice.

PLANCHER   French for floor. Also, the French word for *Plancer* or *Planceer*.

PLANE   European sycamore wood, used for veneer and inlay.

PLANTED MOLDING   A cut and applied molding, as distinct from a stuck molding which is formed on the surface and is an integral part of it. A late-17th-century Jacobean oak chest of drawers with planted or applied moldings is illustrated. See *Applied Molding* and *Stuck Molding*.

PLANTSCAPING   The art of decorating an area with plants.

PLAQUE   A plate or panel of wood, metal, glass, stone, pottery, etc., with a surface ornamentation or inscription. In furniture, an ornamental disc or plate of porcelain, lacquer, finely chased ormolu, inlay, Wedgwood, etc., used as an enhancement. Illustrated is a wall plaque in the François I room at Fontainebleau, designed by Rosso in the mid-16th century. See *Cartouche*.

PLAQUE STRIÉE   A striped plaque, usually of bronze, which appeared as a decorative banding on aprons and legs of tables and commodes in the late Louis XVI period and through the Regency period in England.

PLAQUETTE   A strong shape of contrasting veneer inlay in a veneer surface. The shape usually has a decorative inlaid detail like an eagle, an urn, etc. An inlaid top of a Sheraton pier table is illustrated (late 18th century).

PLASTER   A wall and ceiling surfacing material, usually made of lime, water, sand, and sometimes plaster of Paris. On occasions, hair is added to the plaster as a reinforcing agent. May be a smooth surface or a textured one. Illustrated is a Tudor plaster ceiling.

PLASTER OF PARIS   A composition of calcined and ground gypsum.

PLAQUE

PLAFOND

PLASTER

PLASTERBOARD   See *Building Board.*

PLASTIC   Modeled, as opposed to carved. Also, a general term for a man-made resinous material which is chemically produced. It may be molded, formed, extruded, or shaped by heat or pressure. See *Thermoplastic, Thermosetting,* and the generic names for trademarked plastics.

PLATE GLASS   Glass rolled in large sheets, made with soda, lime, and silica. The surfaces are ground and polished. A mid-19th-century development making possible large window panes and mirrors.

PLATE WARMER   A metal-lined unit equipped with an iron heater which was placed in sideboards of late-18th-century English design. It later became a self-contained unit used on serving tables, similar to the current electric "hot plate."

PLATEAU   A decorative stand, set on low feet, used to raise a centerpiece above the table's surface, popular in the early 19th century. Often made of papier-mâché, but also of wood, brass, or glass. It is similar to a large trivet.

PLATERESCO   The period in Spanish art dating from the first half of the 16th century. The style of ornament that prevailed was an imitation of the fine details of the silversmith's art. Platero means silversmith in Spanish. Illustrated is the inner court of the College of San Gregorio in Valladolid, with its exuberant details, Moorish carvings, twisted columns, and three-centered arches.

PLATFORM BED   A mattress set on top of a wood or plastic platform or pedestal. Sometimes the mattress is recessed into a frame on the top of the platform and there is a shelf which may go partially or completely around the perimeter. In other designs, the mattress may appear to float over a base which is recessed below it. The platform bed may be used against a wall or placed as an "island" in a room. See *Island Furniture.*

PLEATING   The folding or doubling over of fabric to create a fullness below the folds. There are various methods of pleating: pinch pleating, box pleating, accordion pleating, etc. Each technique creates a different heading effect. Pleating is more formal than shirring. Illustrated is a Chippendale four-poster with a pleated valance. See *Linenfold.*

PLEXIFORM   A surface design which resembles basket weaving or plaiting. It was often used to decorate Romanesque and Celtic architecture. See *Nattes.*

PLEXIGLAS   A trademark name for a group of plastic sheet products produced in

PLIANT

PLINTH

PLINTH BLOCK

PLATERESCO

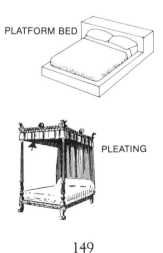

PLATFORM BED

PLEATING

a variety of sizes, colors, thicknesses, and patterns, some transparent.

PLIANT   French for flexible. A cross-legged folding stool, campstool, or deck chair. Illustrated is a stool of the Louis XI (Gothic) period in France. See *Faudesteuil.*

PLINTH   The square part of the base of a column or a pedestal piece of case furniture which is set solidly flat on the floor. It is the molded projection base of a structure or a pedestal without moldings. Illustrated is the base of an Ionic column.

PLINTH BLOCK   A small block of wood used at the bottom of a door trim. The baseboard butts against this block. Illustrated is a 17th-century doorway designed by Inigo Jones. A=the plinth of a Corinthian-type column; B=the plinth block of the door trim.

PLIQUÉ À JOUR ENAMELING   A 14th-century process of enameling which created a small-scale stained-glass effect. Vitreous, translucent glass pastes were set into a fine metal network or mesh, without backing.

PLISSÉ   A crinkled surface in stripes or patterns which results from a method of printing on plain-weave cotton or rayon fabrics.

PLUMWOOD   A dark red wood, like mahogany, which was used up to the 18th century.

PLUSH   A long-pile velvet. Deeper and lusher than velvet or velour, it may be made of silk, mohair, or synthetic fibers. Used as an upholstery fabric. Velvet pile is usually less than ⅛″ thick, and plush pile is longer than ⅛″.

PLUSH CARPET   Carpet distinguished by a slightly higher pile than a velvet carpet; usually less dense. Since the surface is not as smooth as the velvet, some light is absorbed in the pile, resulting in a low reflection level and a warmer, textured appearance.

PLY   The number of twists, folds, strands, or layers in yarns, papers, woods, etc.

PLYWOOD   Strong layered wood panel, consisting of a thick, semiporous core, on both sides of which are laminated exactly equal thin veneers, $\frac{1}{16}$″ thick or less, with the grain of both veneers running exactly perpendicular to the grain of the core. The arrangement is called crossbanding. A finish layer is applied on top: a veneer with the grain running parallel with that of the core. This makes a "plaid" with all tensions pulling in different directions. This crisscross effect makes for the strength of plywood. See *Lamination*.

POCKET DOOR   A standard-size door that is opened by sliding it sideways out of sight, into an opening in the supporting wall. A popular device in the 19th century, when a pair of pocket doors were used to close off a parlor or dining room from each other, or from the main entrance hall.

PODIUM   A pedestal or platform. A continuous base supporting a series of columns. See *Stylobate*.

POINÇON   French for *Hallmark*

POINT D'HONGRIE   Needlepoint with a design which vaguely resembles an irregular series of chevron forms. It is usually made of silk and used as an upholstery fabric.

POINTING   The process of gouging out part of the mortar which was used for the bedding of bricks or masonry (up to ¾″) and replacing it with a compound that has a greater resistance to moisture.

POISSANT, THIEBAUT (born 1605)   A French architect and sculptor. His work appears in most of the palaces built and furnished for Louis XIV.

POLE SCREEN   A fire screen. Illustrated is a Chippendale mid-18th-century design. See *Banner Screen*.

POLE TABLE   See *Pote Table*.

POLISH BED   See *Dome Bed*.

POLLARD OAK (WALNUT)   Oak or walnut trees that are "polled," i.e., cut at the top to secure a bushier grain.

POLYCHROME   Multicolored. Illustrated is a multicolored ceiling of an early English Renaissance house.

POLYETHER   See *Polyfoam* and *Polyurethane Foam*.

POLYETHYLENE   An olefin or polyolefin fiber which can be paraffin-based. It is waxy in hand, and resists dyeing, but it has excellent chemical resistance, and resists the harmful effects of sunlight. Lighter than water, and will therefore float.

POLYFOAM   A synthetic resin which simulates latex foam rubber. Used for upholstery pieces, mattresses, pillow filling, etc. It is also called polyurethane foam or polyether.

POLYMER   A chainlike molecular structure composed of monomers, the basis of synthetic fibers like nylon, Dacron, Acrilan, Dynel, Creslan, etc.

POLYPROPYLENE   Similar to polyethylene, this is a paraffin-based fabric that

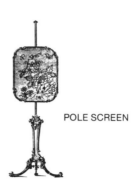

POLE SCREEN

POLYCHROME

POMPEII

POMPEIIAN

is called an olefin. It is stronger, lighter, and less heat-sensitive than polyethylene, and is abrasion-resistant.

POLYPROPYLENE-OLEFIN CARPETS   Carpets made of a synthetic fiber either by pile construction or felting. The material has a high resistance to moisture, mildew, rot, wear from abrasion and stains. Their weather resistance makes them ideal for indoor-outdoor use.

POLYURETHANE FOAM   Also called polyfoam or polyether. A synthetic resin which simulates foam rubber, and can be substituted for it. See *Foam Rubber*.

POLYVINYL CLORIDE   See *PVC*.

POMBALINO   A Portuguese style in mid-18th century based on the French Rococo. It was named after the Marquis de Pombal who was responsible for the rebuilding of Lisbon after it was destroyed by a tidal wave in 1755.

POMEGRANATE   A decorative ornament based on the pomegranate fruit, which is apple-shaped with a hard rind and a pronounced crownlike ending. It was used in classic times as a symbol for fertility.

POMMES   French for apples. A finial shaped like an arrangement of apples on a plate, used on bedstead posts. In the late 17th century, pommes were the ornaments used by Daniel Marot to surmount the corners of his testers. See *Marot, Daniel*.

POMPEII   A Greco-Roman resort city which was completely covered with ashes after Mt. Vesuvius erupted in A.D. 79. In the mid-18th century, extensive excavations at Pompeii and Herculaneum uncovered great decorative works and art treasures that had a strong influence on the designers of that time. These finds were a rich source of inspiration for the Adam brothers of England and the Neoclassic designers of the Louis XVI period.

POMPEIIAN   Based on motifs or designs uncovered by the excavation of Pompeii in the mid-18th century. Illustrated is a French Empire wall treatment in the Pompeiian manner.

POMPONNE   Gilded copper. See *Cuivre Doré*.

PONDEROSA PINE   A light-colored wood with soft, even texture and a faint grain pattern. It is light in weight, easy to work, and takes paint or stains well. This pine is often used as "knotty pine." A product of the western United States.

PONGEE   A fabric of plain weave made from wild silk in its natural, beige-tan color. Has an interesting slubby texture. The name is derived from the Chinese *pen chi*, which means woven at home on one's own loom (*pen*, own; *chi*, loom). Now also produced from synthetic fibers.

PONTEUSE A gaming chair which one straddled. The wide back rail contained compartments for chips, money, cards, etc. See *Fumeuse*.

PONTIL An iron rod used to carry hot materials in the glass manufacturing process. In the hand-blown glass technique, the pontil is often used to support the bottom of the piece being blown.

PONTIL MARK The mark left by the pontil after glass cools. Usually the mark appears at the bottom of handmade glass vases, pitchers, dishes, etc. The pontil mark is sometimes ground off and the bottom is polished flat, or a small dimple remains. See *Pontil*.

PONTYPOOL An English term for a method of japanning on metal originated by Thomas Allgood at Pontypool, England, in about 1660. See *Japanning*.

POP ART Originally, the popular arts of mass culture. Later applied to serious work in the fine arts, using themes conspicuous in the affluent consumer society: movie actresses, sport heroes, film strips, commercial packaging, advertising, photography, and automobiles. Among practioners of this movement were Andy Warhol, James Rosenquist, Roy Lichtenstein, Claes Oldenburg, and Robert Indiana. Pop Art peaked in the late-1950's and early-1960's in the United States.

POPLAR See *Whitewood*. A very pale-colored wood with an exceptionally fine grain, sometimes used for paneling in the Stuart period. In the 16th and 17th centuries, used for inlay work.

POPLIN A plain-weave fabric with fine cross ribs. The warp threads are finer than the fillers. It is similar to broadcloth but it has a heavier rib.

POPPY HEAD The decorative end of a Gothic bench. It was often carved with fleurs de lis, animals, figures, etc.

PORCELAIN A hard, vitreous, nonporous ceramic ware made of kaolin. Illustrated is an early-18th-century English porcelain vase. See *China*, *Hard Paste*, and *Kaolin*.

PORCH An exterior addition to a building. It usually forms a covered approach to a doorway. See *Portico*.

PORPHYRY A form of marble, consisting of a compact feldspathic base through which crystals of feldspar are disseminated.

PORTAIL

PORTICO

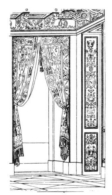

PORTIÈRE

PORTLAND STONE

PORCELAIN

PORTUGUESE BULB

The crystals are lighter than the base, often white. There are red, green, and purple varieties. Popular for architectural and ornamental use.

PORTABLE SERVER A small movable serving cart on casters. It can be equipped with removable trays, shelves, drawers, etc., and can be used as a bar or tea wagon.

PORTAIL French word for portal or chief doorway. Illustrated is the portal of the Brussels Cathedral. See also *Façade d'Honneur*.

PORTAL An entrance to a large, important structure.

PORTE-COCHÈRE French for an extension porch from a building which provided shelter for passengers alighting from carriages. A gateway for carriages leading into the courtyard of a major building, characteristic of French Renaissance architecture.

PORTER CHAIR An enclosed chair of the 18th century with a bowed top and sides, which was often set in entry halls to accommodate waiting porters or footmen and to protect them from draughts in the waiting area. See also *Sedan Chair*.

PORTICO An open space covered with a roof supported on columns. A porchlike structure in front of a building which is fronted with columns. Illustrated is the Doria Palace in Genoa.

PORTIÈRE A curtain or drapery over an arch or doorway, or used in place of a door. A means of separating one area from another, and providing privacy. It can be used to separate an alcove from a room. Illustrated is an Empire portière from the former Palace of the Tuileries.

PORTLAND CEMENT A synthetic cement made from lime and clay.

PORTLAND STONE An English limestone which is white or creamy in color. Illustrated is a vase designed in Portland stone by James Gibbs in the early 18th century.

PORTLAND VASE A Roman vase design of a blue-black glass with opaque white figures superimposed on the glass. It was reproduced by Josiah Wedgwood in black porcelain in the late 18th century, as well as in some typical blue Wedgwood color schemes.

PORTRAIT A painting or sculpture of a person, usually a recognizable representation.

PORTUGUESE BULB A bulbous, knobby turning of Portuguese origin, for furniture supports, used in the William and Mary style in England. The stretcher would usually connect into one of these distinctive knobs, rather than a cube shape. The stretcher itself was sometimes a bulbous prominence.

POST A short piece of wall which is about as long as it is thick. When a post acts as a support, it is called a pedestal.

POST AND LINTEL The basic form of construction that depends upon a horizontal member (the lintel) resting upon two uprights (the posts). Illustrated is the Arch of the Goldsmiths in Rome which shows an opening spanned by a lintel.

POSTERN The back door or entrance as opposed to the portal.

POSTURE FURNITURE Chairs designed to give proper back support, encourage correct body positions for various tasks.

POT AU FARD French for a cosmetic jar.

POT BOARD The lowest shelf (closest to the floor) of a dresser.

POT CUPBOARD See *Bedside Cupboard*.

POTE TABLE A narrow, cylindrical table which sometimes resembled the lower portion of a fluted column. The cylinder was a single pedestal either with exposed shelves on one face, or with a tambour door. An 18th-century design, it is also called a pole table.

POUCH TABLE A small, elegant lady's worktable of the late 18th century. It contained various fittings and a silk pouch to hold needlework. The Sheraton period combined worktables with writing tables in elaborate variations. Sheraton described a pouch table as "a table with a bag, used by ladies to work at, in which bag they deposit their fancy needlework." It is also called a *Bag Table*.

POUDRE D'ÉCAILLE French for powdered tortoiseshell, which was the basis of a highly colored material used for finishing small wood objects.

POUDREUSE A lady's powder or toilet table, often equipped with a mirrored lid in the center which lifts up. A Louis XV period innovation. Illustrated is a design by Roentgen.

POWDER ROOM Originally a corner or small closet in the bedroom of an 18th-century house where one could go to have one's hair powdered. In current usage, a ladies' lavatory.

POWER POLE A wooden or plastic vertical member that goes from floor to

POST AND LINTEL

POWER RACEWAY

POUCH TABLE

POUDREUSE

PREMIÈRE PARTIE

ceiling and carries electrical wires with power within it. Electric outlets can be spaced along the pole into which electrical equipment can be plugged. Particularly useful in open-office layouts or landscapes, since the electric power can be brought from the perimeter wall out to the middle of the space, often through the power raceways in the bottom of the screens used. The various work stations clustered around the power pole can then have their electrical equipment plugged into the pole.

POWER RACEWAY A channel provided in some open-office panels through which electrical power lines can be drawn to provide electrical power in the free-standing, out-in-the-open work stations. Also called an Electrical Raceway. See *Open Planning* and *Acoustical Panels*.

POYNTELL A floor pattern or pavement made up of square tiles or blocks laid diagonally, or diamond shaped tiles.

PRAGUE CHAIR A simple, classic chair made of steam-bent birchwood combined with almost white handwoven cane. The squarish seat and chair back have gently rounded corners. The raked back chair legs continue up to form the frame for the subtly bowed back.

PRAYER RUGS Small rugs originally designed for an individual to kneel on for Moslem prayers. See *Turkish Rugs*.

PREDELLA A footstool. Also, in Italian art, the narrow panel at the back of the altar which served as a base for the altar-piece. Often the entire grouping consisted of several small, related paintings grouped together with the major painting set above.

PREFAB The vernacular term for *Prefabricated*.

PREFABRICATED Units used in construction or decoration which are shaped, formed, and finished in a locale other than the site of construction or installation. Examples are prefabricated windows and doors made to fit doorways and frames being constructed on the site.

PREFABRICATED HOUSES Houses made up of many prefinished parts brought to the building site, and there assembled.

PREMIÈRE PARTIE A Boulle marquetry in which the tortoiseshell predominates and forms the groundwork for the metal inserts. See *Boulle Work* and *Contrepartie* or *Contre Boulle*.

PRE-RAPHAELITE BROTHERHOOD During the second half of the 19th century, a group of English artists, writers, and poets who revolted against the mechanization and eclecticism of the Victorian arts and the decline of craftsmanship. Their movement started a trend back to the styles of the Italian primitives, to nature, and to the handicrafts. In 1848, the Pre-Raphaelite Brotherhood was started by Dante Gabriel Rossetti, Holman Hunt, and John Everett Millais. John Ruskin was an inspiration to the group, and Edward Burne-Jones was sympathetic to their cause. The Arts and Crafts Movement, which was begun by William Morris, was an outgrowth of the Brotherhood.

PRESHRUNK   A term applied to fabrics processed for shrinkage before being marketed. After such treatment (Sanforizing is one trademark process) shrinkage in future washings should be minimum.

PRESS   A cupboard or armoire in which clothes or linens were stored. In the mid and late 17th century, used to describe the case in which books were stored; it has also been used as a term for bookshelves. The press was also known as a press cupboard, great cupboard, or wainscot cupboard. A Chippendale mid-18th-century clothespress is illustrated.

PRESSED GLASS   Glass objects shaped by a fast and inexpensive method of pouring the molten glass into a mold. A plunger is pressed inside the mold and creates the inner contours of the object. An ideal technique for producing flat dishes, bowls, saucers, and plates.

PRICKET CANDLESTICK   An early form of candlestick with a spike projecting above the rim. The candle was impaled on the spike and thus held erect. Illustrated is an ancient Chinese candlestick.

PRIE-DIEU CHAIR   A chair designed to accommodate a person at prayer. A carved armchair with a high back, a low, hinged seat, and a receptacle for a prayer book. Also a low chair, without arms but with a broad upholstered shelf in place of the top rail. A person kneeling in prayer can rest his or her arms on the shelflike projection.

PRIEUR   An 18th-century French designer of interiors, ornaments, arabesques, etc., during the reign of Louis XVI.

PRIMARY COLORS   The basic colors from which all other colors can be mixed. The commonly accepted theory as applied to pigment, as opposed to light, is that red, yellow, and blue are the three basic primary colors. Red and yellow make orange, blue and red produce violet, and yellow and blue form green. (Black and white are not considered colors; they are neutrals.) See *Secondary Colors*. In light theories, red, blue, and green are the primary colors.

PRESS

PRICKET CANDLESTICK

PRINCE OF WALES FEATHERS

PRIMARY LIGHTING   The basic, most elemental lighting in a store or selling area or commercial space. Usually devoid of special lighting effects such as spots, filters, floods, or washers, and thus lacking in any attempt to affect atmosphere or mood. See *General Lighting*.

PRIMAVERA   A yellow-white mahogany with a striped or cross fire figure. Mexico and Guatemala produce a similar pale yellow-brown, birch-colored wood with a mahogany grain. It is a handsome and easily worked fine cabinet wood. See *Acajou* and *Mahogany*.

PRIMING   The application of a primary or first coat of paint, primer, or sealer on a wall, piece of woodwork or furniture, floor, etc. The use of a preparatory surfacing material.

PRIMITIVE ART   Art of either deliberate or unconscious naïveté, characterized by more or less unsophisticated technique. A term also applied to the art of the 15th century in Italy, to the productions of some 17th- to 19th-century American itinerant artists, and the work of such modern artists as Henri Rousseau and Grandma Moses, as well as to prehistoric art and the art of regions remote from European and Western or Chinese art developments.

PRINCE OF WALES FEATHERS   A chair-back ornament of the Hepplewhite period. It was a carved representation of the three ostrich plumes which were the badge of the Prince of Wales. See *Parlor or Parlour* for another illustration.

PRINCEWOOD   A Spanish elm imported from the West Indies. Its reddish color made it popular in late-17th-century English furniture.

PRINT ROOMS   Prints and etchings were stylish wall decorations in mid-18th-century England. Prints were sometimes pasted directly onto the walls with ornamental paper borders around them to serve as mountings or frames. Cutout borders, frets, ribbons, and festoons of wallpaper were used to accent and dramatize wall arrangements. A room decorated in this manner was called a print or engraving room. Horace Walpole had a print room at Strawberry Hill, and Chippendale made use of this form of decoration also.

PRISCILLA CURTAIN   A curtain, usually sheer, with a deep ruffle of the same material on three sides of each panel. Two such panels are usually set on double curtain rods, one behind the other, with the long unruffled side against the side of the window frame. The panels are then pulled back one to each side of the window, creating an overlap or crisscross effect at the window top, and tied to the window frame with loops of fabric, often ruffled pieces of the curtain material. The ruffles cascade down from the tieback point. This curtain may also be a simple pullback curtain with the two panels meeting but not overlapping in the middle, and may be sill length, three-quarter length, or floor length.

PRISMATIC GLASS A translucent rolled glass with one smooth surface, the other surface textured with parallel prisms. Light is refracted through the glass, and the angle of refraction is determined by the way the light hits the prism.

PROFILE The outline of an object as seen from the side or in cross section.

PRONG BOX A receptacle for table silver placed in or on an 18th-century sideboard. See *Knife Box*.

PROPORTION The relative size of one part to the whole or to any of the other parts of a composition.

PROSCENIUM The part of the stage in front of the drop curtain. Originally, in the Greek theatre, the word meant the stage itself.

PROSCENIUM ARCH The frame or arch that holds the drop curtain. See *Proscenium*. Illustrated is a theatre of the time of Louis XIII of France (mid-17th century).

PROTEIN FIBERS Synthetic fibers derived from peanuts, soybeans, caseins, cornmeal, or other protein sources.

PROVINCIAL Of the provinces. Country-made and/or country-styled. Simple, unsophisticated, and rustic. See *French Provincial*.

PROVINCIAL FRENCH See *French Provincial*.

PRUD'HON, PIERRE-PAUL (1758–1823) A celebrated French painter and designer of the Empire period. He painted in the classic style, and often used allegorical or mythological subjects. Illustrated is a crib designed for the King of Rome.

PSYCHE An Empire cheval mirror which stood on the floor and could be tilted forward or backward. See *Cheval Glass or Mirror* and *Grand Miroir à la Psyché*. Illustrated is a psyche designed by Prud'hon for the Empress Marie-Louise. Also, an upholstered sofa, with Greek curves, of the first part of the 19th century.

PUCE From the French word for flea. A dark brown or brownish-violet color.

PULL BRACKETS

PULL-UP CHAIR

AUGUSTUS WELBY PUGIN

PULLDOWN FRONT

PROSCENIUM ARCH

PIERRE-PAUL PRUD'HON

PSYCHE

PUENTE STAND A carved trestle table which was designed to support the Vargueño.

PUGIN, AUGUSTUS WELBY (1812–1852) English architect and writer, the prime architectural force in the Gothic Revival period. Illustrated is a prie-dieu designed by Pugin, carved of oak and enriched with color and gilt.

PULL BRACKETS Movable arms located on either side of and below a pullout writing surface of a desk or secretary. When pulled out, the brackets support the writing surface. Illustrated is an early-19th-century Sheraton design.

PULLDOWN FRONT A lid or covering on a secretary or bureau which, when lowered, covers the writing area and its fittings. Other types of pulldown front are cylinder, roll, and tambour fronts. A Sheraton design is illustrated.

PULLMAN KITCHEN A shallow alcove or recess, often screened off from a living area, equipped with a compact arrangement of kitchen fixtures (sink, stove, refrigerator, etc.). It is sometimes one wall of a room which is camouflaged to hide its utilitarian features.

PULLS Handles for drawers, cabinets, etc. See *Hardware*.

PULL-UP CHAIR A small, light-scaled chair used in living rooms and bedrooms. An occasional chair which can be designed in a period or contemporary style. Illustrated is an 18th-century barrel-type pull-up chair.

PULVINARIA The pillow-like elements on the side of an Ionic capital which end in the volutes. Pulvinar (the singular form) also refers to the pillow on which the statue of a god was set in the classic temples.

PULVINATED Describing a frieze with a convex profile.

PUNCHWORK A form of simple carved decoration. The background is made stipple-textured by the use of a fine steel punch.

PURFLED Having a surface ornament of drapery, lacework, or embroidery or one which simulated such an effect.

PURPLE WOOD A purplish-colored Brazilian wood used for inlay work, popular in the 18th century. Also called violet wood. See *Amaranth*.

PUTTO A figure of a very young boy, somewhat like a wingless cherub or cupid. Popular subject for decoration and sculpture in the Italian Renaissance and appeared in painting.

PVC (POLYVINYL CHLORIDE)   A rigid, tough plastic material which is extruded in tube lengths and used for indoor-outdoor "pipe" furniture. Available in a wide range of colors and tube diameters; resistant to color fading, moisture, and mildew.

PYRAMID   A geometric solid shape composed of inclined triangles which meet at a point. The noted structures in ancient Egypt, which have a square base and four triangular sides meeting at an apex.

PYROXYLIN   A cellulose product which when applied to cotton or rayon fabrics makes them stain-resistant and waterproof.

Q

QAMARIYYAH Arabic for a lattice window or a pierced stone or stucco opening. See *Mashrebeeyah*.

QUADRA A square architectural molded frame sometimes used to accent a relief sculpture. Also the plinth block of a podium or platform.

QUADRANT BRACKETS or QUADRANTS Quarter-circle bands of metal attached to the pulldown front of a secretary or bureau. When the front is down, it is supported by these bands. Illustrated is a bureau bookcase (secretary) of the Hepplewhite and Sheraton period.

QUADRANT BRACKETS

QUADRATURA A 17th- and 18th-century type of trompe l'oeil mural painting. Architectural elements like columns, cornices, entablatures, cupolas, and colonnades were painted on flat walls and ceilings to create strongly foreshortened perspective views of exterior scenes. The painters who specialized in this art were called quadraturisti or quadratisti.

QUADRATURE See *Illusionism* and *Trompe l'Oeil*.

QUARREL or QUARRY A square or diamond-shaped pane of glass. The term also refers to a square paving stone or tile.

QUARRY ORNAMENT A surface treatment of crisscrossing or reticulated lines which form quadrangular or diamond-shaped spaces.

QUARRY TILE A paving tile, of ceramic, unglazed.

QUARTER LANDING A square landing which makes a 45° turn in a stairway.

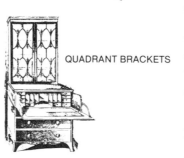
QUATTROCENTO

QUEEN ANNE PERIOD

QUARTER ROUND A convex molding which, in profile, is one quarter of a circle. See *Echinus*.

QUARTER-SLICED VENEER A quarter of a log sliced in parallel lines at right angles to the annual growth rings. This produces striped or straight grains on the slices of veneer.

QUARTETTE TABLES A nest of four light tables made to be stored by nesting one inside the other. See *Nested Tables*. *Sheraton* was one of the originators of this device, and he called them quartetto tables.

QUATREFOIL A four-lobed ornament, like a stylized four-leaf clover. A Gothic symbol for the cross and the four Evangelists, it was often used in Gothic window tracery and carved-wood decoration on interiors and on Gothic furniture. See *Cusps*.

QUATTROCENTO The 15th century of the 1400's. Illustrated is a French chair of that century.

QUEEN ANNE PERIOD The furniture and interior styles of England during the reign of Queen Anne (1702–1714). Early Queen Anne is a continuation of the William and Mary style, while the late Queen Anne heralds the George I period. The cabriole leg with clubbed foot, shell carvings on the knees of furniture supports, and the swan's neck pediment were popular motifs of this period. The web or Dutch foot appears in the Queen Anne style. See *Decorated Queen Anne Period*.

QUEEN-SIZE BED A bed with a single mattress approximately 60″ wide by 76″ to 84″ in length.

QUERVELLE, ANTHONY G.   A 19th-century Philadelphia cabinet-maker.

QUILLING See *Quillwork.*

QUILLWORK Decorative applied wavy bands of glass, especially on American and English glass. The glass is pinched as it is being applied, and thus the wavy line is formed.

QUILTED FIGURE See *Blister.*

QUILTING Two layers of fabric with padding between the layers, held in place by stitches that usually follow a definite pattern. The raised or tufted areas between the stitches give the fabric the characteristic bumpy surface. Papers and fabrics can be embossed to create a quilted effect.

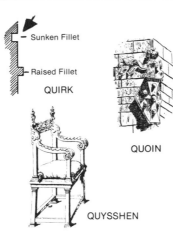

QUIMPERWARE Simple pottery ornamented in bright colors with local scenes and figures produced by local craftspeople during the mid-to-late-18th century in France. A French Provincial decorative accessory.

QUIRK A sharp, incised groove in a molding. It is sometimes referred to as a "sunken fillet."

QUOIN The corner angle of a building. Also, the brick or stone laid at the corner angle. The cornerstone may be a decorative element, as illustrated.

QUYSSHEN A 16th-century term for cushion. Illustrated is a wood chair of the early French Renaissance period with the quysshen added for comfort.

R

RABBET A continuous rectangular groove cut along the edge of a piece of wood or metal. It is usually cut to receive the edge of another piece of wood or metal, e.g., a rabbet is sometimes cut on the inner edges of a chair's seat frame to receive a slip seat.

RABBET JOINT In construction, a form of joinery in which a recess or groove is cut in one piece of wood to form a bed for another piece of wood. Also called a dado joint.

RABESCO Italian for arabesque.

RACHET An 18th-century term for a gearlike construction element used in English secretaries to lower the writing surface. See *Ratchet.*

RACK An angled frame or stand to hold music, books, magazines, etc. A grooved frame or a stand (with or without brackets) to hold guns, cups, etc. Illustrated is a late Victorian combination bookrack and stand.

RADIAL RUBBER FLOORING Heavy-duty commercial rubber tile flooring patterned with raised circles or rectangles of the same color as the background of the tile. The raised pattern provides not only a greater life span for the flooring but also good traction, reducing the possibility of slipping. It has become fashionable for interiors with a high-tech look. See *High-Tech.*

RADIANT HEATING A system of heating rooms by setting heat coils in the floor or walls, or both; when these areas are heated, the whole room warms up.

RADIUS EDGE A rounded corner equivalent to a quarter of a circle which

RABBET

RABBET JOINT

RAFFLE LEAVES

RACK

connects a straight vertical plane with a straight horizontal one. A 6″ radius edge would be ¼ of a circle with a 12″ diameter.

RAEBURN ARMCHAIR An 18th-century English armchair with a simple upholstered rectangular back, short slim upholstered armpieces, and curved wood arm supports which sweep up and back from the front corners of the upholstered seat. The arm supports and the legs are the only exposed wood parts of the chair. The legs may be cabriole or straight, molded with carved or pierced brackets.

RAFFLE LEAVES An 18th-century English motif of ornamental foliage with serrated edges similar to the acanthus leaf. Originally found in Italian designs, and adapted by the English designers. Illustrated is an Adam example.

RAFRAÎCHISSOIR or SERVANTE A small Louis XV rectangular serving table set on casters, often marble-topped, with rounded corners and a drawer below, and two shelves set between the legs. The top was fitted with two silverplated receptacles which could be filled with cold water to keep wine bottles chilled. Canabas designed many such tables in solid mahogany. Variations also appear in the Louis XVI period. See *Dumbwaiter.*

RAFTERS The sloping beams that support the upper part of a roof, sometimes kept visible for design purposes in an interior.

RAG RUG A rug woven of strips of rags or fabric scraps. The fabrics are sometimes plaited or braided and then sewn into a circle or oval area rug. It is now made to resemble provincial Early American rugs made by hand.

RAIL   The horizontal strip of a frame or a panel. The horizontal tie bar in the framing of a piece of furniture, such as the top of a chair back, or a stretcher rail.

RAINCEAU   The 18th-century English spelling of rinceau. Illustrated is an *Adam* design for a panel.

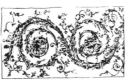
RAINCEAU

RAKE   An inward slant or slope from an upright, like the slope of a chair back (R in the illustration). An outward slope is a splay (S in the illustration).

RAKING CORNICE   In architecture and furniture, the series of moldings on the angled sides of a pediment.

RAMIE   A fiber, similar to flax, which is derived from a stalk plant grown in the United States and in the Orient. See *Bast Fibers*.

RAMP   An inclined surface which joins two different levels, or the part of a staircase handrail which rises at a sharper angle than the normal handrail. In furniture, a sharp curve ending in an angle at the end of the upright. Illustrated is an early-18th-century English Hogarth chair, in which this often appears.

RAM'S HEAD   A classical decorative motif, reintroduced in the 18th century by Robert Adam on his furniture and in his decorative accessories.

RAM'S HORN STUMP   A double curved arm support which resembles a twisted ram's horn. Illustrated is a mid-18th-century English chair.

RANCH WINDOWS   Wide but short windows placed higher up from the floor than the traditional double-hung or casement window. This permits the placement of furniture beneath them, but ranch windows do not usually afford much of a view, and could be a safety hazard in case of fire. Also called strip windows.

RANCH-STYLE HOUSE   In contemporary usage, a house built completely on one level. All the living, sleeping, and service rooms are on the ground. The house may have a cellar or basement and a crawl-space attic.

RANDOLPH, BENJAMIN   A late-18th-century Philadelphia cabinet-maker. He designed highboys, and made chairs in the Chippendale style. See *Philadelphia Chippendale*.

RANDOM MATCH   In veneering or decorative surfacing, a casual, unmatched effect with no attempt at a symmetrical or repetitive pattern.

RAKE

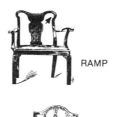
RAMP

RAM'S HORN STUMP

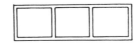
RANCH WINDOW

RANDOM MATCH

RANDOM RUBBLE   In masonry, stones of assorted shapes and sizes, roughly surfaced, which are set in not clearly defined courses.

RANDOM WIDTH   In woodworking, assorted widths of planks used vertically or horizontally to create an irregular pattern.

RANGE TABLES   A late-18th-century term for rectangular tables of the same size which could be combined to form a longer table. The outer corners of the end sections were sometimes rounded.

RANSON   An 18th-century French designer of furniture, floral decorations, and trophies in the Louis XVI style. Many beds of that period were made from his designs.

RAPHAEL (RAPHAEL SANZIO) (1483–1520)   A leading artist and architect of the High Renaissance in Italy. He decorated many rooms (stanze) with frescoes and paintings for Popes Julius II and Leo X. He succeeded Bramante as the architect of St. Peter's in Rome. Among his many noted religious paintings are the Sistine Madonna, the frescoes and tapestry designs for the Farnesina in Rome, and the "Transfigurations" in the Vatican. See *Loggia*.

RATCHET   A tooth or detent which is used in conjunction with a ratchet wheel for many purposes, including the raising and lowering of desk surfaces, lids, etc., on 18th-century furniture. The ratchet wheel has many inclined teeth around the outer rim. When the ratchet is released, it catches onto one of the angled teeth, and thus keeps the wheel from turning any farther. This would keep a writing surface at a set angle or height. For Sheraton's ratchet mechanism for working his late-18th-century harlequin table, see *Harlequin Table*.

RATCHET CHAIR   An 18th-century English reclining chair. A high-backed wing chair with Marlborough legs and curved arm stumps supporting covered arm rests. The movable back was attached to the arm rest by means of a ratchet device which made possible several changes in the degree of incline.

RAT-CLAW FOOT   A mid- and late-18th-century English and American furniture foot which resembled the sharp spiny claws of a rodent clutching a ball.

RATINÉ   A loose, plain-weave fabric with a nubby, uneven surface. The warp of the fabric is a special knotty yarn.

RATTAN   The long, solid, round stems of a species of palm found in India and the East. The unbranched stems are pliable and tough, and are used in wickerwork furniture. Though it does not stain readily, rattan can be lacquered. See *Lacquer*.

RAYON The trademark name for a synthetic fiber having a cellulose base. It is more lustrous, stiffer, and less expensive than silk, and may be used in combination with other synthetic or natural fibers.

RAYONNANT The French word for radiant or beaming. The name given to 13th-century French Gothic architecture which was characterized by wheel tracery and circular windows such as were used in Bourges, Amiens, and Rheims (illustrated).

READING STAND or READING DESK A popular piece of furniture of the late 18th century. Hepplewhite described one of his designs as a "tripod stand having a staff slide on the stem (fixed with a screw), supporting an adjustable book holder or table."

REBATE See *Rabbet*.

REBUS A form of expression in which words are not spelled out in letters but are represented by pictures of objects whose names the words resemble. A picture of an eye would represent "I," and a rose could represent the act of rising.

RÉCAMIER In furniture, a French 19th-century Directoire or Empire chaise longue named for Mme Récamier. A classic type of reclining couch, with one end slightly higher than the other and gracefully curved. Illustrated is an Empire or Regency version by Sheraton. The Récamier was also called a Grecian sofa.

RECESS A niche or alcove. An area set back from or into a wall. Illustrated is a recess in the 14th-century Gothic church of St. André in Bordeaux.

RECESSED STRETCH In furniture, the cross stretcher which unites with the two side stretchers rather than with the front legs. This creates a setback which allows room for the sitter's heels. See *H Stretcher*, *Stretcher*, and *X-shaped Stretcher*.

RÉCHAMPI A French term for relief decoration in gilt or color, or a combination of the two. Illustrated is a Louis XIV armchair covered in tapestry, with gilded carved decoration.

RECLINING CHAIR A mechanically operated chair which has a back that lets down and often a footrest that rises up. By dropping the back and raising the footrest, the person in the chair places himself in a horizontal position, as in a modern barber chair. A late-19th-century example is illustrated.

RECTILINEAR PERIOD

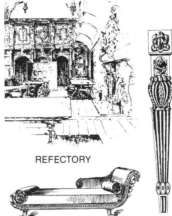

REFECTORY

RÉCAMIER   REEDING

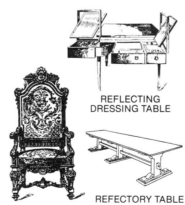

RECESS

RECLINING CHAIR

REFLECTING DRESSING TABLE

RÉCHAMPI

REFECTORY TABLE

REGENCY (ENGLISH)

RECTILINEAR PERIOD The late Gothic period in England (approximately 1377–1485). See *Perpendicular Style*. Illustrated is Westminster Hall in London, England.

RED FILLER An Early American furniture finish used until about 1830. It was applied on country-made pieces, and consisted of Spanish brown pigment mixed with raw linseed oil.

RED GUM A fine-grained wood of a reddish-brown color used for veneer for doors, and general interior finishes. Red gum can be stained to imitate walnut, mahogany, or maple, depending upon the figure of the particular species used.

REDWOOD A handsome, uniformly red-colored wood which takes paint and stains well. Wide widths of planking are available. Native to the western United States, especially California.

REEDING Rows of beading or semicylindrical convex moldings used in close parallel lines. When concave moldings are used it is called fluting. Illustrated is a Sheraton chair leg which is reeded.

REFECTORY The dining room in an institution, or school. Illustrated is an Elizabethan (1571) dining room in a charterhouse. Note the long refectory table. The oak screen in the background is typical of this period, as is the minstrel's gallery in the upper right-hand corner of the illustration.

REFECTORY TABLE A long, narrow dining table. In the early Gothic period it was a slab of wood or several fitted planks on trestles. This developed into a firm, massive table with bulbous legs, heavy stretchers, and ornate carving. Illustrated is an Italian trestle table.

REFLECTING DRESSING TABLE A complex, mechanically ingenious dressing table of the mid-18th century. Illustrated is a Shearer design. See *Rudd's Dressing Table*.

RÉGENCE See *French Régence* or *Regency*.

REGENCY (ENGLISH) The period in England from 1811 to 1820 when the future George IV was Regent. In furniture and interior designs, the period resembles the concurrent French Directoire and Empire. Noted for its extensive use of painted stucco and Greek, Roman, and Egyptian motifs. Thomas Hope and Sir John Soane were the leading designers. John Nash's work, especially his Brighton Pavilion, was a particularly fine achievement of the period. A Thomas Hope interior is illustrated. See *Hope, Thomas* and *Soane, Sir John*.

REGLET   A narrow band or fillet which separates two moldings.

REGOLO   Italian for mullion.

REGULA   The short band between the tenia and the guttae in a Doric entablature.

RÉGULATEUR   French term for a grandfather clock or a long hanging case clock. A *Regulator*.

REGULATOR   A large wall-hanging case clock. Illustrated is a mid-19th-century German example made of pearwood. See *Régulateur*.

REIGNIER WORK   Decorative inlays of colored woods similar in concept to buhl or *Boulle Work*. See *Reisner Work*.

REINFORCED CONCRETE   Concrete which has been strengthened with steel members or wire mesh. These are embedded in the concrete when it is being poured. This is also called ferroconcrete.

REISNER WORK   A 17th-century German ornamenting technique of inlaying colored woods, similar to Boulle work and Reignier work.

REJA   A Spanish wrought-iron grille, used to enclose a chapel or shrine.

RELIEF   A carved or applied ornament above the level of a surface. It may be a high or a low relief. Illustrated is a carved running leaf pattern over the main portal of Notre-Dame in Paris.

RELIQUARY   A small container, usually of precious metals and ornamented with jewels, used to hold a sacred relic. A French Gothic design is illustrated.

RENAISSANCE   The period in Europe, from about the 15th century to about the end of the 17th century, when art, architecture, philosophy, and literature had a rebirth based on classic Greek and Roman models. The intellectual movement began in the 14th century with the writings of Dante, Petrarch, and Boccaccio. Vitruvius' *Treatise on Architecture*, originally written in the time of Augustus, was issued in Rome in Latin, in 1486, and translated into Italian in 1521. This became one of the bibles of Renaissance architecture, and through it, of design. Illustrated is the Italian Renaissance Scuola di San Rocco in Venice. See *French Early Renaissance*, *French Late Renaissance*, and *French Middle Renaissance*.

RENAISSANCE REVIVAL   One of the several design revivals of the eclectic 19th century. The architectural designs were reminiscent of famous Renaissance structures. Sir Charles Barry was one of the

REGULATOR

RENT TABLE

RELIEF

RELIQUARY

REPOUSSÉ

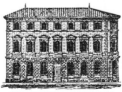
RESPOND

RENAISSANCE

RENAISSANCE REVIVAL

noteworthy architect-exponents of this revival. Illustrated is his Reform Club.

RENT TABLE   A round or octagonal pedestal table with drawers set into the apron under the tabletop, usually seven in number, marked with the days of the week. This design was used in the 18th century in England by landlords for collecting and filing rents. Sheraton designed several in mahogany.

REP   A plain-weave fabric with a heavy filler thread giving the fabric a corded effect, a definite crosswise rib. Rep can be made of most natural or synthetic fibers, and can be used for upholstery and draperies.

REPLICA   An exact reproduction or copy.

REPOUSSÉ   Relief work on metal materials. The design is produced by hammering or pressing on the material on the reverse side so that the design appears raised on the front. See *Chasing* and *Embossed*. Illustrated is a 13th-century half-life-size head done in silver-gilt repoussé.

REPP   See *Rep*.

REPRODUCTION   A faithful copy acknowledged as such, of the form, workmanship, and ornamentation of an original, not an attempt at a counterfeit or a fake.

RÉSEAU   French for tracery.

RESILIENCY   The natural capacity of a fabric or material to spring back after being crushed or bent; the capacity to resist creasing. Fabrics can be made more crease-resistant by chemical treatment.

RESISTANCE DIMMER   See *Dimmer*.

RESPOND   In architecture, the corbel or half column which supports one end of the last arch in an arcade. Illustrated is the Basilica of Santa Agnese in Rome, an example of early Christian church architecture.

RESTORATION   Repairing of broken parts or replacing of missing pieces or worn materials, to return an antique object or building as close as possible to its original appearance and condition. If done openly and not done to deceive, restoration is an ethical practice.

RESTORATION CHAIR   A high-backed, cane-paneled chair of the Carolean period (late 17th century in England). The legs as well as the uprights were usually spiral turnings. The chair often had a carved cresting representing the crown, supported by cherubs and adorned with acanthus leaves and roses. The motif was sometimes repeated on the front stretcher. See *Restoration Period*.

RESTORATION PERIOD The period from 1660 to 1688 in England. In 1660 the monarchy was restored, Charles II became king and the Age of Walnut began in furniture. Though the furniture remained relatively simple and rectangular in outline, it became more ornate and decorative in finish. This was the antithesis of the puritanical quality of the preceding Cromwellian or Commonwealth period. French and Flemish designs were popular. Illustrated is a chair made of walnut with the crown carved on the stretcher and top rail.

RESTORATION PERIOD

RETICELLA A type of lace using a combination of drawn and cut work. See *Lace.*

RETICULATED A surface decorated with a latticelike design similar to the meshes of a net.

RETURN A change in direction of any continuous surface. An example would be the turning of a cornice at the angle of a building and its continuance on the adjacent side of the building. This continuation would be the return. Illustrated is the 15th-century house of Jacques Coeur at Bourges.

REVEAL The vertical wall area which is not hidden by the frame of a window or door, and is at right angles to the wall surface.

RÉVEILLON, JEAN-BAPTISTE A French wallpaper manufacturer of the mid-18th century. He commissioned outstanding artists like Jean-Honoré Fragonard and François Boucher to execute designs for large panel decorations. His papers had a strong Neoclassic influence, though he also produced floral and arabesque designs. The delicacy and variety of coloring approximated those of true mural paintings.

REVERSE BOX MATCH A decorative veneer technique similar to a reverse diamond match, but angled to create a cross-patterned center with right-angled patterns going off in four directions.

REVERSE DIAMOND MATCH Four wedges of wood or veneer set together to form an X at the center with consecutively smaller V's radiating out from the center in all four directions.

REVERSE SERPENTINE The opposite of a simple serpentine curve. The ends and center are concave while the area between is convex. Illustrated is an 18th-century Sheraton kneehole table. See *Serpentine.*

REVETMENT A veneering, facing, or sheathing of stone or metal on a structure or architectural element for protection or

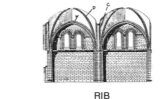

RIB

RETURN

RIBBAND BACK

RIBBON BACK

JEAN-HENRI RIESENER

REVERSE SERPENTINE

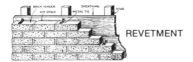

REVETMENT

adornment. This is also called a retaining wall. Illustrated is an example of brick veneering.

REZ-DE-CHAUSSÉE French for the ground floor or ground level.

RHENISH The German Romanesque style.

RIB A projecting band on a ceiling or vault. In the illustration, W is the wall rib, D is the diagonal rib, C is the cross rib. See *Groin Rib* and *Vault.*

RIBBAND BACK A Chippendale chair style. The chair back is carved to resemble a pattern of interlacing ribbons. The ribbon motif also appears in the Louis XVI style and in German Rococo ornament. See also *Ribbon Back.*

RIBBON BACK A carved chair back representing puckered ribbons tied in bows, a decorative splat for a chair or settee. Popular in the Louis XV period, and adapted by Chippendale and Manwaring. A Manwaring design is illustrated. See *Ribband Back.* Also, a wood grain or figure of wide, unbroken, alternating light and dark stripes, mainly found in quarter-sliced mahogany.

RIBBONS Narrow finished widths of fabric used for trimming, manufactured in many widths, weaves, fibers, and colors. As a decorative motif, ribbons appear with foliage and flowers in garland and festoons. Ribbons are called labels when they bear an inscription. Antique labels are often simple and terminate in balls. Gothic labels are curled and quaint. Renaissance labels are free and elegant and are often divided at the ends like pennons. The labels of the Louis XVI period have a crinkled quality. See *Festoon* and *Pennon.*

RICKRACK A flat braid in a chevron motif. A zigzag pattern used as an applied trimming.

RIESENER, JEAN-HENRI (1735–1806) A French master cabinet-maker. He trained under Jean François Oeben during the Louis XV period, but his work had the classic look typical of the Louis XVI period: exquisite proportions, graceful lines, architectural motifs, and roses. Marie Antoinette favored roses. Riesener's designs included fine marquetry details in deep tones on mahogany. He also used pictorial center panels, with allover patterns on the sides of his units. Illustrated is a writing table (scritoire) designed for Marie Antoinette. See *Bureau à Cylindre.*

RIFT CUT A method for slicing oak wood. A comb grained effect is produced by cutting perpendicularly to the medullary rays which radiate from the center of the log like wheel spokes.

RILIEVO STIACCIATO A shallow relief produced by scratches and incisions, described by Vasari as a "low or flattened relief."

RIM In furniture, a border, edge, or gallery around a tabletop, molded, carved, or fretted. Illustrated is a Chippendale table.

RIM

RINASCIMENTO Italian for Rennaissance.

RINCEAU French for scroll ornament. Sometimes called an arabesque. It is usually a symmetrical, horizontal composition of scroll and leaf ornaments applied to a frieze, panel, or other architectural feature. It is often combined with cartouches and grotesques. A Venetian Renaissance example is shown.

RINCEAU

RISER In a stairway, the vertical or rising part of a step.

RISING STRETCHERS X-shaped stretchers (the connecting cross pieces between the legs of furniture) that curve upward toward the intersection. A single stretcher that curves upward is called an arched or hooped stretcher. Rising stretchers are also called saltires. Illustrated is an 18th-century Italian Renaissance chair.

RISER

RISOM, JENS A 20th century Danish designer/manufacturer who emigrated to the United States and produced fine modern furniture with high standards of craftsmanship. Many designs are scaled to the smaller home or apartment. Also a designer of contract furniture.

RIYA RUG See *Rya Rug.*

ROBBIA, DELLA The family name of eminent Italian sculptors of the 15th and 16th centuries: Luca, Andrea, Giovanni and Girolamo. The name is usually associated with a faïence finish, and ceramic relief round plaques or medallions with polychromed fruit and foliage garland frames surrounding, usually a white figure on a blue ground.

ROBERT, HUBERT (1733–1808) A French painter of romantic landscapes of the Louis XVI period. Often these scenes included imaginary Roman ruins (follies). Robert created a series of six paintings for the bathroom of the Château of Bagatelle. He also designed the little "hamlet" of Normandy-like half-timber thatched cottages set around an artificial lake, where Marie Antoinette and her ladies played at being dairymaids.

RISING STRETCHERS

ROCOCO

ROGNON

ROBSJOHN-GIBBINGS, TERENCE HAROLD A 20th century furniture and interior designer in the classic tradition: pristine simple and elegant case goods and fine-lined seating units inspired by antique Greek and Roman models.

ROCAILLE A French term for an outdoor artificial grotto decorated with odd-shaped stones and shells. The term is applied to the stone and shell decorations of the Rococo period, and to the Louis XV period of the early 19th century.

ROCKING CHAIR A chair set on bowed runners, allowing the sitter to rock to and fro. A popular chair in the United States since 1800.

ROCOCO The name applied to the Louis XV period. The word is derived from rocaille (rockeries) and coquille (cockleshell), motifs that appeared in pottery designs of Bernard Palissy in the 16th century. Juste Aurèle Meissonier, an Italian who came to Paris in 1723, is credited with being largely responsible for developing the rococo style. He produced a book of engraved designs using the shell as a decorative motif. The period was distinguished by ornate, asymmetrical carvings and painted decorations using foliage, shells, scrolls, and fantastic whorls. Chinese or other exotic motifs were often combined with them.

ROENTGEN or RÖNTGEN, DAVID (1743–1807) A great marquetry and furniture designer of the Louis XV and the Louis XVI periods. He used light, bright-toned woods as inlays in mahogany, and his marquetry work has been compared to marble mosaic work. Roentgen, also known as David, contrived numerous compartments in his cabinets and secretaries which opened and shut by means of clever mechanical devices. His furniture was produced mainly in a factory at Neuwied in Germany. Chrétien Krause and Michael Rummer are credited with doing much of the marquetry, and Johann Roetig the mechanical devices. Roentgen was patronized by Marie Antoinette. See illustration for *Poudreuse.*

ROGNON French for kidney. Used to describe kidney-shaped designs. Illustrated is an 18th-century Sheraton kidney-shaped kneehole desk.

ROLL In wallpaper, 36 square feet. Wallpaper varies in width and may be 18″, 22″, 28″, 30″, or 36″ wide, and the length varies, but the roll will usually average 36 square feet. Several rolls are included in a bundle or stick.

ROLL MOLDING   A round molding. In Gothic architecture it is referred to as a bowtell.

ROLLED GLASS   Glass which is extruded between two rollers in a continuous viscous strip. The strip is passed through a heating process, and then it solidifies. A pattern may be pressed on one of the surfaces.

ROLL-OVER ARMS   Upholstered chair arms which start at the side seat rails and turn over in a full, bold sweep. Padded scroll arms which join the chair back and thus form an enclosed seat area. Originated in France in the early 16th century, and adapted by the English in the Restoration period (1660–1689). Illustrated is a late-17th-century English chair.

ROLL-OVER ARMS

ROLLTOP DESK   See *Pulldown Front.* A late-18th-century English design is shown.

ROMAN ARCHITECTURE   The architecture of the Roman republic and empire, based on the classic orders: Tuscan, Doric, Ionic, Corinthian, and Composite. The arch, vault, and dome are all prominent features in Roman architecture. Illustrated is the Colosseum in Rome which shows the three main orders (Tuscan, Ionic, and Corinthian) with Corinthian pilasters on the uppermost tier. These orders are used in a superimposed manner.

ROMAN ARCHITECTURE

ROMAN EAGLE   A decorative motif used by many countries and for many centuries. The classic Romans used the eagle as a symbol of the deification of their emperors, and also for the standards of their armies. Napoleon I, emulating the Roman emperors, gave his armies the French eagle in 1804. The eagle appears in Louis XVI, Directoire, and Empire designs. Illustrated is an eagle from the bas-relief in Trajan's Forum, an ancient Roman edifice.

ROMAN EAGLE

ROMAN SHADE   A window shade, which, when raised, is accordian folded. It does not work on the usual spring roller associated with window shades; raising and lowering is controlled by cords at one end. Can be made of many different fabrics; uses a special tape. It is decorative, and is sometimes used in place of curtains for a window covering.

ROMANESQUE   The period of the Dark Ages in Europe (about the beginning of the 9th to the end of the 12th century), predominantly a period of ecclesiastic arts and building. According to Sir Banister Fletcher: "Romanesque may be said to include the phases of European architecture which were based on Roman art from the

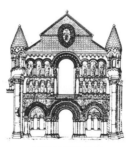

ROMANESQUE

departure of the Romans up to the end of the 12th century, when the pointed arch was introduced. It includes the Norman, Lombard and Byzantine periods, and was the basis for the ensuing Gothic styles." Illustrated is the church of Notre-Dame-la-Grande at Poitiers.

ROMANISCH   German for Romanesque.

ROMANTIC EPOCH   The period of romanticized medievalism which started in France around 1830, an attempt to break away from the old classic school. In the arts, the Gothic trend was picked up by Eugene Viollet-le-Duc.

ROMAYNE WORK   Carved medallions, heads, or knobs used in the Jacobean and Restoration period as furniture knobs or pulls. Also an early Renaissance motif (16th century) of classic Roman-type heads carved in medallions.

RONDEL   A round outline or design in a flat pattern.

RÖNTGEN, DAVID   See *Roentgen* or *Röntgen,* David.

ROOF LIGHT   A skylight or glass area in a roof which allows outside light to pass through to the area below.

ROPE BED   A bed frame with rope laced back and forth to form a spring upon which a mattress is set.

ROPE MOLDING   A half-round or quarter-round molding which is carved or embossed to resemble a rope. See *Cable Molding.*

ROSACE   A decorative rosette or circular centerpiece in a ceiling.

ROSE WINDOW   A circular window with tracery mullions radiating like spokes of a wheel from a central point. The areas between the mullions are filled with stained or colored glass. A feature in Gothic architecture. Also called a wheel window.

ROSETTA STONE   A black basalt stone uncovered in 1798 near Rosetta in Egypt. The same inscription is written in hieroglyphics, demotic, and Greek. This stone became the key to the hieroglyphic records of ancient Egypt. It was found during Napoleon's campaigns in Egypt, which were responsible for introducing the Egyptian motifs into the Directoire and Empire styles.

ROSETTA WOOD   An East Indian wood used by Spanish and Indian craftsmen during the 17th and 18th centuries in the Americas. It was also used for panels on some early American chests because of its brilliant red color and black graining.

ROSETTES French for little roses. A floral decorative device, usually a circle with petals developing out from a central point. The outer contour may be round, elliptic, or square. The rosette has been a popular motif since the Gothic period, and was favored by Adam and Hepplewhite. See *Patera*.

ROSEWOOD, BRAZILIAN A hard, heavy wood, mainly of a purplish-brown hue with almost black streaks. When freshly cut, exudes a roselike aroma. Also called jacaranda. Popular during the English Empire period for cabinets and musical instruments.

ROSEWOOD, HONDURAS A lighter and more uniformly grained wood than Brazilian rosewood. See *Palisander*.

ROSTRUM A raised speaker's platform. The raised tribune in the Roman Forum from which the orators spoke was decorated with the prows of ships which were trophies of war. One of the meanings of the Latin word rostrum is beak of a ship.

ROTARY-CUT VENEER A slice of veneer made by cutting a log in a circular manner around the circumference. It is similar to the unwinding of a roll of paper. A bold, variegated grain is produced since the cut follows the log's annual growth rings.

ROTTENSTONE A finely powdered soft stone (originally called Tripoli after the country of its origin). It can be used with oil to polish wood, and also for grinding and polishing sculpture, etc.

ROTUNDA A round building such as the Pantheon in Rome, or the main central part of a round building. A rotunda may also be a round central hall, usually surmounted with a dome, as in the Capitol in Washington, D.C. Illustrated is a section view of the early Christian church of S. Costanza in Rome.

ROUNDABOUT A 19th-century three-seater unit. In plan, the three seats form a circle, and the three individual chair backs radiate and curve out from the central point of the circle. The seated persons must turn their heads toward the center of the circle to see and talk to the others who are seated on the same piece of furniture. See *Tête-à-Tête*.

ROUNDABOUT CHAIR Usually designed to fit into a corner, the square seat diagonally set and the back extending across two adjoining sides. Thus the chair has a leg in front, one in back, and one at either side. It is sometimes referred to as a

ROSETTE

ROTUNDA

PETER PAUL RUBENS

RUDDER

ROUNDABOUT

ROUNDABOUT CHAIR

corner or writing-arm chair. See *Fauteuil de Bureau*.

ROUNDEL A round, flat form like a patera, medallion, or plaque. The term also refers to a circular disk of stained glass in a leaded window.

ROUSSEAU DE LA ROTTIÈRE, JEAN-SIMÈON (1747-c.–1822) A French designer of interiors and accessories of the Louis XVI period. He decorated the boudoir of Marie Antoinette in elegant, refined forms using golden tones. The panels ("Love Assisting at the Toilet of Grace"), which he used in this room, were done in subtle gradations of gold and silver. He also decorated the Queen's room at Versailles.

ROVANA Dow Chemical Company's tradename for synthetic products which include Saran microtape. Can be extruded as a fiber, and used in fabrics. Flame-resistant, has excellent resistance to abrasion, and keeps its shape. Used mainly for warp threads in drapery fabrics.

RUBBED BRICKWORK An English Renaissance type of brickwork which used soft bricks which could be cut into exact shapes and sizes. The finely fitted bricks were rubbed down to make a smooth, even surface. Sir Christopher Wren used this technique at Hampton Court.

RUBBER TILE A synthetic rubber floor-covering material which is made in a continuous roll or as tiles. Nonporous and more resilient than most tiles, as well as quiet and comfortable underfoot. It remains flexible over wide temperature variations, but is adversely affected by oil, grease, and some solvents.

RUBBLE Irregularly shaped stones set into a wall, with or without mortar.

RUBENS, PETER PAUL (1577–1640) A great Flemish painter. He also decorated the Luxembourg Palace in Paris for Marie de Medici. Illustrated is "Children Carrying Flowers" by Rubens.

RUDDER A wooden support for the leaf of a drop-leaf table or shelf which resembles a ship's rudder. It is similar to a butterfly support.

RUDD'S DRESSING TABLE A mid-18th-century English dressing table which was described by Hepplewhite as "possessing every convenience which can be wanted; or mechanism and ingenuity supply." It was named for a noted personality of the period. See *Reflecting Dressing Table* for illustration.

RULE JOINT A dustproof and draft-proof hinged joint on late Queen Anne furniture, screens, tabletops, etc. A hinged joint. See *Knuckle Joint.*

RUNIC KNOT An ornamental motif of the Celtic, Scandinavian, and German Romanesque periods. It is an interlaced design using the magical symbols of ancient North European countries.

RUNNER In furniture, a guide strip of wood, metal or plastic under the center or at the sides of a drawer. Also the curved member of a rocking chair. In carpets, a narrow rug used in hallways or foyers. In accessories, a long strip of fabric used as a decorative cover over the length of a table.

RUNNER FOOT A pair of straight legs which are connected at their base by a horizontal rail or stretcher. The legs appear to end on this crosspiece. A popular chair support in the Italian Renaissance period. Sometimes the ends of the crossbar were decorated with carved lion's paws.

RUNNING BOND See *Stretcher Bond.*

RUNNING DOG A continuous scroll or wavelike design. It is also called the *Vitruvian Scroll.*

RUSH A long grass which is twisted and woven to make seats for provincial chairs. The seats are also known as flag seats. Rush seats have been used from earliest times, and rush has often been woven into mats. See *Flag* Illustration.

RUNNER

RUSH SEAT

RUSTIC FURNITURE

RUNNING BOND

RUSH SEATS. See *Rush.*

RUSKIN, JOHN A 19th-century English writer and art critic, who wrote that "ornamentation is the principal part of architecture."

RUSTIC FURNITURE English garden furniture of the mid-18th century which simulated natural twigs and branches, gnarled with an effect of fantasy. Manwaring and Chippendale (illustrated) were among those who designed pieces in this style.

RUSTIC STONEWORK Masonry in which the face of the stone is roughened, but the block is carefully shaped, leveled, and set in straight courses. The edges are often smoothed out to emphasize the rough face of the block.

RUSTICATION A form of masonry using stonework or bricks which have recessed or chamfered edges. A decorative, wide-jointed appearance is created. It was popular in the Baroque and Mannerist periods.

RYA RUG A high-pile, shaggy rug. From the Scandinavian word for rough or shaggy. A Scandinavian craft that goes back to before 3000 B.C. It was originally a dowry item, and was used as a blanket for warmth. Used today in contemporary or provincial rooms as a decorative area rug.

S

SAARINEN, EERO (1910–1961) An influential modern architect and designer who was born in Finland and arrived in America in 1923. He regarded each problem as a new and individual challenge, and he sought to answer it with a free, original form, creating world-famous buildings and widely used furniture. Saarinen designed the pedestal chair, as well as other architectural furniture. He introduced the *Womb Chair* in 1946.

SAARINEN PEDESTAL TABLE A simple elegantly proportioned round pedestal table designed by Eero Saarinen. The pedestal is a graceful, trumpet-like element that spreads out at the base, gets thinner as it rises and flares out again where it meets the table top.

SABER LEGS Fine splayed legs often found on early-19th-century Sheraton chairs in the Grecian manner. The front legs flare forward, the rear legs curve out behind.

SABICU A pink to red wood which resembles mahogany. It is hard and heavy and has a low luster. The wood is native to Cuba and Central America.

SABOT FOOT See *Spade Foot.* An Adam chair is illustrated.

SABOTS French for wooden shoes. Decorative metal coverings for the feet of wood furniture. They were designed to enhance as well as protect the foot, and serve the same purpose that Chutes do on the angles and legs of wood furniture. They appeared in the 18th century, and were made of bronze doré, bronze, brass, etc. An 18th-century secretary by Pionniel is shown. It was made of amarynth and embellished with a Sèvres plaque.

SAARINEN
PEDESTAL TABLE

SADDLE SEAT

SALON

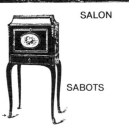

SABOTS

SACK BACK The double-bowed back of a Windsor chair.

SADDLE See *Sill.* Board or stone slab at the bottom of a door.

SADDLE SEAT A scooped-out seat which resembles the contour of a saddle. The seat is convex from the sides and back to a raised central ridge. It is often found in Windsor chairs with thick pine seats. A Chippendale chair is illustrated.

SADDLE-CHECK A bedroom easy chair of the wing or "forty-winks" type designed by Hepplewhite and others in the mid and late 18th century in England and America.

SAILCLOTH A strong, durable, firmly woven cotton canvas.

SALEM ROCKER An early-19th-century New England rocking chair with a heavy scrolled seat, top rail, and arms. The spindle back is usually straight and not as high as that of a Boston rocker.

SALEMBIER A French 18th-century designer in the Louis XVI style. He designed overly ornate small furniture.

SALON A great apartment in a large house or palace, the room used for entertaining and conversing. It was the center of cultural and political society from the late 18th through the 19th centuries. Many salons were made famous by the hostesses who presided over them. Illustrated is a Louis XVI salon.

SALT GLAZE A surfacing of thin glass for pottery or brick which is produced by throwing salt into the oven while the firing process is taking place. The glass finish is produced by the thermochemical reaction

167

of silicates of the clay body with the vapors of the salt or chemicals.

SALTIRE   An X-shaped *stretcher* of Italian origin, used to reinforce the legs of tables, chairs, etc. See *Rising Stretchers* and *Stretcher.*

SAMARA   A trademark name for a reddish-brown hardwood from French Equatorial Africa. It is rotary-cut, and usually has a large swirled grain pattern. Also called gaboon wood.

SAMBIN, HUGUES (c. 1520–1600) A French architect, furniture designer, cabinetmaker, and engraver. He worked in the tradition of the Italian Renaissance, and in 1572 he published a book of designs which featured rich French Renaissance or Burgundian forms with Italian overtones. He used the human figure and other carved motifs for his heavily embellished furniture designs.

SAMITE   A heavy silk fabric of the Middle Ages, usually interwoven with gold and heavily embroidered. It was used mainly for upholstery and garments.

SAMPLER   A needlework exercise performed by a child or novice in embroidery. Especially in vogue during the 18th and 19th centuries, the sampler usually showed an alphabet or a quotation embroidered in a variety of stitches and colors.

SAND SHAKING   A 17th-century Dutch technique for deepening or shading the color of pieces of wood inlay by dipping them into hot sand.

SANDALWOOD   An East Indian and Pacific islands wood, hard, yellow, close-grained, and used for ornamental objects and inlays rather than furniture. Illustrated is a late-18th-century door panel carved out of sandalwood, from Travancore, India.

SANDBLASTING   A method of cleaning or polishing stone surfaces by a bombardment of sand particles propelled by jets of steam or air. It is also a technique for cutting or engraving glass or crystal in a similar manner. The blasted area is usually cloudy and gray and not as smooth to the touch as polished glass.

SANGUINE   From the French for bloody. A reddish-brown or terra-cotta color chalk used for drawing. Many Renaissance drawings or studies for paintings were executed in this soft, pastel-like material.

SAPELE or SAPELI   An African wood which resembles mahogany in color and texture, but is more evenly striped and harder, heavier, and tougher than African

SALTIRE

SARCOPHAGUS

SANDALWOOD

SASH WINDOW

mahogany. Sapele is usually dark red-brown in color. It is also called tiama.

SAPPANWOOD   A wood which closely resembles brazilwood, and is native to Java, Ceylon, and India. Used for furniture produced in the Dutch colonies during the 17th and 18th centuries, based on models and designs supplied by the Dutch.

SARABEND RUGS   A style of Persian rugs with a rose or medium blue background, with palm leaves the major decorative motif.

SARACENIC   Showing a Mohammedan influence. The Mohammedan Saracens greatly influenced Spanish arts and architecture from the 8th century when they swept from Morocco into Spain. Saracenic Spanish arts are also called Moorish. Motifs were chiefly abstract geometric and interlaced patterns.

SARAN   A term for the plastic vinylidine chloride from which multifilaments are extruded for use in tough, heavy-duty fabrics. A Dow Chemical compound product. Stiff, sunlight- and weather-resistant, and excellent for outdoor use.

SARAZIN, JACQUES (1590–1660)   A French sculptor of decorative elements during the reign of Louis XIV.

SARCOPHAGUS   A stone coffin originated by the ancients. In the 18th century, a wine cooler usually made of mahogany with a lead liner, and often part of a sideboard. It was also called a cellarette or "garde du vin."

SAROUK RUGS   A style of Persian rugs which are predominantly knotted in deep, dark blues and reds with floral designs that stand out in lighter colors.

SASH BAR   The strip of wood or metal which subdivides the panes of glass in the frame of a window. See *Mullion* and *Tracery.*

SASH CURTAINS   Sheer or semi-sheer curtains mounted on a rod attached to the sash or frame of a window or door. Sometimes the curtain has two slots for rods, on both the top and the bottom, and the fabric is shirred and pulled taut between them.

SASH WINDOW   Usually a double-hung window which is opened and shut by raising or lowering one of the windows.

SATEEN or SATINE   A cotton fabric with a satin weave, a lustrous face and a dull back. Commonly used as a lining material for draperies.

SATIN   A fabric originally made of silk and imported from China. It was known as Zaytūn, after the Chinese seaport. It is a basic weave, and the face of the fabric is smooth and glossy while the back is dull. The fabric is stronger when the silk fibers are blended with linen or cotton wefts. There are many types of satins. See *Satin: Antique, Charmeuse, Hammered, Ribbed,* and *Slipper.*

SATIN, ANTIQUE   A rich, heavy fabric with a dull, uneven texture. It is used for upholstery, drapery, etc. It may be made of silk, cotton, rayon, silk and cotton, etc. See *Satin.*

SATIN, CHARMEUSE   A satin fabric with an organzine warp and a spun silk weft.

SATIN FINISH   A smooth, low-luster finish on fabric, paper, paint, etc.

SATIN, HAMMERED   A satin fabric which has been treated to have a textured surface effect similar to that of beaten or hammered metal.

SATIN, RIBBED   Bengaline or faille fabric woven with satin face ribs which gives the fabric a lustrous unbroken surface. It can also be given a moiré finish. See *Moiré.*

SATIN, SLIPPER   A heavyweight fabric of silk or synthetic fibers with a cotton back, originally used to make slippers in the 18th and 19th centuries. It is currently used as an upholstery and drapery fabric.

SATIN WEAVE   One of the basic weaves, producing a face almost completely of warp, evenly spaced and therefore lustrous.

SATINE   See *Sateen* or *Satine.*

SATINE RUBANNE   A straight-grained, strong, durable South African wood which has ribbon-like markings. Used for inlays and decorative banding. Also called capomo.

SATINWOOD   A highly figured, close-grained, hard, durable wood native to Ceylon and the East Indies. It is light yellow to golden brown in color with a lustrous satin-like quality. A favorite wood in the Louis XV and Louis XVI periods, and was also favored by Adam, Chippendale, and Sheraton for inlay and veneering. Hepplewhite used satinwood as a background for painted medallions. A Robert Adam sideboard of the mid-18th century is illustrated. Note the *knife urns.* Also see *Age of Satinwood* and *Seddon, George.*

SATYR MASK   Germanic motif which reached the height of its popularity in England from 1730 to 1740. Carved on the knees of furniture legs, and also used decoratively on other areas. Originally a

PIAT JOSEPH SAUVAGE

WILLIAM SAVERY

SAVONAROLA CHAIR

SAVONNERIE

SATINWOOD

classic motif, it also appears in French and Italian Renaissance designs.

SAUNAS   Rooms, roomettes, or closets, usually lined in wood and provided with benches for sitting or stretching out. Can be filled with dry heat, thermostatically controlled, or produced by hot bricks or stones, contained within the sauna. Originally, a Scandinavian innovation to relax and refresh its users.

SAUNIER, CLAUDE CHARLES   An 18th-century French master ébéniste (cabinetmaker) who worked for Louis XV and Louis XVI. His marquetry was in the style of Jean François Oeben.

SAUSAGE TURNING   A wood turning which resembled links of sausages, typical of German Renaissance turnings. Also appeared in 19th-century American furniture.

SAUVAGE, PIAT JOSEPH   An 18th-century French painter of the Louis XVI period. He created trompe l'oeil paintings which simulated sculptured bas-relief in grisaille. Were used on overdoors, overmantels, etc. See *Grisaille.*

SAVERY, WILLIAM (1721–1787)   A Philadelphia cabinetmaker who worked in the ornamental Chippendale style. His highboys and lowboys are considered among the finest produced in Colonial America. See *Philadelphia Chippendale.*

SAVONAROLA CHAIR   An early Italian Renaissance X-shaped chair. The seat was often made of interlaced strips of wood, and the back was usually carved or decorated with inlay work. The chair was named for the martyred Italian monk Girolamo Savonarola (1452–1498).

SAVONNERIE   A famous rug and tapestry factory in France, founded in 1604. Also high-pile, hand-woven rugs produced in this factory, often decorated with pastel floral and scroll designs. Illustrated is a carpet design by Robert de Cotte prepared in the early 18th century for the Savonnerie Factory.

SAWBUCK TABLE   A 17th-century simple tabletop which rested on X-shaped trestles or two-legged standards. It was also called a trestle table and appeared in Europe and America.

SAXONY   A carpet texture longer than a plush but shorter than a shag. No twist is set into the pile. The pile is tall enough to stand up but may flatten out if subjected to heavy traffic. Usually produced with thick yarns for a nubby or casual look.

SCAFFOLDING   A temporary skeletal framework built around a structure or object, or on one side of it. It provides a means of working on the outside of a building, or inside a large unplatformed area. The word also means a framework around a piece of sculpture.

SCAGLIOLA An imitation of marble made of gypsum or plaster of Paris, chips of marble, and coloring matter, invented in Italy in the 17th century. Scagliola was used to make chimneypieces in the 18th century in England, and the Adam brothers used this technique on their interiors. Illustrated is an 18th-century scagliola chimneypiece designed by Thomas Milton.

SCALE The dimensions of a unit of furniture in relation to the height and width of the area in which it is to be placed. The relationship between one piece of furniture and another in size and proportion. In a scale drawing, the drawing is proportionately reduced or enlarged in relation to a given ratio, for example ¼″ = 1′.

SCALE-BACK CHAIR A Queen Anne chair with an imbricated pattern carved onto the chair's splat and uprights. See *Scaling* and *Imbricate*.

SCALING A surface finish which resembles the scales of a fish. A technique used by architects and designers to fill in the background of small panels. See *Imbricate*.

SCALLOP SHELL Semicircular shell shape with ridges radiating from a point at the center bottom, used as a decoration. Very popular in the late Renaissance, Louis XIV, Louis XV, Queen Anne, and Georgian periods. It was often found on Goddard 18th-century kneehole desks and cabriole-legged highboys (see *Goddard, John*), and on the knees of cabriole legs, on aprons, on crests of furniture, and also as a hood on architectural pieces of case goods. A Queen Anne chair is illustrated.

SCALLOPED ARCH An arch having more than five foils, a design found in *Moorish* architecture.

SCALLOPED BORDERS See *Cutout Borders*.

SCALLOPED EDGE An edge or border that has been marked or cut into segments of a circle. An outer profile which resembles the wavy, fluted contour of a scallop shell.

SCALPTURATUM OPUS A Latin term for a technique of inlay with colored marble, introduced into Italy in the first century B.C.

SCANALATO Italian for fluting.

SCANDINAVIAN MODERN A simple, chaste, refined, version of the tradi-

SCAGLIOLA

SCALLOP SHELL

SCISSORS CHAIR

SCONCE

SCANDINAVIAN MODERN

SCOOP SEAT

tional Empire style, introduced in the 1930's as Swedish or Danish Modern. The furniture has a sculptured quality with gracefully tapered legs and gently curved arms and backs. Walnut and teak are the woods most often used. There is an almost complete lack of applied decorative elements; hardware is simple.

SCARAMOUCHE A decorative representation of a buffoon or clown of 17th- and 18th-century Italian comedy. The figure was usually represented in black with a black cape and hat and a grotesque mask. A decorative element in 18th-century English, French, and Italian designs.

SCARF JOINT In cabinetry, two beveled edges laid one over the other to form a continuous level plane. An overlapping joint.

SCATTER RUG A small area rug used as an accent, often at the bedside or in entries and hallways. Available in many sizes, shapes, colors, patterns, and fibers, e.g., wool, nylon, Acrilan, cotton and sisal.

SCENIC A wallpaper mural, usually made up of three or four panels that create a continuous scene, vista, or design. Printed in a variety of colors on any number of background papers, vinyls, or cloths.

SCHOOL A group of artists or designers, whose work shows similar characteristics owing to the influence of an individual master, region, or body of theory; the art of a country. See *Hudson River School*.

SCHREINERING A process for producing a high luster on fabric by passing it between rollers, one smooth and one engraved with fine lines, to increase the surface for light reflection.

SCISSORS CHAIR A folding X-shaped chair, used in ancient Egyptian, classic Greek, and Roman times. The prototype of the Dante and Savonarola chairs. Illustrated is an ancient Greek example. See illustration for *Early French Renaissance*.

SCONCE An ornamental wall bracket used to hold candles or electric bulbs. The word derives from abscondere, Latin for "to hide;" originally a sconce was a shield or protection for a flame, or a lantern to protect a light. See *Applique* and *Girandole*.

SCOOP SEAT A slightly concave seat, dipped to accommodate the contour of a seated person. It is found in classic chairs, and reappears in the late 18th century in Sheraton's work (illustrated) and the Empire style. A variation appears in present-day contour and molded plywood chairs. Also called a "drop seat."

SCOTCHGARD A trademark name for a fluorochemical process applied to fabrics to make them resistant to stains from dirt, water, or oil. The process allows the fabric to breathe and does not impair the hand or color. Produced by the Perma Dry Company, Inc.

SCOTIA A concave molding which resembles the S curve made by two connecting curves of different radii.

SCRATCH CARVING A simple country-style carving done with a V-shaped chisel.

SCRATCH COAT A rough first coat of plaster which is scratched and scored before it is thoroughly dry. The finish, or smooth coat will adhere better to this coarse texture.

SCREED The guide band applied to a surface before the application of plaster, the final layer of a concrete floor, or the finishing material of a roof: tile, asphalt, etc.

SCREEN A separating device. A divider. A partition or enclosure of wood, metal, or stone which can be decorative, functional, or both. See also *Papier-Mâché* for an illustration of a Victorian design.

SCREEN TABLE A late-18th-century Sheraton design for a lady's desk with a screen set behind the desk surface. It permitted the lady to work near a fire and yet be protected from flying embers, etc. The screen let down into a slot opening, making a level surface when it was not in use. A drawer was placed below the slider.

SCREW STAIR A spiral staircase that twists around a slender pole.

SCRIBANNE An imposing desk-cupboard of the Louis XIV period.

SCRIBE In carpentry, to fit one material to another, as the side of a shaped wooden strip to an uneven wall surface. The strip has to be shaped to fit the irregular surface contour of the wall.

SCRIBE MOLDING A small pliable strip of wood used to cover up an irregular joint or crack.

SCRIBING A technique of fitting frames, moldings, etc., onto irregular surfaces. The unit to be applied must be cut and shaped to fit these irregularities.

SCRIM A lightweight, open-weave, coarse cotton fabric similar to marquisette, usually white, cream, or ecru, used for needlework. Sometimes scrim has larger openings (¼″ × ¼″) and is heavily sized. A form of scrim is also used to cover and hold

SCRINIUM

SCROLL

SCROLL FOOT

SCREEN TABLE

SCROLL PEDIMENT

SCROWLED CHAIR

the joints between plasterboards before plastering.

SCRINIUM A round box of the classic Roman period which was used to hold scrolls. Such boxes were generally made of beechwood, and could be locked or sealed when necessary, and carried about. A scrinium, as illustrated, would be a library case, or a collection of scrolls.

SCRITOIRE French for writing table. See *Secretary* and *Riesner, Jean-Henri* for an illustration.

SCRODDLED WARE Marbelized pottery produced at the Fenton Pottery in Bennington, Vermont, from 1853 to 1858. The ground is beige and the mottled pattern is in terra-cotta, brown and greige.

SCROLL An S or C curved design. An artistic invention in ornamentation, used with acanthus leaves, laurel, oak, ivy, and wheat. A spiraling and convoluting line, like a rolled piece of paper, makes the scroll.

SCROLL BED See *Gondola Bed* and *Sleigh Bed*.

SCROLL FOOT A flattened scroll at the end of a cabriole leg originated in the Louis XIV period. Appears in England in the William and Mary and Chippendale periods.

SCROLL MOLDING A molding which resembles a curled piece of paper; popular in English Gothic architecture.

SCROLL PEDIMENT A broken pediment with each half in a reverse curve ending in a scroll at the outside ends. The open center area usually is trimmed with a finial.

SCROLLED TOP MIRROR A Chippendale design found in America in the mid-18th-century, similar to a silhouette or fretwork mirror, but is usually characterized by a broken pediment with a centered carved ornament. Often made of mahogany with gilt decoration.

SCROLLWORK Ornate, lacelike wood cutouts made with a jigsaw. It was a popular decoration in the Steamboat Gothic period in the 19th-century United States. See *Jigsaw Detail*.

SCROWLED CHAIR An English chair of the mid-16th to the mid-17th centuries, with a heavy, high, panel back. It usually had a heavy top rail and cresting partly supported by brackets attached to the upper sides of the stiles, and flat-shaped arms attached to the front supports, baluster legs and low-placed stretchers. See *Wainscot Chair*.

SCRUBBED PINE A provincial furniture finish for Early American and French "antiques," consisting of light oil on a natural pine wood, which approximates an unfinished look.

SCRUTOIRE   A writing desk. Often a slope-front desk which has a lid that opens to form a horizontal writing surface.

SCULPTURE   The art of creating forms and decorations in three dimensions or in relief. Carving is the process of freeing the form from the material. Modeling is the building up of the form from some plastic material like clay or plasteline. Both are techniques of sculpture. Carving is usually done in wood, stone, or marble. Modeling is done in clay or wax, and then cast in plaster or metal, usually bronze. Illustrated is the head of the famous French Gothic statue "Le beau Dieu" of the Amiens Cathedral (13th century).

SCULPTURE

SCULPTURED RUG   See *Carved Rug.*

SCUTCHEON   See *Escutcheon.*

SEAM   The joining of two surfaces: the butt or overlap of two pieces of wallpaper, the sewed line of two pieces of fabric in a drapery, the hairline between two joined pieces of wood or pieces of veneer.

SEASONED LUMBER   Wood that has been dried in the air or in a kiln to improve its durability for furniture construction, and to control warping and checking. See *Kiln-dried.*

SEAWEED MARQUETRY   A popular form of ornament during the William and Mary and the Queen Anne periods in England. An inlay of various woods in an arabesque pattern of small leaves and seaweed forms, also called "endive." Probably based on the look of Boulle work. Illustrated is a Queen Anne press of the early 18th century.

SECESSION MOVEMENT   See *Sezession.*

SECOND EMPIRE or LATE EMPIRE
The period in France, approximately between 1852 and 1871, which produced massive scrolled and rollover-type furniture which blended the Empire with Louis XV motifs rather than classic elements. In America, Duncan Phyfe produced ungainly "butcher" furniture in this style.

SECONDARY COLORS   Colors produced by mixing any two of the three primary colors. Red combined with yellow produces orange. Blue and yellow make green, and blue mixed with red will form a violet color. Therefore the three secondary colors are orange, green, and violet.

SECONDARY LIGHTING   Additional lighting of an interior that goes beyond the

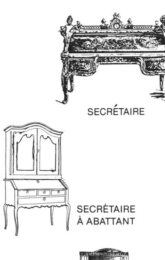

SECRÉTAIRE

SECRÉTAIRE
À ABATTANT

SECRETARY

SEAWEED MARQUETRY

GEORGE SEDDON

basic, primary, or general lighting plan. The use of spotlights, floods, filters, wall washers, and indirect lighting techniques to add depth, dimension, and atmosphere. See *Ambience Lighting* and *Indirect Lighting.*

SECRÉTAIRE   French for desk. See *Gouthière* and *Kingwood* for illustrations. See *Secretary.*

SECRÉTAIRE À ABATTANT   A drop front desk. See *Scrutoire* and *Secretary* illustration.

SECRETARY   A desk surface with a space for writing appliances which is combined with a drawer base below and a bookcase cabinet above. In the 17th century, it was essentially a bureau (a writing table on a chest of drawers with a hinged desk arrangement equipped with brass quadrants). During the 18th century, the bookcase or shell units were added over the desk surface. See *Bureau, Scritoire,* and *Scrutoire.* A Sheraton design is illustrated. See *Trelliswork* for another illustration.

SECTION   A vertically sliced view through a structure or a formed part, such as a molding. Gives a clear impression of the silhouette as well as the internal construction of the object. The section view can also give dimensions.

SECTIONAL FURNITURE   Upholstered or case furniture made in modules or small units which can be pulled together in a variety of ways to make larger units that turn corners, etc. Usually refers to a sectional couch which is composed of two, three, or more parts, one of which is a curved or angled corner piece. It is possible with this type of modular furniture to have a continuous couch on two adjacent walls. Each part of the sectional couch can be a completely finished piece that may be used individually.

SEDAN CHAIR   An 18th-century enclosed chair which was a form of transportation, usually carried by four men. Originated in Sedan, France, in the 17th century. Popular in England in the 17th and 18th centuries. The French name for this chair is chaise à porteur. See *Palanquin.*

SEDDON, GEORGE (1727–1801)
An English cabinetmaker, furniture designer, and upholsterer, who worked with his sons George and Thomas, and his son-in-law Thomas Shakleton. Seddon made rich, elegant pieces and favored satinwood. Illustrated is a satinwood dressing table made by the firm of Seddon and Shakleton at the end of the 18th-century.

SEDDON AND SHAKLETON   Late-18th-century English cabinetmakers who made fine carved and painted furniture in the Sheraton, Louis XVI, and Directoire or Regency styles. Much of Seddon's work has been attributed to Sheraton. The firm made many of the furnishings used by George IV at Windsor Castle. For illustrations see *Satinwood* and *Seddon, George.*

SEDIA The Italian word for chair. Illustrated is an early-19th-century Italian Directoire chair designed by Guiseppe Soli.

SEGMENTAL ARCH An arch shaped as part of a circle but less than a semicircle. An elliptical arch.

SEGMENTAL CORNERS The corners of a rectangular panel that are broken into curves. The cutout corners are frequently decorated with patera or rosettes. Often used by the Adam brothers for ceilings, walls and doors. Illustrated is a Hepplewhite sideboard which has segmental corners on the doors and panels.

SEGMENTAL FRONT See *Bow Front* and *Swell Front*. A Sheraton pier table is illustrated.

SEHNA KNOT Method of hand-tying pile yarns in Oriental Rugs, over one warp thread and under a second. Also called the Persian Knot. See *Ghiordes Knot*, the other traditional knot.

SEIGNORIAL CHAIR A chair of state which in the Gothic and Renaissance periods was usually high-backed and had solid arm supports and a solid base. The chair was often canopied and elaborately carved. Less imposing versions were used for the master of the manor or castle. Illustrated is the Coronation chair from Westminster Abbey in England. See *Canopy Chair*.

SELVAGE or SELVEDGE The reinforced up-and-down outer edges of a fabric. Also the unpatterned or unprinted margin of wallpaper (on either side of the design), usually imprinted with the name, number, manufacturer's name, and any instructions.

SEMAINIER A tall bedroom chest with seven drawers, introduced in the Louis XV period. The seven drawers were originally one for each day of the week. It was similar to a chiffonier, which is wider and does not have a specified number of drawers.

SEMÉ The French for sown, as seeds are sown. A minute floral motif scattered over the background of a brocaded fabric. In the Louis XVI period, tiny rosebuds were often found within or around satin and faille stripes woven on the fabric.

SEPIA PRINT A print of a reddish-brown tint. Sepia is a brownish pigment originally made from the cuttlefish.

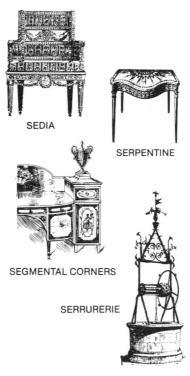

SEDIA

SERPENTINE

SEGMENTAL CORNERS

SERRURERIE

SEGMENTAL FRONT

SEIGNORIAL CHAIR

SERVITEUR FIDÈLE

SET

SERAGLIO An enclosed or protected area in a house. A harem in a Turkish palace.

SERIOGRAPHS Silk-screened prints. See *Silk-screened.*

SERPENTINE Snakelike. The juxtaposition of a concave and a convex form to create a sinuous line. Two connected cyma curves. Usually the center curve is convex and prominent. When the center curve is concave and receding, the line is called a reverse serpentine. The serpentine line was used in Louis XV commodes, and also in 18th-century English cupboards, desks, and chests. A *Hepplewhite* table is illustrated.

SERRATED EDGE A zigzag, toothed, or dentil edge. A series of inverted V's in a continuous band.

SERRE-PAPIERS See *Table à Gradin.*

SERRURERIE The French term for wrought iron. Illustrated is a Renaissance well.

SERVANTE See *Rafraîchissoir* (or *Servante*).

SERVER or SERVING TABLE An auxiliary piece of furniture in a dining room, used to hold or contain dishes, glassware, silver, napery, bottles, etc. It usually has drawers, and may also contain cabinet space. The larger units are similar to buffets, and the smaller pieces are like rafraîchissoirs, servantes, or dumbwaiters. The top surface is used to hold food, platters and service pieces for use at the dining table.

SERVITEUR FIDÈLE From the French for loyal servant. The French version of a dumbwaiter; a multitiered table. Illustrated is a Louis XVI design by Martin Carlin. See *Dumbwaiter* and *Rafraîchissoir.*

SET A matched group of furniture, coordinated to be used together, like a headboard, night tables, dresser, and chest of drawers all made in the same decorative style, ornamented in the same manner and finished in the same color. Also called a suite. Illustrated is a matched set of carved and gilt upholstered furniture of the period of Charles II of England (second half of the 17th century).

SETTEE A seating device which developed from the *settle*. Long with a carved or *upholstered* back, arms, and a soft seat, it was originally designed to hold two or more persons. Usually matched the individual chairs of the period in contour and chair-back decoration. They were often described as two-, three-, or four-chair-back settees. A front leg was provided between each chair back, therefore a three-chairback settee would have four legs in front to delineate the three seats. Popular in the late 17th and early 18th centuries.

SETTLE Bench, usually of oak, for two or more persons. A settle was usually provided with a high back and arms, and sometimes there were ears or wings at either end. Originally, a popular seating device in the Middle Ages, often carved, paneled, and richly decorated. A settle with a hinged seat over a chest is called a box settle. A canopied settle was called a canapé. Illustrated is an English carved oak settle of the second half of the 17th century (the reign of Charles II).

SETTLE

SÈVRES A porcelain factory at Sèvres near Paris, founded in 1756. Mme de Pompadour obtained royal patronage for it during the reign of Louis XV. Here were produced magnificent vases and plaques for furniture and table inserts. The term "Sèvres" is also used to identify the products of the factory, including the vases and urns of a special rose color, as well as King's blue. Illustrated is a Sèvres vase from the Grand Trianon. See *Kingwood* for an illustration of Sèvres plaques used as a furniture embellishment.

SÈVRES

SEWING TABLE A popular small working table of the mid and late 18th century. Usually equipped with drawers, trays, spool racks, and a cloth bag below for sewing materials. Sheraton (illustrated), Hepplewhite, and others designed many such pieces, which were also called "pouch tables." French Louis XVI and Empire designs were also created to satisfy this need.

SEWING TABLE

SEYMOUR, JOHN An 18th-century American cabinetmaker who worked in Boston.

SEZESSION A series of artistic revolutions which occurred in Germany and Austria during the late decade of the 19th century. The avant-garde artists left the old academic societies, and organized exhibitions of their own progressive new Impressionist or Art Nouveau styles. The three major eruptions took place in Munich in 1892, in Vienna in 1897, and in Berlin in 1899. See *Art Nouveau*.

SFUMATO The Italian word for smoky. In painting the blurring or hazing of the outline of an object so that it tends to blend in with the background. Leonardo da Vinci was a leading painter who used this technique.

SGABELLE or SGABELLO A small 16th-century Italian Renaissance chair usually identified by its carved back splat, octagonal seat and carved trestle supports instead of legs.

SGRAFFITO (GRAFFITO) Italian for scratcher. A decorative technique of 16th-century Italy, in which tinted plaster was covered by white plaster (or vice versa), and the top layer was "scratched" to reveal the color of the bottom layer through the pattern. Arabesques were popular designs in this technique.

SHADE A color with black added, as opposed to a tint, which is a color with white added. Also a protection or covering: lampshade, window shade, etc. See *Lampshade* and *Window Shade*.

SHADE CLOTH See *Holland Shade Cloth*.

SHAFT The central portion of a column or pilaster, between the capital and the base.

SHAG RUG Rug with a long pile, usually highly textured looped or cut, or a mixture of the two. The longer the pile, the more it will have a tendency to lie down and "mat." In luxurious shag carpeting, the pile is both long and dense, and does not flatten as readily when walked on. Nylon and various polyester shags are most popular, though shag rugs are also available in wool and acrylics.

SHAGREEN The untanned skins of horses, mules, or sharks which were finished with a granular surface and dyed green, sometimes used for covering small pieces of furniture in the 18th century.

SHAKE A rough split-wood shingle much favored in the western part of the United States.

SHAKER A religious sect in America at the end of the 18th century and early 19th century who preferred simple, plain, functional furniture devoid of "wicked decorations." The line of their designs is almost 20th-century modern in its clean straightness and their concept of built-ins is also prophetic.

SHAKER

SHAKER MODERN A simple, chaste, up-to-date version of early-19th-century Shaker furniture. Clean, straight-lined, gentle tapers and the pegging and dovetailing details are the only embellishments. Maple, cherry, and other fruitwoods are often used and given an oil finish.

SHANTUNG A heavy grade of pongee originally made in Shantung, China. It is usually manufactured of wild silk, cotton, or a combination of the two.

SHAVING MIRROR

SHAVING MIRROR A popular device of the 18th century. A framed mirror that can be tilted within a stand, often fitted with drawers below to hold razors, jewelry, etc. The unit could be set on top of a chest.

A Sheraton design is illustrated. See *Standing Mirror*.

SHAVING TABLE   A clever, complicated, and involved dressing-shaving table of the Chippendale period (illustrated). Often equipped with hinged side-table surfaces, a basin area, a spring-up mirror, and drawers, compartments, etc. Also called a reflecting dressing table. See also *Rudd's Dressing Table*.

SHAW, NORMAN   A 19th-century English architect who designed domestic architecture in a romantic Queen Anne style based on the *Stick Style* construction. He introduced new freedom in the interior space arrangements, with reception rooms opening from a wide living hall.

SHEAF BACK   A delicate late-18th-century French chair back design of a bundle of stylized wheat which fanned out to meet the top rail. These chairs usually had rush or cane seats. Similar to the Hepplewhite chair backs of the same time.

SHEARER, THOMAS   An 18th-century English cabinetmaker and designer and contemporary of Sheraton. Shearer was influenced by Hepplewhite's work. In 1788 he published a book of designs, and he is credited with designing the sideboard as it is known today. Illustrated is part of one of his sideboard designs and a demilune buffet. See *Table* for another illustration of his work.

SHED CEILING   A slanted ceiling that starts at a lower wall and rises to meet a taller wall on the opposite side of the room.

SHEEN RUGS   Also called lustre rugs. A shine is chemically produced on these usually inexpensive rugs.

SHEER   Name for lightweight, gauzy, transparent fabrics like china silk, marquisette, net, maline, etc. May be woven of natural or synthetic fibers.

SHEET GLASS   Glass produced by drawing in long strips or by the cylinder glass process. Cut into sheets.

SHELDON'S TAPESTRIES Tapestries produced in the time of Elizabeth I by Flemish weavers working in England under the supervision of William Sheldon.

SHELF   A horizontal, fixed platform of wood, glass, or other rigid material, set onto a wall or in a cupboard, bookcase, dresser, etc., usually meant to hold objects. Chippendale designed many elegant hanging shelf units, some with glass doors, others carved or inlaid. Illustrated is a 17th-century carved oak German buffet unit. Note the stepped shelves between the lower closed cabinet and the open cupboard above.

SHAVING TABLE

SHELL

THOMAS SHEARER

THOMAS SHEARER

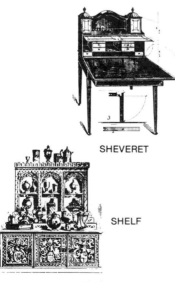

SHEVERET

SHELF

SHELL   A decorative motif. In furniture construction, the framework or basic structure. The unadorned, unsheathed unit. See also *Cockleshell*, *Rocaille*, and *Scallop Shell* for the specific shell motifs.

SHELL CHAIRS   Molded fiberglass chairs with sides, backs, and seats formed of plastic material. May have metal pipe legs or a molded plastic pedestal base. See *Tulip Chair*.

SHELLAC   A natural resin soluble in alcohol. When applied to wood, it produces a shiny surface. Often used as a prime coat on unfinished wood pieces, as a sealer.

SHERATON, THOMAS (1751–1806) The last of the great 18th-century furniture designers. He published *The Cabinet-Maker and Upholsterer's Drawing Book* from 1791 to 1794. Sheraton was greatly influenced by Hepplewhite and Chippendale, but even more so by the Louis XVI style in France. He used satinwood veneers, straight lines, and inlays rather than painted decorations, and there was an overall elegance, grace, and refinement in his early and middle years. In his later works, he tried to introduce an extravagant version of the French Empire style. Urns, rosettes, festoons, scrolls, and pendant flowers were some of the motifs favored by Sheraton.

SHEVERET   An elegant drawing-room writing table with a small shelf in back for books. The front portion of the top was hinged so it could be turned over, and the front legs pulled out to support it, thus forming a writing surface. Originally a Louis XVI design, Anglicized at the end of the 18th century. Illustrated is a late-18th-century Sheraton variation. The writing surface falls over like a card table, and it is supported by the drawer in the frame rather than the legs.

SHIELD BACK   The shape of a chair back popularized by Hepplewhite in the mid-18th century in England. The chair back resembles a shield-shaped frame with a tapered point at the center bottom. The frame would sometimes have a carved splat representing the feathers of the Prince of Wales, or a sheaf of wheat. See *Prince of Wales Feathers* for illustration.

SHIKI   In fabric, a heavy silk or rayon rep made with irregular-shaped filling threads. In wallpaper, a paper-backed fabric with silk threads on the face which simulates the actual shiki silk, or an embossed paper which simulates the texture of the fabric.

SHINGLE STYLE   A domestic architectural innovation of about 1870 based on the Queen Anne *Stick Style* of Norman Shaw of England, and on Japanese forms.

Buildings were sheathed in shingles over a wood frame in curved and straight sweeps. Ground-floor plans were open, and porches became noticeable external features.

SHINGLES Thin wood tiles, usually of cedar, used as overlapping plaques for facing outer walls and roofs. Produced today in synthetic materials.

SHIRRING A gathered effect of fabric drawn on a thread or a rod; many small folds result. An *Austrian Drape* is a fine example of a controlled shirred effect.

SHISH A fretted wooden lattice in Egyptian buildings. See *Qamariyyah*.

SHOE or SHOE PIECE The part of the back seat rail of a chair that projects out to support the bottom of the splat, often found on brace-back Windsor chairs (see illustration). Also the disk often found under the foot of a furniture leg. A ferrule. A mid-17th-century Jacobean stool is illustrated.

SHOJI A simple Japanese geometric frame, subdivided into smaller rectangular panels. The framework is usually made of narrow black lacquered wood strips, and the open rectangular spaces are filled in with translucent materials like rice paper, poly-plastex, plastics, fabrics, etc. Shoji panels are used as screens, dividers, doors that slide behind one another on a track (Japanese style), or as window coverings.

SHORING A temporary wooden framework used to support a building which is being repaired or an unstable wall.

SHOT In carpet construction, the relationship of weft threads (across the loom) to the tufts or loops of surface yarn. A "two shot" means two weft threads between each row of surface tufts. The larger the number, the more material, and the closer the carpet construction, and therefore the stronger the weave.

SHOULDERED ARCH An arch with a rectangular lintel supported by shaped corbels. The curved inner edges of the corbels create the archlike effect.

SHOW WOOD The exposed, finished wood on upholstered furniture. Illustrated is a Louis XVI armchair.

SHUTTER An interior or exterior covering for a window made of wood or metal, flat, paneled, louvered, or a fabric covered frame. Once largely protective, shutters are now often used largely as decoration, both interior and exterior.

SHUTTERING The use of temporary walls of wood or metal to enclose poured

SIAMOISE

SHOE

SIDE TABLE

SILHOUETTE

SHOW WOOD

concrete. These temporary pieces are removed after the concrete sets.

SIAMOISE An S-shaped two-seater of the mid-19th century, either an upholstered sofa or a double armchair. When seated, two persons are facing in opposite directions and they must look over their shoulders in order to converse with each other. This design was named after the Siamese twins, Chang and Eng, who created a sensation at that time. See plan-view illustration. Also called a "Tête-à-Tête." See the illustration for *Tête-à-Tête*.

SIDE CHAIR A term used to distinguish the armless chair from the armchair. The side or armless chairs were evolved in the 17th century when they replaced the stools and benches which were provided for persons other than nobility or the heads of families. See *Hall Chair* and *Light Chair*.

SIDE TABLE Originally an ornate serving table which was often combined with pedestals (as in the Adam designs) to form sideboards. William Kent, in the 18th century, designed many magnificently carved and decorated tables, and often they were topped with marble. Illustrated is an early-19th century Duncan Phyfe design. See *Satinwood* for an illustration of an Adam sideboard with side tables.

SIDEBOARD As known today, an auxiliary case piece in the dining room, which consists of drawers and cupboards that hold the items needed to furnish the dining table. Its present form was evolved by Shearer and perfected by Hepplewhite and Sheraton in the late 18th century. See *Satinwood* for an illustration of an Adam design which was a forerunner of the current design. Also see *Buffet*, *Crédence*, and *Credenza*.

SILHOUETTE The outline of an object. A profile or outline drawing, the outline completely filled in with a single color. Illustrated is a silhouette of a German Romanesque molding with an elevation view of the same molding.

SILHOUETTE MIRROR A scrolled mahogany mirror frame of the Chippendale period. The frame was usually carved and/or gilded. A decorative ornament was often applied to the cresting. It was also called a fretwork mirror.

SILK A natural fiber extruded from the silkworm as it spins its cocoon. The name is probably derived from that given to the people in the part of China where silk was first known. Silk may be used alone as a fiber or blended with other natural or synthetic fibers. It has a fine hand, drapes beautifully, and takes a brilliant dye.

SILK FLOSS   The tangled waste fibers of silk. The term is often misused to describe kapok, an upholstery filling.

SILK-SCREENED   Originally an old Chinese method of hand-printing colors through stencil-like designs on screens made of fine silk tautly stretched on rigid wooden frames. As in lithography, wood blocks, and etchings, each color requires a separate screen with only that part of the design which is to appear in that particular color drawn on the screen. For more details see *Hand Screening*. Seriographs are fine silk-screened prints, usually created in a limited number.

SILL   In construction, a horizontal strip forming the bottom of a structure; most usually, the board at the bottom of a window frame. A door sill is called a saddle.

SILVERING GLASS   A late-17th-century process for making looking glass. A sheet of tin was laid on a backing and covered with a layer of quicksilver and then with a piece of glass. Pressure was applied to fix the quicksilver to the glass. The silvering was easily injured.

SINGERIE   A decorative motif with the monkey as an ornament or an element in a mural, fabric, or wallpaper design. The monkey was often combined with chinoiseries in gay, delicate designs. Such murals were often used to decorate dadoes and cornices. Singerie was popular in France and England during the 18th century because of the popularity of the exotic and Oriental. See *Huet, Christophe*.

SINGLE ARCH MOLDING   A small half-round molding strip used around drawers in case furniture of the William and Mary period in England. Illustrated is a dressing table of this time. See *Cock Beading*.

SINGLE BED   A bed that is usually 39″ wide by 78″ to 84″ long. Some single beds may be as narrow as 30″, 33″, or 36″. Two standard-size twin beds can be used together to make a king-size bed.

SINGLE GATE TABLE   A drop-leaf table with only one leaf, which can be raised to a horizontal plane by extending the one "gate" or supporting member. It is also called a tuckaway table.

SISAL   A hard fiber, larger and stiffer than jute, flax, or hemp, used to make summer carpets, hard floor mats, etc.

SIX-LEGGED HIGHBOY   A highboy design peculiar to the William and Mary period in England.

SIZE   A gelatin-like solution used for stiffening textiles and glazing papers. Sizing is

SILL

SKIRT

SINGLE ARCH MOLDING

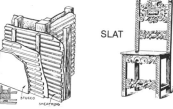

SLAT

SLAT

SLAT-BACK

also used to prime coat a wall before painting and papering it. A new paper or paint holds better on a wall that has been treated with sizing. See *Buckram*.

SKEIN DYED   The fibers are dyed before they are spun into a yarn.

SKEIN DYED YARN   Surface yarn spun from white wool or worsted staple, and then dyed in skein form by immersion in kettles or vats.

SKETCH   A rough draft for a composition or a design. A trial run by the artist. A preliminary attempt which may later serve as reference material. A pictorial note or memo.

SKEW ARCH   An arch where the axis is not at right angles to the face of the arch. The courses that make up the arch are not parallel with the axis, but at right angles to the face. The resultant arch is inclined inward toward the horizon.

SKIRT or SKIRTING PIECE   The wood strip or panel, usually shaped, below a sill, shelf or tabletop. It is also called the *apron* or *frieze*. Also a fabric valance around the base of an upholstered chair, couch, etc., to hide the legs and wood construction of the seat. The skirt may be pleated, shirred, or tailored (fitted and plain).

SKIRTING   A molded strip which covers the joint where the wall and the floor meet, often made of wood, or of vinyl, tile, rubber, etc. Illustrated is a carved skirting designed by Sir Christopher Wren, and executed by Grinling Gibbons in the late 17th century. See *Coved Skirting*.

SKYLIGHT   A window or glass structure set into the ceiling of a room (under a roof) to provide additional light without detracting from the privacy of the room.

SLANT TOP DESK   A desk, usually 18th-century English or American with a drop-front writing section, set at an angle, which rests on a base made up of several drawers. Similar to a Secretary without the bookcase element. See illustration for *Secretary*.

SLAT   A horizontal bar connecting the upright members of a chair back. It is sometimes used as a single feature, or it may be used to hold the vertical splat. The top rail is considered a slat. The slat is also called a horizontal splat. Also, a thin, narrow piece of wood like a lath, of one of the many metal or wood strips in a Venetian blind. In the illustration the sheathing is made up of slats.

SLAT-BACK   A chair back with several horizontal rails or crossbars. Chippendale and Sheraton (illustrated) designed more formal versions of this country-style chair. The slat-back was popular in Early American furniture. See *Ladderback*.

SLATE   A fine-grained stone formed of compressed clays, which readily splits into plates or tiles. Slate is used as a roofing material, usually set in an overlapping manner, and it is also used for flooring and pavements.

SLEEPY HOLLOW CHAIR   A mid-19th-century American chair which is upholstered and has a curved back and low, comfortable arms. The seat is usually scooped out. The Sleepy Hollow chair is typical of the Louis XV influence on Victorian design.

SLEIGH BED   A 19th-century American adaptation of the Empire scrolled-end bed. The resemblance of these scrolled or roll-over elements to the front and back ends of a sleigh gave the bed its name. Illustrated is an early-20th-century New Colonial style variation called a scroll bed.

SLEY   A term used to specify the number of warp threads or ends per inch of woven fabric.

SLIDE   The pullout shelf of a desk, secretary, writing table or serving table. Illustrated is a Shearer, mid-18th-century writing table.

SLIDING CASEMENTS   Windows that open and close by sliding from side to side on horizontal tracks.

SLING CHAIR   A 20th-century canvas (or leather) and metal rod chair. The wrought-iron base is shaped like two bent butterfly paper clips with two peaks in the front and two higher peaks in the back. The canvas cover or sling has four pockets which fit over these peaks. The sling makes a concave sweep from the back peaks to the front peaks. Also called a butterfly chair. See *Hardoy Chair*.

SLIP   Clay and water which have been mixed to a creamlike consistency, applied to pottery to produce a glaze or colored effect.

SLIP COVER   A removable fitted cover made to protect upholstery fabric, or to cover worn upholstery, or to provide a change for a new season. May be made of cotton, linen, chintz, silk, or synthetics. The idea of slip covering became popular in the Louis XV period.

SLIP MATCH   A veneering pattern created by joining the veneer sheets side by side so that the figure is repeated over and over in a continuous manner.

SLIP SEAT

SLEIGH BED

SLOPE-FRONT DESK

SLIDE

SMALL CHAIR

SNAKE FOOT

SLIP SEAT   A seat which can be lifted out from the frame of a chair and be readily re-covered. See *Fauteuil à Châssis*.

SLIPPER CHAIR   Any short-legged chair with a very low seat. The seat is usually only 12″ to 14″ off the ground. A regular seat height is about 18″.

SLIPPER FOOT   A club foot with a more pointed and protruding toe. It was a popular furniture foot in the Queen Anne period in England.

SLODTZ BROTHERS   Five master furniture designers of the 18th century. Three of them worked for Louis XV of France in the rococo style: Antoine Sébastien (c. 1695–1754). Paul Ambroise (1702–1758), and René Michel or Michel-Ange (1705–1764).

SLOPE-FRONT DESK   A drop-front or drop-lid desk. The desk surface slants upward and backward when closed, thus creating a sloped or angled front. It appeared in 18th-century English and American designs. Illustrated is a Sheraton design.

SLUB YARN   A yarn with a thickness caused by wrapping or twisting one yarn around another several times. This irregularly thickened yarn adds a distinctive quality when woven into a fabric. Slub yarn is also called nub yarn and thick-and-thin yarn.

SMALL CHAIR   An armless chair. A side chair. Illustrated is a Hepplewhite ovalback chair of the late 18th century.

SMITH, GEORGE   A late-18th-early-19th-century English cabinetmaker and furniture designer. He published a book on household furniture showing the then prevalent Regency style. Smith worked with Thomas Hope, and in 1808 was made Upholder Extraordinary to H.R.H. the Prince of Wales. His work showed his strong preference for things French.

SNACK TABLE   Small lightweight folding table, portable and usually available in an easily stored set of four, with stain-resistant finishes. Sometimes decorated.

SNAKE FOOT   A furniture foot carved to resemble a snake's head. It is actually a club foot with an elongated toe like a slipper foot, and it is found in 18th-century English and American furniture. A Hepplewhite bookstand is illustrated. Also, a yellow-brown or red-brown wood with dark spots and markings, popular for inlay work in the latter part of the 18th century.

SNAP TABLE   A small tripod table with a hinged top held in a horizontal position by a spring catch. Also called a tip-up table.

Designed in the mid-18th century in England and America.

SOANE, SIR JOHN (1753–1837) An English architect, and one of the group chiefly responsible for introducing classic Greek architecture into England. He studied in Rome, and found inspiration in the temples of the Caesars, which were built in the Greek style.

SOCKETING A cheap method of joinery. The end of one piece of wood is shaped to wedge tightly into a cavity cut in a second piece, like a chair leg pegged into the round cavity on the bottom of a wood seat of a kitchen chair.

SOCLE A plain, unmolded square pedestal for a statue or superstructure. Also the base of case furniture.

SODIUM VAPOR LAMP A light source used mostly in street lighting. An electric discharge into sodium vapor produces a yellow light, approximating the maximum luminosity in the spectrum. Very efficient and can have a lamp life of up to 20,000 hours, but is not a desirable lighting for merchandise presentation and not complementary to the human complexion, since it changes the color of the object it lights.

SOFA An upholstered daybed or couch, sometimes with two arms and a back. From the Arabic word suffah. The sofa appeared in France in the Louis XIV period. A Louis XVI sofa is illustrated.

SOFA BED A sofa whose back drops down, becomes parallel with the seat, and makes a sleeping surface about 43″ to 49″ wide. This type of unit is also called a jack-knife sofa bed.

SOFA SLEEPER A convertible sofa with a concealed sleeper unit (mattress, etc.) beneath the seat. May be designed in a traditional or modern style, and may vary in size from a love seat (48″ sleeping area) to a standard 7′ or longer couch which usually opens to a 54″ or 60″ sleeping surface.

SOFA TABLE An oblong table with flaps at the short ends which are supported by hinged brackets, similar to a Pembroke table. The drawers are in the longer side of the table frame. This particular type of table appeared at the end of the 18th century. A Sheraton design, c. 1804, is illustrated.

SOFFIT The underside of an arch, cornice, beam, or lintel.

SOFT PASTE A base for ceramics that lacks the whiteness and hardness of true porcelain, which is made of kaolin. See *Hard Paste*.

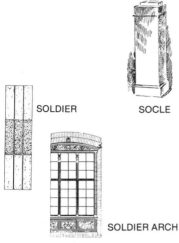

SOLDIER   SOCLE

SOLDIER ARCH

SOFA

SOFA TABLE

SPADE FOOT

SOFFIT

SOFTWOOD See *Hardwood*.

SOLAR LAMP A mid-19th-century fuel-burning lamp based on the Argand lamp. The fuel supply was set under the burner. The lamp usually consisted of a metal or marble column topped with a large globe. Prisms were frequently used to decorate the base of the globe. See *Argand Lamp* and *Astral Lamp*.

SOLARIUM A room or porch enclosed with large areas of glass to allow in the sun's rays and light.

SOLDIER A brick laid on its end so that it appears vertical in the bond.

SOLDIER ARCH A flat arch made up of bricks that are laid on edge. It is often used as a facing for a lintel-type construction (over window and door openings).

SOLUTION DYED A synthetic fiber dyed while in its liquid stage. See *Vat Dyed*.

SOMNOE A night table.

SONORA A Philippine yellow-white to pale brown, heavy hardwood with a medium-fine texture.

SOUTACHE A narrow, rounded braid with a herringbone effect, used as a trimming or edging material.

SPACE HEATER A portable gas or electric unit which can be used when needed to provide extra heat. Sometimes installed semi-permanently, to provide for extra warmth where the overall heating system is not completely effective under extreme conditions.

SPACKLING A plaster or a putty-like substance used to fill up holes or correct surface imperfections in a piece of wood or on a wall, ceiling, etc. When the spackle has dried, the excess material is sanded off, and the smooth surface is ready for the finishing coat.

SPADE FOOT A rectangular, tapered foot often found in Hepplewhite designs and also in Sheraton's work (illustrated). It is separated from the rest of the leg by a slight projection. See *Sabot Foot* (illustration). *Taper Leg, Therm Leg,* and *Thimble Foot*.

SPALLIÈRE A decorative painting on a chair back. The stenciled top rail of a Hitchcock chair.

SPAN The open or clear space between two supporting elements. The space between two columns, piers, etc. The space covered by an arch.

SPANDREL In furniture, a triangular piece spanning the space between a vertical support and a horizontal piece or rail.

SPANDREL WALL In architecture, the part of the curtain wall above the top of the window of one story and the bottom of the windowsill of the story above. This area may consist of several courses of masonry, or it may be glass, metal, plastic, or combination spandrel panels such as are used in modern curtain wall constructions.

SPANDRIL STEPS Steps of which the treads are triangular in shape.

SPANISH CHAIR A late-16th-century English chair with a high upholstered back and seat. The top rail or cresting was usually ornate and richly carved. Illustrated is a Spanish Renaissance chair which was a prototype for the English model described above. Note the Spanish foot and the giant nailhead trim.

SPANISH COLONIAL FURNITURE The provincial furniture of the American Southwest. Based on Spanish styles, the furniture is often heavy, crudely made, massive and quite rectilinear, with simple, naive carving and decorations. The native woods are used and finished in a dark brown color. Used in largely white washed and/or stuccoed, low ceilinged rooms, trimmed with heavy exposed ceiling beams. Decorative accessories are a combination of Indian, Mexican and Moorish motifs in bright colors: geometrics, primitively drawn birds, animals, and flowers.

SPANISH SCROLL FOOT A hooflike, grooved and flared foot which ends in an inward curving scroll. It was introduced from Portugal during the Restoration period and used in 18th-century English and American furniture. It was also called a Braganza toe. Illustrated is a late-17th-century cane chair with Spanish scroll feet.

SPARKING LAMPS Small lamps of the early 19th century which burned sperm or whale oil and gave off a small, flickering light. Particularly favored by courting couples, hence the name, from the slang word for courting.

SPARVER A canopy or tester over a bed. A Sheraton camp bed is illustrated.

SPECIFICATIONS The exact details, measurements, materials, etc., stipulated for a given project, job, or construction.

SPECTRAL COLORS Colors produced by a beam of white light as refracted through a prism. They are usually called violet, indigo, blue, green, yellow, orange, and red.

SPHINX A mythical monster that combines a human head and woman's bust with the body of a lion. Originally an ancient Egyptian motif. In the Roman era, wings

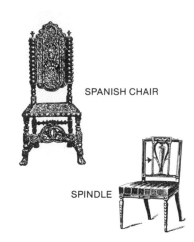

SPANISH CHAIR

SPINDLE

SPINET

SPANISH SCROLL FOOT

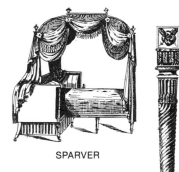

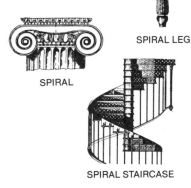

SPARVER

SPIRAL

SPIRAL LEG

SPIRAL STAIRCASE

were added. During the Renaissance, Adam, Empire, and Regency periods the sphinx was used as a carved or painted decoration. It was particularly popular as a furniture support during the Empire and Regency periods when things Egyptian were mixed with classic Greek and Roman motifs.

SPIDER-LEG TABLE An 18th-century English drop-leaf table of Sheraton design with eight thin legs. A variation on the gateleg or eight-leg table.

SPINDLE A long, slender rod often ornamented with turned moldings or swellings. A Sheraton chair is shown.

SPINDLE AND BEAD An ornamental molding, resembling a string of sausage-like members separated by round or elliptical beads.

SPINDLED PANELS Interior shutters made of delicate spindles. Common in Spanish window treatments.

SPINET From the Italian spinetta which means little thorn. A musical instrument of the 16th to 18th centuries, later superseded by the harpsichord. The strings were plucked in the same way as on the harpsichord. The case was usually highly embellished with paintings, gilding, carvings, and inlays. An 18th-century French spinet is illustrated. In contemporary usage, a small upright piano. It is usually about 4′ tall by 5′ wide and 2′ deep, with a standard keyboard.

SPIRAL A curve that winds around a fixed point and does not backtrack on itself. Each whorl is a complete turn of the curve around the axis, and may be on one plane, or in an ascending or conical shape like a shell. The spiral is the basis for the volutes of classic capitals (illustrated), scrolls, or twisted rope turnings.

SPIRAL LEG A leg resembling a twisted rope, or a support with a winding descending flute or groove. It was originally of Portuguese and Indian origin, and became popular in England during the Restoration. A Sheraton, late-18th-century furniture leg is illustrated. See *Barley Sugar Turning.*

SPIRAL STAIRCASE A stairway that winds around a central shaft as it rises from one level to another. Illustrated is a 19th-century cast-iron spiral staircase. It is also called a winding staircase.

SPIRAL WHORL See *Paper Scroll.*

SPIRE The pointed termination of a structure, such as a finial, usually conical or pyramidal in form.

SPLAD An 18th-century English spelling of splat. Illustrated is a mid-18th-century Chippendale chair.

SPLANCH A split-level, ranch-style house, on two-levels, but with only half a story between the two. See *Ranch-Style House* and *Split-Level House*.

SPLAT The central, upright wood panel of a chair back, serving as a back rest. May be carved, vase- or fiddle-shaped, embellished with carving and marquetry, or decorated with fretwork, pierced designs, or tracery.

SPLAY A bevel or chamfer. A surface that is spread out or set at a slant. A large chamfer or diagonal surface formed by cutting away an angle of a wall. A shortened form of the word "display."

SPLAY LEG A leg which angles or flares out from a chair, table, chest, etc. Illustrated are an ancient Greek klismos and a mid-19th-century Biedeimeier table.

SPLINE In cabinetry, a method of strengthening a joint by means of a small strip of wood inserted between and projecting into the two pieces of wood that form the joint. Illustrated is a spline miter joint.

SPLINT SEATING Chair seats made of thin slats or splints of wood woven into a wood webbing. Used on rustic or provincial furniture. Similar to caning but much coarser.

SPLIT SPINDLE An applied ornament of 17th-century English and American furniture. A delicate, slender turning was cut in half lengthwise, thus creating two half-round moldings. It was applied to cabinets, cupboards, etc. In Jacobean furniture split spindles were used for chair backs with the smooth cut side toward the sitter's back.

SPLIT-LEVEL HOUSE A house built on a series of levels rather than complete stories. The main level usually has the living and dining rooms, the kitchen, and sometimes a study. Several steps up from this level are the sleeping quarters, while several steps down one usually finds the utilities, recreation or family room, maid's quarters, storage, etc.

SPOOL FURNITURE Turned furniture which was mass-produced in the United States in the mid-18th century, distinguished by turnings which resemble a string of spools or buttons, often made of pine, and stained to resemble mahogany. The better pieces were made of maple, cherry, or walnut. See *Jenny Lind Bed*.

SPOON BACK A high chair back shaped to fit or conform to the curvature of

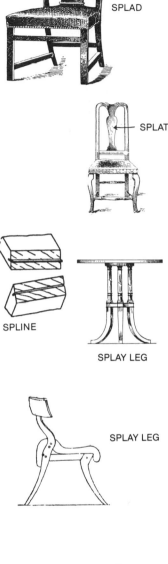

SPLAD

SPLAT

SPLINE

SPLAY LEG

SPLAY LEG

S-SCROLL

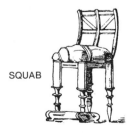

SQUAB

the human back. The back gently slopes backward as it goes up, and it is slightly concave. Introduced by the Dutch, and appeared in England during the period of William and Mary. It became more popular in the Queen Anne period and faded out with the Chippendale style.

SPOON FOOT A club or Dutch foot. The foot of a cabriole leg which flares and spreads out at the base; usually it is set on a pad. Popular in the Queen Anne period.

SPOON-BACK CHAIR An early-19th-century Regency and Biedermeier chair with a curved wood back. The low-set arms rise from the seat above the front legs, and make a continuous and rising sweep up to form the top rail. The center splat is plain, or it may be urn- or vase-shaped. The spoon-back is similar to the American Empire chair called the Mme Jumel.

SPRINGS Flat, zigzag, or coiled constructions of high-quality steel which add to the resiliency of upholstered furniture, or of beds when used under the mattress, or in its construction.

SPRUCE A type of pine closely related to fir. A soft, light, strong, straight-grained wood used for interior and exterior work.

SPUN SILK Silk yarn which is made from waste fibers and damaged or pierced cocoons. Heavier and less lustrous than first-grade yarn.

SPUR The triangular filler between the round shaft and the square base of a Gothic column. A filler might be a spray of foliage, a tongue, or a grotesque.

SPUR STONE A stone specially shaped and set at the corner of a structure to prevent injury to the corner from passing traffic.

SQUAB A loose, stuffed cushion used for seats of chairs, settees, and long stools. Squabs were replaced by upholstered seats toward the end of the 17th century, but they are still used on luxurious armchairs and sofas. Illustrated is an ancient Pompeiian chair with footstool.

SQUINCH In furniture, a corner cupboard. See *Coin* and *Encoignure*.

S-SCROLL A popular cyma curve of the French Rococo (Louis XV) and Chippendale periods. Sometimes used broken or stepped in the center. A Chippendale design is illustrated.

S-SCROLL LEGS A 17th-century furniture support of Dutch design. It was S-shaped and ended in an S-shaped scroll. Usually heavily embellished with carving.

STABRE, LAURENT A noted cabinet-maker, "joiner and carpenter in ebony" to Louis XIII in the 17th century, when ebony was often glued onto blackened pearwood to obtain added strength or size.

STACKING CHAIRS Chairs designed to be stacked atop one another and nested when stored. Used in contract design for setting up temporary auditoriums, fashion shows, dining accommodations.

STAINED GLASS Designs or pictures made of colored glass and held together by strips of lead which also form the outlines of the design. It was a Byzantine invention, but became a distinctly medieval art form. The colored glass is made by adding metallic oxides to molten glass (pot metal) or by fusing colored glass on plain glass (flashing).

STAINLESS STEEL A steel alloy which is a bright silvery color, and is resistant to tarnish, rust, and corrosion.

STAIR RODS Metal rods, often brass, to hold a carpet runner on a flight of stairs. Holds the carpet in place without need of nails or tacks by being secured close to the bottom of each riser, across the face of the carpet. The carpet installation is easy to change or move.

STALACTITE WORK Small vertical, polygonal, or curved niches projecting in rows above one another to create a stalactite-like formation. Illustrated is the Hall of the Abencerrages in the Alhambra. This type of ornament was also used to create Moorish capitals.

STALKER, JOHN With George Parker, published *A Treatise of Japanning and Varnishing* in 1688. Japanning was of great interest to the English, even at this early date.

STANCHION A vertical, metal member (usually a rolled-steel joist) which supports a load carried onto it by a beam.

STAND A framework, small table, or lowboy upon which chests, cabinets, drawers, basins, and such were placed. Daniel Marot, Grinling Gibbons, and William Kent carved many magnificent gilded stands in the 17th and 18th centuries.

STANDARD-SIZE BED A double bed, usually 53"–54" wide by 75" long.

STANDING MIRROR An oval, shield-shaped, or rectangular framed mirror set on a chest or table, usually equipped with a drawer. An 18th-century design, it was also called a shaving mirror.

STANZA The Italian word for room.

STAR BURST A five-pointed star with raylike emanations. A decorative motif.

STAR MOLDING

STACKING CHAIRS

STALACTITE WORK

STEPPED CURVE

STANDING MIRROR

STEREOBATE

STAR MOLDING A decorative sculptured molding with a star motif, popular in Romanesque architecture.

STEAMBOAT GOTHIC A style using lacey ornate, overembellished woodwork, turnings, balls, finials, gables, bargeboards, and "gingerbread" on wood and shingle structures built in America at the end of the 19th century. The inspiration for this extravagant use of the jigsaw was the "floating palaces" on the Mississippi in the middle of the 19th century, hence the name. See *Jigsaw Detail*.

STEEL ENGRAVING An art reproduction technique introduced in the second quarter of the 19th century. A microscopic film of steel is deposited on the softer copper plate by means of electrolysis. The hard steel plate made it possible to print large editions without destroying the fine details of the plate. Soon superseded by photoengraving methods.

STEEL FURNITURE Pieces produced in very limited quantities in the 17th and 18th centuries in Europe by gunsmiths and ironworkers. Most of the known designs are of the Directoire or Early Empire style and were created for Napoleon's campaigns, in which the strong and easily transportable folding chairs and collapsible tables, beds, and desks were particularly useful. The designs were often embellished with bronze doré rosettes and medallions as well as chiseled and chased details.

STELA or STELE A stone slab or pillar used as a commemorative or grave marker in ancient Greece.

STENCIL A pattern made by brushing or wiping ink or paint over a shield of metal or paper in which the required design has been cut. The paint will go through only the cut-out areas. The design can be reproduced many times over on walls, ceilings, furniture, floors, etc. In the 19th century, it was used in place of wallpaper as a method of getting an allover design on walls. The top rails of Hitchcock chairs were usually stenciled in gold.

STEPPED CURVE In furniture, a sudden break or stop in the direction of a curve, or the junction of a curve with a straight line, used in the uprights of the Queen Anne and Early Georgian periods. It appears in a modified form in the Hepplewhite chair back illustrated here.

STEREOBATE The basement or foundation of a building. The word also means a continuous pedestal under a plain wall. Illustrated is the mid-15th-century Italian Renaissance Palazzo Ricardi in Florence.

STEREOCHROMY A technique of painting on stone or marble with pigments in water glass, (a sodium-silicate compound).

STERLING A standard of pure silver content. Also silverware, jewelry, etc. which is made of silver that is at least 92½ percent pure, meeting the standard.

STICK In wallpaper, a set of several rolls.

STICK STYLE A romantic 19th-century English style of architecture with "emphasis given to structural and visual multiplication of the framing sticks." It is a variation on the half-timber house, with the wood strips forming the major pattern and decoration, being left completely exposed.

STICK TABLE A combination pedestal table and lamp. The lamp base is usually a turning or column which appears to be a continuation of the table support, extended through the table surface. A lampshade is set atop this stick or base. Interpreted in most traditional styles as well as modern designs.

STICK-BACK The back of a Windsor chair, made up of many rods or spindles. These elements are called sticks or fiddle strings.

STICKLEY, GUSTAVE See *Mission*.

STILE In furniture, the vertical strips of the frame of a panel or case piece of furniture. Also the outer uprights of some panel-back chairs.

STILL LIFE A painting or representation of an arrangement of flowers, fruit, books, musical instruments, vases, etc. In certain periods a still life included hunt trophies.

STINKWOOD A South African wood with a distinctly unpleasant odor when freshly cut. Resembles walnut, and has a reddish cast. Used in the 17th and 18th centuries by the native craftsmen of the Dutch East India Company in South Africa to reproduce Dutch furniture designs.

STIPPLE or CRAYON ENGRAVING A combination of etching and intaglio engraving especially popular in the 18th century for reproducing portrait drawings of famous personalities. The stippling consisted of making dots on a grounded plate with an etching needle. See *Intaglio* and *Intaglio Engraving*.

STIPPLING A painting technique for surfacing a wall or object with a multitude of tiny dots, spots, or blobs. It can be accomplished with the stiff bristles of a brush, a fine sponge, crumpled tissue paper, etc.

STITCHED UP A French upholstery technique of the 17th century. The uphol-

STICK-BACK

NICHOLAS STONE

STILE

STONEWARE

STOOL

STITCHED UP

stery of the seat is drawn over the seat rails and attached to the rails underneath the chair. Illustrated is a Louis XIV chair. See *Stuffover Seat*.

STOA A colonnade around an agora (an ancient Greek marketplace). A detached colonnade or portico. See *Colonnade*.

STOCK DYEING The dyeing of a fiber before it is spun into thread or yarn.

STOEP The Dutch word for Veranda (Verandah).

STONE, EDWARD DURREL An American architect born in 1902, who has designed many important buildings in and out of the United States. His pierced screen and deep eaves, pierced concrete and clay tiles, as well as pierced metal facades, have influenced interior designers.

STONE, NICHOLAS (1586–1647) An English stone carver who produced many of Inigo Jones's designs for fireplaces, mantels, etc. In 1626, he was appointed Master Mason to Charles I. He worked in marble, alabaster, touchstone, and Portland stone. Some of his work was inlaid with other colored marbles (intarsia) or embellished with chased brass mounts. The gateway to St. Mary's Church at Oxford is one of his finest works.

STONEWARE A heavy opaque nonporous nonabsorbant pottery made from siliceous paste. Illustrated is an early-17th-century jug made in Germany.

STOOL A backless and armless seat which was replaced by small or side chairs in the 17th century. A stool is now used as a small decorative seat, or a very low design will serve as a footrest. See *Piano Stool*.

STOPPED CHANNEL FLUTING A series of equidistant concave flutes with straight or rounded ends. Originally a decoration on classic architecture, in the 18th century it was used as a frieze decoration on cabinets and furniture.

STORAGE BED A platform bed with storage space below. The mattress is placed on a base fitted with drawers or cabinets. A contemporary version of the old Captain's Bed—the bunk bed with drawers below which was used on 19th-century whaling ships.

STORAGE WALL A series of modular units which can be set up in a variety of combinations as a wall, or against one. A 20th-century invention introduced by George Nelson and Henry Wright in 1945, as a space-saving answer to storage problems for apartment dwellers. It was later refined into a collection of units produced by Herman Miller in the form of a "basic storage component" system. Many variations are now available, from wall-hung to self-standing, and from modern styles to medieval and Spanish-inspired units.

STORY or STOREY   The space between two floors or between the top floor and the roof.

STORY POST   A weight-carrying post that extends through the story.

STRADDLE CHAIR   A chair one straddles or sits spread-legged across. See *Cockfight Chair* and *Voyelle.*

STRAIGHT STAIR   A flight of stairs uninterrupted by turns or landings.

STRAINING   An early-17th-century technique of tightly stretching and gluing the upholstery fabric to the whole of the woodwork, as in the stately beds designed by Daniel Marot in the William and Mary period. Illustrated is a late-17th-century state bed from Knole Park in England. Note the tester. The fabric has been pulled taut and sharp across the wood framing.

STRAPONTIN   A bracket or jump seat used in carriages, cars, or in public buildings. A flap or fold-down seat.

STRAPWORK   A carved wooden arabesque pattern having a flat stem of a scroll in section and/or an ornament which resembles a pattern cut from a sheet of leather. An interlaced pattern which resembles a crisscross folded or plaited design which might be created from strips of leather. Elizabethan and Jacobean carved-wood decorated panels with ribbon-like bands in repeating and interlacing designs. In the Chippendale period, flat and sometimes elaborately carved strapwork was used for the splats of chairs. See *Ribband Back.*

STRAW CHAIRS   Originally provincial chairs with rush or woven straw seats. They were adapted to more formal and decorative uses in the 17th and 18th centuries.

STRAW MARQUETRY   An Eastern or Oriental technique which was used in France in the 17th century. Two layers of flattened and tinted straw were placed one on top of the other and cut through together, as in marquetry, and the cutout shapes were applied to wooden or papier-mâché objects. Some straw designs were executed like mosaics, others were engraved, and in some extraordinary units minute pieces of straw were built up into low-relief decorations.

STRAWBERRY HILL   A house built by Horace Walpole at Twickenham, England, in the mid-18th century. It gave im-

STRETCHER

STRAINING

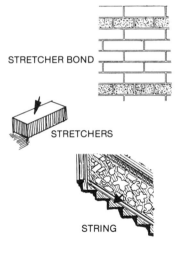

STRETCHER BOND

STRETCHERS

STRING

STRINGING

petus to the Gothic revival, and was filled with fan-ribbed vaulting, tracery patterns, and details from medieval tombs.

STRETCHER   The crosspiece which connects, braces, and strengthens the legs of tables, chairs, chests, etc. Illustrated is a 17th-century English chair. See *Arched Stretcher, Rising Stretchers, Saltire,* and *X-shaped Stretcher.*

STRETCHER BOND   In masonry, a method of bricklaying with only the stretchers showing. The stretchers in the succeeding courses appear to overlap one another, and the vertical joints fall in alternate courses instead of one directly under the other. The overlap may be only ¼ of the brick in length. See *Bond.*

STRETCHER COURSE   See *Stretchers.*

STRETCHERS   In masonry, the two surfaces of a brick bounded by the longest and the shortest sides, rather than the short end, which is called the header. A stretcher course is one which is composed only of stretchers laid in a continuous row.

STRIÉ   A fabric with an uneven color or streaked effect produced by using warp threads of varying tones. It is possible in this manner to produce a two-toned effect in taffeta, satin, or corded upholstery fabrics. See *Jaspé.*

STRIGES   The vertical fluting on a classical column. See *Fluting.*

STRING   In stair construction, the angled member into which the treads and risers are fixed.

STRINGING   A narrow band or strip of contrasting veneer used as a decorative border, the same as lining.

STRIP LIGHTING   A metal or plastic strip with a series of exposed sockets and a single plug and/or switch. Can be used to frame a mirror, outline a window, follow a ceiling line or create a decorative pattern of lamps in lines. Usually used as an accent light.

STRIP WINDOWS   See *Ranch Windows.*

STRIPPING   Removing old paint, lacquer, varnish or any other finish from a piece of furniture or treated surface, the first step in refinishing.

STRIX   A channel or groove in a fluted column. See *Fluting.*

STRUCTURAL CLAY TILE   A hollow masonry unit with parallel air cells. It may be made of burned clay, shale, fire clay, or mixtures of the above.

STRUT   A horizontal building construction member which is set between two verticals (or vice versa) to hold them apart. A chair or table stretcher acts as a strut.

STUART STYLE   The architecture and design of England from the reign of Charles I into that of William and Mary (approximately 1625–1690). See *Jones, Inigo,* and *Wren, Sir Christopher.*

STUBWASSER, JOHANN HEINRICH (1740–1829)   An 18th-century German craftsman who in 1758 originated a method of lacquering. He produced snuff-boxes, cofferets, and small pieces of furniture in wood and papier-mâché which were lacquered and decorated by fine artists.

STUCCO   A plaster or cement used for interior or exterior walls. It can be decoratively textured and/or coated. The surfacing material can be tinted. See *Composition* and *Gesso.*

STUCK MOLDING   A molding forming part of the surface it adorns rather than one applied to the surface and not an integral part of the unit. Illustrated is a 15th-century English oak buffet. See *Planted Molding.*

STUD   A wooden post, usually 2″ × 4″, used to form the skeleton of a wall or partition. The posts support the joists, and receive the lath or sheet material which finishes the wall. A stud is also a copper, brass, or gilt nailhead used for decorative purposes on chests, cabinets, door panels, etc., or for securing leather or fabric to chairs, panels, chests, cabinets, etc. Originally nailheads were functional rather than decorative, but the heads became more ornate and larger, and eventually a form of repetitive embellishment. Introduced in Spain, Portugal, and Italy in the Middle Ages and in the 17th century used in France and England. Illustrated is a chair of the Louis XIII style.

STUDENT LAMP   A late-19th-century brass lamp with the fuel reservoir higher than the burner; it is similar to the astral lamp. The chimney, which was set around the projecting burner, was partially covered by a tole shade to direct the light downward. The lampstand itself sometimes had a ring on top to make the lamp portable. Electrified versions of the student lamp are available.

STUDIO APARTMENT   A compact living space, often located in an urban high-rise building. Usually one room which also serves as the living room, bed-

STUDY

STUCK MOLDING

STUFFOVER SEAT

STUMP BEDSTEAD

STUD

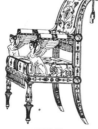
STYLE

room, dining room, and study. There may be a small kitchen area or a Pullman kitchen, closets, a bathroom, a dressing room, and a foyer which can be adapted to other uses.

STUDIO COUCH   A seating device which converts into a sleeping unit by means of removable cushions or bolsters and retractable springs. An informal bed unit. A studio couch with an auxiliary set of spring and mattress kept, trundle-bed fashion, under the main spring and mattress converts into two twin beds.

STUDY   In art, a drawing or painting of a detail made to be studied and perhaps used as part of a larger composition. In interior design, a library or den, usually a room with a desk, comfortable chairs, and bookshelves. A retreat. Illustrated is a Renaissance study.

STUFFER   In carpet construction, a strong coarse fiber like jute which runs lengthwise on the loom and is woven in with the weft and warp threads. It adds a thick protective backing to the finished carpet.

STUFFOVER SEAT   The fixed seat of a chair upholstered by drawing the fabric or leather over the seat rails and securing it with nails along the underside of the rails. The join is finished off with a galloon or a brass molding. Illustrated is a late-17th-century English chair. See *Stitched Up.*

STUMP   See *Buttwood Veneer.*

STUMP BEDSTEAD   A bedstead without posts. A medieval example is illustrated.

STUMP FOOT   A furniture leg that goes directly down to the floor without any special foot, pad, or disk.

STUMPWORK   A relief effect in embroidery created by stitching with wool or silk threads over padding. A quilting or trapunto effect in vogue during the late Tudor and Jacobean periods.

STYLE   The characteristics of a design. The motifs, techniques, and materials typical of a certain period of time or of a particular designer. Illustrated is an example of the French Empire style. The design is by Charles Percier and Pierre Fontaine, the style setters of the period.

STYLOBATE   The stone blocks or steps of a Greek temple upon which the columns rest. A basement or platform upon which columns are placed to raise them above the level of the ground or floor. A continuous unbroken pedestal for a range of columns, an arcade, etc.

SUEDE CLOTH   A synthetic fabric with the look and feel of suede leather. Also, any fabric with the raised nap and matte finish that suggests suede.

SUFFAH   The Arabic word from which "sofa" is derived, defined as "a place or couch for reclining before the doors of Eastern houses." Illustrated is a Sheraton sofa.

SUGAR PINE (WHITE PINE)   Product of California and southern Oregon, which ranges in color from creamy white to pale brown faintly tinged with pink. It has little flecks and intermittent lines of a darker shade running parallel with the grain. Knots have a purplish band around their edges. A close-grained wood that works well and holds a shape.

SUGI FINISH   A Japanese wood-finishing technique. The surface is charred and rubbed with a wire brush to create a driftwood effect.

SUITE   See *Set.*

SULLIVAN, LOUIS (1856–1924) The "father" and first truly creative genius of modern American architecture. He evolved the skyscraper design, and combined new technical means with aesthetic ideals. In 1873 he worked for William Le Baron Jenney, who was later to build the first all-steel-frame building. In 1881, Sullivan became a partner of Dankmar Adler, who was the engineer-constructer of the partnership. They completed the Auditorium Building in Chicago in 1889; the structure was an opera house combined with an office block. This was the last of his "masonry" period. The Wainwright Building in St. Louis in 1891 and the Bayard Building in New York City in 1898 are early attempts by Sullivan at steel-frame structures which widely influenced American architecture. The Carson, Pirie & Scott Department Store in Chicago (1899–1904) was a tremendous step forward in "cage" construction, and even today it has a fresh, modern look with the horizontal emphasis in its façade which reflects the framework of the building. In his book *Ornament in Architecture* in 1892, he stated, "Ornament is mentally a luxury, not a necessary."

SUMMER BEAM   From the French "sommier," a rafter. A large horizontal timber used as a bearing beam. It usually spans the width of a room. In the Colonial American home, the beam ran from the central stone chimney to a post.

SUMMER BED   A Sheraton design which consisted of two single four-poster beds, separated by a space but connected at

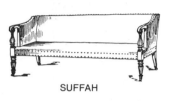

SUFFAH

SUNBURST

SUNK TOP

SUPPORTING COLUMN

the cornice which ran straight across the two beds.

SUNBURST   An ornamental motif, carved, painted, or inlaid, with straight or jagged rays radiating from a central point. It was associated with the style of Louis XIV, "the Sun King." Illustrated is a Chippendale chair back.

SUNFAST   Describes a dyed fabric which does not fade appreciably under normal exposure to sunlight.

SUNK PANEL   See *Panel.*

SUNK TOP   A table surface which is set below an edge or rim, as in gallery tables. See *Piecrust Table.*

SUPER LAMP   A new compact fluorescent lamp created by Phillips to replace incandescent lighting. Promises a life span seven to ten times longer than the traditional incandescent bulb and an energy saving of up to seventy percent. From North American Phillips Lighting, Highstown, N. J. 08520.

SUPERGRAPHICS   Environmental designs of huge scale, often executed with a bright rainbow palette. Generally simple, bold repetitive lines and forms. Used on walls, ceilings, columns, and doors to "break" the dullness of box-like interiors, accentuate areas, create movement or flow between rooms or spaces, camouflage dated architectural details, or decorate a wall without using wallpapers, graphics, or wall arrangements. A late-20th-century concept.

SUPERIMPOSED ORDER   Each successive story of a colonnaded building having its columns, pilasters, or anta treated with a different classic order. Doric is usually on the lowest level, Ionic on the second, and Corinthian on the third story. The Romans used this device in decorating the Colosseum in Rome, and it was reintroduced in the Renaissance period. Illustrated is a section of the Roman theatre of Marcellus, which has a combination of Doric and Ionic orders.

SUPERMULLIONS   The upright bars or mullions above the starting point of the foliation of a Gothic tracery window.

SUPPORTING COLUMN   A column at a front corner of a cabinet or chest which supports an overhanging frieze drawer. This motif is usually associated with Empire, Regency, and Biedermeier styles. Illustrated is an Empire secretary.

SURAH   A soft silk fabric, usually twill woven in a plaid design. It can be made from synthetics or a combination of fibers.

SURBASE MOLDING   In cabinetry, the pedestal of a piece of furniture treated with a carved, inlaid, or otherwise decorated molding. The pedestal is often treated with drawers.

SURREALISM   A 20th-century school of art which had its ancestry in the weird and fantastic works of Hieronymus Bosch, Francisco Goya, Guiseppe Arcimboldo, Odilon Redon, and Henry Fuseli. It was also influenced by the nihilism of Dada and certain aspects of early-20th-century Cubism. The word was first coined in France and was defined by André Breton as "pure psychic *automatism,* by which it is intended to express verbally, in writing or in any other way, the true process of thought. It is a dictation of thought, free from the exercise of reason and every aesthetic or moral preoccupation." Some of the leading surrealist artists are Salvador Dali, Paul Klee, Giorgio di Chirico, and Pablo Picasso.

SWAG   Cloth draped in a looped garland effect. A carved or painted decoration in a pendant curve. The swag may be a festoon or a garland of fruit, flowers, leaves, or ribbons. See *Festoon.*

SWAG LIGHT   A lamp or light fixture hooked into the ceiling with the electric cord, usually decorated with a metal chain, swagged from the hanging point to the nearest wall, and then down to the floor outlet where it is plugged in. Provides overhead light without installing electrical outlets or boxes in the ceiling.

SWAN, ABRAHAM   An early-18th-century English cabinetmaker noted for his mantels, doors, window trims, and staircases. In 1745 he published The *British Architect, or the Builder's Treasury of Staircases* with simple, understandable methods of drawing the classic orders. A source of inspiration and instruction for the Colonial American builders in the 18th century.

SWAN BED   A French Empire bed with carved swans on either side of the headboard. The front or footboard consisted of a pair of cornucopia-type legs, and usually a carved fruit arrangement. The entire bed was raised up from the floor on a heavily carved base or dais.

SWAN NECK   A general term for moldings or members with an ogee curve, as in the shape of a curved handrail ending.

SWAN NECK PEDIMENT   A broken pediment in which the raking lines are composed of two opposed S curves. The upper ends are scrolled over with paterae on their faces. The pediment usually has a

SWASTIKA

SWAG

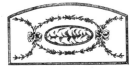

SWEEP FRONT

SWELL FRONT

SWIVEL

SWAN NECK PEDIMENT

small central pedestal, sometimes topped with an ornamental feature like a vase or pineapple. An 18th-century Chippendale design is illustrated. Also popular in the earlier Queen Anne period. Also called a Gooseneck.

SWASTIKA   A cross composed of four equal L-shaped arms at right angles to each other. It is an ancient symbol of good luck, often used in the classic Greek and Roman times as part of a fret or Greek key design. Illustrated is an ancient Pompeiian frieze.

SWATCH   A small sample of cloth or material, also called a clipping or cutting. Used as a specimen of the color, pattern, and texture of a fabric, as an aid to making choices.

SWEDE CLOTH   A napped fabric that resembles suede leather.

SWEDISH MODERN   A style of furniture and furnishing that features simple, clean lines, light woods, and avoids carved, applied, or painted decoration. Simple curves, a sculptural use of the wooden elements, and refined tapered legs add to the beauty of this style. See *Scandinavian Modern.*

SWEEP FRONT   A piece of furniture with a flat, bowed, or slightly curved front. Illustrated is a plan view of a Hepplewhite commode tabletop.

SWELL FRONT   A cabinet, credenza, chest of drawers, etc., with a segmental or bow front. Illustrated is a Sheraton dressing table. See *Bow Front.*

SWING GLASS   See *Cheval Glass* or *Mirror.*

SWING-LEG TABLE   Table with a hinged rail with a single leg which sweeps out to a right angle and supports a dropped leaf raised parallel with the floor. See *Flap Table, Eight-legged Table, Gate-Leg Table, Thousand-legged Table,* and *Tuckaway Table.*

SWIRL   A wood grain effect which usually appears around knots or crotches. An irregular eddying grain.

SWISS   A very fine sheer cotton fabric which was first made in Switzerland. It may be plain, embroidered, or patterned with dots (dotted Swiss). It is often used for glass curtains.

SWIVEL   A revolving mechanism below the seat of a chair or below the surface of a tabletop, as in lazy Susans or dumbwaiters, to swing the surface around in a wide arc, sometimes a full 360°. The swivel is also used for desk chairs, piano stools, television bases, etc. Illustrated is a German revolving armchair, c. 1870.

SYCAMORE, ENGLISH A white to light brown wood which is heavy, tough, and strong, usually used for finishing work. When stained with oxide of iron it becomes a greenish-gray color. Popular as a veneering wood in the late 18th century. Also called Harewood.

SYLMERIZED A chemical treatment for fabrics to make them stain-resistant. The process does not affect the color, feel, or hand of the fabric.

SYMBOL In furniture and interior decoration, a pictorial representation of an intangible, i.e., of an idea, quality, virtue, group, or trade. A decorative grouping of typical tools and instruments which represents a concept such as art, science, music, astronomy. Used as a carved, painted, and

SYMMETRICAL

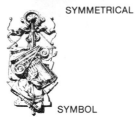

SYMBOL

appliquéd decoration. See *Palette* and *Trophy.*

SYMMETRICAL A balance of mirror images. Two units of exactly equal shape, size, mass, etc., set on either side of a central point or line and at equal distance from it.

SYMOND, JAMES An early-18th-century American cabinetmaker in Salem, Massachusetts.

SYNTHETIC RESINS Chemical compounds used in finishing textiles to give desired resiliency, hand, fade-resistance. Also used on coated plastic fabrics.

SYNTHETICS Man-made fabric fibers, carpet fibers, etc. Materials which are produced chemically rather than from natural growth or development. New materials can be made from such natural elements as cotton, wood pulp, coal, etc., combined with chemicals, tars, resins, etc.

T

TABARET A stout, satin-striped silk fabric used for upholstery.

TABBY A watered silk or moiréd effect on fabric. Also the name of an 18th-century English wallpaper ground. See *Moiré*.

TABERNACLE FRAME The entire trim or decoration of a door, window, niche, or chimney which consists of columns or pilasters with an entablature and pediment over them. It is an early-18th-century term defined by Robert Adam in his *Works of Architecture*.

TABERNACLE MIRROR See *Constitution Mirror*.

TABERRAY See *Tabaret*.

TABLE Before the mid-16th century, an index, a pocketbook, or a tablet. In the 14th century, religious carvings and paintings in churches. Now, a flat, horizontal surface, raised on legs, trestles, or a pedestal, its size and shape determined by its use. Illustrated is a late-18th-century English Pembroke table by Shearer.

TABLE À COIFFER A dressing table, introduced in the period of Louis XV. Usually the center sliding panel contained a mirror with a drawer below. Deep wells on either side contained cosmetic containers, washbasins, etc. Also called a coiffeuse or poudreuse.

TABLE À ÉCRAN A table with a sliding screen. See *Screen Table*.

TABLE À GRADIN A tiered desk of the 18th century. A second tier of boxes and/or compartments was set on the flat writing surface. It was similar to a *Bonheur du Jour*.

TABLE À MILIEU

TABLE À OUVRAGE

TABLE

TABLE CHAIR

TABLEAU

TABLE À JEU A gaming or card table.

TABLE À L'ANGLAISE An extension dining table of the *Louis XVI period*.

TABLE À L'ARCHITECTE A table with a hinged top. See *Architect's Table*.

TABLE À MILIEU A *Center Table*. Illustrated is an early-19th-century English Regency design.

TABLE À OUVRAGE A worktable. Usually a small table with an undershelf or drawer, often equipped with spaces for writing materials. Illustrated is a French Empire version. See *Pouch Table*.

TABLE À ROGNON A kidney-shaped table, a shape especially popular in the Louis XV period. See *Kidney Desk* or *Table*.

TABLE CHAIR An armchair or settle of the 16th and 17th centuries which had a hinged tabletop for a back. When the back was swung up and lowered over the arms, the table came into being. Illustrated is an oak chair of the Jacobean period. A drawer was placed below the seat.

TABLE DE CHEVET A night table which was probably originated in the period of Louis XV. See *Chevet*.

TABLE DE DAME A lady's small dressing or powder table of the 18th century, especially popular in the Louis XV period. See *Poudreuse*.

TABLE JARDINIÈRE A table with a sunken well in the surface to hold a plant container. The earliest were sometimes decorated with Sèvres plaques.

TABLEAUX French for pictures, paintings, or scenes. Illustrated is a painted win-

189

dow of the 13th century in Chartres Cathedral.

TABLEAUX TENTURES   A set of wallpaper panels which, when put up together, makes one large panoramic scene or a series of coordinated scenes. A wallpaper mural of many panels, popular in the early 19th century.

TABLET CHAIR   A chair with a wide flat arm which serves as a shelf or writing surface. It appeared on 18th-century American Windsor chairs, and a popular early-20th-century version appeared in many schoolrooms. The design is also called a writing armchair.

TABONUCO   A light-colored, beautifully grained, West Indian hardwood.

TABOURET   A low upholstered sitting stool. In the 17th century in France it was a distinguished seat for a lady of the court to sit on before the King and Queen, and in the court of Queen Anne as well. In the 18th century, the tabouret was replaced by the side chair. May also be an unupholstered stool which can function as a stand or table.

TABRIZ RUGS   Rugs with classic Persian border designs, many dating back to the 16th century. Often with a central medallion, sometimes incorporating shapes of stylized hunters, animals, flowers, and birds. Colors are usually soft and muted.

TAFFETA   A plain, basic weave, as well as the crisp fabric produced with this weave. The warp and weft threads are of equal size, and the resulting fabric is smooth on both sides with a lustrous surface. Named for the Persian fabric, taftah. Taffeta may be woven in such a manner as to produce a changeable, iridescent effect. It is also called taffety. See *Plain Weave.*

TAFFETA, ANTIQUE   A stiff, plain-weave fabric made of duppion to simulate 18th-century taffeta. See *Douppioni* or *Duppion.*

TAFFETA, FAILLE   Taffeta woven with a pronounced crosswise rib.

TAFFETA, MOIRÉ   Rayon or silk taffeta with a watered or moiré effect. See *Moiré.*

TAFFETA, PAPER   A lightweight taffeta which has been treated to produce a crisp, paper-like finish.

TAFFETA, TISSUE   A very lightweight, semitransparent fabric.

TAILLE-DOUCE   French for line engraving. See *Engraving.*

TABLET CHAIR

TABOURET

TALLBOY

TALON-AND-BALL FOOT

TAMBOUR

TAPER LEG

TAILPIECE   A projection on the back of the seat of certain Windsor chairs, which receives the spindle braces.

TALIESIN   The late Frank Lloyd Wright's summer home in Taliesin, Wisconsin. The first house was designed in 1914, and the second house burned down in the early 1920's. In 1925, the present structure was started in wood and local stone. The building is composed of low-slung lines which appear to be growing out of the surrounding terrain.

TALL CASE CLOCK   See *Grandfather (long case) Clock.*

TALLBOY   One chest of drawers set on top of another larger chest. This piece of furniture was introduced at the end of the 17th century. Illustrated is a design by Ware. See *Chest on Chest* and *Highboy.*

TALON-AND-BALL FOOT   See *Claw-and-Ball Foot.* Illustrated is a Hogarth chair of the Queen Anne period.

TAMBOUR   French for drum. A flexible rollover top, or rolltop desk or table. Small molding strips or reeds are transversely glued onto a heavy canvas backing, the ends of which fit into grooves on the inner sides of the piece of furniture. It may also be used as a vertical rolling or sliding door on a cabinet, chest, etc. A Hepplewhite desk is illustrated. See *Demilune* illustration.

TAMBOUR CURTAIN   Panels of fine sheer cotton fabric (batiste, muslin, or lawn) which usually have embroidered borders or allover patterns.

TAMBOUR EMBROIDERY   A chain-stitch form of embroidery which is done on special tambour frames. At present it is a machine technique which is made to resemble the handmade product. It is used to decorate fine lawn, batiste, and muslin fabric panels used as curtains. See *Tambour Curtain.*

TAMO   Japanese ash. A figured blond wood with patterns that may vary: fiddleback, mottle, swirls, and "peanut-shell" figures. Tamo bends easily, glues well, and takes a beautiful finish.

TANGUILE   A Philippine dark, red-brown hardwood similar to *Lauaun.* It is sometimes marketed as Philippine mahogany.

TAPA CLOTH   A fiber cloth made in the South Seas, and usually block printed in bright allover native designs with vegetable and animal dyes. The fibers used are usually derived from the bark of the mulberry.

TAPER LEG   A straight, rectangular furniture leg which tapers and thins down evenly as it approaches the bottom or foot. A Hepplewhite chair is illustrated. See *Therm Foot*.

TAPESTRY   From the French tapisser, to line. A handwoven fabric with a ribbed surface like rep, and a design woven in during the manufacturing, making it an essential part of the fabric structure. Pictorial tapestries were originally made of wool accented with silk and metallic threads. They were used to line the cold, draughty walls of medieval castles and fortresses. A handmade tapestry is reversible if the loose threads are snipped off. At the end of the 19th century, there was a revival of this art in England under the guidance of William Morris. The earliest wallpapers in England were referred to as "paper tapestries." Illustrated is a 16th-century wall tapestry from the Fontainebleau Palace. See *Arras* and *Mortlake Tapestries*.

TAPESTRY CARPET   Carpet made with an uncut pile fabric woven on a velvet loom; often referred to as a hooked-type carpet. Special textured effects can be achieved on the tapestry carpet.

TAPET   A late-Gothic, early-Renaissance term for a carpet, which at that time meant a table covering. Illustrated is the interior of a late-14th- early-15th-century French château (after Viollet-le-Duc). Note the carpet (tapet), the built-in furniture, canapés, woodwork, and fireplace.

TAPISSERIES   French for tapestries or arras.

TARLATAN   A stiff, gauzelike fabric.

TARSIA   See *Intarsia* or *Tarsia*.

TASK LIGHTING   Specific lighting for special purposes; brighter, more direct or more concentrated light at a specific area where a task is being performed or an object is on display. Specific and concentrated light.

TASK SEATING   Chairs designed for a specific purpose: e.g., a typing chair, a tall stool for a drafting table, a chair with a writing arm, a swivel and/or tilt chair. Seats are designed to accommodate to the work to be performed and to make the worker as comfortable and as productive as possible.

TASLAN   A trademark name for Dupont's textured air-bulked yarn.

TASSEL   A pendent ornament, usually twisted threads around a roundish core with a thick fringe of the twisted threads falling below the core. Applied to the corners of pillows on upholstery pieces, along the edges of draperies, on cornices, etc.

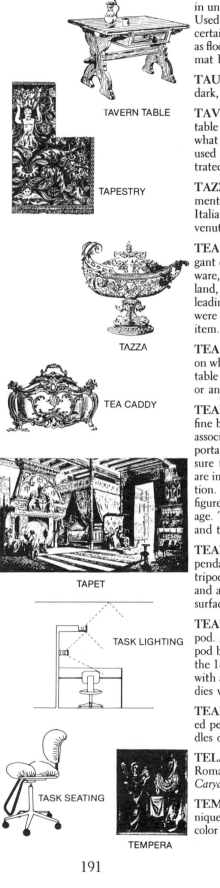

TAVERN TABLE

TAPESTRY

TAZZA

TEA CADDY

TAPET

TASK LIGHTING

TASK SEATING

TEMPERA

TATAMI   A natural straw matting woven in uneven rows, often bound in black tape. Used by Japanese architects, arranged in certain patterns, for wall coverings as well as floor coverings. The texture of the tatami mat has been reproduced in vinyl.

TAUPE   French for mole or moleskin. A dark, brownish, gray-purple color.

TAVERN TABLE   A simple, leafless table of the 17th and 18th centuries, somewhat like a refectory table. The term is also used for a stretcher or turned table. Illustrated is a German Renaissance example.

TAZZA   An Italian term for a large ornamental cup or a footed tray. Illustrated is an Italian Renaissance design credited to Benvenuto Cellini.

TEA CADDY   A tea container of elegant design made of wood, china, earthenware, pewter, or silver. In 18th-century England, these pieces were designed by the leading decorators and designers, and they were considered an important household item. A Chippendale design is illustrated.

TEA WAGON   A small movable table on wheels with a shelf or two below the top table surface. Often equipped with handles or an extension to facilitate manuevering.

TEAK   A light tobacco-brown wood with fine black streaks. (The blackish cast often associated with teak is a stain.) Teak is important in tropical countries where exposure to moisture, heat, and insect attacks are important factors in furniture construction. The wood has a rippled or mottled figure, and the color becomes deeper with age. Teak is native to India, Burma, Java, and the Malay Peninsula.

TEAKETTLE STAND   In the Chippendale period (mid-18th century), a small tripod table with a central column support and a gallery around the edge of the table surface.

TEAPOY   The Hindustani word for tripod. A small, low table, most usually a tripod but sometimes four-legged, popular in the 18th century. A large tea chest on legs, with a lift-up top under which the tea caddies were kept.

TEARDROP BRASSES   Teardrop-shaped pendants or drops used as pulls or handles on drawers, doors, etc. Drawer pulls.

TELAMONES   Male caryatids. The Roman term for Atlantes. See *Atlantes* and *Caryatids*.

TEMPERA   A common painting technique up to the 16th century. Powdered color is mixed with fresh egg yokes, thinned with water, and then applied to a panel well prepared with gesso. It dries quickly, and the color lightens; it is a tough and permanent finish. Tempera is much like the current gouache technique. See *Gesso* and *Gouache*. Illustrated is a German mid-14th-century tempera painting on a panel.

TEMPLET　A pattern for a construction or decoration. A contour drawing of the exact shape and size of a form to be created.

TEMPORA　A trademark name for a nonwoven, feltlike woolen upholstery and drapery fabric.

TENIA　The flat band at the top of a Doric architrave upon which the triglyphs rest.

TENON　In carpentry, a projection at the end of a piece of wood which is shaped to fit into a special opening (a mortise) of a corresponding shape in another piece of wood. It is used in joinery. See *Mortise and Tenon Joint*.

TENSILE STRENGTH　The ability of a material to resist breaking under stress.

TENT BED　An 18th-century variation of the camp or field bed. A four-poster with a tester that resembles a tent top. A Chippendale design is illustrated. See *Field Bed*.

TENTURE　The French term for tapestry, wall hanging, colored wallpapers, or a set or series of tapestries on one particular subject.

TERM　A pedestal which usually tapers toward the base; sometimes not only the pedestal but also the bust that stands on it. The term was used as a decorative device in the Renaissance period, and especially in the French Rococo period.

TERMINAL FIGURES　Human figures, natural or grotesque, often carved in high relief, and used to embellish prominent features on furniture. See *Term*. See Illustration for *Torso*.

TERN FOOT　Triple scrolled foot. Illustrated is a mid-18th-century Chippendale design.

TERRACE　A raised, out-of-doors area or platform usually surrounded by a balustrade or low fence. A continuous row of houses. Also a graded bank of earth covered with sod.

TERRA COTTA　Italian for baked earth. Clay fashioned into ornaments, vessels, tiles, etc., and then baked. Finished pieces vary in color from a gray brown to a brick red. The clay may be colored with paint or a glaze may be baked on. Terra cotta baked in molds can be used as a facing material for buildings, flooring, etc. Illus-

TENT BED

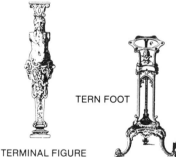

TESSELLATED

TERMINAL FIGURE

TERN FOOT

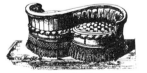

TÊTE-À-TÊTE

TERRA COTTA

trated is a German Renaissance terra-cotta plaque.

TERRACESCAPE　The end result of landscaping an area by creating various levels, or terraces and enhancing them with plants, shrubs, and paving materials.

TERRAZZO　A concrete made up of small pieces of crushed marble and cement, used for pavements, floors, and walls, and sometimes accented with metal feature strips. The color will vary with that of the crushed marble used.

TERRE-CUITE　See *Faïence* and *Terracotta*.

TERRY, ELI　An early-19th-century American clockmaker. See *Pillar-and-Scroll*.

TERTIARY COLORS　Colors produced by mixing a primary color with an adjacent secondary color; red and orange produce a red-orange. See *Primary Colors* and *Secondary Colors*.

TESSELLATED　Describes a surface, e.g., a wall, treated with a mosaic design composed of small cubes (tesserae) of stone, glass, marble, etc. A Pompeiian tessellated wall decoration is illustrated.

TESSERAE　Little cubes of glass, marble, stone, ceramic, etc., used in mosaic designs. See *Tessellated*.

TESTALIN, LOUIS　A 17th-century French portrait painter and tapestry designer at the Gobelins Factory.

TESTER　A canopy on a four-post or draped bed from the French term testière, or headpiece. Originally, a flat wooden canopy, paneled and carved, used as a roof for four-post Tudor and Stuart bedsteads. This was replaced by a wooden framework heavily draped and swathed with valances. In the mid-18th century it became a small wood cornice with a fabric valance and curtains.

TÊTE DE NÈGRE　French for Negro's head. A dark blackish-brown color.

TÊTE-À-TÊTE　An S-curved sofa for two, also called a Siamoise. A 19th-century design in which the seated persons sit shoulder to shoulder but facing in opposite directions.

TÊTES D'ANGES　Angel heads with wings. Decorative sculptured forms, sometimes set in medallions or rondels or on pilasters. Used in Renaissance architecture and furniture, and also in the late 18th century in France and England.

TEXTILES　Fabrics. Woven or unwoven materials used in interiors for upholstery, drapery, wall coverings, etc. Made of natural fibers (wool, silk, cotton, linen), synthetics (rayon, nylon, dacron, etc.), or combinations of natural and synthetic fibers.

TEXTOLITE A trademark name for a plastic material manufactured by General Electric in a wide range of colors, patterns, and textural effects. Easy to clean, resists stains and scratches, and used for laminating on table and counter tops, walls, and shelves.

TEXTURAL DESIGN In fabrics and carpets, a design created in the texture of the weave rather than by the use of printed patterns.

TEXTURE The feel and the appearance of the tactile effect of the surface of a material, e.g., smooth, rough, pebbly. Also grain in wood. See *Embossed*.

THATCH A roof covering of straw or reeds.

THEATRICAL GAUZE A plainweave, open, lightweight semisheer cotton or linen fabric, usually stiffened with size to give it body. Produced in a wide range of color and in wide widths. It is also called opera gauze, and is mainly used for glass curtains.

THERM FOOT A rectangular, tapering foot for a chair, table, or cabinet leg, also called a spade foot, favored by mid- and late-18th century designers like the Adam brothers, Hepplewhite, and Shearer.

THERM LEG A four-sided tapering leg. A favorite furniture support of Hepplewhite (illustrated) and other mid- to late-18th-century English designers. Could be highly decorated with carving or inlay work. See *Taper Leg*.

THERMOPANE A trademark name for a double-glass insulating pane used on doors and windows.

THERMOPLASTIC Plastic materials and synthetic resins that soften at high temperatures.

THERMOSETTING Plastics and synthetic resins that harden and set at high temperatures. The opposite of thermoplastic.

THIMBLE FOOT A spade or sabot foot, but one that is usually turned rather than rectangular.

THIRTEEN-STATE TRACERY A late-18th-century fretwork or tracery made up of thirteen elements. The idea was originally Chinese, and the concept of the original thirteen states was superimposed on the established design. Used to decorate glass

THOUSAND-LEGGED TABLE

THERM FOOT

THERM LEG

THUMB MOLDING

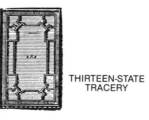

THIRTEEN-STATE TRACERY

panels of secretaries and bookcases of the late 18th century.

THOMIRE, PIERRE PHILIPPE (1751–1843) A French, Empire metal chaser and engraver who specialized in making plaques with figures in low relief, which were applied to furniture. Besides these gods, goddesses, and caryatids, he created gilt bronze mountings which were sometimes credited to his contemporary, Pierre Gouthière. Thomire was a student of the sculptor Jean Antoine Houdon.

THONET, MICHAEL See *Bentwood Furniture*.

THOUSAND-LEGGED TABLE A variation of the gateleg table which dates back to the first half of the 17th century. It had a central drawer, two extra swinging legs which folded in under the braces of the tabletop, and two leaves that dropped down. When the table was fully opened, it could be as much as five feet in diameter. See *Eight-legged Table* and *Gateleg Table*.

THREE-BACK WINDSOR CHAIR See *Comb Back*.

THREE-QUARTER WIDTH A term in carpet construction. One quarter of a yard or 9″ is a unit of loom width, and a standard carpet is "three-quarters" or 27″ wide. In Europe "three-quarters" is referred to as an ell.

THRU-VU VERTICAL BLINDS Vertical strip blinds used over windows, made of lightweight metal or fabric. Used to control light and air much as the traditional horizontal Venetian blinds do. Originally designed by George Nelson and Henry Wright. Since imitated, adapted, and improved under other trademark names. Sometimes called Boston blinds.

THUMB MOLDING A convex molding with a flattened curve also referred to as lip molding.

THUYA A hard, dark, red-brown wood native to North Africa, usually with a bird's eye figure. Takes a high polish, and is used for cabinetwork. Used by the ancient Greeks and Chinese, and a popular veneer wood in 18th-century England.

TIAMA See *Sapele* or *Sapeli*.

TICKING A closely woven cotton fabric with a twill or satin weave, usually woven with stripes. May be printed. A sturdy fabric for mattress covers, and also decorative for drapery, upholstery, and wall covering. The fine striped quality of ticking has been reproduced on wallpaper.

TIDIES Small doilies, often crocheted or elaborately embroidered, or large runners, used on chair backs and arms. Popular decorative conceits during the Victorian period. Also called Antimacassars. See *Antimacassars.*

TIE BEAM A horizontal beam which connects the rafters, and keeps them from spreading. The tie beam is used in truss construction to counteract the outward thrust of the slanting members. May be left visible in an interior.

TIEBACK A fabric sash or cord with tassels, or a decorative metal, glass, or wood hook, rosette, or bar to hold back a drape. When the drape is tied back to the sides (or one side only) of an opening, a decorative swelling of fabric appears above the tieback, and the fabric below cascades down, usually to the floor.

TIEPOLO, GIOVANNI BATTISTA (1696–1770) An outstanding Venetian artist, designer, and decorator of the 18th century. He painted many wall frescoes and ornate ceilings filled with light, brilliant color, with remarkable perspective and foreshortening, often with sunny skies, clouds, cherubs, and classical gods and goddesses. He personified the Venetian Rococo period, though he also worked in Würzburg (the royal palace) and Madrid.

TIER CURTAINS Two or more rows of short curtains hung one over the other to cover a window. Sometimes the lower tier is longer, and sometimes made of a more decorative or more opaque fabric.

TIER TABLE A small round table consisting of two or more surfaces or shelves set one over the other with the largest one at the bottom. A serving table. See *Serviteur Fidèle.*

TIGERWOOD Also called African walnut and Nigerian golden walnut. A West African wood of a grayish-brown to golden-brown color, accented with black streaks and a definite ribbon stripe, used for cabinetry and paneling.

TILE A thin slab of baked clay. May be glazed and/or ornamented. Used for roofs, walls, floors, counters, etc.

TILL A small drawer or compartment in a table, desk, chest, etc., for money, jewelry, or special papers, often equipped with secret springs or locks.

TILT-TOP A pedestal table with a hinged top which can be dropped vertically when not in use. See *Snap Table.*

TINT A color with white added, which in effect lightens or pales the color to a pastel. The opposite of "shade," which is a color with black added.

TIRETTE

TIEBACK

TODDY TABLE

TILL

TILT-TOP

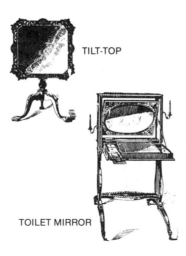

TOILET MIRROR

TINTORETTO, IL (Jacopo Robusti) (1518–1594) A Venetian painter who created great emotional effects by the play of light and shadow in his paintings.

TIP-UP TABLE A double-leaved table which folds like a book (the hinged leaves hang down on either side of a central spine). It is similar to a *Snap Table* or *Tilt-Top* table.

TIRETTE The French term for extension or pullout leaf or slide to provide a larger table surface.

TISSUES Semisheer crisp fabrics made of silk or synthetic yarns.

TITIAN (TIZIANO VECELLIO) (1477–1576) A Venetian painter with the sensuous quality of the Renaissance, who was influenced by the work of Giorgione. In his later years he developed a free, almost impressionistic style, in which form was rendered in patches of color rather than contours.

TODDY TABLE A small table of the Georgian period in England. A Hepplewhite design is illustrated. See *Urn Stands.*

TOILE French for a linen- or canvas-like cloth. Also a fabric for painting, or a painting or picture. A fabric with pictures printed all over it. See *Toile de Jouy.*

TOILE DE JOUY Originally a hand-blocked cotton or linen fabric with pastoral scenes printed all over, in one color, on a white or natural background. The printed fabrics, called indiennes, were produced in a factory operated by Christophe-Philippe Oberkampf at Jouy, near Versailles, in the mid-18th century. Oberkampf designed pictorial groups in large repeats in one color (red, blue, green, or eggplant), and printed them on natural cream-colored cotton. They showed groups of peasants or aristocrats dressed in their different costumes and engaged in their everyday activities, as well as bourgeois scenes, fables, and historical scenes. Later, discoveries at Pompeii and changes in the French government influenced Oberkampf's designs, as did the ornamental motifs of Napoleon's designers Charles Percier and Pierre Fontaine. All the original Jouy prints were marked Bon-Teint on the selvage, which means fast dye.

TOILES D'INDY Printed cottons and linens with floral or pictorial designs imported into France during the late 17th century from India and Persia. See *Indienne Fabrics.*

TOILET MIRROR A cheval mirror with dressing table compartments. Illustrated is a Sheraton design. The toilet mirror is also called a dressing mirror.

TOILET TABLE See *Dressing Table.*

TÔLE French for sheet iron. Objects made of sheet metal or tin and ornamented with painted or enameled patterns. 18th-century lamps, boxes, trays, etc., were often made of tôle.

TÔLE SHADE A lampshade made of sheet metal, often decorated with painted or decal artwork. Usually associated with Early American, early 19th century, and provincial lamp designs. See *Bouillotte Shade.*

TONAL VALUE The relative strength of a color based on its degree of absorbtion of light.

TONDINO Italian for circular molding. See *Tondo.*

TONDO A circular picture, a shape popular in Italy in the mid-15th century. A tondo by François Boucher is shown.

TONGUE AND GROOVE A joint in which a long narrow, straight projection (the tongue) fits into a corresponding groove in the adjacent piece. T is the tongue, G is the groove. Used extensively in flooring. See *Joinery.*

TONTINE A trademark name for Dupont's washable window-shade fabric.

TOP COLOR In printed or screened fabrics, papers, etc., the color or colors applied over the basic or ground color of the material to produce the design or decoration.

TOP RAIL A horizontal bar or rail which connects the uprights of a chair back, and supports the cresting, if any. Also called the cresting rail. In some historical periods, the top rail appears to be a continuation of the uprights in that it is a curve, serpentine or bow-shaped. Also the top horizontal member of a door.

TOPIARY ART The clipping and shaping of plants, shrubs, and trees into formal or fanciful shapes: geometric, bird, or animal forms. Topiary trees have been featured in formal gardens from the 16th century to the present.

TORCH A flambeau. A flaming brand. A Roman motif which reappeared in the Renaissance, Directoire, and Empire periods.

TORCHÈRE Originally, a small table designed to hold a candlestick, candelabrum, or other light-giving object. The table surface was usually mounted on a pillar or light framework, and often embellished with carvings and gilt. Originally a French design of the Louis XV period. Now a standing floor lamp, usually with a

TORSO

TORCHÈRE

TONDO

TORUS

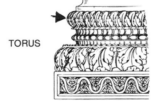

TOP RAIL

JOB TOWNSEND

T-PILLOW

bowl shade to cast light toward the ceiling. Illustrated is a Chippendale design. The torchère was also called a *Guéridon.*

TORSADE A molding with a twisted ropelike or cable design. See *Cable.*

TORSO The trunk of the human body. Illustrated is a drawing by Hans Holbein of Erasmus with his hand resting on a sculptured torso and head.

TORTOISESHELL The back plates of a sea turtle flattened out and joined together under heat and pressure. Used in antiquity as a veneering material for furniture. It again became popular, thanks to Charles-André Boulle and his inlay technique, during the period of Louis XIV. Usually a mottled brown, gold, and black material, semitranslucent. See *Boulle Work.*

TORUS A convex, semicircular molding, often found at the base of a column. A Roman example is illustrated.

TOUCHSTONE A black marble from Namur, Belgium, used on chimneypieces and mantels in the late 16th and early 17th centuries. Nicholas Stone often used touchstone in his work.

TOWEL HORSE or TOWEL RAIL A slender wood frame with several crossbars used to hold towels, usually on two or more legs. In vogue in England in the mid-18th century.

TOWNSEND, JOB An 18th-century American cabinetmaker, considered the dean of the Newport furniture makers.

TOWNSEND, JOHN An 18th-century American cabinetmaker who worked in and around Newport, Rhode Island. See *Goddard.*

T-PILLOW A seat pillow or cushion for a chair or sofa which is wider in front than at the back because the arms of the upholstered unit do not extend to the front of the seat. The two rectangular projections of the pillow (the crosspiece of the T) fill up the space between the end of the armpiece and the front of the chair or sofa seat. A sofa with two pillows will have only one projection or ear on each pillow.

TRACERY Originally the stone mullions in Gothic windows. A decorative form composed of circles, with arcs formed by the intersection of circles. Thus every line is either a circle or the broken arc of a circle, and the composition of these elements makes for intricate patterns. See *Bar Tracery.* In the Chippendale Gothic period, tracery appears in chair backs, door panels, etc.

TRACHELION The neck of a Greek Doric column, between the annulets and the hypotrachelion. In the illustration, A is the annulets, T is the trachelion, and H is the hypotrachelion.

TRACK LIGHTING The arrangement of spot- or flood-lights in decorative housings on a channel or track attached to a ceiling, wall, or other surface, with one end plugged into a source of electrical current. The length of channel can be extended as necessary. Fixtures can be moved anywhere along the track, aimed at different positions, and be turned on and off individually as needed. Used for selective or task lighting. Can be either primary lighting or secondary lighting in an interior. Also called Overhead Track.

TRADITIONAL In interior decoration, a term usually applied to a style of a bygone age, in contrast to a contemporary or modern style.

TRAFORO Italian for tracery or fretwork.

TRANSEPT In church architecture, the part that crosses the nave at right angles near the apse of the building. The plan of Amiens Cathedral is given here.

TRANSFER PRINTING A method of applying one-color designs to pottery. The pattern is printed on paper by means of a copperplate engraving, and then transferred to the pottery like a decal. See *Decalcomania*.

TRANSITIONAL A style which combines elements already established with those newly appearing. An example is the French Régence, which was a transition from the Louis XIV style to the Louis XV style.

TRANSLUCENT A material (fabric, glass, etc.) which allows light to pass through, but diffuses it so that objects cannot be seen clearly. See *Obscure Glass*.

TRANSOM The upper part of a window, or the window over a doorway, usually constructed to allow in air.

TRANSVERSE RIBS In arch vaulting, the main ribs which mark or delineate the contour of a vault.

TRAPUNTO A type of quilting which gives a raised relief effect to a stitched design. The design is usually outlined with single stitches, and then filled from behind. Trapunto is often used to embellish the pillow backs of upholstered pieces.

TRAVERTINE A cream-colored, onyx-like stone which is usually pockmarked or full of irregularly shaped depressions. Reproduced as a vinyl floor-covering design.

TRACHELION

TRAY-TOP TABLE

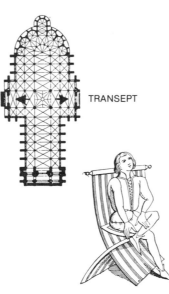

TRANSEPT

TRECENTO

TRELLISWORK

TRAY TABLE A collapsible stand which, when opened, supports a tray. The tray serves as a table surface.

TRAYLE A running vine with grape clusters and leaves which appeared as a decorative element in Tudor England. See also *Vinette*.

TRAY-TOP TABLE A small table with a low gallery or skirting around three or all four sides, popular in the mid- to late-18th century. A Sheraton design is illustrated.

TREAD In stair construction, the flat, horizontal part of the step between two risers. See *Riser* illustration, where arrow points to the tread.

TREAUMAU A noted embroiderer of the Louis XV and Louis XVI periods. He created and executed beautiful designs for pillows and cushions. Among his most ambitious works were the "Four Seasons" and the "Four Elements" on the cushions of the two carriages sent to Marie Antoinette in 1770.

TRECENTO The thirteen hundreds, or the 14th century. Illustrated is a 14th-century English folding chair.

"TREE OF LIFE" PATTERN Motif based on a tree or vine with branches, leaves, flowers, and small animals, originated by the ancient Assyrians and used as a decorative motif by the Persians, Indians, and English Renaissance craftsmen. See *Hom* and *Palampores*.

TREFOIL A three-lobed, clover-like ornament used with Gothic tracery and decoration. The three arcs are separated by the cusps. The Gothic symbol for the Holy Trinity.

TRELLISWORK A crossbarred or lattice effect in wood. A pierced or fretted woodwork design with a reticulated appearance. Adam, Chippendale, and others used brass trelliswork for inserts in bookcase doors. Illustrated is a Sheraton "gentleman's secretary." See also *Fretwork*.

TRENAILS Literally "tree nails." Wooden pegs which have been rounded and tapered to a point, used in the construction of finer 18th-century pieces.

TRENCHER A large wooden serving platter. (Originally, a slice of bread upon which food was placed.)

TRESTLE A supporting frame. The term is derived from the Old French trestel, a beam. In the Tudor period, large boards were supported by these trestles to form trestle tables.

TRESTLE TABLE See *Sawbuck Table*. For illustration, see *Arkwright*.

TRIANGLE SEAT Sometimes called a corner seat or a boffet or buffet chair. The latter was a Scandinavian design which was made in England in the early 17th century. Triangular chairs were also made in the Queen Anne period and afterward, with splats on the two sides under the semicircular arm and backrest which encircled the two sides of the triangle. See *Barber's Chair.*

TRICOT An inexpensive tapestry fabric, the underside of which is different from the top side, usually made of cotton or rayon. A warp-knit fabric, also having different sides, usually made of nylon.

TRICOTEUSE A small sewing table or worktable, usually with a gallery around the top. The table often had several shelves under the top surface. Appeared in the Louis XVI period, and continued through the Directoire and on into the 19th century. See *Pouch Table* and *Worktable.*

TRICTRAC TABLE A backgammon table. A popular gaming table of the Régence, Louis XV, and Louis XVI periods. In the Louis XVI period, they were made of mahogany with removable tabletops. Sometimes one side of this removable top was covered with leather and the reverse side was covered in baize. See *Baize.* The top was removed to reveal the interior, a gaming area with a backgammon board, sockets for candles, and small drawers or compartments for dice and counters.

TRI-DARN A Welsh court cupboard of the 16th century, with two tiers of cupboards, and above them an open, spindle-sided dresser. See *Deu-Darn.*

TRIFID A three-toed furniture foot of the 18th century which was used in England and America. See *Tern Foot.*

TRIFOIL A form of tracery consisting of three lobes or arcs. See *Trefoil.*

TRIGLYPHS In the Doric entablature, the triple upright grooves channeled in the spaces between the metopes. The triglyphs and metopes together form the frieze.

TRILOK A trademark name for corrugated, three-dimensional fabric made of monofilament yarns. A durable, serviceable fabric used for upholstery in homes, autos, and public areas. Patented by the United States Rubber Company.

TRIM A term usually applied to the woodwork of rooms designed in a traditional style. Dadoes, wainscots, paneling, cornices, coves, chair rails, picture moldings, window and door moldings are all considered trims. Marble or stonework, as on mantels, could also be considered trim. Il-

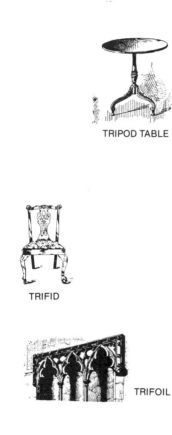

TRIPOD STAND

TRIPOD TABLE

TRIFID

TRIFOIL

TRIM

TRUMEAU MIRROR

lustrated is an early-18th-century wall design by Isaac Ware.

TRIPOD STAND A very small table with a flat or gallery top surface which rests on a column-like shaft that ends in a triple spread-legged support. A favorite of the 18th century in England and America. Illustrated is a Chippendale design.

TRIPOD TABLE A pedestal table supported by three outward-curving legs. Adam and Chippendale designed many.

TRIPTYCH Any three-panel or three-fold picture, screen, or mirror, especially three-panel religious paintings used on altars.

TRIQUETRA An ornamental interlaced pattern which consists of three pointed lobes.

TRIVET A small, openwork, three-legged frame in metal, originally hung on the bars of a grate to keep a kettle or dish hot. Today, a three-legged stand which raises a hot container off the surface of a table or server. A larger trivet is called a footman. Trivets became fashionable in the mid-18th century.

TROMPE L'OEIL French for deceive the eye. A polished technique of using pictorial elements, perspective, foreshortening and shadows, to render objects in paint or inlay so realistically that they appear to be actually three-dimensional. The Italian form of trompe l'oeil is called quadrature.

TROPHY Tokens of victory. A decorative painted, carved, or inlaid arrangement of symbols of battle, weapons, horns, banners, spears, shields, laurel leaves, etc., set on a panel or a pilaster. Renaissance artists' trophies were executed in intarsia, woven fabrics, and tapestries. Other types of trophies were also developed: musical instruments, flowers, fruit, fish, animals, and professional symbols. See *Gibbons, Grinling,* and *Symbol.*

TROTTER See *Philadelphia Chippendale.*

TRUCKLE BED See *Trundle Bed* or *Truckle Bed.*

TRUMEAU The French word for pier, or the wall between windows. Overmantel or overdoor paneling, usually filled with mirrors or paintings. The paintings were often made to look like relief sculpture in the 18th century. See *Grisaille.* The trumeau was part of the exquisite boiserie of the Louis XV and Louis XVI periods.

TRUMEAU MIRROR A framed mirror of the late 18th century, usually a tall rectangular mirror set into an overmantel.

A characteristic element is a painted scene in the upper section or a carved panel. The decoration was usually more prominent than the mirror. Illustrated is a mid-18th-century chimneypiece designed by Thomas Johnson of England. See *Constitution Mirror*.

TRUMPET TURNING   A turning with a flaring end that resembles the bell of a trumpet. A 17th-century motif.

TRUNDLE BED or TRUCKLE BED A trundle is a roller or caster, and the trundle or rollaway bed was originally a Gothic design. It was a small-scaled bed on casters for children or servants, which was rolled under a full-size bed when not in use. It was often used in Colonial and early American homes. Now, a pullout bed on casters somewhat smaller than the bed under which it is set. Similar to a hideaway bed.

TRUSS   In furniture construction, a bracket, console, or corbel.

TUB CHAIR   A late-18th-century English easy chair with a rounded back and wide wings, similar to a barrel chair, but is wider, taller, and more enveloping. A Sheraton design is illustrated. In the Regency period (early 19th century) the design changed, and it more closely resembled the spoon-back chair except that, instead of having a splat, the entire back was enclosed with cane or upholstery.

TUB FRONT   See *Blockfront*.

TUB SOFA   A fully upholstered French design. The ends sweep around in curves, and they are provided with arm pads or manchettes. The persons seated at either end of this couch are slightly turned toward each other. It is similar to a kidney-shaped couch.

TUBULAR FURNITURE   Contemporary furniture with structural parts made of plastic or metal rods or tubes including the chair and table legs, chair arms and back rests. Outdoor furniture is often made of PVC plastic or aluminum tubes with plastic webbing or plastic-covered pillows.

TUCKAWAY TABLE   An 18th-century American folding table with crossed or scissored legs. The top leaves dropped close together, making a compact storable unit. A forerunner of the snack table.

TUDOR ARCH   A four-centered, flat-pointed arch, characteristic of the English Gothic and early Renaissance period.

TUDOR FLOWER   See *Brattishing*.

TUDOR PERIOD   The reign of the Tudor family in England from Henry VII through the reign of Elizabeth I (1485–

TUDOR ROSE

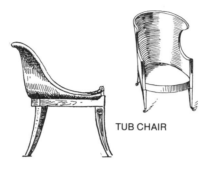

TUB CHAIR

TUFTING

TULIP CHAIR

1603). It was a transitional period in architecture and decoration from the late Gothic to the Renaissance. A time of secular building which combined elements of the late Gothic perpendicular with Norman castellated motifs.

TUDOR ROSE   An English Renaissance decorative motif which consisted of a conventionalized five-petal rose with a smaller rose set in its center. It was the royal emblem of England, and symbolized the marriage of Henry VII of Lancaster (the red rose) to Elizabeth of York (the white rose).

TUFA   A lightweight volcanic stone, or a rock of a rough, irregular, cellular structure. It may also be formed as a calcareous deposit from water. The ancient Romans used tufa to make concrete.

TUFFT, THOMAS   A late-18th-century American cabinetmaker of Philadelphia, most noted for his simple lowboys.

TUFT   In carpet construction, a single yarn in a surface pile of a carpet. The tuft or yarn is produced by twisting together the fiber strands.

TUFTING   An upholstery technique. The covering fabric and the padding are tied back in a definite pattern, creating little "pillows" between the depressions. The tieback process is usually fastened with self-covered buttons. Tufting makes the upholstery fabric conform to the curves of the unit. It is often used on leather (or imitation leather) where the material is not as easily worked as most upholstery fabrics. An early-18th-century English armchair is illustrated. Tufting reached the peak of its popularity during the opulent, "overstuffed" Victorian period. Also, a new form of carpet construction. The pile yarns are sewn onto a wide fabric by means of multineedled machines. A heavy jute or canvas backing is used. The yarn ends of the tufted fabric are usually applied to the backing with latex.

TULIP CHAIR   An influential chair design by Eero Saarinen. A curved, molded plastic form continuous with a pedestal base, and with an affixed upholstered seat pad. Similar to a *Cognac Chair*.

TULIPWOOD   A yellowish wood with red and purple stripes from a small Brazilian tree, a member of the rosewood family. Used mainly for inlays and banding. See *Bois (or Boise) de Rose* and illustration for *Kingwood*.

TUNBRIDGE WARE   A kind of veneer which was made at Tunbridge Wells in England. It resembled minute mosaic work. Many small rods or dowels of wood were arranged in a design, and they were then glued in place (like so many pieces of spaghetti glued together vertically). This cluster of rods was then thinly sliced, horizontally, through the collection of rods, and the design appeared on each fine sectional slice of veneer.

TUNGSTEN HALOGEN LAMP   An incandescent lightbulb which contains halogen gas in addition to the tungsten wire filament. The gas recycles the tungsten (which would ordinarily collect on the bulb wall) back onto the filament. Supplies an almost constant light output throughout the life of the bulb. Emits a slightly whiter light than the usual incandescent lamp.

TUPELO   A gumwood of a light gray color which has a tendency toward warping unless properly dried. Will take a mahogany or walnut stain. Often used for inexpensive furniture, interior trims, and plywood construction.

TURKEY ROCKER   An overstuffed, liberally tufted easy chair on a spring base, popular at the end of the 19th century. See *Tufting*.

TURKEY WORK   An Oriental type of fabric or rug, or an imitation of it. Worsted yarns were pulled through a coarse, open-textured cloth, then knotted and cut. The patterns were usually executed in bright colors, and the fabric was used to cover the backs and seats of chairs after the mid-17th century.

TURKISH CORNER   An exuberant, overstuffed, overdecorated, overpillowed, and overcanopied area in a late Victorian home. It was an attempted re-creation of the informal, luxurious, exotic East, in this already ornate and heavily patterned period. The corner was usually equipped with a large daybed, sometimes with a canopy, myriad bright cushions, Indian carved tables and stands, incense burners, vases with peacock feathers, water pipes, pictures, trophies, and an occasional animal skin.

TURKISH KNOT   See *Ghiordes Knot*.

TURKISH RUGS   Hand-knotted rugs which are more geometric in character than the traditional Persian Rug designs, even when floral patterns are used. Small versions of the rugs are used by Mohammedans to kneel on in prayer. This type of rug has a niche or mihrab element included in the overall design which is always pointed towards Mecca when used for Moslem prayer.

TURKOMAN RUGS   Short, close pile wool rugs made by nomadic tribes of Turkestan in Central Asia, now part of the Soviet Union. Their dominant color is

TURNING

TURNIP DOME

TURQUOISE

TUSCAN

blood red, often combined with cream, black, brown, and blue in overall geometric patterns that vary with the different tribes. Bokhara is the most noted name among designations of the Turkoman Rugs, but is often used inaccurately in the West.

TURNING   An ornamental or structural element of furniture produced by rotating a wood dowel on a lathe, and shaping the dowel with cutting tools into a series of nodules, swellings, disks, etc. See *Spindle*.

TURNIP DOME   A dome or cupola most often appearing in Russian, Near Eastern, and Arabic architecture and ornament. It resembles an inverted turnip, bulbous and overlapping the turrent or drum below, and tapering to a graceful point above. Illustrated is a group of turnip cupolas of a Russian church.

TURNIP FOOT   A 17th century variation on the ball foot. The general appearance is that of an inverted turnip with a flattened end. A collar usually separated the ball from the floor.

TURPENTINE   A resinous fluid used as a solvent and dryer in paint mixing.

TURQUOISE   From the Old French for Turkish. A type of daybed or settee introduced in the Louis XV period based on the Oriental divan. The piece had a mattress-like cushion, no back, and equally high ends or side pieces. The daybed was usually placed with the long end against the wall, and two bolsters were set against the wall for additional comfort. Round bolsters were placed next to the rising end panels. A forerunner of the studio couch.

TUSCAN   See *Etruscan Order*. A Roman variation of the Doric order. See *Doric Order*.

TUSSAH SILK   Silk made from the cocoons of wild silkworms, usually light brown in color. Used for weaving pongee, shiki, and shantung. Coarse, strong, slubby, and uneven in texture.

TUXEDO SOFA   A clean-lined, simple, upholstered sofa with thin sides that flare out slightly. The upholstered sides are the same height as the sofa back, creating a continuous line. Can be finished with a skirt.

TWEED   A rough-surfaced material with a homespun effect. The yarn is usually dyed before weaving, and it is often woven in two or more colors to obtain a pattern: plaid, check, or herringbone.

TWEED CARPETS   Carpets loomed with shag, looped or twisted yarns in a variety of colors mixed together. The surface may be an even texture or a mixture of high and low pile. Tweeds are usually recommended where soiling may be a problem, since the mixed colors can camouflage stains and dirt.

TWILL   A basic weave, and also the fabric produced by this weave. It has a distinct diagonal line owing to the *weft* yarn passing over one or more warp yarns, then under two or more. The herringbone is a variation on this weave.

TWINING STEM MOLDING   A molding which simulates a stylized tendril wound around a stem.

TWIN-SIZE BED   A standard twin-size bed is 39″ wide by 75″ long. Two twin-size springs may be used with one large headboard to make a unit about the size of a *King-Size Bed*.

TWIST CARPET   A floor covering made of uncut pile. Yarns of different col-

TWIST TURNING

TWO-CHAIR-BACK SETTEE

ors are often twisted together to form the pile loops.

TWIST TURNING   A spiral turning used in France and Holland in the late 16th and early 17th centuries. It was introduced into England in the mid-17th century, and used during the Restoration period for legs, uprights, etc. Illustrated is a chair of the Louis XIII period. See *Spiral Leg*.

TWISTED COLUMN   A decorative column which appears to be twisted around its vertical axis. Popular in the French Renaissance period and also in the 19th century. Also called a wreathed column.

TWO-CHAIR-BACK SETTEE   See *Courting Chair*. Illustrated is a late-17th-century English design.

TYMPANUM   The triangular surface of a pediment bounded by the lower molding and the sloping sides.

U

UMBRELLA SETUP An architectural firm which consists of architects, engineers, landscape and interior designers, plus various other specialists, able to provide a complete design coverage for a structure, internally as well as externally.

UNDERBRACING The arrangement of stretchers, braces, or spandrels under chairs, tables, and chests, used to reinforce and strengthen the units. See *Stretcher.*

UNDERFRAME The part of furniture supported by the legs or feet, which carries the superstructure. For example, the frame under a tabletop, or the frame under a chair seat, called the seat frame or the seat rails. The underframe may be painted or carved or decorated with an apron, pendants, etc. Illustrated is an early-17-century Jacobean design. See *Apron* and *Skirt* or *Skirting Piece.*

UNDERGLAZE COLOR A mineral pigment used for pottery decoration. It is applied before the glazing, and resists the high temperature of the firing process.

UNICORN A single-horned mythological animal that looks somewhat like a white horse with a long gold horn sticking up from its forehead.

UNIDURE A trademark name for a permanent wrinkle-resistant finish applied to spun rayon and blended fabrics. It is patented by The United Piece Dye Works.

UNIVERSAL JOINT A joint which allows one or both of the connected units to move in all directions.

UNIVERSAL TABLE A Sheraton design of the late 18th century for an all-

UNDERFRAME

UPHOLSTERY

UPRIGHTS

UNIVERSAL TABLE

purpose table which could be used as a dining table, or converted into a breakfast table or used to store condiments, tea, sugar, etc. Usually made of mahogany, and equipped with two leaves which slipped under the main table surface. A drawer, set at one side, was fitted with twelve storage bins plus a writing shelf.

UPHOLDER An 18th-century term for an upholsterer.

UPHOLSTERED WALLS Walls that are covered with a soft filler material and then with a finishing fabric. Sometimes tufted with buttons, or marked off into billowing panels or squares. Soft and giving to the touch, and adds some sound-absorption to a room. Ceilings may also be upholstered.

UPHOLSTERY The act of stuffing, padding and covering chairs, sofas, etc. Also the materials used in this operation. Leather, velvet, petit point, gros point, tapestry, brocade, damask, brocatelle, horsehair, and Naugahyde are used as upholstery fabrics. Illustrated is a 17th-century upholstered English armchair.

UPRIGHTS In chair construction, the outer vertical rails or stiles that extend up from the back legs of the chair and support the chair back. These vertical members are braced and connected by the top rail. The uprights can be turned, straight, or shaped, depending upon the period and the style of the furniture. Uprights do not appear in the oval, shield, and heartback chairs of Hepplewhite and Adam. A Sheraton design is illustrated.

UPSON BOARD See *Fiberboard.*

URAEUS   A serpent used as the symbol of royalty in ancient Egyptian art and decoration.

URN   A large decorative container made of metal, pottery, stone, etc. In furniture, a large wooden vaselike container which was usually set on a pedestal on either side of a side table. This was characteristic of the 18th-century Adam designs and also of Hepplewhite's work (see illustration). Urn shapes were also used as decorative turnings at the cross points of stretchers in 16th- and 17th-century furniture designs. The urn and the vase were often set on the central pedestal in a swan's neck pediment. See *Knife Urns* and *Vase*.

URN STANDS   Small tables designed to hold silver or Sheffield plate urns. They

URN STAND

URN

URN-SHAPED SPLAT

were often provided with a pullout shelf to hold a teapot or coffeepot. These stands made their appearance in the 18th century, and Chippendale designed many fanciful urn stands.

URN-SHAPED SPLAT   A wood chair back, cut out and shaped like a vase or urn, a popular decorative device in 18th-century English and American furniture, sometimes pierced for an openwork or lattice effect. Illustrated is an 18th-century Queen Anne chair with cabriole legs, claw-and-ball feet, and an urn-shaped splat.

UTRECHT VELVET   A mohair velvet with a pattern created by pressing down some of the pile. The pile which has not been pressed down has the usual soft velvet or plush touch.

V

VAISSELIER An 18th-century French dining-room cabinet or dresser with shelves. See *Ménagère*.

VALANCE A decorative finishing device over the top portion of draperies. It may be made of fabric, wood, mirror, etc. It can also be designed to go over window frames, doorways, or the hangings of the tester of a bed. See *Cantonnière, Lambrequin,* and *Pentes.*

VALENCIENNES LACE An elaborate bobbin-made lace pattern in which the ornaments and fabric are of identical thread, similar in technique to those used to make Cluny, Duchesse, and Chantilly lace.

VALOIS PERIOD The Renaissance period in French architecture which dates from about 1483 to 1589, the reigns of Charles VIII, Louis XII, François I, Henri II, Henri III, and Charles IX.

VALUES The gradations of tone from light to dark on a solid object under the play of light.

VAN CLEVE, CORNIELLE (1645–1732) A Flemish artist who worked as a sculptor in France in wood, metal, and marble.

VAN DE VELDE, HENRI A 19th-century Belgian artist turned architect, who campaigned for art moderne in Belgium, France, and Germany. He was impressed with the importance of machinery and its ultimate effect on the design and ornamenting of architecture. He was greatly influenced by John Ruskin and William Morris.

SIR JOHN VANBRUGH

VALANCE

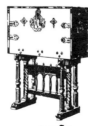

VARGUEÑO

VANBRUGH, SIR JOHN (1664–1726) An architect and designer of furniture in the 18th century, the architect of Castle Howard and Blenheim Castle, and a scenic designer. He did not adhere closely to the Palladian concepts introduced by Inigo Jones. Illustrated is a portion of a chimneypiece designed by Vanbrugh for Castle Howard.

VANE A weathercock.

VANITIES See *Vanitories.*

VANITORIES Modern dressing surfaces which surround the washbasin in bathrooms. Usually marble, tile, formica, or other washable material. Drawers are sometimes set into the apron and a cabinet under the sink area.

VARGUEÑO A Spanish cabinet and desk with a drop lid. It was introduced during the Plateresco period (16th and 17th centuries). A movable piece with the interior subdivided into many drawers and compartments. Vargueños were originally made of walnut, later in mahogany. The drop-lid front was elaborately carved or inlaid with lacy pierced metal mounts, velvet panels, nacre, etc. Hardware was often very large, elaborate, and gilded.

VARNISH A finishing coating applied to woodwork to create a glossy, transparent, washable surface, made of resinous matter in oil or alcohol. In the 16th and 17th centuries, an oil varnish that sank into the wood was used. In the early 18th century, lac dissolved in wine spirits was used. *Vernis Martin* became a popular finish in Europe in the mid-18th century. See *Lacquer.*

VASE A decorative vessel or urn. A shaped container made of precious metals, bronze, brass, porcelain, china, glass, etc. A popular decorative motif in the 18th century. A fiddleback was also called a vase-shaped chair back. Illustrated is an Italian Renaissance faïence vase from the town Savona, Italy.

VASE

VASE-SHAPED SPLAT An urn-shaped splat which appears in the center of a chair back, under the top rail and between the uprights. Similar to the fiddleback. Illustrated is a mid-18th-century Chippendale chair.

VASE-SHAPED SPLAT

VASSELIER See *Ménagère*.

VAT DYE A dyeing process that gives a permanent fast color. Each fiber of the fabric has the colors of the vat chemically induced and fixed into it. The fastness will vary from color to color. Used mainly for cotton, rayon, linen, and some blended fibers; not for silks, vinyls, nylons, polyesters, and glass fibers.

VAULT A roof constructed on the principle of the arch. The word also means an underground room or burial place.

VAUXHALL The location of the noted mirror and glass factory established near London, England, in 1670 by the Duke of Buckingham.

VEDUTA The Italian word for view. A painting or drawing of a place, town, or vista. Giambattista Piranesi was an outstanding vedutiste, witness his "Views of Rome," prints that are much used in decorations of interiors.

VEILLEUSE From the French word for Watcher, or one who sits up to watch or look after. It was a chaise longue of the Louis XV period.

VELARE Italian for a glaze or a thin coat of color.

VELCRO A fastener that, like the zipper, connects two pieces of fabric. Two strips of specially devised fabric, each with thousands of tiny grippers on its surface, are sewn on the pieces to be connected. The strips adhere to each other. To "open" one just pulls the strips apart. They readily reconnect. Trademark of Velcro Corporation. Used for Slip Covers.

VELLUM An ancient writing material made from the skin of a calf, lamb, or kid, treated with lime. Today, a parchment-like paper. See *Parchment*.

VELON A trademark of the Firestone Plastics Company for extruded plastic filaments used in making fabrics and webbing. Also a plastic upholstery fabric available in

VELOURS-DE-GÊNES

VELVET

VENEER

a wide range of colors, textures, patterns, and weights.

VELOUR French for a velvet fabric. A soft, closely woven, smooth fabric with a short thick pile.

VELOURS D'UTRECHT A 17th-century wool velvet produced in Utrecht, Holland. See *Moquette* and *Utrecht Velvet*.

VELOURS-DE-GÊNES A silk velvet made originally in Genoa. It usually has an allover pattern. See *Genoa Velvet*.

VELURE An 18th-century American word for velour.

VELVET A fabric with a thick short pile, less than ⅛″ on the top surface, and a plain back. True velvet is made with two warps, one of which loops over a wire which later cuts the loop into pile. Velvet can be plain, striped, or figured, and can be made of wool, silk, cotton, nylon, etc.

VELVET, BROCADED Velvet on which a pattern is created by removing part of the pile by means of heat and chemicals. It is also called façonné.

VELVET CARPET Plain velvet is a cut pile fabric woven on the velvet loom, the simplest form of carpet construction. Figured velvet is a cut pile fabric woven with wool or worsted surface yarns. All the pattern colors have been drum-dyed before being placed on the loom. Bladed pile wires form the surface texture as they do in plain velvet.

VELVET, CHIFFON A lightweight, soft velvet with a cut pile. It has a closer weave than transparent velvet.

VELVET, CISELÉ A velvet with a pattern created by the contrast between the cut and uncut loops.

VELVET, LYONS A stiff, erect, thick pile velvet usually made of silk, with a cotton or rayon back.

VELVET, NACRÉ Velvet which has one color for the backing and another for the pile, thus creating an iridescent, pearly appearance.

VELVET PAPER See *Flock Paper*.

VELVET, TRANSPARENT Lightweight, soft, draping velvet which is made of silk or rayon with rayon pile.

VELVETEEN Cotton velvet, woven like a sateen with weft threads floated loosely over the warp, and must be sheared to produce a fine, close pile. Used for upholstery and drapery.

VENEER Usually slices of wood between ⅟₁₆″ and ⅟₃₂″ in thickness sliced through the cross or vertical section of a

VEILLEUSE

flitch. These thin, continuous slices are fairly identical as to grain and figure, and can be matched in various ways to create interesting surface patterns. Veneers are applied over a sturdy backing of a coarser, less decorative wood. The effect of veneered furniture or walls is that the area has been constructed completely of a finely grained or interestingly colored wood. During the 16th century in Southern Europe, veneers were cut by hand to $\frac{1}{10}''$ in thickness. In the reign of William and Mary (the end of the 17th century in England), burr walnut veneers were applied over oak. Chippendale, Sheraton, and Hepplewhite used mahogany and satinwoods as veneers, as well as in solid construction. Illustrated is a veneered Hepplewhite bureau bookcase.

VENEER MATCHING   See *Book-Match Veneering, Box Match, Center Match, Checkerboard Match, Diamond Match Veneer, Four-Way Center and Butt Match, Herringbone Match, Random Match, Reverse Box Match, Reverse Diamond Match, Slip Match, Vertical Butt and Horizontal Book-Leaf Match,* and *V-Match.*

VENETIAN   The arts, architecture, and crafts of Venice, a seaport city, once a major trading center. In the early Renaissance, there was a blending here of European and Eastern motifs. Italian Rococo is sometimes referred to as Venetian because of the flamboyant, fanciful, and ornamental quality of the Venetian designs of the mid-18th century. The furniture was often elaborately painted, japanned, and/or gilded, and exaggerated bombés were prevalent.

VENETIAN BLINDS   Window coverings or shades made up of many horizontal wooden or metal slats strung together on tapes. May be raised or lowered as a unit, or the slats can be angled up or down to ensure privacy, at the same time allowing air and some light to seep in.

VENETIAN CHINOISERIE   The Rococo furniture of the 18th century which was produced in Venice; it was based on the Louis XV style. The Venetians added to this an embossed quality, and satin lacquer finishes of oriental design. Though chinoiserie was adopted throughout Europe, Venice, with her advantage of direct trade with the Orient, created many of the finest orientally inspired designs in the 18th century.

VENETIAN DOOR   A door with glass side panels incorporated into the door frame.

VENETIAN FURNITURE

VENETIAN GILT

VENETIAN

VERMEIL

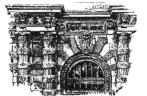

VERMICULAR

VENETIAN FURNITURE   Late Italian Renaissance furniture, highly ornate and extravagantly curved and carved. It is a blend of the grandiose baroque, the frivolous rococo, and the exotic Oriental. Illustrated is a wood frame of the period. See *Venetian* and *Venetian Chinoiserie.*

VENETIAN GOLD or GILT   A gilt finish developed by the early Italian Renaissance craftsmen of Venice and Florence. Gold leaf was applied over a red paint preparation, and then burnished. Some of the red undercoat came through to add more brilliance and richness to the finish. Illustrated is a 16th-century carved center table finished with Venetian gilt.

VENETIAN SHUTTER   A louvered shutter.

VENETIAN WINDOW   A three-panel glazed window with one large central panel and two narrow side panels.

VERANDA or VERANDAH   A long, covered porch, usually built against one side of a building.

VERDIGRAS   A grayed blue-green coating or patina that with time forms on metals like copper, brass, and bronze. Also the same color used as a finish for wrought-iron furniture.

VERDITER PAPER   From the French for green of the earth. A term for 18th-century English wallpapers printed in cool bluish-green colors made from chalk and precipitated copper.

VERDURE TAPESTRY   A leafy tapestry design featuring forests, bushes, trees, and meadows, with only an occasional bird, animal, or figure.

VEREL   A trademark name of the Tennessee Eastman Company for a modified acrylic fiber which has a soft hand and drapes well. High resistance to abrasion and the effects of sunlight. Used in carpeting, for fire-resistant drapery, and for synthetic fur fabrics. It is similar to *Dynel.*

VERMEIL   A French term for silver gilt. Illustrated is a French 18th-century candelabrum originally executed in silver and then washed in gilt. Gilded metal. Also a vermilion-red color.

VERMICULAR   Stonework which is marked with squiggly, wormlike lines. An irregular textured design carved on the facing material of Renaissance buildings.

VERMILION   Also called padouk. A highly decorative Indian wood with a brilliant red-orange hue on a pinkish ground. Also a pigment of the same color.

VERNIS DE GOBELINS A Japanese lacquer process introduced into France and the Gobelins Factory by Dagley in the late 17th century.

VERNIS MARTIN A lacquer finish invented by the Martin brothers during the reign of Louis XV. It was an imitation of Chinese and Japanese relief work rendered in lacquer. Illustrated is a Louis XV commode decorated in Vernis Martin with ormolu mounts. See *Martin Brothers.*

VERRIER A glassware cabinet or a glass showcase with shelves. See *Vitrine.*

VERRIÈRE French for stained-glass window.

VERRIO, ANTONIO (c. 1639–1707) An Italian artist who painted great allegorical scenes at Hampton Court Palace under the supervision of Sir Christopher Wren. He produced overwhelming, giant-size compositions of gods, goddesses, nymphs, cupids, and satyrs.

VERTICAL BLINDS Vertical strip blinds made of lightweight metal, vinyl, fabric, or wood slats, used to cover windows, as dividers or as screens or interior separators. Can be closely coordinated to an interior in color and pattern. The strips are removable and interchangeable. Also called Boston Blinds.

VERTICAL BUTT AND HORIZONTAL BOOK-LEAF MATCH Small pieces of veneer (from a small log) are matched in two directions, vertically and horizontally. A series of rectangles which create a butt design vertically also form a book-leaf match horizontally.

VERTICAL FILES The standard office file cabinet which may be 15″ wide (letter size) or 18″ wide (legal size), and in which one arranges papers, records, etc., in a convenient order, usually one behind the other —from front to back. Vertical files may be had in several tiers: 2, 3, 4, or 5 drawers high.

VESICA PISCIS A pointed oval shape. An almond-shaped halo. See *Aureole.*

VESTAL LAMP A mid- to late-19th-century paraffin lamp in the shape of an antique oil lamp set on a base and stand. The burner was raised above the fuel supply, and covered with a chimney and a glass shade. It somewhat resembles a *Student Lamp.*

VESTIBULE An entrance hall or waiting room.

VICRTEX Trademark for electronically fused vinyl sheeting for upholstery or wall

VERNIS MARTIN

VICTORIAN CLASSIC

VICTORIAN GOTHIC

VICTORIAN JACOBEAN

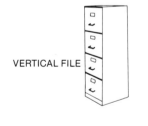
VERTICAL FILE

VICTORIAN RENAISSANCE

covering, produced by L.E. Carpenter and Co.

VICTORIAN Pertaining to the reign of Queen Victoria of England (1837–1901). See the following Victorian periods.

VICTORIAN CLASSIC A revitalization of the Louis XVI designs in Europe and America in the 1860's. The furniture had simple, delicate lines with restrained decorations. Illustrated is a Victorian classic table.

VICTORIAN GOTHIC American and English furniture design from 1830 to a peak in 1840, after which it continued for another twenty or thirty years. The designs were light and small in scale, but decorated with Gothic pointed arches and tracery. Illustrated is a cabinet in the medieval style by John Gregory Crace of London, c. 1850.

VICTORIAN JACOBEAN An unimportant furniture style of the 1870's characterized by strapwork, interlaced flat bands of carving, and the use of myriad small spindle turnings. Illustrated is a dining room designed in 1870.

VICTORIAN ORIENTAL The latter part of the 19th century brought a revived interest in Chinese and Japanese art. Lacquered pieces and Chinese fretwork appeared in Victorian designs, as well as bamboo and bamboo turnings and moldings. Oriental prints also had an effect on the Art Nouveau which was then entering the design field. See *Turkish Corner.*

VICTORIAN RENAISSANCE The period from 1850 to about 1860 when the Italian *Renaissance* became the source of inspiration for the eclectic Victorian furniture makers. The pieces were massive and heavy in scale, with moldings, carvings, and marble lavishly applied. The classic motifs used were ponderous and overly embellished. Illustrated is a carved ebony bedstead c. 1850, designed by M. Roulé of Antwerp.

VICTORIAN ROCOCO A popular furniture style from about 1840 to 1860, also called the French style since it was adapted from the Louis XV Rococo. The designs were full of curves, scrolls, and heavy carvings of birds, flowers, and fruits, often executed in rosewood, mahogany, and black walnut. Marble was freely employed for tabletops, ledges, etc. John Belter of New York is probably the most famous American designer of this style. See *Belter, John Henry.*

VIEIL From the French for old or old-fashioned. The name of a silk brocade.

VIGNETTES From the French for small vines. In Gothic ornament, a leaf and tendril decoration. A vignette is also an ornamental motif, pattern, or design which is centered on a large field, and not confined by a border or edge. The design fades subtly into the background, and the entire composition has an unfinished quality.

VIGNOLA, GIACOMO BAROZZI DA (1507–1573) An Italian architect who, from the careful study of antique examples, formulated a set of rules and diameters for reproducing the classic Roman orders. He used half of the lower diameter of a column shaft as his unit of measure or module. His rules and proportions are still used as a guide, open to interpretation and revisions for particular requirements. He based his original theories on the works of the Roman Vitruvius.

VILE, WILLIAM An 18th-century furniture maker to George III. A partner of John Cobb, he designed in the rococo style.

VINCI, LEONARDO DA (1452–1519) One of the great "universal men" of the Renaissance; painter, sculptor, architect, scientist, engineer, writer, and musician. Among his best known works are "Mona Lisa" and "The Last Supper."

VINE A popular motif in classical and medieval ornament. In antiquity it was associated with grapes, wine, and the god Bacchus. Ivy leaves were often combined with the vine. In the Middle Ages, the vine was used in ecclesiastical art, combined with ears of corn, to symbolize Christ. Illustrated is a 16th-century wood carving.

VINETTE A continuous ornamental band of leaves and tendrils.

VINYL ASBESTOS TILE A tile similar to asphalt tile. Has excellent wearing qualities, is resistant to grease, oil, and mild acids. Vinyl asbestos is much less expensive than homogeneous vinyl tile, but not as resilient nor as quiet underfoot. It is easy to maintain, and wears well under most normal circumstances.

VINYL FABRICS Textiles fused or coated with vinyl plastic. In the coated types, the vinyl is opaque, and the surface is printed or embossed.

VINYL TILE A nonporous, homogeneous flooring material resembling rubber tile. It has excellent wear resistance, and is comfortable to walk on. Resists oil and grease, moisture and mild acids, and is very resilient. Laminated or backed vinyl is not as expensive as homogeneous vinyl, and though it has many of the advantages of vinyl it does not wear as well and indents more easily. Produced in a great range of brilliant and pastel colors, in a wide selec-

EUGÈNE EMMANUEL
VIOLLET-LE DUC

VISE

VINE

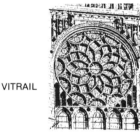

VITRAIL

VINETTE

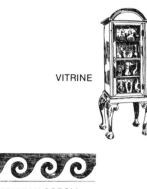

VITRINE

VITRUVIAN SCROLL

tion of patterns, textures, gauges, and tile sizes.

VIOLET WOOD See *Amaranth.*

VIOLLET-LE-DUC, EUGÈNE EMMANUEL (1814–1879) A 19th-century French architect, archeologist, and writer noted for his dictionary of architecture. He was much enamoured with the Gothic, and he engaged in restoring important buildings like the Notre-Dame in Paris. Illustrated is a medieval bed and bedroom of the 14th and 15th centuries after research by Viollet-le-Duc.

VIRGINAL A spinet. An instrument popular with young maidens in the 16th and 17th centuries, hence the name. See *Harpsichord* and *Spinet.*

VIS-À-VIS A 19th-century S-shaped two-seater. The two seats faced in opposite directions, but were attached in the middle. Also called a *Dos-à-Dos, Siamoise* and *Tête-à-Tête.*

VISCOSE RAYON See *Rayon.*

VISE or VICE An archaic term for a spiral staircase around a column called a newel. The staircase was usually constructed of stone.

VITRAIL A French term for glass set into windows. Also a stained-glass window. Illustrated is the rose window of the north transept of Chartres Cathedral.

VITREOUS ENAMEL A shiny porcelain enamel fused upon metal.

VITRIFIED Hardened clay products (tiles, etc.) which have been sufficiently fired so that all grains are fused and pores are closed. The end product is impervious to water.

VITRINE A curio cabinet with a glass front, used for the display of china, glass, or objets d'art. A verrier.

VITRUVIAN SCROLL A series of undulating, wavelike scrolls. A continuous band of horizontal scrolls. It was named after Vitruvius, the classic Roman architect.

VITRUVIUS The Roman authority on architecture in the time of Augustus. He considered three things vital in every construction: "utility, durability, and beauty . . . Beauty will result from the form of correspondence of the whole with respect to the several parts, of the parts with regard to each other, and of these again to the whole." Palladio, in 1570, published his *Five Orders of Architecture* in Venice, based on Vitruvius' work. This book became the textbook of Renaissance architecture in Europe. See *Palladio, Andrea,* and *Vignola, Giacomo Barozzi da.*

V-MATCH Two slices of wood or veneer butted together like facing pages in a book. The graining resembles a series of V's set one over the other.

VOIDER A tray used for carrying dishes and utensils to and from the table. An 18th-century English term.

VOILE A light transparent fabric of plain weave, usually piece-dyed, and then striped or figured. Can be made of cotton, wool, silk, and some synthetic fibers. See *Sheer.*

VOLUTE A scroll line or spiral form such as that used on Ionic and Corinthian capitals. A flat or rising spiral in furniture decoration, at the end of furniture legs, etc. See *Earpiece* and *Scroll.*

VOUET, SIMON (1590–1649) A French artist appointed first painter to Louis XIII. He created many tapestry designs, and was a great promoter of the Renaissance in France.

VOUSSOIR A wedge-shaped block used in arch construction. The central voussoir is the keystone, and it is marked "clef" in the diagram. The lintel in the diagram is marked "linteau."

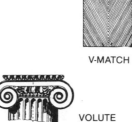

V-MATCH

VOLUTE

VOUSSOIR

VOYELLE A cockfight chair of the Louis XVI period. One straddles the chair, facing the chair back, and rests one's arms on the upholstered shelflike top rail.

VOYEUSE See *Cockfight Chair* and *Voyelle.*

VOYSEY, CHARLES FRANCIS ANNESLEY One of the most important links between the ornamentation of Morris at the end of the 19th century and the 20th-century modern movement. Voysey believed in "discarding the mass of useless ornament." See *Morris, William.*

VYART, BAUDREN A 17th-century French painter in charge of models and designs at the Gobelins Factory during the reign of Louis XIV. He designed many tapestry cartoons.

VYART, JOSEPH The son of Baudren Vyart and his successor at the Gobelins Factory.

VYCRON A dacron-like fiber produced from Goodyear's "vitrel" polyester resin by Beaunits Fiber Division. It is produced as a polyester. The name Vycron is used on only fabrics which meet the requirements established by Goodyear.

W

WACHSTUCH-TAPETE An 18th-century German variation on gilded leather tapestries. A heavy linen or canvas fabric was used as the base, and the artwork was done on it in durable brilliant color. Chinoiserie was a popular motif for Wachstuch-Tapete. It was actually a forerunner of modern plastic- or vinyl-ground wall coverings. At the end of the 18th century, this technique was imitated in England.

WAGGON VAULT A semicylindrical vault or barrel vault.

WAGNER, OTTO (1841–1918) An Austrian architect, one of the first in the late 19th century to admire the machine and to understand its essential character and relation to design and ornament. He was impressed with the comfort and clean lines of English industrial art. "All modern forms must be in harmony with the new requirements of our time . . . Nothing that is not practical can be beautiful."

WAG-ON-WALL A weight-driven clock with exposed weights and pendulum.

WAINSCOT A wooden lining applied as paneling to interior walls. May or may not continue up to the ceiling. Made up of stiles and rails which form frames for large or small panels. The name refers to a superior grade of oak, close-grained and without knotholes, originally used before the Tudor period in England.

WAINSCOT CHAIR An early-17th-century English and American chair which was also called a "panel-back" chair because of its similarity to a wainscot wall. The panel splat was often carved or inlaid, and the seat was usually high and required a footstool. The chair was a sort of "chair

WALL FURNITURE

WALL HUNG UNIT

WAINSCOT CHAIR

WALL LIGHTS

of state" in the Tudor and Jacobean periods.

WALL BED See *Murphy Bed.*

WALL FURNITURE Architectural furniture, cabinets, cupboards, seats, etc., which are built as an integral built-in part of the room, in contrast to portable chairs, small tables, and such. Before the Renaissance period, seats and beds were often stationary units. Illustrated is a mid-19th-century bookcase.

WALL HUNG UNITS Chests, cabinets, and shelves supported from a wall by means of brackets, without touching the floor. The brackets usually insert into slotted upright bars, or standards bolted into the wall, which provide a number of possible positions, thus making the units adjustable. The furniture appears to "float" off the floor. See *Floating Furniture.* Illustrated is a classic design by George Nelson for Herman Miller.

WALL LIGHTS See *Sconce.*

WALL MIRROR See *Pier Glasses.*

WALL SYSTEM Any device or system that is bolted, screwed, or fastened into a vertical surface such as a wall, and does not depend upon legs or a base for support. A wall hung unit or set of units.

WALL TREATMENT The decoration applied to a wall, rather than its actual surface. It may consist of a grouping of paintings, graphics, medallions, tiles, bracket clocks, mirrors, lavabos, etc., in various arrangements (symmetrical or asymmetrical). The wall arrangement can also be as simple as a large painting or mural papered or painted on a wall. In small foyers or entries, the treatment might include a mirror and console shelf with several accessory plaques, objets d'art, and such, depending upon the wall space.

WALL WASHERS Lights used to bathe the walls rather than the floor or the general area. May be angled track lights or indirect lights turned towards the wall. Cove lighting is often used. See *Cove Lighting.*

WALLBOARD See *Building Board.*

WALLIS, N. An 18th-century English designer. In 1771, he published *A Book of Ornaments in the Palmyrene Taste* with designs for ceilings, panels, paterae, and moldings. In *A Carpenter's Treasure* he combined Chinese and Gothic motifs. In 1772, Wallis published *A Complete Modern Joiner* with designs for chimneypieces and cabinets, their moldings and decorations.

WALLPAPER Paper printed by hand or machine methods in a variety of patterns, textures, and colors, and applied to walls as a decorative and utilitarian covering. The earliest papers were Oriental imports in the 17th century. See *Chinese Wallpaper* and *Domino Papers.* Wallpaper today is also printed on vinyl and fabric grounds. See *Flocking.*

WALNUT A light-brown wood grown throughout Asia, Africa, Europe, and America. American walnut has coarser grain than the European varieties. It presents a tremendous range of figures, depending upon the method of slicing. Illustrated is a walnut bureau of the early-18th-century Queen Anne period, it is typical of the Age of Walnut. See *Age of Walnut.*

WALNUT, BLACK A richly colored wood whose fine-grained quality makes it easy to carve. Takes a high polish; fairly expensive because in limited supply. Also called English walnut.

WALNUT, CIRCASSIAN A beautiful curly-grained brown wood from the Black Sea area. It is relatively expensive, and used for furniture and interior paneling.

WALNUT, OILED Walnut treated with a linseed oil finish, instead of varnish or lacquer. The oil finish gives the wood a smooth, dull satin feel, and it is usually more resistant to stains, heat, and alcohol than a varnish or lacquer finish.

WALNUT, ORIENTAL Eucalyptus wood. A pale reddish-yellow figured wood.

WALNUT PERIOD See *Age of Walnut.*

WALNUT, WHITE See *Butternut.*

WARDROBE

ISAAC WARE

WASHSTAND

WALNUT

← WATER LEAF

WARDROBE As known today this is basically the Sheraton design for a clothes press and hanging cupboard in one unit. The wardrobe evolved from the medieval ward room (a place for hanging garments) to the 17th-century hanging cupboards and closets, to the 18th century tallboys and clothes presses. See *Armoire, Garde-robe,* and *Kas.*

WARE, ISAAC An 18th-century English architect-designer of buildings and furnishings. In about 1749, he published *Complete Body of Architecture,* and collaborated with William Kent on the interior decoration at Holkham in Norfolk. See *Trim* for another illustration.

WARIN, JEAN (1595–1672) A French decorative and figure sculptor of the Louis XIV period.

WARP The threads that run lengthwise on a loom. The vertical threads of a fabric. See *Weave.* In furniture or woodworking, the twisting or bulging of a piece of wood, which can be caused by a certain change in the moisture content of the wood.

WASHSTAND A stand for a washbasin. Prior to the 18th century, the basin was often placed on a small table or lowboy. Chippendale designed special stands, often corner units with hinged covers and with a drawer to hold a minute basin. Hepplewhite (here illustrated) and Sheraton also designed special stands for small 18th-century washbasins.

WASSILY CHAIR A chair designed by Marcel Breuer in 1925 and still in production today. The frame is made of tubular steel with a polished chrome finish and the seat, chair back, and arm rests are leather slings or bands that wrap around the metal frames. Named for the artist Wassily Kandinsky who used this chair in his staff house on the Bauhaus Campus.

WATER BENCH See *Dry Sink.*

WATER LEAF An ornamental motif which resembles an elongated laurel leaf, and is often used to enrich a cyma reversa molding. In the 18th century, the water leaf was usually represented in low-relief carving on moldings. Illustrated is a chair splat designed by Sheraton.

WATERCOLOR A painting technique which uses colored pigment ground up with water-soluble gums. When the color is moistened with water, a transparent stain is obtained which is applied in washes to paper. The ground or paper is usually left unpainted to provide white highlights, and gradations of color and tone are accomplished by adding washes. In the 18th and early 19th centuries, Joseph Turner and

Alexander Cozens were the masters of the watercolor.

WATERED SILK　See *Moiré.*

WATERFORD GLASS　Fine Irish glassware and crystal.

WATTEAU, JEAN-ANTOINE (1684–1721)　A great painter and stylist of the French Régence period. His art was light, coquettish, and graceful, full of idyllic shepherdesses and attenuated decorative borders. Watteau painted musical parties, balls, masquerades, and pastoral scenes.

WAVE PATTERN　A continuous horizontal band made up of conventionalized wave crests, also called a wave scroll. See *Vitruvian Scroll.*

WEATHER BOARDING　Horizontal boards, which overlap one another, placed over the framework of a building. It is an exterior wall-facing technique.

WEAVE　The process of making fabrics by interlacing threads (the lengthwise threads) with the weft or filler threads (horizontal or across-the-fabric threads) at right angles. Different patterns and textures are possible depending upon the type of loom, the weaving pattern and yarns used.

WEB FOOT　A heavy, clumsy foot similar to the cloven, hoof, and club foot. It was sometimes used as an ending to a Queen Anne cabriole leg.

WEBB, JOHN (1611–1672)　An English architect and designer. He was a student of Inigo Jones and executed some of Jones's designs.

WEBB, PHILIP SPEAKMAN (1831–1915)　An English architect, who, with Shaw and Nesfield, brought about a revival of residential architecture based on Queen Anne and Georgian styles. Their aim was to create the artistic effects by means of the intrinsic values of the materials used. Webb was a friend of William Morris, and designed the Red House at Bexley Heath (1859) for him. The planning and furnishing of this historic structure led to the establishment of the firm of Morris, Marshall, Faulkner and Company, in 1861, a group important in the formation of the Arts and Crafts Movement. Webb was a member of this firm, and he designed furniture, tiles and stained glass. See *Morris, William.*

WEBBING　Strips of tightly woven burlap used in upholstery construction as a reinforcement and support for springs and cushions. The strips can also be made of linen, plastic, or nylon. In some skeletal-type seats of lawn or beach furniture, the

JOSIAH WEDGWOOD

JEAN-ANTOINE
WATTEAU

WAVE PATTERN

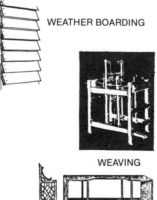

WEATHER BOARDING

WEAVING

WHATNOT

WEBBING

webbing forms the finished seat or back rest.

WEDGE　A shaped piece of metal, stone, or wood with two faces tapering down to a fine edge on one side, making an acute angle.

WEDGWOOD, JOSIAH (1730–1795)　A distinguished English potter. He produced plaques, medallions, and rondels to adorn the classic designs of the Adam brothers. Wedgwood established his factory at Stoke-on-Trent in 1769. It was called the "Etruria" works. He also produced jasper ware and other fine pottery pieces. Illustrated is an Adam commode which has been enhanced with Wedgwood plaques.

WEFT　The threads that run across the loom from selvage to selvage. These are woven in and out among the warp threads. The weft threads are also called the fillers or the woof. See *Filling.*

WEGNER, HANS　A 20th-century Danish furniture designer of exquisitely simple modern furniture. His designs combine comfort with function and are executed with exemplary craftsmanship.

WEISWEILER, ADAM　A great cabinetmaker of the late Louis XVI period. He was strongly influenced by Egyptian as well as classic designs; in a console table which he executed for Marie Antoinette, he used caryatid figures for the leg supports. Weisweiler favored Sèvres plaques as embellishments on his furniture designs.

WELDWOOD FLEXWOOD　A trademark of the United States Plywood Corporation for a wide selection of wood veneers on cloth backing, used for wall covering installations. Adaptable to curved and straight surfaces, and is applied like wallpaper. Installed, it resembles fine wood paneling.

WELSH DRESSER　A side table with cupboards and drawers with a pot board below and shelves above, popular in England in the 17th century. Based on the 16th-century French dressoir de salle à manger and the English *tri-darn.* See *Dutch Dresser* and *Tri-Darn.*

WELTING　A strip sewn between two pieces of upholstery fabric to give a more finished appearance to the seam. Usually made by covering a cord with a tube of fabric and sewing it into the seams so that the stuffed tube appears on the right side between the two joined pieces.

WHATNOT　An ornamental shelf unit used to display bric-a-brac and objet d'art. It was usually designed to fit into the corner of a room. Chippendale designed some of these, but it is best known as a Victorian piece. See *Encoignure*.

WHEAT EAR   A decorative, carved, painted or inlaid motif on Hepplewhite designs which resembles an ear of wheat. Note the design on the top rail of the Hepplewhite chair back illustrated.

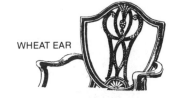

WHEAT EAR

WHEEL WINDOW   A large circular window with tracery radiating from the center. It is similar to a rose window, but the spokes are not as pronounced. A Gothic design.

WHEEL-BACK CHAIR   Chair whose back resembles a wheel with spokes radiating from a central boss, patera, or plaque. It is characteristic of the Adam, 18th-century school, and Hepplewhite also used the wheel-like feature to decorate Windsor chairs. Sometimes the circle was replaced by an oval.

WHIPLASH LINE   The typical curved line of the Art Nouveau period. It is a slow, lazy S which sinuously curves back on itself, and resembles the snap curve of a whip which has been flicked. Illustrated is a magazine decoration in the Art Nouveau style.

WHIRLPOOL TUB   See *Jacuzzi* and *Hot Tub*.

WHITE LEAD   A heavy, non-water-soluble substance used as a base in house paints when mixed with linseed oil.

WHITEWOOD   A trademark name for yellow poplar and cottonwood. It has a uniform, uninteresting grain, and is used for the interior parts of furniture and as the core for veneer work. Soft, easy to work, and excellent for painted or lacquered finishes.

WHORL   A scroll or spiral effect on the feet or top rails of furniture. Illustrated is an early-17th-century Jacobean English chair.

WICKER   Small twigs or flexible strips of wood which are woven into chairs, tables, screens, and baskets. See *Rattan*.

WIG STAND   A 17th- and 18th-century tripod stand fitted with a small basin and drawers to hold wig powder, etc., and a form to hold a headdress or wig. It was also called a demoiselle.

WILLARD, SIMON (1753–1848) American clockmaker of Roxbury, Massachusetts. In 1802, he designed the *banjo clock*, which was meant to be hung on the wall. The case was shaped like an inverted banjo, and was usually made of gilt metal with an eagle or finial set over the dial. Painted decorations rarely appeared on the rectangular glass panel below the dial.

WILLIAM AND MARY

WHIPLASH LINE

WILLOW BRASSES

WHORL

WINDING STAIRCASE

Other clockmakers made similarly shaped clocks, but the panel was invariably painted. Simon Willard's younger brother Adam, who had his business in Boston, used the painted panel to decorate his hanging clocks.

WILLIAM AND MARY (1689–1702) King and Queen of England. William III was a Dutch prince. This period in furnishings is sometimes referred to as Early Queen Anne. They introduced into English design Dutch, Spanish, and Oriental motifs, and made welcome French refugee artisans. See Marot, Daniel. This conglomeration gave rise to a distinctly English school of furniture. Illustrated is a walnut tallboy with early cabriole legs and canted corners.

WILLIAMSBURG, VIRGINIA   Established in 1699, the town was originally laid out by Governor Nicholson in a plan delineating the letters "W" and "M" for William and Mary. Sir Christopher Wren is said to have contributed to some of its buildings. Much of Williamsburg was restored by the Rockefeller Foundation from 1928 to 1934. The restoration has influenced the production of careful reproductions of 18th-century furniture and accessories, now widely available.

WILLOW BRASSES   Furniture hardware with plates that have scrolled outlines. An 18th-century decorative motif.

WILTON   A pile carpet fabric woven on the special Wilton loom, which is controlled by a jacquard pattern device. The loom draws up all yarns of a single color at a time, while the pile and the other colors remain hidden beneath the surface. The pile may be cut or uncut, or a combination of the two, and thus can accommodate a variety of textures. Wool Wiltons wear well under severe conditions, and have a sturdy foundation construction. A worsted weave Wilton is a luxury fabric, and fine details and delicacy of design are possible in it. See *Wires*.

WINDER   In stair construction, a tapered step used at the angle where a stairway makes a turn but has no landing.

WINDING STAIRCASE   A staircase which spirals around a central shaft as it rises from one level to the next. It is also called a spiral staircase. Illustrated is the famous spiral staircase of the Château de Blois, built during the reign of François I of France in the early 16th century.

WINDOW BREAST   Particularly in Gothic architecture, the term refers to a thin screen wall below a window. The mullions of the clerestory window may be carried by this screen which may, itself, be decorated with a blind arcade.

WINDOW FRAME A frame around a window opening often ornamental. A mid-18th-century English design by William Joseph Halfpenny is illustrated.

WINDOW FRAME

WINDOW MANTEL A cornice of wood and fabric trim set over a window as a finishing piece for draperies or curtains. Illustrated is a Robert Adam mid-18th-century design. See *Cornice* and *Lambrequin*.

WINDOW MANTEL

WINDOW SEAT A small upholstered stool or bench made to fit into a window recess or alcove. Adam and Chippendale designed units of this type in the mid-18th century. Now, a built-in bench in a bay, bow, or window alcove. The unit is usually covered with pillows, and the top is sometimes made to open to permit use for storage.

WINDOW SEAT

WINDOW SHADE A window covering, usually made of heavy fabric, placed between the glass and the curtain or drapery treatment. The shade fabric is attached to a roller with an internal spring mechanism. The roller is fixed to the inner surfaces of the window frame at the top. The shade is made to unroll and cover all or part of the window by a pull on the cord attached to the lower hem of the fabric. A quick tug at the cord will cause the fabric to roll back on the roller. See *Austrian Shade Cloth* and *Holland Shade Cloth* for two types of shade cloth fabrics. See *Roman Shade* for an accordion-type folding fabric shade.

WINDOW STOOL A Hepplewhite term for an upholstered settee or bench made to fit in a window recess. See *Window Seat*.

WINDSOR CHAIR A domestic chair introduced in the early 18th century in England. The chair back was filled with vertical rods which created a fiddle-string back or a stick-back appearance. The legs were originally cabriole in shape; later they were made of turnings. The arms and rail were sometimes connected around the back in a hooped-back effect. Chippendale introduced a pierced splat between the rods of the back. Hepplewhite added a wheel-like feature in the center splat. The withes and bowed shapes that formed the spindles and back were turned and cut originally near Windsor, England, hence the name. See *Comb Back*, *Fiddle-String Back or Stick-Back*, and *Stick-Back* and *Windsor Chairs, American*.

WINDSOR CHAIRS, AMERICAN
Versions of the Windsor Chair produced in the 18th and 19th centuries in America,

WINE COOLER

WING-AND-CLAW FOOT

WINDSOR CHAIR

and reproductions still being made today. The early New England variations were lighter, more graceful, and without the wide splat in the back of some of the English forms. Some Pennsylvania designs had ball feet. The many variations are usually designated by the chair-back type: bow- or loop-back, fan-back, low-back, and comb-back. Some had a writing arm. Many 19th-century chairs were characterized by bamboo turnings. The nine-spindle, hoop-back chair, with spindles and turned balusters supporting the bent armrests was typical of New England.

WINE COOLER A small, metal-lined stand designed to keep wine bottles chilled during a dinner. An 18th-century Hepplewhite design is illustrated. See *Cellaret* and *Sarcophagus*.

WINE TABLE A horseshoe-shaped table designed to stand in front of a fireplace, with a curtain across the open end which faced the fire. Persons sat around the convex end of the table. A small decanter holder on a pivoting arm was often attached to the curtain support so that the wine bottle could be easily reached from all parts of the horseshoe. See *Horseshoe Table*.

WING BOOKCASE See *Blockfront* and *Broken Front*.

WING CHAIR A high-backed, upholstered easy chair with side wings or ear-pieces on either side of the chair back. It was originally a mid-17th-century design, and a forerunner of the 18th-century grandfather chair. Also known as forty-wink chair, saddle-back chair, and grandfather chair.

WING-AND-CLAW FOOT A massive carved foot used on Empire couches and other large pieces. Used in England and America in the early 19th century. Also called a winged paw foot.

WIRED GLASS See *Fire-retardant Wire Glass*.

WIRES In carpet construction, metal rods inserted across the loom at the same time the weft yarn is shuttled across the warp threads. When the wires are withdrawn, a series of loops remain which are the pile of the carpet. In Wilton carpets, the wires have a knife edge which cuts the loops into tufts as the wires are withdrawn. Wiltons usually have 13 wires per inch.

WOLFE, ELSIE DE A leading interior designer of the early 20th century. She had a great influence both in America and in Europe fostering 18th-century elegance, especially the French versions.

WOMB CHAIR A curved, enveloping, plastic chair with upholstery covering designed by architect-designer Eero Saarinen for Knoll Associates, Inc., in 1946. A very modern version of a wing chair. See *Saarinen, Eero.*

WOOD ENGRAVING A method of printing in which a design is cut with a graver or burin (a sharp, pointed tool) on a block of wood (like boxwood) which has been cut across the grain. The furrowed lines are filled with ink, the block is set against the paper to be printed, and pressure is applied. The ink records the design of engraved lines on the paper. This technique was popularized by Thomas Berwick in the mid-18th century in England.

WOODCUT A method of printing. From the surface of a block of wood, all parts of the design but those which are to be reproduced in ink are gouged out. The untouched parts are covered with printing ink and the block is pressed onto a sheet of paper or fabric. The ink prints only the level, ungouged, top surface of the wood block; whatever has been cut away does not print. Thousands of impressions are possible from a woodcut block. Used to print the earliest wallpapers, fabrics, and gilded leather tapestries. A multicolored design can be made with a separate printing block for each color, using a multiplate technique like silk screening.

WOOF See *Weft* and *Weave.*

WOOL A natural crumped fiber from the hair of sheep and goats. The scaly surface of the fibers makes it possible to felt wool. Wool is warm and resilient. Used for upholstery, drapery, casement fabrics, and carpets.

WOOL SUEDE A trademark for an all-wool, nonwoven fabric produced by the Felters Company. Used for drapery or upholstery or as a wall-covering material. Soil- and flame-resistant, with excellent acoustical and insulating properties.

WOOLEN YARN In carpets, woolen yarn is spun from short fibers which are interlocked as much as possible and tightly twisted.

WORK STATION An enclosure or compartment made up of screens or panels. One unit in an open-office system, with furnishings appropriate to the specific work that will be performed there, such as a CRT unit, a desk with or without a return, a drafting table, a conference table, chairs, files, bookcases. (A programmer may share a work station with one or more workers; an engineer or draftsperson may have an 8′ ×

WORKING DRAWING

WORKTABLE

WREATH

SIR CHRISTOPHER WREN

8′ work station furnished with the tables and storage units needed.)

WORKING DRAWING A carefully detailed scale drawing used in the construction of the object drawn.

WORKTABLE See *Pouch Table.* Illustrated is an 18th-century design.

WORMHOLES Tiny, pinhead-sized, crooked holes often found in old pieces of furniture made of soft woods. Usually the holes are the result of beetles, or the worms of beetles, eating into the wood. In faked antiques, the wormholes are artificially created and go straight through the wood rather than being crooked, having been made with buckshot or fine dental drills.

WORMY CHESTNUT Chestnut wood which is holey and pitted as though affected by the chestnut blight. The rough, irregular texture and pleasing light-brown color make it popular for paneling and provincial tabletops and cabinet panels. It is too weak for actual structural woodwork.

WORSTED YARN In carpets, worsted yarn is spun from the longer types of staple, and then carded to lay the fibers as nearly parallel as possible, and finally combed to extract the shortest fibers for use as noil. See *Wilton.*

WOVEN SHADES See *Woven Wood.*

WOVEN WOOD A trademark name for thin slats of wood woven with various fibers (wool, linen, cotton, nylon, Lurex, etc.) into window shades, draperies, and roll-up shades. The wood can be left its natural color, or lacquered with other colors. The vertical yarns woven in can create exciting patterns.

WREATH A closed or partially closed ring of foliage, fruit and/or flowers. A classic Roman motif, it was adopted in the Renaissance and Classic Revival periods. In the Empire period it became an important ornamental feature, often enclosing the initial "N," Napoleon's personal badge, or an eagle.

WREATHED COLUMN See *Twisted Column.*

WREN, SIR CHRISTOPHER (1632–1723) The noted classic architect of St. Paul's Cathedral in London. He was an architect-designer of interior decorations rather than movable furniture: mantels, fireplaces, wall treatments, pews, stalls, etc. Grinling Gibbons was the foremost wood carver of Wren's "school." Wren designed and supervised the execution of the state apartments at Hampton Court Palace, and he was responsible for fifty-three colleges, churches, and town halls, as well as credited with being the overall designer of the architecture of Williamsburg, Virginia. He was influenced by the Louis XIV baroque and Renaissance forms and his contact with Giovanni Bernini in France, as well as the Dutch craftsmen in England. Illustrated is the interior of St. Stephen Walbrook, in London, England. See *Williamsburg, Virginia.*

WRIGHT, FRANK LLOYD (1869–1959)   A great midwestern American designer, architect, historian, and critic. He believed that a building should be part of a site, and he expressed a great love and respect for nature and natural materials. In his youth, in Chicago, he worked for and with Louis Sullivan. In domestic architecture, he endeavored to break down the cubicles in which people confined themselves, and bring the outside inside and vice

WRITING ARMCHAIR

WROUGHT IRON

WRITING TABLE

versa. Wright employed continuous casement windows, lowered ceilings, and projecting, streamlined, horizontal overhangs. He designed furniture especially for the interiors he created.

WRITING ARMCHAIR   See *Roundabout Chair* and *Tablet Chair.*

WRITING TABLE   See *Desk.* Illustrated is a late-18th-century kidney-shaped writing table designed by Sheraton.

WROUGHT IRON   Iron which has been worked, bent, twisted, and formed. Iron contains a low percentage of carbon, and is malleable (can be drawn out and extended by beating), and can be used for decoration as well as the functional parts of furniture. Illustrated is a mid-17th-century German Renaissance candlestick. See *Lanthorn* illustration.

XYZ

X-SHAPED CHAIR   A folding chair similar to the current camp stool or yacht chair made with or without a back. This design is found in antiquity, also in Italian medieval furniture of the 14th century. High-backed, armed, and heavily sculptured X-shaped chairs were used in the 17th century. See *Curule Chair, Dante Chair,* and *Savonarola Chair.*

X-SHAPED STRETCHERS   Cross stretchers made flat or curved upward in serpentine form, with knobs or other ornamentation at the intersection. They were used to connect the four supports of a chair or piece of furniture, and to reinforce them. See *Saltire.* Illustrated is a Louis XIV chair.

YARN-DYED   Dyed before the yarn is woven into fabric.

YESERIA   Small, colored, lacelike patterns of plaster relief used in Moorish interiors. See *Composition Ornament.*

YEW, ENGLISH   A hard, durable, pale reddish-brown wood with a fine, even, lustrous grain, used for furniture in England from the Tudor period on. In the late 17th century, yew was used for veneer as well as for long case clocks.

YOKE BACK   A crossbar with two S-shaped curves used as the top rail of chair backs in the Georgian period. The silhouette is that of an ox-yoke.

YOKE-FRONT CHEST   An 18th-century chest of drawers with a reverse serpentine front. The sides swell out, and the center area is concave. It is also referred to as oxbow or U-shaped.

YORKSHIRE CHAIR   A small Jacobean chair with knob-turned legs and

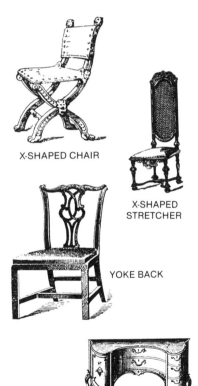

X-SHAPED CHAIR

X-SHAPED STRETCHER

YOKE BACK

YOKE-FRONT CHEST

YORKSHIRE CHAIR

straight uprights ending in inward scrolls. The broad carved top rail and seat below were arched above and crescent cut below.

YORKSHIRE LADDER-BACK CHAIR   An 18th-century domestic or provincial chair with a rush seat and a high ladder back usually composed of five slats, plain or slightly shaped and curved to fit the back.

ZEBRAWOOD OR ZEBRANO   An African wood with a vigorous brown stripe on a light brown ground, used for ornamental cabinetwork and banding. The striped figure is most pronounced, and it is heavy and hard, with a rather coarse texture.

ZEFRAN   An acrylic staple fiber produced by the Dow Chemical Company. A light, bulky fiber, it has a soft, woolly hand. Zefran is much like Acrilan and Orlon, and is stronger and more stable than many acrylics, but present some dyeing problems.

ZEFTRON   A trademark name for a nylon fiber produced by the Badische Corporation; wool-like soil resistant, fast colored fiber that has permanent shock control and wears well. Used to produce contract carpets. (Originally called Zeflon.)

ZELAN   Trademarked name of a finish applied to fabrics to make them resistant to water-based stains.

ZEPEL   A registered trademark name for a special finish applied to fabrics to make them soil and stain resistant. See *Scotchguard.*

ZIGGURAT   A feature of Assyrian and Babylonian architecture. A tower made up of a series of setbacks with ramps connecting one level to the next. Each stage was set back, and usually terraced. The stages were also differentiated by color (the exterior surface was often finished in colored glazed tiles). The lowest stage was the black platform for the underworld, the red was the earth, the blue was the sky, and the gold was the heavens.

ZIGZAG   A chevron pattern; a Norman motif.

ZOOPHORUS   A sculptured frieze that combines animals with human figures. Il-

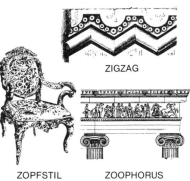

ZIGZAG

ZOPFSTIL   ZOOPHORUS

lustrated is the frieze of the Erechtheum in Athens.

ZOPFSTIL   German for the mid-18th-century Rococo style. Illustrated is a German rococo armchair.

ZUCCHI, ANTONIO PIETRO (1726–1795)   A Venetian painter who did decorative paintings for interiors, as well as panels, plaques, and medallions for furniture designed by Adam. He was married to Angelica Kauffmann, who did similar work. See also *Kauffmann, Angelica.*